Racism in the Nation's Service

Racism

IN THE Nation's Service

Government Workers and the Color Line
in Woodrow Wilson's America

ERIC S. YELLIN

The University of North Carolina Press

Chapel Hill

Designed by Jacquline Johnson

Set in Arno Pro

by Tseng Information Systems, Inc.

The paper in this book meets the guidelines for permanence and durability of the Committee on Production Guidelines for Book Longevity of the Council on Library Resources.

The University of North Carolina Press has been a member of the Green Press Initiative since 2003.

Library of Congress Cataloging-in-Publication Data

Yellin, Eric Steven, 1978–

Racism in the nation's service : government workers and the color line in Woodrow Wilson's America / Eric S. Yellin.

p. cm.

Includes bibliographical references and index.

ISBN 978-1-4696-0720-7 (cloth : alk. paper)

ISBN 978-1-4696-2838-7 (pbk. : alk. paper)

ISBN 978-1-4696-0721-4 (ebook)

1. African Americans in the civil service—History— 20th century. 2. African Americans— Segregation. 3. Wilson, Woodrow, 1856–1924. I. Title.

JK723.A34Y45 2013

331.6'396073009041—dc23   2012037473

Portions of this book have been reprinted with permission in revised form from "'It Was Still No South to Us': African American Civil Servants at the Fin de Siècle," Washington History 21 (2009): 22–47.

THIS BOOK WAS DIGITALLY PRINTED.

For Nathan Henry and the people for whom he was named

Contents

Illustrations

Acknowledgments

Luck comes to mind when I think about the incredible help I have had in writing this book. Telling the stories of people whose fortunes changed has reminded me continuously that we are all subjects of circumstances over which we have little control. And so it is wonderful to have the chance to express gratitude in print to the people and institutions that have made this book better and the writing easier.

This project began at Princeton University under the sharp and empowering mentorship of Nell Irvin Painter. Her kindness and generosity made the day-to-day writing possible, but her scholarship on the meaning of being human in a nation obsessed with race inspired the project's larger inquiry. Her work, bound or on canvas, continues to move me. Crucial, too, has been the support and incisiveness of Daniel T. Rodgers. Dan's willingness to read multiple drafts, ask hard questions, and entertain failure has made me a more thoughtful historian and a more dedicated teacher. His insistence that we connect ideas with experience and experience with ideas confounds and animates my work every day. Others at Princeton have been invaluable teachers and mentors, especially Hendrik Hartog, William Chester Jordan, Kevin Kruse, Valerie Smith, Christine Stansell, and Richard Turits.

Scholars elsewhere have also made this project better. Gretchen Boger read drafts at every stage, and any clarity in the writing is thanks to her. Gary Gerstle, Howard Gillette, Steven Hahn, Sarah Igo, and Touré Reed played key roles in sharpening ideas and improving prose. Special thanks go to Joshua Derman for his help with the work of Max Weber. For their valuable comments on conference papers, on drafts, and in conversations, I thank Cathleen Cahill, Christopher Capozzola, Dan T. Carter, Benjamin Fordham, David Greenberg, William P. Jones, David Krugler, Adriane Lentz-Smith, Kate Masur, Mary-Elizabeth Murphy, Roy Rosenzweig, Samuel Schaffer, Zachary Schrag, Martin Shefter, Jeffrey Stewart, and Chad Williams.

At my new home at the University of Richmond, I have had the privilege of joining a rich community of scholars and teachers. I did not expect to receive the same level of caring mentorship on the job as I did in school, but

Hugh West is an extraordinarily gifted department chair with the brain for administration and the heart for developing young academics. Like Hugh, Bob Kenzer read this manuscript at its most bloated stage and gave me the confidence to make it shorter. The fact that so many other colleagues have blurred into friends is another reason to be grateful. Special thanks go to Bert Ashe, Joanna Drell, Debbie Govoruhk, Ray Hilliard, Woody Holton, Amy Howard, Glyn Hughes, Tze Loo, Manuella Meyer, Nicole Maurantonio, Rob Nelson, Kevin Pelletier, David Routt, Monika Siebert, John Treadway, Sydney Watts, and Yücel Yanikdağ for support, inspiration, and good humor. My thanks, also, go to the many wonderful students I have had at Richmond; in particular, Chris Florio, Kara Schultz, and Luke Victor have given me great faith in the future of historical studies.

As I try to show in this book, money matters. I am grateful for the financial support of the history departments at Princeton and Richmond. Thanks go to the Princeton University Graduate School for its university fellowship, the Rollins and Davis Prizes, and the Charlotte Elizabeth Procter Fellowship. The University of North Carolina at Chapel Hill provided a John Eugene and Barbara Hilton Cay Research Stipend. Stanley Katz and the Fellowship of the Woodrow Wilson Scholars gave two years of financial and intellectual support. The School of Arts and Sciences at Richmond provided summer and sabbatical funding. A postdoctoral fellowship at the John W. Kluge Center allowed for a long swim in the deep research pools of the Library of Congress. I treasure my chats with Mary Lou Reker, who, along with Director Carolyn T. Brown and the other Kluge staff, helped to make my time at the library very productive.

Sometimes shelter magically comes without money, but never without the kindness of friends. Rob and Polly Wright provided a home in which to live and unwind after long days of researching at the National Archives in College Park. Karen and Alan Senter provided a wonderful berth in New York, and Arthur Sackley gave a home and companionship in Washington. Other close friends offered shelter in the metaphorical sense: my tremendous thanks go to Dan Burstein, Sander Cohan, Josh Derman, Dave Ekbladh, Abby and Michael Goldman, Abby Heald, Tom King, Gene Perelson, Juliet Ross, Don Saelinger, and Sherwood Waldron Jr. for just about everything.

As any historian knows, research is only as good as the archivists you meet along the way. My greatest debt is to Lisa Boykin at the National Personnel Records Center in St. Louis, Missouri. Lisa answered an email many years ago and made this whole book possible. My three trips to St. Louis were terrific, thanks to Lisa's personal warmth and hard work. I also thank all of the NPRC staff members who helped Lisa comb the records center for the personnel files of early-twentieth-century civil servants. At the National Archives and Records Administration, I was fortunate enough to work with Rodney Ross in Washington and Walter B. Hill in College Park, Maryland. At the Library of Congress, Adrienne Cannon connected me to Joseph Kendrick Brooks and his family's incredible story. Jim Gwin has been a bedrock of research support at the University of Richmond's Boatwright Memorial Library. Also at Boatwright, Chris Kemp and his team did heroic work on the book's illustrations. At the Washingtoniana Division of the District of Columbia Public Library, Margaret Goodbody offered wonderful resources and advice. Daniel Linke at the Manuscripts Division of the Princeton University Library gave me access to Arthur Link's intricate filing system for the Woodrow Wilson Papers Project. Grace Palladino at the Samuel Gompers Papers Project helpfully answered a query about black unionists. Finally, this project would not have been possible without the special collections staffs at Howard University's Moorland-Spingarn Research Center, Harvard University's Houghton Library, the University of Virginia, and the Virginia Historical Society.

At the University of North Carolina Press, Sian Hunter took an interest in this project at an early stage, and Chuck Grench and Paula Wald made the process of bringing it to fruition as smooth as possible. I thank them, Dino Battista, Julie Bush, Sara Jo Cohen, and Beth Lassiter for helping a neophyte author with patience and kindness.

Last, I thank my family. This book is dedicated to Helen and Norman Yellin, who made much of my education possible, and to Nathan Henry Yellin, who makes sure I learn something new every day. My parents, Laura and Joel, have provided just about every kind of support there is. Their reliable interest in my life and career is a constant source of comfort. My brother, Michael, has been my intellectual and emotional partner since my first teary phone call about a college term paper. Debi, Tzipora, and Zosia have put up with our endless, meandering debates/conversations, and so they deserve thanks too.

It is not easy to explain gratitude for the most important person in your life, especially when she is central to both your work and your personal happiness. I am thankful for everything Nicole Sackley is: partner, mother to Nathan and Lena, chef, scholar, teacher, editor, therapist, best friend. Like I said, I have been lucky.

Racism in the Nation's Service

Aside from the trails we are blazing for those who are to enter the Civil Service after us, we have our families to support, homes to purchase and properly equip and preparations to make for larger and higher service in the cause of the uplift of the race.

—W. Calvin Chase, *Washington Bee*, September 27, 1913

Introduction

In 1913, several hundred black men and women working as clerks in the nation's service were a rare reminder of the rights and citizenship African Americans had won nearly fifty years earlier. Between the 1880s and 1910s, thousands like them passed civil service exams, pulled political strings, and traveled to Washington, D.C., to take up work in the executive offices of the federal government. They produced reports in the Census Bureau, managed appropriations in the Treasury Department, and sorted in the Post Office Department. With decent paychecks, they built middle-class lives and sent their children to college. But that spring, the complex and tenuous political arrangements that had made their positions possible were undone by the racism of a new regime. "I have plans that are all ruined, utterly ruined," despaired Census clerk William Jennifer.[1] The opportunities and stability he and so many others had come to expect from government employment would all but vanish. This is a book about how that world of possibility, work, politics, and mobility was snuffed out. It is a story of how "good government" became the special preserve of white men.

The standard narrative about racism and the U.S. civil service in the early twentieth century is that Woodrow Wilson, a southern Democrat, segregated black workers in federal offices in 1913.[2] The real story is not so simple. The fact of spatial segregation cannot capture the experiences, struggles, and national significance of workers like William Jennifer. What concerned African American employees most was the increasingly apparent relationship between segregation and stunted opportunity. Even if they could find autonomy in "Negro corners," the corners were necessarily on the margins, offering, in the words of historian Earl Lewis, "more space than power."[3] Economics, not space, lay at the heart of what we call segregation. The goal of Wilsonian discrimination was not just racial separation but the limitation of black people to a controlled and exploitable class of laborers. It meant channeling civil servants into a racially tiered system with less mobility and less money for black Washingtonians.

Segregating the civil service had economic consequences but also political and civic ramifications. Wilson's administration combined institutionalized racism with progressive reform in a way that devastated not only careers but also the very foundation of full citizenship for African Americans. Historians have not adequately connected this kind of racial segregation with the state's power to bureaucratize racism and shape class formation.[4] As Wilson and his managers cut down African American civil servants, they undermined an actual as well as a symbolic black middle class in the nation's capital and nationalized a white supremacist social order too often presumed to exist only in Wilson's native South.[5]

Racism in the Nation's Service reveals a key shift in national racial regimes during Wilson's presidency. By regime, I mean the ways in which white and black federal employees interacted and the ways in which bureaucrats conceptualized racial distinctions as they organized government employment. Wilson's government was no more racialized (that is, involved in maintaining racial categories and distinctions) than preceding administrations, but it was more dedicated to white supremacy. By denying appointments, promotions, and even dignity to African American workers, Wilsonians limited the ability of African Americans to obtain stable employment and build the kind of wealth, not just income, that is required to rise in American society. The attrition of African American clerks in federal offices was not simply a routine political purging of loyal Republicans at the hands of newly empowered Democrats. It was a deliberate subversion of a small but growing class of African American middle-class professionals. Under a segregationist regime, being black meant being economically vulnerable, just as it meant suffering social and political inequality.

In public memory, Woodrow Wilson stands alone at the center of this story. While Wilson strongly supported segregation, there is no evidence that he oversaw its implementation or ensured consistency through a clear directive.[6] Wilson was an aloof and shadowy chief executive when it came to personnel management, even in the area of racial discrimination. Instead, it was the men Wilson appointed to run his government who threaded white supremacy into the federal bureaucracy. A few, such as Assistant Secretary of the Treasury John Skelton Williams, were especially steadfast and exuberant discriminators. Yet the progressive aims of Wilsonians and the resistance of African Americans forced most bureaucrats to work haltingly and often in negotiation with each other, government workers, and even civil rights leaders. The result was a more complex regime with a larger cast of characters. Wilson's most remarkable role came after the dirty work was well underway, when he blessed the marriage of progressive politics and state-sponsored racism as necessary for good government.

Racism is too often walled off as an ugly and vestigial outlier to the efficient and equitable state that progressives sought to build. Fair elections, untainted food, and a stable currency stand as essential goods, while the racism of leaders like Wilson is usually lamented but ultimately set aside as personal prejudice unconnected to policy.[7] A few scholars have located the origins of an extensive American "racial bureaucracy" in the Wilson administration.[8] Yet the U.S. civil service was ordered by racial constructions from its inception. It was the practice and force of racism that changed with the progressive politics of the 1910s. In fact, bureaucratic rationalization provided white progressives with a way of explaining their actions against black civil servants that seemed to fit their progressive politics.[9] We cannot explain these changes without a longer view and a deeper understanding of the experiences of black federal employees, whose longstanding claims to citizenship and employment in the national state provoked Wilsonian Democrats.

The histories of black politics, progressive reform, and state-making are crucial to understanding racial discrimination under Wilson, and so my account stretches from Reconstruction to the late 1920s. Its chief actors are those black and white Americans who together forged national politics and urban life in Washington. I examine the capital's relatively egalitarian society at the turn of the twentieth century as well as the forces that led to its destruction. In particular, political patronage's incessant swapping of partisanship for jobs in the late nineteenth century was a central factor of African American federal employment, the establishment of Washington's black middle class, and white progressives' complaints about black politicians.[10] The new political regime of the 1910s, supposedly free of patronage and inaugurated at a moment of expanding state power, did more than harm a few elite black men and women. It undermined the claims to citizenship and economic security of all African Americans.

FOR DECADES AFTER THE CIVIL WAR, federal employment was a powerful means of social mobility for African Americans. The decent salaries of government clerks paid for a full and dynamic life in a capital city with comparatively little racial discrimination. Washington was an island of possibility for ambitious black men and women at a time when racism cordoned them off from vast sectors of the economy and set ceilings on the jobs they could manage to get. Never free of hardship, the District of Columbia and its federal offices nonetheless offered a promising future for African Americans in a nation in which disfranchisement, peonage, violence, and terror were hallmarks of black life.

Government employment and Republican politics safeguarded Washington as a place of relative opportunity for black Americans. To be sure, racism circumscribed black life in Washington well before the Wilson administration. Historian Kate Masur has revealed how the revocation of the District's franchise in the 1870s was racially motivated and crucial to the story of Reconstruction's demise.[11] Losing the vote was a major blow to the citizenship and liberty that Radical Republicans had promised Washington's freed people. Even so, the social mobility, wealth, prominence, freedom, and power of Washington's black middle and elite classes in 1900 were remarkable. Black Washingtonians testified to a distinct contraction of possibility with the coming of the Wilsonians, suggesting that what occurred was not merely the topping off of the process Masur describes.

Black men and women who worked for the government in 1900 were functional members of the state apparatus doing the nation's business. Their numbers grew steadily well into the new century.[12] In 1912, every dollar printed by the Bureau of Engraving and Printing bore the signature of the black man who served as register of the Treasury. Black men also served as auditor for the Navy Department, U.S. consul in Cognac, France, and collector of the Port of New York. More than 400 African Americans, mostly men, worked as white-collar clerks in Washington, some in supervisory positions over white workers. The politically savvy, educated, and reasonably well-off black population in the capital represented the highest ideal of progress for African Americans. That they made their living in government offices placed them at the very center of the American republic.

Such vital citizenship required political power. Against mounting odds, African Americans maintained a voice in the Republican Party after Reconstruction. Even as disfranchisement began to bring a white supremacist order to the political chaos of the 1870s and 1880s in the South, northern Republicans did not yet imagine their party without black politicians. Through actual votes, mostly outside the South, and the patronage manipulation of Booker T. Washington and his "Tuskegee Machine," black Republicans exerted pressure on the national party even as southern states were blocking black voters.[13] The roots of the modern civil rights movement have been found recently in nineteenth-century black nationalism, the early NAACP and its forerunners, and working-class radicalism, but these discoveries should not diminish the political party activities of black Americans after Reconstruction. The self-uplift ethic of middle-class African Americans in this period required not just the stability of federal paychecks but the protection of interracial political connections.[14]

The significance of political patronage becomes apparent when it is seen in the context of the racist labor market of late-nineteenth-century America. Patronage is typically characterized as a malignant system of graft, corruption, and undemocratic politics. Thanks, in part, to the progressive ideology of leaders such as Woodrow Wilson, the patronage system that produced black federal employees has a bad reputation.[15] Most historians assume that African Americans played no role beyond being the mere tools of spoilsmen. The old view of Reconstruction as a political sewer still survives — if implicitly — in the literature, which can make it difficult to shed light on the ways in which black politicians operated shrewdly (and morally) according to the rules of their era, rules white politicians created for their own benefit.[16] Not that every black politician was a saint. Black spoilsmen were self-serving in just about the same proportion as white spoilsmen, but the preoccupation with patronage's undeniable problems obscures the ways in which African Americans used politics and the state productively to protect their well-being even after Reconstruction.

Indeed, patronage greatly facilitated African American citizens' claims to decent jobs, social mobility, and civic equality in circumstances that denied them other ways to express these claims.[17] Patronage did not float all boats and may have even forestalled a broader collective black politics by turning some leaders into conservative ward heelers.[18] Yet federal patronage did more than serve a few individualistic elites. Legal historian Risa Goluboff has noted that the demands African Americans made on the expanded New Deal state for their safety and security "prove false the historiography's dichotomy between patronage and rights consciousness."[19] I argue that this dichotomy was undercut from the moment African Americans engaged the state as full citizens in the 1860s. For a time, black civil servants in Washington were treated as equals and moved up in the bureaucracy to positions of decent pay and real responsibility. Their mobility allowed for investment in the city's institutions that benefited all black Washingtonians. The public schools in the capital, topped by the famed Dunbar High School, were one obvious example, but so too was the ability of black lawyers and Republican administrators to maintain a relatively unsegregated city into the 1910s.

THE PROMINENCE AND PROSPERITY of educated black Washingtonians attracted a racist backlash after the turn of the twentieth century. As legal disfranchisement shut down persistent pockets of black and Republican voting in the South, as racist thinking scaled the heights of modern science, as disputes between capital and labor grew more urgent, and as Reconstruction-era politicians—black and white—exited the stage, white Republicans began to shed their egalitarianism. White supremacy then arrived in Washington in full force with Woodrow Wilson and his Democrats in 1913.

When Wilsonian progressives pledged to clean up Washington, they meant its offices and its streets. They posed as "Redeemers" of a government and its capital gone astray under Republican rule. Bureaucratic reform in federal offices proceeded apace with racial discrimination under Wilson, and with similar arguments and language. Progressive reformers demanded racial segregation as part of their efforts to make the federal government more efficient and the capital a happier, more attractive city. Powerful black people in the national capital made the government vulnerable to corruption, "friction," and even racial conflagration. White supremacy was a necessary precondition if the United States was to be a model nation, if the federal government was to be a model employer, and if Washington was to be a model city.

The racism of white Americans in the early twentieth century should not surprise us, but the practice of racism still requires exploration and explanation by historians. Racism has been a profoundly protean phenomenon, one driven by human beings in specific contexts and with evolving ideologies.[20] Progressive ideas about friction and efficiency did not cause Wilsonian racial discrimination; racism led Wilson to exclude black people from his "New Freedom." But Wilsonians hit upon discriminatory and discursive practices that allowed them to claim simultaneously the mantles of progressive politics and white supremacy. Politics is made up of methods of talk as well as policy ideas, and Wilsonians narrowed issues of citizens' rights to managerial concerns of "efficiency" versus "corruption." They racialized efficiency (made it white), just as they racialized Republican corruption (made it black). Progressive critiques of patronage thus maligned black Republicans as corrupt and associated racial integration with dirty politics. Patronage, especially black patronage, lost out to managerial bureaucracy, and African Americans, once skilled players, were left without access to the game.

The changes that Wilsonian management practices ushered in are indicated by the treatment of black workers when the Republicans returned to power in 1921. Whereas William Howard Taft never fully abandoned his connections to black patronage, the Harding and Coolidge administrations saw no reason to return to pre-1912 levels of black employment. They too adopted the Wilsonians' assumption that black and white workers could not and should not be expected to work as equals in the same offices. They did so not simply as racists but, following patterns set by the Wilsonian racial regime, as modern administrators interested in managerial questions of efficiency. These concerns about efficiency did not bring about segregation, but they did become powerful and important ways of talking about segregating—just as they became key ways of talking about administration in general.

African Americans were profoundly disturbed by discrimination in federal offices, and they never stopped protesting it. But most of the black civil servants working in Washington when Wilson took office in 1913 did not live to see the color line erased. That generation experienced both the opportunities of the Republican era and the betrayal of those opportunities as the racial regime shifted. No longer did their abilities, education, and political loyalty to the GOP serve as productive elements in a government career. Black civil servants could not repel the racial exclusion that the more powerful Wilsonians were intent on enacting. They resisted but did not overcome.

THIS BOOK TRACES THE RISE AND FALL of African American civil servants in three sections. The first section establishes the world of black politics and federal employment in Washington, D.C., before Woodrow Wilson's election in November 1912. Chapter 1 takes us on a walk through Washington and its federal offices around the turn of the twentieth century, and chapters 2 and 3 follow national politics and its connection to federal employment from Abraham Lincoln's administration to William Howard Taft's. The next section charts the rise of the Wilsonian regime between 1913 and 1917. Chapter 4 explores the ideologies and discourse swirling around the Wilson administration, in particular the relationship between progressive politics and white supremacy. Chapter 5 lays out the ways in which Wilson's administrators went about discriminating against African American federal employees in Washington, from separating and isolating employees to limiting career prospects. Chapter 6 examines the methods of resistance and protest deployed by black employees and civil rights activists, as well as Woodrow Wilson's response to the protests. Finally, the last section, chapter 7, follows the story into the late 1920s, when the generation of federal employees who experienced Wilsonian discrimination began to die out. This chapter returns us to ordinary life in federal offices and in Washington's streets, to see the ways in which the changes under Wilson's administration became institutionalized after Republicans returned to national power.

The achievements of African American civil servants at the turn of the twentieth century show how federal employment and political patronage provided avenues to social and economic mobility, especially for those discriminated against elsewhere. In turn, tracking the deliberate destruction of this system reveals how racial discrimination was experienced by black Americans, justified by white Americans, and both rationalized and nationalized by the federal government. Because they had been so privileged, because the government kept so much paperwork about them, and because some Wilsonians worked so deliberately, the stories of African American civil servants in Washington offer an unusually complete and eloquent record of the process and pain of drawing the color line in the United States.

The bureaucratic segregation and discrimination that metastasized in Washington's offices in the 1910s involved a new racial system, one that just a few years later would seem timeless. Federal discrimination was not simply the establishment of segregation in federal offices by one Democratic president. Rather, it constituted a dramatic change in national politics, one that encompassed bureaucratic rationalization, progressive politics, and African American disfranchisement. This history illustrates how the American state has been complicit in racism and black poverty. If Radical Reconstruction offered a chance for the United States to fulfill its founding promises, Wilsonian discrimination revealed the extent to which the state continued to be implicated in the nation's failures.

Part I

THE REPUBLICAN ERA, 1867–1912

As long as I have been colored I have heard of Washington Society.
—Langston Hughes, *Opportunity*, August 1927

Chapter One

No South to Us

African American Federal Employees in Republican Washington

Washington, D.C., was the nation's most important city for African Americans at the turn of the twentieth century. Black Washingtonians' cultural and educational institutions, political connections, and prospects for stable employment stood out against the penury, terror, and segregation that plagued black lives elsewhere in the United States. Four decades of decent employment in federal offices had made Washington a city of opportunity and relative freedom for black men and women, a place where respectability and status could be earned by work in the nation's service. The salaries paid to black federal clerks fueled a growing black middle class, and its power and prestige limited racial discrimination in the city. Life in the District was hardly free of racism or struggle. But for ambitious African Americans, the social as well as economic value of federal positions was incalculable.

In 1911, twenty-seven-year-old Swan Marshall Kendrick traveled from the Mississippi Delta to Washington because a clerical job in the War Department promised decent and reliable pay. He was emblematic of the capital's striving black middle class. A Fisk University graduate, Kendrick was soon promoted and placed in charge of managing the Small Arms and Equipment Division's complex filing system, corresponding with munitions and manufacturing firms, and preparing reports for Congress.[1] On warm weekend afternoons, he joined the young people on the Howard University hill talking about their futures, "the work we want to do, of the lives we want to live, of the possibilities of achieving some of our desires."[2] His work hours—9 A.M. to 4:30 P.M. on weekdays; 9 A.M. to 1 P.M. on Saturdays—left him time to stroll the capital's streets, read at the congressional library, and dream up life goals. Most days ended with some satisfaction and "the usual 'pie and glass of milk.'"[3] Soon, he began describing his life to his beloved Ruby Moyse back home in Mississippi: the city's "eternal rumble of the cars, ringing of bells," his plans to travel the world "in first-class style," his hopes of giving his wife and children "every opportunity," and the inspiration he took from reading W. E. B. Du Bois to "help along, even in a small way, a cause [of civil rights] which is the greatest since the anti-slavery crusade of [William Lloyd] Garrison and [Wendell] Phillips."[4] It was not a bad life, if a bit humdrum: "Easy work; short hours; good pay; lifetime job; What more could a sane man want?"[5] One thing was "sure as fate," he declared in February 1913, a month before Woodrow Wilson moved into the White House. "I'm bound to win."[6] Washington was not Mississippi.

When Kendrick arrived in Washington, the capital had only recently come into its own as a city. The mud-filled nineteenth-century streets mocked by Charles Dickens and Henry Adams had given way to asphalt boulevards and elegant parks. In the years after the Civil War, a flood of new residents, black and white, had come for government employment and to take part in the ascendant American state. The prosecution of a war and the management of a huge army had swollen the federal government and employed new wageworkers, especially women. In the early 1860s, the city's population doubled and never shrank back to its prewar size. The provincial and largely undistinguished District was poised to become a metropolitan capital.[7] In the following decade, Washington officials and civil servants began working and spending money—enormous amounts of money—to modernize Washington. Alexander "Boss" Shepherd, through his post as director of public works and later as governor, disbursed $20 million, considerably over his $6 million budget, to lay pavement, sewer lines, and gas pipes; to erect streetlights; and to plant trees.[8]

By the 1880s, charming social clubs, dazzling department stores, and grand palace theaters were beginning to replace the smokers and saloons that had marked the city as foul and profane to visitors in the past. Elegant late-Victorian homes and apartment buildings proceeded in impressive rows across the western quadrants. The city proudly promoted its scenic beauty, mild winters, and educated society.[9] It had become a place where dignified women could embody the city's essence. "Washington," rhapsodized journalist Alfred Maurice Low in 1900, "is like a woman whose very presence radiates happiness, whose beauty and grace and charm make the world better for her being." Unlike other American cities, Washington had not been disfigured by factories, leaving it clean and cordial. In that way, concluded Low, "Washington is not America."[10] And yet it was also the central worksite of the American state, a city of civil servants doing the nation's business.

The work federal employees did varied greatly, from postal employees carrying letters to chemists conducting experiments at the Department of Agriculture to laborers at the Navy Yard unloading steel. The term "clerk," noted civil service reformer El Bie Foltz in 1909, was actually a capacious category that included "copyists, stenographers, typewriters, transcribers, indexers, cataloguers, assistant librarians, certain kinds of attendants, translators, statisticians, section chiefs, abstracters, assistant chiefs of division, and a large number of miscellaneous employe[e]s whose duties are of a clerical nature."[11] In other words, the clerks administered modern government by doing its paperwork.[12] "A cynic must not think that because Washington makes very little smoke, it does not hold an important place in the national economy," a local journalist reminded the nation in 1908.[13] The Washington Board of Trade imagined the city sitting atop the entire southern economy, serving as a gateway to the North.

As the progressive state began to expand in power and size, it increasingly connected Washington to the nation. National government, all agreed, *was* Washington. By 1900, nearly a quarter of all jobs in the capital were with the federal government.[14] "It is our daily bread; it is the thread which runs through the woof and warp of our lives," sang Low. The result, he said, made the capital "the paradise of the poor man with brains."[15] The steady paychecks of the clerks, generally between $1,000 and $1,600 a year, began to support new real estate and retail markets. These roughly 10,000 men and women were the city's "backbone," declared former District commissioner Henry L. West in 1911. "Whatever is done for the government clerks," he said, "is done for the whole city."[16]

Swan Kendrick, circa 1909, and Ruby Moyse, circa 1915. Though he was invited by the family to court her older sister, Swan Kendrick met and fell in love with Ruby Moyse in Greenville, Mississippi, around 1911. When government work took him to Washington, Kendrick romanced Moyse by letter for nearly five years before she agreed to marry and join him in the capital. Often critical of what Moyse called "High Colored Society," both had relatively privileged childhoods in the Mississippi Delta and received the best education available to African Americans at the turn of the twentieth century. As their fine clothes and confident poses attest, these young people, born in the mid-1880s, faced the future with prospects and ambition. (Kendrick-Brooks Family Papers, Library of Congress)

African Americans lived in every quadrant of the city and worked in every department of the government. They made up about one-third of the population and over 10 percent of federal employees at all levels.[17] More than 350 black men and women held clerical positions, meaning that African Americans, too, were a part of the city's elite backbone. While black Washington contained exceptional contrasts, with its famous "colored aristocrats" standing out against a backdrop of laboring and underemployed masses, the experiences of its middle strivers, the white-collar clerks, embodied the aspirations of the capital city in the new century. Black government employees like Swan Kendrick earned more-than-decent salaries of $1,200 a year. They were experiencing social mobility.[18]

The nation's African American press carried news of black Washington's china and crystal banquets across the country every week.[19] While never dominant in the capital at large, this black bourgeoisie — with its connections to government and politics — was more prominent and more remarked upon by black and white Americans alike than any other group of African Americans anywhere. "The eyes of the entire country are upon the 100,000 Negroes in the District of Columbia," announced Booker T. Washington in 1909, with his typical combination of aggrandizement and didacticism. "The nation looks to the happily environed, intelligent, well-paid and dignified colored people of the capital for inspiration, example, and instruction."[20] New York, Baltimore, and New Orleans contained prominent black elites, and Norfolk had government laborers in its navy yard, yet in no other American city did black people collaborate with the state as productively as in Washington.[21] That the District of Columbia was administered by the federal government made all the difference, because it meant that black Washington's civic virtues lasted long after white supremacists crushed similar societies elsewhere.

The Black Capital

Thousands of African Americans were enjoying the newly vibrant capital at the turn of the twentieth century. Washington's black population of 86,000 not only outnumbered that of any other American city in absolute size but also far surpassed most major cities as a proportion of the total population.[22] Though black city boosters correctly decried the District's loss of the franchise in 1878 as an effort to undermine black political participation, they continued to proclaim Washington a place of real opportunity for African Americans.[23] Black men and women might read comfortably

in the city's public library, sit in integrated audiences at the Belasco Theatre, or even share a drink with white Washingtonians at some saloons.[24]
Black and white city papers announced the doings of the black government
workers, politicians, and businessmen who sat in Martin's Café, a black-run
restaurant, to participate in the meetings of the city's famous Mu-So-Lit
Club. They also reported on the myriad scholarly papers and manifestos
read at the Bethel Literary and Historical Society, the intellectual home of
Du Bois's "Talented Tenth."[25] Black Washingtonians built businesses and
established innumerable orders of Freemasons, Odd Fellows, Elks, Knights
of Pythias, Woodmen of America, Mosaic Templars, and True Reformers.
Washington was also the organizing site of the National Association of
Colored Women's Clubs, created in 1895 for the moral and social uplift of
"the race."[26] The grand pulpits of the Metropolitan AME Church, Fifteenth
Street Presbyterian Church, and Nineteenth Street Baptist Church not
only spoke for the souls of black Washington but also were key organizing
stations for political, civic, and philanthropic movements. But these were
only the most famous: less prominent sanctuaries included Shiloh Baptist,
Plymouth Congregational, and John Wesley AME Zion.[27]

Washington was home to the nation's most elite black Americans, including former Mississippi senator Blanche K. Bruce, North Carolina author
Anna Julia Cooper, the stylish and outspoken social reformer Mary Church
Terrell, and former Louisiana governor P. B. S. Pinchback.[28] Accomplished
men and women announced their power and affluence by promenading
down Connecticut Avenue on bright Sunday afternoons, building hotels
and restaurants, paying for expensive church pews, and hosting endless re-
ceptions.[29]

For the city's children, the black elite erected good schools that exemplified modern education. Congress had created the Washington public school
system in 1864, and even though students were segregated—or perhaps because of it—African Americans maintained substantial autonomy in their
part of the system in the twentieth century.[30] The M Street High School
offered black children a superior high school education; teachers with degrees from Harvard, Dartmouth, and Oberlin taught students who went
on to attend Amherst, Brown, Yale, or the capital's own Howard University, "the capstone of Negro education." Doctors, lawyers, economists, and
social workers poured out of Howard's classrooms, many to stay on, living
and working in Washington.[31] Describing the famous Washington "Negro
Society" in 1901, poet Paul Laurence Dunbar wrote, "Here come together
the flower of colored citizenship from all parts of the country." The result was

Law Library, Howard University. Founded in 1867, Howard was "the capstone of Negro education" by 1900, producing thousands of African American professionals. Many entered government service, where they could make use of their training and fulfill their expectations of decent white-collar work. (Library of Congress)

grand: "The breeziness of the West here meets the refinement of the East, the warmth and grace of the South, the culture and fine reserve of the North."[32]

In the wake of the Civil War, Washington had become a kind of laboratory for government-sponsored civil rights measures. The experiments began with the payment of nearly one million dollars in 1862 to masters for the freedom of their slaves. It continued with federal support for black schools to usher freedpeople into civic life, antidiscrimination rules for public transportation in the District, the extension of voting rights to black residents in 1866, and civil rights legislation in 1870. African Americans and a willing Republican Congress turned the District of Columbia into a crucible of equality.[33] As historian Kate Masur has shown, many of the District's experiments failed by the end of the 1870s, and with them went civil rights across the South. Indeed, as the depression of the mid-1870s and attendant labor troubles drew northern white attention away from black rights, a white oligarchy arose across the region to suppress black voters and reestablish antebellum labor practices. Peonage was the most extreme form of black exploitation in the New South, but sharecropping and tenancy could easily devolve into debt and violence. The vast majority of families were tenant farmers earning less than $400 a year.[34]

Washington, however, remained apart from the rest of the South after Reconstruction. In the District of Columbia, the loss of the vote was not the end of black political power, economic viability, or personal liberty. Former congressmen and other politicians, literally run from their homes and offices by southern racists, retreated to the nation's capital and to its federal offices, bringing with them connections to the highest levels of the Republican Party. The black men in the District of Columbia who held national positions, like assistant attorney general and register of the Treasury, illustrated that relative power. Of particular importance, the register was the government's internal accountant, keeping track of spending, income, and outstanding debts involving the public money. The office paid $4,000 a year and employed a staff of seventy, including an assistant register, the chiefs of the Division of Loans and the Division of Notes, Coupons, and Currency, and more than fifty clerks, messengers, and laborers.[35] The job, too, offered a perch in the Treasury Department, placed one's name on the U.S. currency, and granted a good deal of status in black America.

At the turn of the twentieth century, African Americans also held important local appointments, such as U.S. attorney in the District of Columbia, recorder of deeds for the District, and municipal judge, and black men were comfortably serving on Washington's police force.[36] Men were not the only ones benefiting from District resources. Thousands of black women came seeking good public schools for their children and decent-paying work in government offices, schools, and the homes of well-off white statesmen. They served as the core of the city's black philanthropic ventures and activism for the rights of family and children. In fact, Washington was very much a city of black women; they noticeably outnumbered black men.[37]

In all, Washington stood out for its relative lack of statutory segregation and racial violence. The nation's capital did contain terrible examples of black poverty, however. Most of the city's black workers were not elite professionals, teachers, or civil servants. Even better-off black Washingtonians could experience humiliation just by walking the streets.[38] Yet as one migrant remembered, "Washington wasn't South. It's the capital, and you had more chances for things. Jim Crow was there, but it was still no South

to us."[39] This was a crucial distinction. There were always enough northerners and Republicans in Congress, even after the Democratic triumph of
1910, to ensure that bills to segregate Washington never became law. A bill
proposed by Alabama congressman "Cotton Tom" Heflin to segregate the
city's streetcars in 1908, for example, was defeated soundly. Washington remained the southernmost city in which black and white customers mingled
freely on public transportation. Alexandria, just on the other side of the
Potomac River, relegated black riders to segregated cars.[40]

Perhaps nothing spoke to the complicated culture of race in Washington better than the city's leading paper, the *Washington Evening Star*, which
catered to a largely white readership. The paper walked a complex racial
line, vacillating in almost every issue between racist assumptions and color
blindness. The paper endorsed Booker T. Washington's ideas about industrial education and bought wholesale the implications of his gradualist message of racial uplift: that most black Americans were not worthy of equal
participation in American social, economic, or political life.[41] And yet before scientific racism coalesced into general white opinion, the *Star* declared that race was largely a social construction: "There are no strictly black
men any more than there are strictly white men."[42] After 1900, it could be
counted on for a Republican egalitarianism, even as its pages carried racist
depictions of African Americans in crime reports and in the popular comic
Sambo and His Funny Noises.[43] White southerners regularly came under
criticism in the *Star* for lynching, but African Americans who defended
themselves against racism by violence were equally castigated. Black men
and women were usually identified as "colored," but black civil servants
listed in articles about personnel changes were not. While the paper's editors generally accepted social segregation, they often rebuked the Democratic Party's overt racial discrimination and race-baiting.

Thus, the *Star* was not remarkable because it was free of racism; rather,
it was the frequency with which the paper betrayed sympathy and respect
for black Americans that reflected the District's distinctiveness. The *Star's*
praise for black officials, its coverage of African American churches and cultural events, and its vociferous objections to lynching and disfranchisement
in southern states (a particularly sensitive issue in the voteless District)
contributed to the atmosphere of black opportunity in the city.[44] In 1901, for
example, the *Star* repeatedly expressed surprise and impatience with white
southerners' haymaking of President Roosevelt's dinner with Booker T.
Washington, a supposed breach of Jim Crow etiquette. And when a white
mob terrorized black residents in Atlanta in 1906, the editorial page rang

out in disgust: "Thus was lashed into madness one of the leading cities of the country by office-seekers and inflammatory newspapers." The solution, declared the editors, could be found only in legal justice. "A Cracker rhetorician calls for a separation of the races! And he is a fair specimen of the men who are trying by lawlessness to force on this country a new negro problem infinitely more difficult than African slavery ever was."[45] The newness of twentieth-century racism was not lost on the paper, and its reportage and editorial pages contained opinions that would have been dangerous to publish farther south.

As segregation spread across the United States, African Americans remained far more able to fight and win battles in Washington. A powerful community of black lawyers, some of whom had fled the South, ensured that antidiscrimination laws dating from Reconstruction were still functioning.[46] For example, in November 1887, in a fairly ordinary encounter with the color line, attorney Emanuel Hewlett was refused service in a business-district restaurant at 13th and E Streets NW, a few blocks from the White House. In response, a police officer visited the proprietor to enforce the District's equality laws.[47] Twenty years later, Hewlett found similar redress against a color bar at the heart of the city's government. When a Mrs. A. Lambert decided to serve only white customers at her lunch concession in City Hall, Hewlett complained to the U.S. marshal, who informed Lambert she would have to serve everybody or nobody.[48] Dining rooms run by the federal government served black clientele. Southern congressmen who became "irate" at the sight of Register of the Treasury William T. Vernon and a guest eating in the dining room of the House Office Building could do no more than complain in 1909.[49]

In addition to holding back the color bar, black Washingtonians sought to maintain equal protection in the judicial system. In March 1909, Census Bureau clerk Robert Pelham Jr. came across a white police officer beating a black woman he was arresting. As Pelham gathered the names of witnesses to the assault, the officer arrested him as well. On the appointed court date, Pelham brought Republican senator William Alden Smith of Michigan as his attorney, a surprise that earned the story a headline in the *Atlanta Constitution*.[50] Pelham was acquitted, only burnishing his reputation, according to the *Washington Herald*, as a "worthy citizen."[51] The officer in question was found guilty of "conduct unbecoming an officer and prejudicial to the good name of the Metropolitan Police Force of the District of Columbia."[52]

As these stories indicate, black Washingtonians faced plenty of racial hostility at the turn of the twentieth century. What made their experiences different from elsewhere in the South was their ability to find redress from the city's authorities.

In the Nation's Service

Perhaps most important for African Americans everywhere, Washington was distinguished by its integrated government offices. Black men and women, enslaved and free, had always worked as laborers for the government. They had laid the first cornerstones of the new capital on the Potomac at the turn of the nineteenth century. But civil service after emancipation conferred new status, and black Americans leaped at the opportunity.[53] Solomon Johnson led the way when President Lincoln arranged for Johnson, his barber during the war, to be placed in the Treasury Department in 1864. Johnson quickly earned several promotions, working his way up to a $1,400 clerkship in the Third Auditor's Division. Johnson would serve as a Treasury clerk until his death in 1885. During his career, 620 black men and women joined him in Washington's various department offices, laying the foundation for black civil service for the next quarter century.[54]

Black men and women operated in a job market very different from the one white people worked in, and government employment was among the best options, especially for those with some education. By the end of the nineteenth century, routinized clerical work offered little chance for entrepreneurship and increasingly appeared unmanly and deadening to white men. For white workers, clerical jobs had become women's work. But for African American men, the stable salaries of civil service employment offered a rare chance at upward mobility and respect.[55] "I really like stenographic work, yet it is not a man's work," admitted Swan Kendrick. "Of course, if I could get to be a court reporter or something of that sort, it would be quite different. But when I attempt to enter that field, I meet the color bar."[56] The opportunity to work in a clean suit in an important office with relatively clear rules for pay and promotions made federal employment unusual and immensely desirable.

After the Civil War, Republican administrators turned the government into a pioneering employer, pushing managerial and racial boundaries faster than other industries did. The civil service system established in 1883 systematized, and to some extent democratized, access to government employment. Between 1883 and 1909, over a million people took civil service examinations, with nearly 80,000 earning appointment to government positions.[57] The exam could be a serious barrier to black southerners, who frequently lacked elementary education, and the lowest and most menial jobs, such as charwomen, who emptied the trash and swept the floors, were exempt from the exam.[58] But to those with the right preparation, the exam was an opportunity. Applicants for the highest grade of clerks were generally well-educated men like Fisk alum Kendrick or Thomas Dent, who had graduated from Atlanta University and earned a law degree from Howard.[59] Lower-level clerks did not need to be quite as well educated. George Cox of Washington, D.C., who moved from working as a waiter to government laborer and then to minor clerk in 1900, had graduated from high school and completed a stenography course.[60]

For all, federal employment was more stable and progressive than jobs in other fields. The rush and strain of modern industrial capitalism, proclaimed El Bie Foltz in *The Federal Service as a Career* in 1909, was missing in the more wholesome government offices.[61] Foltz surely had only the white-collar clerks in mind, but it is worth noting that even those who worked in governmental factories like the Government Printing Office (GPO) and the Navy Yard were usually granted an eight-hour day long before private industry accepted the standard. The federal government was also a forerunner in the hiring of female workers, even for those who did not fit the profile of young middle-class women working until marriage.[62] Census clerk Lucretia Mott Kelly, for example, bore a proud heritage in a namesake, a family lineage of free blacks in Philadelphia, and a husband who was a Union Army veteran. Yet her husband had returned from war with malaria and no way to support her and her four children. She found some security in the Interior Department in 1879, where she worked as a laborer and then as a clerk for forty-two years.[63] White women benefited far more from white-collar work in the expanding government, but federal agencies like the Freedmen's Hospital, the GPO, and the Bureau of Engraving and Printing did offer the prospect of steady pay for black women.

The civil service also provided a safety net that most American workers, not merely black workers, lacked at the turn of the twentieth century. After 1897, dismissals required demonstrable and just cause.[64] Federal employees who reached permanent appointment in the early twentieth century might continue to earn money well into old age. Before the pensions system created by the Federal Employees Retirement Act of 1920, men and women in their eighties still worked in federal offices.[65] The most common reward for seniority was the right to die while still employed, and personnel records reveal that a great many did so.[66]

Although black government workers had been earning positions since the Civil War, the presidency of William McKinley (1897–1901) was a particularly fruitful period. The last U.S. president to have fought in the war, McKinley made a series of high-profile appointments and welcomed black Republicans into Washington's government offices. The *Star* highlighted the story in "Draw Good Salaries; Several Thousand Colored Men in Uncle Sam's Employ." William Powell, for example, had been appointed minister to the Republic of Haiti, making him the most "honored" of a cadre of prominent black presidential appointees. The article's emphasis on salaries pointed to the real value of this integrated government service. Milton Holland, "a remarkably capable colored man," was at work in the Treasury Department, directing the division of mails and files in the sixth auditor's office. Holland was described as "light in color, with straight black hair, and resembl[ing] a Latin rather than an African." Holland's complexion might have accounted for his large $1,800 a year salary, though in fact, plenty of well-paid black civil servants could not claim such "high color." In addition, noted the *Star*'s reporter, black clerks with stories of pluck and uplift came from all over the country. J. William Cole of the Pension Bureau, earning $2,000 a year, had joined government service in 1871 as a mere messenger. "He was educated in the Quaker Schools [of Philadelphia], and has since profited from their highly refined influence." Cole too was a "light mulatto" color with a "very intellectual face." Henry E. Baker of Mississippi had earned even more, $2,500 a year.[67]

What is remarkable about the *Star*'s feature story is not merely the extent of black federal employment, its concern with complexion, or the impressive salaries. In 1897, a year during which 123 black men and women were lynched for violating codes of black subservience, the capital's paper of record and a key mouthpiece of the nation's ruling party was boasting of black government officials.[68] This feature story on government employment offered something other than race neutrality, a doctrine more often used to subtly discriminate than to create advancement.[69] Here the *Star* was implicitly pointing to the power of a race-sensitive system to offer opportunity to black people. The real purpose was to give McKinley due credit for the hundreds of thousands of dollars being put in the pockets of black men and women by the new administration. The paper calculated that with 180 black appointments and another 125 promotions, "the new administration has benefited over 300 Afro-Americans to the extent of over $215,000 a year within eight months."[70]

Over the next decade, ambitious black men and women answered McKinley's call from all over the country. By 1907, the number of Afri-

GOVERNMENT CLERKS

Have received appointment as Clerks in Civil Service

Departments United States Government through

Competitive Examinations.

This collage of photographs of African American civil servants was assembled by
W. E. B. Du Bois for the "Exhibit of American Negroes" at the Paris Exposition of 1900.
The exhibit was intended to portray the progress made by African Americans since
emancipation. (Library of Congress)

can American civil servants working in federal offices reached 2,785, or
just about 11 percent of the total federal workforce in the District, some
415 serving as executives, professionals, technicians, scientists, and clerks.[71]
They were part of the "galaxy of young men of our race proving that brains
and energy will do and that merit and not color will be a [talisman] of suc-

cess for us in this country," wrote W. Calvin Chase, editor of the city's leading black weekly, the *Washington Bee*.[72] Outside of Washington, another 5,567 black men and women were working in field offices of the executive departments, while thousands more worked in navy yards.[73]

Civil servants migrated to Washington from elsewhere, a move that could prove difficult, particularly for those coming from rural areas. Government watchman Jesse Porter of Arkansas found himself "1500 miles from home, for the so[le] purpose of discharging [his] duty as a watchman."[74] Most workers did not have to travel so far. In 1907, close to 75 percent of black government workers were appointed from the District or the nearby states of Delaware, Maryland, Virginia, or West Virginia.[75]

Some black clerks came from established Washington families. Thomas H. R. Clarke was the third member of his family to work for the federal government. The *Bee* termed him "handsome, debonair, capable."[76] The son of Cornelius and Emily Clarke, free blacks, Thomas had attended the District's public schools, graduated from the M Street High School, and fought in Cuba in 1898. He returned to Washington as Lieutenant Clarke and soon married a woman from a good family. In 1901, Clarke began working as an assistant messenger in the War Department for $720 a year. A month later, he was transferred to the Treasury Department.[77] Clarke managed to earn a law degree from Howard in 1904, after which he flew through the ranks of the department, doubling his salary to $1,400 by 1910. If the education and war service were not enough to ensure his career, Clarke carefully maneuvered to work exclusively under prominent black Republicans in the office of the register of the Treasury.

Taking full advantage of connections and hard work, black men like Clarke and many others found opportunities for self-advancement in federal employment. Robert Pelham Jr., born in Petersburg, Virginia, and raised in Detroit, Michigan, moved to Washington in 1903 for work in the Census Bureau. With credentials in journalism and Republican politics in Michigan, his starting salary was $1,200 a year. He earned a law degree from Howard a year later. Despite increasing discrimination in the 1910s, Pelham held a position of authority in the Census Bureau and, by the time he retired in 1929, an impressive salary of $2,400 a year.[78] Pelham also joined Washington's elite black society, with membership in the exclusive American Negro Academy. Pelham's career suggests the catalytic power of education, Republican politics, and government work.[79]

Some government workers hoped that decent employment would lead to success in other realms. "I am still looking forward to the day when I can leave here, and go somewhere in the business for myself," Swan Kendrick confessed. "All about me work lawyers, doctors, etc., colored and white, who have gone thru school while working and have not nerve enough to give up their [government] jobs, and try it alone." He wondered, "Perhaps they are right, perhaps I ought to be content to be a very insignificant cog in this great machine, but *I am not.*"[80] Nonetheless, Kendrick worked in the War Department into the 1920s.

William LePre Houston did better. In 1891, Houston left a teaching position in Paducah, Kentucky, to work as a copyist for the Record and Pension Division of the War Department.[81] He quickly earned promotion to clerk and began studying law at night. Meanwhile, he joined the Grand United Order of the Odd Fellows in America and rose to National Grand Master. His position in the Odd Fellows led to travel around the country and a voice in national politics. In Washington, he became a leading faculty member at Howard Law School and was continually courted for his help and influence by friends and political leaders. He offered papers at literary club meetings and socialized with powerful Republicans. In short, Houston became a leader in the capital, even as he spent his days as an undistinguished clerk in the War Department. By 1909, however, he had saved enough money to pursue a private law practice full time. Opening office space on F Street, between 6th and 7th Streets NW, Houston joined the city's most prominent black attorneys working just blocks from federal office buildings.[82]

The path pursued by Houston's son indicated even further the opportunities opened by Washington, D.C., and government employment at the turn of the twentieth century. Charles Hamilton Houston was born in 1895, attended the M Street High School, and was named class valedictorian at Amherst College in 1915.[83] Rather than have Charlie face the dim job market for educated black men in the 1910s, William arranged a teaching position at Howard. After a stint in the military, Charlie earned a law degree at Harvard Law School and returned to Washington to join his father's law practice. From there, Charles Hamilton Houston rose to dean of the Howard Law School and became the architect of the NAACP's legal strategy against segregation. "We wouldn't have been any place if Charlie hadn't laid the groundwork for it," explained his student, Supreme Court justice Thurgood Marshall.[84]

Superior schools, national political connections, and social mobility made Washington attractive to ambitious black families, and they fostered achievement from elite black children. Census clerk Thomas Dent's son followed a path similar to Houston's from M Street to Amherst, earning accolades there and later as an officer in World War I. Messenger John A. Davis sent his daughter to Wellesley and his son to Williams.[85] Treasury clerk Shelby Davidson moved from Lexington, Kentucky, for an education at Howard University and an assistant messenger position in 1893. By 1911, he was a well-regarded clerk, lawyer, and inventor of accounting machinery, earning $1,600 a year.[86] The pay kept the Davidson children in school: daughter Ophelia became a teacher at the District's Armstrong High School, and son Eugene earned his bachelor's degree from Harvard and a law degree from Howard. Eugene later served in Franklin Roosevelt's administration.[87] All of these people worked hard, possessed uncommon natural abilities, and rose above racist and economic adversity that most people could not overcome. But ordinary federal jobs were the reason the Kendricks, Houstons, Dents, Davises, Davidsons, and so many others were in Washington and could find the means to send their children to schools and on to careers out of reach for most Americans, white or black.

No "Colored Man's Paradise"

White boosters sometimes called Washington a "colored man's paradise," but this was going too far.[88] The heady days of egalitarian ideals in the 1860s had faded quickly and given way to outright discrimination and petty harassment throughout everyday life.[89] Just as their achievements and ambitions made black Washingtonians vital parts of the capital, racism and fear kept those achievements under surveillance. Racism is everywhere in the historical record—from continual efforts to draw the color line, to newspaper reports in the mainstream press of black crime and near "race riots," to portrayals of black citizens as sources of disease, to white obsession with "social equality."[90] Although black men and women sat on the city's school boards, played important roles in the District's Republican clubs, and held some municipal offices, the power structure of the city was always dominated by white people. All Washingtonians lacked a democratic voice in their city's affairs after 1878, when Congress was made responsible for funding the city's resources in exchange for residents' right to vote. A board of three city commissioners oversaw the day-to-day operations of municipal administration, but not one of the three commissioners appointed by the president of the United States to manage the city was ever African American.[91]

Black women, in particular, saw even less that resembled paradise. Though there were more teaching opportunities for black women in the

District than elsewhere, they were less likely than men to find work in government service—and far less likely to hold white-collar positions.[92] Black women in Washington who did make it to executive department offices usually worked as charwomen. Thus, most black women in Washington entered domestic service and spent long days toiling for little money.[93] These women, working in other people's homes and living in the alleyways behind, became emblematic of the hardships of urban labor and poverty at the turn of the century. And it was getting worse. Thousands of black southerners moved to cities like Washington, Baltimore, Atlanta, Chicago, and New York after 1900 only to find a different form of the destitution they had left behind.[94]

Like disfranchisement, many of the problems black Washingtonians faced were common to everyone in the developing District. Urban housing, usually rented apartments, imposed financial burdens on all migrants. The city had difficulty paying for its upkeep, and congressional control seemed to make just about everything slower and more difficult for everybody.[95] Yet African Americans clearly took the brunt. Thousands of black men, women, and children were jammed into Washington's alley homes behind the stately townhouses and brownstones that defined the residential parts of the city, especially in the northwest quadrant. Enterprising property owners, sensing a need in the postwar population boom, had opened for tenants the huge alleyways created by Washington's large street blocks. In 1905, the District's 286 alleyways housed nearly 20,000 people. Such crowded conditions fostered crime, despair, and disease. In one infamous alley court of "forty-seven houses," police made 114 arrests for "drunkenness, disorderly conduct, assault, unlawful assembly, larceny, cruelty to animals and accusations relating to sexual crime" in 1912 alone.[96] Perhaps one in three children born in the alleys died in infancy. Famed investigator Jacob Riis declared Washington's alleys, teeming with the pneumonia, tuberculosis, and dysentery bred by poor nutrition and poverty, the worst slums on earth.[97]

Government work at the lowest levels, such as charwomen and unskilled laborers, did not pay well (or even consistently), and supporting a family on a laborer's salary of $360 a year was next to impossible. Of black government workers in 1907, 83 percent were making less than the senior messenger salary of $840 a year. Moreover, 54 percent of the unclassified positions in Washington—low-paying jobs not protected by civil service rules—were held by African Americans.[98] Pay rates for clerkships (generally $900 to $1,000 for a sub-clerk, $1,200 for Class 1, $1,400 for Class 2, and $1,600 for Class 3) were set in the 1840s, though messenger and laborer pay rates were updated in the 1860s and 1870s. By 1912, most federal workers earned wages that had been set at least forty years earlier.[99] Consumer prices fell throughout the late nineteenth century so that a stable wage in this period was a rising wage in real terms. But after 1897, prices began to rise precipitously, culminating in extreme inflation during and after World War I. By the 1910s, the steady salary of clerks represented a falling real wage.[100]

Federal workers frequently complained about their low wages, though often when faced with a threat of demotion or pay reduction. In February 1913, Capers F. Rogers, a watchman in the Treasury Department, begged his supervisor not to reduce his pay. "I would ask in the name of God who is the Creator of us all, to give me one more chance." Rogers was against a wall. Any further reduction could mean doom. "My obligations are great, and on my present salary [$720] I don't live but simply exist—that's all."[101] Certainly, the 125,000 people a year who took the civil service exam in the early twentieth century seemed to find civil service pay attractive, and only with the extreme inflation during World War I did demands for higher government wages actually gain traction.[102] Still, for the majority of black government employees, life was hard.

Working conditions inside government departments, even clerical divisions, could be unpleasant. Offices in the early twentieth century were dark, dusty, and uncomfortable places. The *Star* declared that overcrowding and poor ventilation regularly consigned clerks to bed "with colds and the grip."[103] In 1914, the *Civil Service Advocate*, a publication of the United States Civil Service Retirement Association, protested the insalubrious environments. "In some offices, particularly in rented quarters, the clerks are huddled together too closely for good work and decidedly too closely for good health."[104] Offices in this period could be noisy and leave people feeling jittery. "I never knew how much noise had to do with making me tired until lately," a young woman told the *Star* in 1913. "I used to be tired out in the middle of every afternoon. I would be so nervous I wanted to scream and my head would ache so I hardly knew what I was doing."[105] Women's working conditions were of a particular concern for social reformers. Advocates like Charlotte Hopkins and others in the Women's Welfare Department of the National Civic Federation wrote regularly to cabinet secretaries, passing along complaints of "sickening smells" and unsanitary conditions in toilet rooms.[106]

Government laborers did not even enjoy the comforts of clerical work. In the government divisions that were essentially factories, such as the Bu-

Employee record of Philip Shippen, clerk, D.C. City Post Office, 1887–1928. Before the 1910s, there was no standard place to note race on most civil servant employment cards. However, "Colored" or "Col." was handwritten on the paperwork for nearly all black employees. (National Personnel Records Center, St. Louis, Mo.)

reau of Engraving and Printing (BEP), the work was generally dirty, the pay low, and the hours long.[107] Labor laws governing working conditions in the civil service system were still in their infancy in this period. General work hours were not yet legally set, even if tradition limited clerk hours. In 1909, Gertrude McNally managed to organize the women of the BEP and gain affiliation with the American Federation of Labor (AFL), while a similar group formed in the GPO.[108] But even though postal workers and skilled craftsmen were organizing in this period, there was no general federal employees union until 1917.

Most important, racism did mark the experiences of black civil servants before the Wilson administration.[109] Treasury Department employee forms did not have a place to mark race prior to 1904, but the word "Colored" or simply "Col." can be found handwritten on the forms of most black employees, and such racial designation could bar promotion. Even under the best of circumstances, racial marking was everywhere. A recommendation arguing his case stated that one clerk, Robert Coleman, "is a young colored man but very intelligent and capable."[110] Ultimately, the dispersed nature of power in departmental offices meant that individual bosses made an enormous difference in how far black civil servants could go, a fact the *Washington Bee* recognized, as it regularly singled out supervisors who could be credited with advancing the careers of African Americans. The newspaper offered praise as well as instruction to applicants and employees about who could be trusted and who could not.[111]

Republican administrators' promotion of black civil servants sometimes led to real conflict in the South. In July 1898, Ernest Dillon of the Eclipse Printing Company in Atlanta scolded an assistant secretary of the Treasury for sending the wrong man. "Which is worse," Dillon asked rhetorically, "to carry a letter of introduction to a 'coon' or to have one present a letter to you?" Dillon continued, "When yesterday morning a huge footed, horny fisted, lantern jawed and bullet headed nigger presented to me his appointment as my assistant, I lost several ounces of respect for the powers that be."[112] The Treasury Department regularly received inquiries asking whether several important offices, like the register of the Treasury or the D.C. recorder of deeds, were really held by black men. Motivated by curiosity or indignation, these letters suggested that the racial circumstances in Washington were both strange and visible to Americans elsewhere.[113]

Within government offices in Washington, discrimination was generally subtler. Black clerks complained of unfairness well before the 1910s. The existence of employers like Ernest Dillon made administrators loath to press the issue beyond Washington, limiting the kinds of fieldwork open to black employees. The careers of hundreds of clerks like Charles E. Hall increasingly ran into the color bar after the turn of the twentieth century.[114] Requesting reassignment in 1903, Hall explained to the appointment clerk that he would prefer "a Northern or Northwestern state where race prejudices would not embarrass me or militate against the proper performance of my duties."[115] Administrators, however, felt that no place was safe for black clerks from Washington. When Hall was allowed finally to travel to Chicago on assignment almost two years later, supervisors there were specifically told "to keep him in the office."[116] Administrators feared that the discomforts black clerks faced outside the District might curtail their ability to be efficient workers. "A colored man is not able to occupy a seat in a parlor car or a berth in a sleeper, without the possibility of disagreeable experiences, so that he generally avoids these necessary conveniences."[117] The fact that Hall and other black clerks were willing to endure these indignities was beside the point. Within a decade, a discourse about maintaining efficiency and preventing racial "friction" would also be put to use to justify segregation within Washington's federal offices.

Some black clerks chose simply to leave race behind by passing for white in the capital. "The would-be white Negro who comes to Washington seeks the society of common white clerks in the departments," mocked Calvin Chase in the *Bee*.[118] Chase took great pleasure in the apparent outing of Treasury clerk Theodore Green in 1910. Chase said Green was notorious for socializing only with white clerks, even of low social class.[119] Passing offered some white-skinned black Americans a way into the protected station of white society. Novelist Edward Christopher Williams suggested that passing grew more common among government workers in the 1920s.[120]

Instead of disappearing, much of the black elite cultivated social superiority. Consciousness of class was a distinguishing feature of Washington in general, leaving some to lament the fussiness of the District's status-obsessed elite. (Indeed, Mark Twain set his satire of late-nineteenth-century arrivistes, *The Gilded Age*, in Washington.)[121] For black Washingtonians, this concern was exacerbated by a population that included some of the richest and poorest African Americans in the country. Under increasing pressure from racists, elite blacks became ever more concerned with cultivating their respectability. Paul Laurence Dunbar noted in 1901 that among the Washington elite, "some of us wince a wee bit when we are all thrown into the lump as the peasant or serving class. In aims and hopes for our race, it is true, we are all at one but it must be understood, when we come to consider the social life, that the girls who cook in your [white people's] kitchens and the men who serve in your [white people's] dining rooms do not dance in our parlors."[122] Public events, such as political and religious parades, emancipation celebrations, and presidential inaugurations, were all opportunities to display the respectability of the "better class" of black Washington.[123] That they succeeded in standing apart made the capital remarkable to some white people: "Nowhere but in Washington is this educated, well-to-do, light-colored class so numerous that it can form a society in distinction from the shiftless negroes," declared Mary Logan, wife of the Illinois senator John A. Logan.[124]

The elite held themselves up as leaders and exemplars of "the race." But their concern with uplift merged powerfully with self-regard. "It would be as difficult for a bore or a moral leper to obtain social recognition among the educated, refined colored people of Washington," explained Mary Church Terrell, "as it would be for a camel with a hump to pass literally through a cambric needle's eye." Terrell did not mention skin color, but many others did in their list of necessary refinements. Light complexion, with its obvious connection to white privilege, denoted exceptionalism, particularly exceptional beauty in women.[125] Ruby Moyse's light skin—a legacy of her French father—was part of what attracted ambitious Swan Kendrick. "I like the physical Ruby Moyse," Kendrick confessed in a particularly passionate and candid love letter, "your color especially, and your hair."[126] Certainly her "good hair," which she referred to as her "glory," showed a length and smooth wave that many used chemicals to produce. The result of all of this ranking was a decidedly undemocratic exclusion of people with less physical and social capital.[127]

It was the black elite's obvious accomplishments and status that set white supremacists to work chopping them down. Segregation became a way of circumscribing black men and women who could not be stopped from taking part in civic life and modern mass consumption.[128] White residents began to erect barriers to intermixing in a small city in which the movement from black to white often involved merely crossing the street. In 1891, the white residents surrounding Iowa Circle petitioned to have the benches in the circle's garden walks removed to prevent black neighbors from gathering in the park.[129] Though segregation was by no means complete, D.C. residents were more likely to live on racially homogeneous blocks after the turn of the twentieth century than they had been before. Moreover, even though the 350 or so black government clerks walked and rode street cars with their white peers as they commuted to work, it is likely that residential segregation was reinforced by a kind of temporal segregation, since most black and white citizens made their way to work at different times. "There is one time of day when colored folk have almost exclusive use of the street cars," Belle La Follette, wife of the Wisconsin senator, noted in *La Follette's Magazine*. "In my early morning walks I notice as the cars stop the shovelers, masons, carpenters, cooks, laundresses, housemaids, nurses, get off and go in different direction to begin their day's work."[130]

Capital Investment

Despite Washington's racism, black men and women like the Kendricks and the Houstons continued to move to the city in the belief that they could advance their careers, earn good money, and invest in their futures. No city in the United States after 1900 could be said to have lacked a color line. Boston had circles of black and white intellectuals, many associated with Harvard

University and descendants of abolitionists, but residential segregation and unequal social relations were commonplace even there.[131] Government jobs and the failure to institute legalized segregation meant that opportunities for black people in Washington persisted after Reconstruction.[132] For all the hardship, Washington was the best place in the United States for African Americans seeking economic security.

The financial stability of federal clerkships—and the attendant industries built to support this developing middle class—created expectations for a decent life among many black Washingtonians. Black families with wealth, the stable long-term capital necessary for economic security, were rare in America. But nowhere was that minority as well represented as in Washington.[133] At the turn of the twentieth century, white-collar government workers, black as well as white, generally earned nearly double that of most Americans.[134] In Jim Crow America, a steady paycheck issued by Uncle Sam carried both monetary and social value. And as residents of the national capital and workers in the federal government, those who succeeded were extremely visible symbols of black social mobility.

The Hood family typified the economic stability enjoyed by many black clerks. In 1911, the year Swan Kendrick arrived in Washington to lay the foundation for building his family, city postal clerk Henry Hood was supporting two daughters and his wife, Emma. His $1,100 a year salary was close to the average for permanent civil service employees. They were renting a house on 10th and Q Streets NW, and Emma Hood did not work outside their home.[135] Emma's occupational status stood for a social advancement. The wives of government clerks, even some earning less than Henry Hood, regularly listed no occupation, putting them in a minority of black women in the District. When they did so, they were making public statements about their husbands as providers and their family's respectability.[136] Swan Kendrick could not imagine marrying until he could "offer my wife a little more than 'board and keep,' which is what most wives get."[137] Even more important than the opportunity to live as a single-income nuclear family, however, was the fact that government salaries were relatively stable.[138] Government work transferred millions of dollars in weekly pay to black men and women who worked hard, in striking opposition to the debt cycles and constant cheating of sharecropping that trapped nearly all black workers in the rural South.[139]

City living did come with new costs. Urban consumerism put many of these well-paid workers in debt, as they attempted to interact as equals with middle-class workers, some for the first time in their lives. Stylish clothes from Saks & Company could drain even a decent salary. Swan Kendrick rued the sartorial expenses brought on by "the siren voice" of newspaper advertisements.[140] Many felt an obligation to display their middle-class aspirations. In the context of extreme racism, such social capital was symbolic not simply of status but of freedom and existence. More than just a burden, spending for black Americans was also a chance to exhibit the material rewards of overcoming racism.[141]

That black clerks defended their spending, like most Victorian middle-class consumers, as necessary or unavoidable spoke to their desires to be seen as people with status.[142] The federal government seemed to agree: failure to pay debts was against government policy, but debts themselves were not the problem. The rules made it a violation only to fail to keep up with them.[143] Government pay was public information, and creditors targeted federal employees especially. The interactions between creditors, bosses, and employees revealed the very personal nature of life inside federal offices. Supervisors regularly defended employees against debt claims and even served as go-betweens. Far from the rationalized, impersonal bureaucracy imagined by Max Weber, government employment at the turn of the twentieth century was full of human interaction.[144]

Violating the strict terms of bourgeois propriety could be costly and embarrassing, as when Thomas H. R. Clarke was forced to explain his marital circumstances to Treasury appointment clerk Charles Lyman. By 1901, Clarke's marriage was in shambles. The couple was separated, and Clarke was living with his mother but seeking to hide the realities of his situation "in order to avoid a public scandal in this community." With the *Washington Post* reporting Lucille Clarke's allegations of desertion, Thomas ultimately agreed to pay her fifteen dollars a month in a divorce settlement. A man of Clarke's public and financial prominence had social—as well as moral—responsibilities to meet.[145]

Washington's expanding economy could also be erratic. "Eight years ago I owned my home, was free from debt, and had a small balance in the bank," wrote Treasury clerk Richard Tompkins in 1902. "Had I let real estate speculations alone, I would have acted wisely."[146] Like many government employees, Tompkins had been involved in the Capital Savings Bank, the first bank in the country controlled and operated by African Americans. The bank was founded in 1888, with numerous high-profile government officers on its board of directors, including Charles R. Douglass, Census clerk and son of Frederick Douglass, and John R. Lynch, a former congressman and Treasury auditor for the Navy Department.[147] Within five years of opening, the bank had taken in over $300,000 and was paying investors handsomely. The Capital Savings Bank failed in 1902, however, with federal employees its most common clients.[148] That Washington's economy was volatile did not make it unique in turn-of-the-century America. That it included so many black investors did.

Government employees' most important property and investments were in their homes. They poured capital into Washington real estate.[149] Fewer than 25 percent of African Americans throughout the United States owned their homes in 1910 (the rate for the total population was almost 50 percent), and most federal employees in D.C. rented rather than owned.[150] But when Washington became a center for black economic opportunity in the decades following the Civil War, it saw a 300 percent rise in the number of African Americans who owned at least $2,000 worth of real estate, and a 551 percent rise in the value of their property.[151] Even black clerks like Kendrick and his roommate Lewis Neill, who rented their apartment on the corner of 9th and T Streets NW, invested their hard-earned wages in making their residences comfortable and their furnishings dignified. Federal clerks had a particular opportunity to have their homes serve as measures of progress for black America.[152]

Despite the increasing residential segregation into racial blocks, black civil servants in the first decade of the twentieth century lived in nearly every established neighborhood of the city and in all four quadrants.[153] Immediately following the Civil War, most Washingtonians, black and white, lived in the city's oldest neighborhoods: Georgetown in the southwest and Washington City in the central downtown area. Thanks to the extension of streetcar lines northward up 7th and 14th Streets in the late nineteenth century, the northwest quadrant became the most important residential area.[154] The streetcars also allowed for greater organization along class and ethnic lines, as the wealthy secluded themselves in planned communities of houses and brownstones like Dupont Circle and LeDroit Park. Poorer Irish, German, and African American workers settled into the townhouse apartments of Foggy Bottom, and better-off African Americans followed the 7th Avenue line due north to U Street and the area surrounding Howard University, established in 1867 along Georgia Avenue.[155]

By the twentieth century, U Street and the blocks to the south, later known as Shaw, had become the center of black Washington.[156] Black clerks generally lived near working-class African Americans, perhaps due in part to a desire to live in majority black enclaves where they would not encounter racist white people. Kendrick and Neill's neighborhood, just south of Howard and U Street, was originally home to middle-class white residents. But between 1870 and 1900, the neighborhood's black residents doubled in number.[157] Wealthier black residents built elegant brownstones northeast of Dupont Circle, around 17th and U Streets, that soon earned the nickname "Strivers' Row." They also began to move into the stately homes of LeDroit Park, southeast of Howard. LeDroit in the east and Strivers' Row in the west eventually converged into a bustling commercial district known as the U Street Corridor. Over thirty new entrepreneurs opened shops in the first decade of the twentieth century alone. Ware's Department Store supplied residents with necessities as well as the latest fashions, and restaurants and hotels offered places to gather, including Murray's Café on 7th and Q Streets and John Whitelaw Lewis's elegant hotel on 13th and T Streets. Duke Ellington's biographer credits Ellington's childhood in the neighborhood for the musician's faith that color was no bar to success.[158]

BY THE EARLY YEARS OF THE TWENTIETH CENTURY, most Washingtonians had made a racial bargain. Black residents would not have to fear for their safety, but the context of their liberty would always be limited to the prescribed arenas of political and civil equality. It was this compact that African Americans accused Woodrow Wilson's administration of abrogating in the 1910s. The bargain was somewhat simple, but the practices of the racial regime in Republican Washington were complex. It was not merely a race-neutral legal regime that made some space for black equality; it was a regime in which government officials actively encouraged black mobility by offering respect, decent employment, and real chances at promotion. Government salaries and an expanding urban and civic life made the District of Columbia at the turn of the twentieth century an unusually promising city for African Americans. Such opportunity in the nation's capital was maintained and protected by a national political system that offered black men and women an escape from the economic and social oppression elsewhere in the United States. The construction of that system, beginning in the 1870s, is the subject of the next chapter.

I do not intend to appoint any unfit man to office . . . but I cannot consent to take the position that the door of hope — the door of opportunity — is to be shut upon any man, no matter how worthy, purely upon the grounds of race or color.
— Theodore Roosevelt, *The Independent*, December 1902

I never lose sight of the fact that had it not been for the Republican Party, I never would have been an office-holder of any kind — from 1862 to the present.
— U.S. Customs Collector Robert Smalls to Senator Knute Nelson, August 22, 1912

Chapter Two

The Spoils

Politics and Black Mobility

Political patronage was essential to black rights and mobility in Republican Washington. The job security of African American civil servants depended upon a Republican patronage network of black and white politicians born during Reconstruction. Patronage was more than a party scheme for black Americans; it represented the right to a decent livelihood and social mobility. Black men and women worked hard to succeed in federal offices, and they managed their political affiliations carefully and skillfully to ensure that their efforts would be rewarded. Connections to important people and politicians created a web that could keep vulnerable citizens from falling victim to the hardening bigotry in turn-of-the-century America. This chapter explores the nineteenth-century origins of those connections and their functioning into the early years of the new century. It makes apparent the political system that created black Washington's opportunities and would become the target of white progressive reformers.

Politics was a deciding factor in who could earn federal paychecks, even after the civil service reform and meritocratic fever of the 1870s and 1880s.

The economic stability of black Washingtonians—and the mechanisms for its undermining by the Wilsonians—cannot be understood without exploring the relationship between late-nineteenth-century Republican politics and federal employment. Competitive examinations determined eligibility for federal employment, but the right political party affiliations were necessary résumé builders. Making the wrong ones could be occupational suicide. Political fortunes decided whether or not individuals could pay off their mortgaged homes or continue to pursue a law degree at night. They determined whether or not one's wife needed to take on extra work and how much a person could send back to his or her ailing parents in Mississippi or Minnesota.

African Americans had first directed their hopes for equality to Abraham Lincoln after emancipation, and soon a connection formed with his party as well. During the Reconstruction period, approximately 1867 to 1877, Albion Tourgée, Charles Sumner, Thaddeus Stevens, and many other "Radical Republicans" won the hearts of black men and women by imagining and attempting to implement a new civil rights landscape: they were ready to use the power of the federal government to insert people of African descent into an equal place in the Republic through the exercise of law and military power.[1] The freedpeople tied their already existing social and political consciousness to the Republican Party, building institutions at the county and state level that served as training grounds and depots for connecting to the national party. The presence of African Americans at Republican conventions and national inaugurations and in federal offices was symbolic of black freedom and citizenship.[2]

Though the revolution remained "unfinished" by 1877, many Republicans continued to champion African Americans, and the party as a whole continued to support black male suffrage.[3] Frederick Douglass had famously declared that "the Republican Party is the ship, and all else is the sea." Or, as Georgia politician Judson Lyons put it in 1899, the Republican Party "was the instrument of God to free the Black man."[4] And indeed, the party had great power. Republicans won ten of the twelve presidential elections between 1860 and 1912, and with victory came control over the patronage that filled the civil service and executive appointments. By the 1880s, a political coalition had formed that provided avenues for black southerners to reach the safer social and economic ground of Washington, D.C. Powerful black politicians joined liberal Republicans to give black citizens access to government patronage at all levels. Many white Republicans, well into the Jim Crow era, felt this responsibility deeply. They mentored hard-working men and women who used the pay and status of government work to establish themselves in the nation's capital.

Clear racial identification was essential to the preservation of a system in which black employees were given opportunities. Administrators, who either viewed themselves as egalitarians or viewed African Americans as important to the Republican Party, helped the careers of black civil servants not in color blindness or neutrality but with an explicit eye toward race. They regularly took questions of race and politics into account, as one Treasury Department supervisor did when he remarked on the work of a black employee in the Internal Revenue office: "Were he a white man he would probably be more severely criticized," wrote the division chief. "Taking all things into consideration, however, I am of opinion that his appointment at the expiration of his probationary term would not be prejudicial to the interest of the service."[5]

Black voters and leaders saw more than civic participation in this system: they acted always with a concern for economic welfare and social mobility. As many in Washington knew, this material view of politics could not be dismissed merely as greed or corruption. "If we admit that all the lower places are sought for more for the money there is in them than for the glory of their possessions," remarked the *Washington Post* in 1897, "it does not by any means necessarily follow that the men who seek them are spoilsmen." More than honor, such a patronage recipient, white or black, wanted the salary that "will help him to educate his boys and girls and give his family a better social position."[6] Neither a high civil service exam score nor a patronage connection alone was powerful enough to embark upon a government career in Washington, but the combination proved productive time and again for black men and women in the late nineteenth century.[7]

Black power within the Republican Party was the creation of both a commitment by white party leaders and an effective black leadership corps, which battled not only racism but a tiny, if fervent, group of northern black Democrats for the loyalty of black voters. Black Republicans insisted that the national Republican Party was a force for black progress. "The ascendency of the Republican Party means prosperity generally," wrote Judson Lyons on behalf of President McKinley. Republican loss "means depression, stagnation and general destitution." The party had erected a political and economic safety net open for loyal citizens. "Stay in the party," Lyons warned a black constituent, "or else you may be lost."[8]

Patronage politics could not establish a permanent system of civil rights. Only adequately enforced federal laws could do that, and Lyons and others

Judson Lyons, circa 1908. Lyons's bearing in the image makes apparent the Georgia politician's power and seniority. He was one of several African Americans who served as register of the Treasury during Republican administrations. Doubters wrote to the department asking if it was really true that a black person held so important a post. Lyons's position made him an essential figure in the Republican patronage machine as well. (Library of Congress)

admitted that the repeated failure of legislation to stem southern disfranchisement showed that Congress was incapable of overcoming the assertive racism of white southern delegations. But what it could do, African Americans had hoped, was create an economic lifeline. In the late nineteenth century, no institution embodied the Republican Party's commitment to African Americans more effectively than the federal government itself.

Patronage in the Republican Era

"The sweep made by the Republicans in 1861 was the cleanest in our history," declared Carl Russell Fish in the *American Historical Review* in 1902.[9] Since then, scholars have largely confirmed Fish's claim that Abraham Lincoln used patronage aggressively to purge northern Democrats sympathetic to the South and corral his young party.[10] Importantly, Lincoln was the first to maneuver the spoils in favor of both his party and African Americans. The political system the freedpeople entered into in the 1860s was one in which patronage was essential. Assessments on government salaries paid the cost of party management.[11] Careful job placement rewarded a party's troops and ensured administrative loyalty up and down the line. Misuse of this power could lead to vicious internecine battles, such as in Baltimore, Maryland, where Republicans in the 1870s and 1880s fought constantly over the spoils.[12] And finally, public works and public salaries brought black people to the party, the political system, and the civil administration.

To be sure, patronage could be corrupt, venal, and tawdry. It was an exhausting competition that besieged and dominated the first months of every executive administration, and it demanded loyalty through an often cruel giving and taking of livelihoods. When Democrat Grover Cleveland was elected president again in 1892, the *Bee* asked its readers, "Are you prepared to go?" The stakes were real: "How much money have you saved?"[13] But patronage also laid out the rules by which everyone, regardless of party or race, operated. "To a young man becoming aware of public affairs after the Civil War, patronage must have seemed the natural order for a republic," wrote the great institutional historian Leonard D. White. "Tradition, habit, and democratic theory joined with the sentiments of practical politicians to support an almost impregnable assumption that patronage was both necessary and proper."[14] It was not a system Lincoln or Republicans, black or white, invented. But in the late nineteenth century, it was a system black politicians fashioned for themselves into an institutional bulwark against political and economic discrimination.

In the years immediately following Reconstruction, black Republicans used their remaining electoral power to secure government support in two key ways: veterans' benefits and fusion politics.[15] Both functioned to give African Americans, via the Republican Party, connections to economic security as well as civic participation. Black Union veterans took advantage of all that the federal government was providing veterans, including pensions, back pay claims, and veterans' homes, to build what historian Donald Shaffer has called a "de facto social welfare system."[16] Black recipients joined, though not always on an equal basis, the nearly 30 percent of all elderly northerners in 1910 who were receiving federal veterans' assistance.[17] When we consider how African Americans, especially southerners, interacted with both the federal government and the Republican Party, therefore, the ways in which blacks claimed their rights to "social welfare" through the pension system stand out.

Black men were tied to the Republican Party not just because of a principled allegiance to the memory of Abraham Lincoln. Veterans' newspapers and organizations (not to mention attorneys and pension claims agents) kept alive a functional arrangement between ordinary men and women desperate for assistance and the Republican Party's staunch support for veterans. For its part, the Republican Party saw veterans' support as a key patronage link to bring in voters, black and white. For those African Americans who managed to vote, supporting the Republican ticket was a means to supporting a pension system that many had come to count on for their economic well-being in the insecure years after emancipation.[18] This relationship was also brought to jobs patronage, when Republicans wrote into civil service legislation a preference for veterans in government appointments.[19]

Black Republicans in the 1880s, and in some places into the 1890s, could still exercise electoral rights in the Democratic South to gain a form of social security as well. Support for fusionism, a political movement that married black Republicans with white southerners who refused to adopt the Republican mantle, was also as much about economic welfare as politics for African Americans.[20] When Virginia's William Mahone, for example, built a short-lived machine of black Republicans and white "Readjusters" that sent him to the U.S. Senate in 1881, his main offering to black voters (roughly 40 percent of the Virginia electorate in 1880) was a share in government jobs.[21] This was not a vague or insignificant promise. Mahone spent much of his single term in Washington convincing national Republicans to dole out Virginia's spoils through his fusion organization. The results could be seen in Virginia as well as in Washington, where black Virginians were working as

PUCK.

GILLAM

WHY THEY DISLIKE HIM—HE WILL NOT PROVE HIMSELF A CAT'S-PAW IN THE ENTERPRISE.

Illustration by Bernhard Gillam in the September 3, 1884, issue of *Puck*. Democrat Grover Cleveland was running for president as an enemy of the corruption associated with Republican administrations. The racialized figuring of Republican "spoilsmen" like Benjamin Butler and Charles Dana represents an early version of the kind of association Democrats made even more explicitly in the Wilson era. (Library of Congress)

clerks and laborers in all of the federal offices. "My office looks like Africa, because I have so many colored people in it," a federal revenue collector in Danville griped. A third of the postal employees and a quarter of those in the Treasury were black during Mahone's reign.[22] Indeed, it was this relationship that spelled doom for the Readjuster fusion movement. For white southerners, patronage represented citizenship and public power, and black patronage violated the order of white supremacy. Indeed, nothing served the cause of the Democratic Party better than black Republican officeholders. The Readjuster Party in Virginia was ultimately crushed by the same racist fears of "Negro rule" that threatened black suffrage in post-Reconstruction North Carolina, Louisiana, and elsewhere.[23]

What often goes unappreciated in these tales of racism and white political redemption is the material aspect of patronage that was so essential to American politics. There is no question that for black southerners, disfranchisement and political violence were profoundly disturbing violations of their rights as citizens and human beings. They certainly wanted a say in the policies and representation of their government. But African Americans, like white Americans, had also come to see government jobs as part of the privilege that came with citizenship, especially as they were increasingly locked out of other avenues to economic mobility.[24] With the decline of fusionism, there was little left to protect black voting in Virginia and elsewhere in the South. And without the vote, black southerners had little state-level access to the patronage system. By the early twentieth century, a lily-white Republican faction, led by C. Bascom Slemp, would rise up to handle Virginia's patronage under Republican administrations, regularly choosing to hand jobs to white Democrats rather than to black Republicans.[25] Black Virginians were forced to look to the national party administration and to Washington, D.C., and they placed directly before national leaders the question of African American relevance in party life.

The broad plain of black politics inaugurated in the 1860s was severely narrowed by state-level discrimination, but it is a mistake to see 1877, the year federal troops withdrew and Reconstruction formally ended, as a bright line between black politics and black disfranchisement. After a long period of chaos, fusionism, and wide regional diversity, President Benjamin Harrison in the late 1880s set the terms of black Republicanism at the national level that would hold more or less consistently for twenty-five years. Harrison was not a Radical Republican by the standards of Charles Sumner or Thaddeus Stevens, but he was open to black political equality.[26] His administration established a regime of racial egalitarianism in Washington through its support for black government service.

Harrison came to office in 1889, following a single term by Grover Cleveland, the first Democrat elected president since before the Civil War. Cleveland had sought the advice of a coterie of northern black Democrats, and John R. Lynch later pronounced Cleveland "utterly devoid of race prejudice."[27] But the Democratic president had also turned black Republicans out of offices and replaced them with white Democrats.[28] In succeeding Cleveland, Harrison could have continued to write African Americans out of the U.S. government. He had a ready excuse in the decade's civil service reforms, which promoted a race-neutral meritocracy that ignored the extra burdens on black Americans.[29]

Instead, Harrison's administration pushed forward the ball of patronage. He appointed the notorious spoilsmen John Wanamaker and James Clarkson as postmaster general and assistant postmaster general, respectively. Clarkson was personally well regarded by black Republicans, and he could be a fiery defender of black rights.[30] His position allowed him to place 30,000 fourth-class postmasterships around the country in the hands of loyal Republicans, such as Minnie Cox. An educated and esteemed black woman,

Cox was appointed to postmaster of Indianola, Mississippi, in the heart of the southern Black Belt.[31] In his one term, Harrison appointed more African Americans to executive positions around the country than any president before him.[32] Appointees like Cox, Norris Wright Cuney, Frederick Douglass, and Robert Smalls found in the president a willing defender of black politics.

Harrison established that black citizens would continue to play a role in the federal government, regardless of what was happening in the electorate. Even if they lacked representatives in Congress, African Americans expected to be able to call upon the president and his cabinet.[33] Some white congressmen continued to press for black male suffrage, seeing support for black politics as fulfilling the Republican Party's founding principles as well as serving its state-by-state battle against the Democrats. Massachusetts senator Henry Cabot Lodge nearly succeeded in reengaging the federal government in southern elections in 1890 with his "Force Bill," but he was beaten back by a Democratic filibuster and a growing Republican preoccupation with tariff and currency issues. Cleveland's return and the Democratic capture of Congress in 1893 spelled doom for nearly all federal powers to enforce fair elections.[34]

The mechanism for black power in the Republican Party after 1892 was a fragile combination of party maneuvering and ideology. Black politicians into the early twentieth century used the threat of losing black votes to gain patronage, but the numbers were less and less on their side; and although black voters in the North were increasing, their weight was felt in only a scattering of close local races at the turn of the twentieth century.[35] And yet the Republican Party did not fully abandon black Americans. With few white Republicans in the South, party leaders saw their inclusion of black southerners as a symbol that they were a national party.[36] For their part, black Republicans recognized their ideological and structural place within the party, and they played by longstanding rules to maintain it. Into the twentieth century, southern delegations from Virginia, Tennessee, Georgia, the Carolinas, Mississippi, Louisiana, and Texas were led by powerful black men who understood that their delegations were a crucial part of a presidential candidate's hope of winning the Republican nomination. One could not earn the votes of enough delegates at the national convention without bringing in some of the southern delegations, and that meant maintaining cordial relations with black Republicans.[37]

The District of Columbia also sent two delegates, usually one white and one black, to Republican conventions. Deprived of the vote since 1878, Washington residents could still participate in national party politics, and the capital contained a vibrant political scene, including multiple, competing Republican clubs with black and white members. Black Washingtonians had come to count on having a voice at conventions for use in protecting black civil servants.[38] Through administrative inertia or active support for egalitarianism, white Republicans left in place an institutional commitment to black politics.

Ultimately, that commitment came to reside almost exclusively in Washington. William McKinley's election in 1896 began fourteen years of near-total Republican control over the capital, turning it once again into a site of black political power that harkened back to Reconstruction. Black Republicans converged on Washington to revel in McKinley's inauguration, forcing the society pages to stretch for six columns to account for all the visiting notables. The celebration for the elite culminated in a lavish eight-course banquet that ran past midnight. Their enthusiasm seemed justified. In the busy first days of his presidency, McKinley made a point of meeting privately with a group of black politicians at the offices of the *Washington Bee*. Confidence in the egalitarianism of government administrators soared.[39] But black Washington in the Republican Era was built out of broken pieces from the South, or more to the point, the sectional reconciliation of white Americans. The resurgent Republicans, bigger then ever in the North and finding their feet in the West, worried less about southern black votes. His attention focused on white prosperity, empire, and sectional reconciliation, McKinley did nothing to stop southern Democrats from disfranchising 90 percent of the nation's black electorate or white mobs from lynching 520 black men and women during his presidency. Among the murdered in 1898 was a federal official—Lake City, South Carolina, postmaster Frazier Baker—and his infant daughter.[40]

Deposed black politicians sought in Washington refuge from the destruction. In fact, the path from southern politics to federal employment in the capital had been laid near the end of Reconstruction. The once-powerful black South Carolinian Francis Cardozo moved to Washington in 1877 to work in the Treasury Department, and others, like Congressman Joseph Rainey, would follow as their political office terms ended.[41] J. Willis Menard, who had been elected to Congress from Louisiana but never seated, was working in the Pension Bureau in 1890. Former congressman John Adams Hyman of North Carolina was a clerk in the Department of Agriculture.[42] Joining them was a new generation of exiles. Thomas M. Dent, Georgia Republican and schoolteacher who had met Booker T. Washington in Atlanta in 1895, moved to Washington in 1900 for a job in the Census Bureau.[43]

Office of the *Washington Bee*, circa 1899. The *Bee*, edited by W. Calvin Chase, was the District's most important black weekly from 1882 until Chase's death in 1921. The *Bee* earned a national reputation for its coverage of politics, the capital, and the careers of African American federal employees. The paper's motto, "Honey for Friends, Stings for Enemies," was borne out by the editorial page's fierce defenses of black citizenship and Republican politics. (Library of Congress)

When it proved too dangerous to appoint Judson Lyons to a postmaster-ship in Augusta, Georgia, in 1902, McKinley's successor, Theodore Roosevelt, made him register of the Treasury in the safety of Washington. Postmaster I. H. Lofton of Hogansville, Georgia, had already been forced to flee to civil service work in Washington after he was shot and his post office was burned.[44] And when events in North Carolina exiled John C. Dancy, McKinley's customs collector in Wilmington, Roosevelt appointed him recorder of deeds of the District of Columbia, a position held by an African American since President Garfield had appointed Frederick Douglass in 1881.[45] Dancy's son, who went on to a distinguished career with the Detroit Urban League, recalled "being bundled into a horse-drawn carriage by my stepmother to flee from a rioting mob, and of reading in the newspapers that my father had been advised not to come back to town." Dancy's home in Washington became a "mecca for travelers to and from the South."[46]

In addition to offering refuge to black politicians, federal appointment in Washington kept black advisors close to the administration, where they acted as links between the capital and black communities elsewhere.[47] As one Republican committeeman from Alabama explained it to President Taft's secretary: "It is very important that you should have at your hand, a colored man whose loyalty, knowledge, capacity, and experience will enable you to arrive at correct conclusions and discrimination as between those who can and will render real service, and the chaff whose only object be to mislead or to deceive you."[48] The committeeman's suspiciousness of black politicians echoed a similar wariness among national party leaders. White Republicans were always eager to distinguish between African Americans they deemed to be worthy and unworthy.

Presidential appointees were carefully chosen for their status and connections. Register of the Treasury Judson Lyons spoke for convention delegates in Georgia and elsewhere in the South; Assistant Register Cyrus Adams had been a well-known Republican journalist in Illinois; Recorder of Deeds Henry Cheatham was a leader of the North Carolina Republicans; Postage Stamp Agent John P. Green was a leading citizen in Cleveland; and on and on. These state-level networks were especially crucial during campaigns.[49] Blanche K. Bruce had been appointed recorder of deeds and register of the Treasury by Harrison and McKinley because he could help deliver black votes in Mississippi. Cheatham reported on his speaking tours in West Virginia, where "enormous and uncommon crowds" told him that McKinley would be reelected.[50]

Thus, as disfranchisement shredded black politics in the South, black Republicans were settling into a new regime of patronage that belies the standard narrative that Republicans completely abandoned African Americans in the 1890s. Black politicians found that in the nation's capital, they could still find allies to preserve the civic and economic privileges they felt they deserved as citizens. Republican Washington remained out of the hands of southern "Redeemers." The regime reached even into the ostensibly meritocratic civil service. Patronage networks, usually maligned as corrupt and undemocratic, may actually have provided some institutional fairness, at least in a government vulnerable to racial discrimination. As sociologist Theda Skocpol has noted, state officials have sometimes "insulated" their offices against pervasive elements of the surrounding society, such as racism or capitalism.[51] Though administrators usually positioned themselves as race-neutral rather than affirmative for the cause of black mobility, they nonetheless took their roles seriously as arbiters of opportunity.[52]

The Myth of Meritocracy

Patronage, of course, ran against the civil service reforms that white Republicans had been advocating since the 1870s. The civil service was designed to remove executive appointments at the clerical level and below from the political pressures of Congress. Yet it was very difficult to limit the role played by Congress and the parties because of the power of the purse in congressional appropriations and because "directing personnel" were chosen openly based on politics. McKinley exacerbated the situation by adding about 20,000 appointment opportunities to a bureaucracy that had already grown massively since the Harrison administration.[53] But for African Americans, such expansion of patronage brought opportunity. Even after southern disfranchisement, for example, 244 black men and 36 black women held presidential appointments as local postmasters in 1907.[54] In Washington, Charles E. Hall benefited from McKinley's refusal to extend civil service appointment rules to the Census Bureau, a favorite patronage spot for Congress. Though an examination was required for eligibility and Hall was by all accounts a brilliant statistician, his appointment was still dependent on the recommendation of his congressman.[55]

Despite its many flaws, the civil service system did provide the framework for federal employment, and understanding its bureaucracy was a fundamental part of life for clerks like Hall. Passed by Congress in 1883, the Pendleton Civil Service Reform Act established the basic structure, including the Civil Service Commission, the use of competitive examinations, apportionment of employees by state, and an antinepotism clause. This system would enshrine two basic values within the American government: merit and fairness.[56] Seeking merit was not merely an administrative strategy for the system's backers but a moral imperative that would best serve both the state and the individual. Meritocracy, an Enlightenment ideal, was swirling around industrialized nations in the late nineteenth century as they sought to bring both the mechanisms and excesses of capitalism under control. Between 1870 and 1887, Germany, Great Britain, Canada, Japan, and the United States installed competitive examinations to ensure that only the most qualified worked in government.[57] The transparency of recruitment, promotion, and dismissal would allow for scrutiny by the citizenry, represented by an oversight commission. In theory, the spoilsmen of the nineteenth century would be banished in favor of meritorious workers fit for the challenge of managing a modern industrial democracy.

Civil service reform in the United States systematized government employment, but it did not eliminate the role politics played in who was hired. The initial act, in fact, covered only about 10 percent of the government, and even within that small band of regulation, presidents regularly ignored the rules. Amendments in the years that followed, particularly in 1896 and 1898, extended antipolitical provisions and increased the number of offices and jobs covered by civil service rules, but the growth of federal offices in this period seemed to set the goal line further and further away.[58] In Washington's executive departments, a deliberately porous set of regulations undermined rules governing appointment. Public officials were forbidden from writing letters of recommendation, for example, but they were allowed to comment on an applicant's "character and community standing."[59]

Though it is perhaps not surprising to find letters of recommendation in the files of white-collar clerks, who were generally educated and well connected, laborers' personnel files also regularly contained recommendations from congressmen and other prominent citizens. For example, Raymond Fisher, a helper in the Government Printing Office, had been supported by a Democratic congressman from Illinois and a Republican from Indiana. Fisher's mother, Henrietta, had done laundry for the congressmen's families for years, and they took an interest in young Raymond's career.[60] The personnel file of Charles Barker, a laborer appointed in 1902 to the General Land Office (GLO) of the Interior Department, contained recommendations from Senator J. R. Burton from Barker's home state of Kansas as well as from an assistant U.S. district attorney, the chairman of the Shawnee County (Kansas) Republican Central Committee, a local postmaster, and two newspaper editors. Perhaps most important was a letter from Kansas representative Charles Curtis, who happened to sit on the House Committee on Expenditures in the Interior Department.[61] For all of the systemization and concerns about merit that the Pendleton Act introduced into federal employment, appointments—and indeed, most aspects of personnel management—were decided by division and bureau administrators who could easily come under the influence of elected officials.[62]

In addition, administrators regularly took pity on candidates with compelling personal stories, the most common being a woman whose main source of support had worked in the government but had died or become disabled.[63] Black women were just as eligible for this consideration. For example, Maria Johnson's husband, James, an elevator conductor in the Bureau of Engraving and Printing, suffered an accident in 1904 that rendered him unable to work. The chief clerk spoke to James and thought him near death. Believing that James's unemployment would lead his family to starvation, the clerk recommended to the secretary of the Treasury that he waive the appointment regulations so that Maria could be given a position in the bureau immediately. Maria Johnson worked for the Treasury Department for the next thirty-five years.[64]

Joining the civil service did not guarantee such lengthy employment. In some cases, such as when a congressional appropriation called for more printers to help with a new currency issue or census reports were due, temporary appointments were made. These employees were not protected by civil service regulations. Significantly, black workers were overrepresented among the more insecure, temporary appointments. But even for those fully covered, the oft-used term "permanent appointment" could be a misnomer. In fact, the only legally necessary reason for dismissal was "for the good of the service," a discretion exercised by the appointing officer.[65]

Maintaining connections even after appointment was therefore crucial, especially if one hoped for promotion. Generally, a person who passed the clerk's exam and landed a job would be placed at the lowest clerical grade possible. Working one's way up was an essential feature of the civil service, and the records of African American federal employees generally bore the marks of hard work and mobility. Most began work as messengers and subclerks, even those who eventually earned places at the very top of the classified hierarchy. John A. Davis, for example, began his career in 1882 as a laborer in the GPO earning $500 a year. Bearing a recommendation from Iowa senator William Allison, he was making $1,400 a year as a Class 2 clerk by 1908.[66]

A bureaucracy did overlay this patronage network. Efficiency records were kept on every employee, and reports graded performance in areas such as punctuality, diligence, and accuracy. "Our principal source of excitement is wondering when the next efficiency reports will be sent out," Swan Kendrick told his fiancée. "They are made up twice a year, June 30th and Dec 31st and of course knowing that the board has been meeting off and on for the past two weeks, every one is guessing and prophesying."[67] Good reports and seniority were important for earning promotions, but political connections and recommendations were key to deciding which very good employees moved up quickest.[68] Kendrick did not rank in the top fifteen that time. "My real rival is a Mrs. Daniels, who was moved from 22 to 17; hope I will have a friend on the board next time."[69]

The subtle manipulation of people and institutional systems became integral to the game.[70] The preservation of politics in the civil service resulted in a number of "affirmative actions" operating for veterans, black Republicans, and women in cases where administrators felt that they were better suited for the work. They were also beating the bushes to bring in white southerners, who traditionally stayed away from Washington but who were needed to fulfill a regulation that the composition of the civil service reflect the nation as a whole.[71] Hence, though meritocracy was intended to expunge politics and personal connections from federal employment, it produced an inconsistent system that could be more representative but that was no less personal.

The civil service system was designed and established by the party leaders themselves, and they never wanted to deny themselves wholly the spoils of their political triumphs. Politicians and scholars from 1883 to today have continually argued that American democracy requires a relationship between party and administration.[72] Civil service rules never applied to the upper echelons of the U.S. government, for example, because political appointees were expected to be more sensitive to the electorate than an autonomous civil administration would be. Patronage did not simply seep through the cracks of the civil service; it strode in under a banner hailing democracy.

Roosevelt and the Tuskegee Machine

African Americans operated skillfully within this system. By 1900, a group of black journalists, academics, and politicians had coalesced in Washington into a "black cabinet." They met regularly at Gray's Restaurant at 13th and E Streets NW to discuss ways to influence American politics and the state of black America.[73] Most, though not all, were loyal to Booker T. Washington. Washington, principal of the renowned Tuskegee Institute in Alabama, was the most famous and well-regarded black man in America. When an assassin's bullet made Theodore Roosevelt president in September 1901, Washington replaced Republican kingmaker Mark Hanna as the central figure in the black and white Republican coalition. Whereas McKinley had relied on Hanna and a broad group of black advisors, Roosevelt leaned exclusively on Washington for advice and patronage recommendations. The young president placed Washington at the head of the black patronage machine, giving him the power to select and deny appointments. Roosevelt told Washington that he hoped to clean up southern patronage by appointing only the most worthy officeholders, regardless of race or even party.[74] Yet the new president was also motivated by a desire to avoid dealing with Hanna and the rest of McKinley's wing of the party.[75] That Roosevelt could continue to work with black Republicans while simultaneously trying to rebuild and reorient the party spoke to the depth and diversity of black politics at the turn of the twentieth century. When Roosevelt appointed Dr. William D. Crum, a Harrison Republican out of step with McKinley, to U.S. customs collector in Charleston, South Carolina, he did so in part to signal a new departure.[76]

Roosevelt sought to harness the financial and political empire Washington had built in the years following his famous Atlanta Cotton States Exposition speech in 1895, in which Washington argued that the fates of black and white southerners were tied together, with whites in the lead.[77] The speech had won the trust of white elites interested in black uplift philanthropy, and they poured millions of dollars into Tuskegee and Washington's war chests. Washington turned his philanthropic and educational juggernaut into the "Tuskegee Machine," a powerful political institution capable of rewarding friends with political office, punishing enemies with public humiliation, and holding at bay the growing lily-white movement within the Republican Party.[78] When Alabama Republicans tried to create an all-white convention in 1902, it was Washington who spurred Roosevelt's swift action against the white delegates. In a "private and confidential" letter to a Roosevelt lieutenant, Washington thundered, "[White] republicans all at once have become so righteous and pure that they now say they cannot permit even a dozen or a dozen and a half of Negro representatives, and these of the highest type, to appear in the convention with them, when for nearly forty years these hypocritical republicans have been assembling in convention with hundreds of colored people and they of the most ignorant type." The Alabama movement was snuffed out, at least temporarily.[79]

Theodore Roosevelt and Booker T. Washington at the Tuskegee Institute, circa 1902. During the Roosevelt administration, the black patronage machine came under Washington's firm control. The "Tuskegee Machine" held sway not only over presidential appointments but also over civil service positions. (Yale Collection of American Literature, Beinecke Rare Book and Manuscript Library)

Through the zealous and officious activity of his lieutenants — most important, his private secretary, Emmett J. Scott — Washington attempted to draw the entire world of black patronage into Tuskegee's orbit. Scott — who had served as secretary to another great black Republican operator, Norris Wright Cuney — monitored newspapers and Washington's correspondence looking for signs of friendship or disloyalty across black America, and he doled out rewards and punishments according to Washington's will.[80] From his desk in the small Alabama town that served as home to Washington's famous school, Scott mailed checks and strategic editorials to black newspapers all across the country. Calvin Chase's *Washington Bee*, for example, was generally a dissident, anti-Tuskegee voice, but this could change dramatically when Chase needed money to keep his paper going.[81] Tuskegee and its allies provided avenues to the capital and government jobs by forming a network of party players and administrators who would watch out for black job candidates and shore up black Republicanism. Writing to Roosevelt's attorney general, Philander Knox, in October 1901, Washington offered a list of names for a civil magistrate position and assured Knox that all were "good, clean, first class colored people and competent."[82]

A regime established under Harrison and centralized by McKinley reached a kind of maturity under Roosevelt and Washington. Roosevelt had always approached the civil service as a reformer, a modern thinker who would rationalize the bloated and lazy bureaucracy. Yet the fundamentally human system of affirmative action for chosen classes — veterans, African Americans, friends — persisted, especially within the classified civil service. In 1905, for example, Roosevelt himself issued an executive order transferring and promoting William S. Fuller, an African American messenger. Before joining the government, Fuller had been the butler of a friend of the president.[83] His interest in bureaucratic and civil service reform aside, Roosevelt's party and personal loyalty drove him to leave the Republican patronage machine largely intact.

Roosevelt, like most white Americans at the turn of the twentieth century, was a white supremacist. His refusal to publicly acknowledge the heroism of black troops who had served with him in Cuba is stark evidence of his fantasy that black people were incidental to American life. Even more, Roosevelt was a national spokesman for the preservation of the white race; he worried incessantly about the possibility of its decline in the face of industrialization, world peace, and immigration.[84] And yet like many Republicans, Roosevelt made a distinction between black people's racial or "social" inferiority and their basic political right to be a part of the nation.

His willingness to dine with Booker T. Washington and support the Tuskegeean's political agenda bore testimony to his belief that African Americans he deemed to be "worthy" deserved recognition.[85]

Thus, Roosevelt bolstered a Republican patronage machine that both served his own partisan interests and provided places for African Americans in Washington. Thomas H. R. Clarke entered government service in 1901, for example, fresh off campaign work for McKinley's reelection. He had gotten out black voters in the Mid-Atlantic states and written a pamphlet advocating the Republican ticket, all of which attracted the attention of Representative Joseph Sibley of Pennsylvania and Register of the Treasury Judson Lyons. After the election, Clarke began as an assistant messenger in the War Department at $720 a year. Within five years, he was making $1,200 a year as a Class 1 clerk in the Treasury Department.[86] Clarke could not have navigated Washington without men like Sibley and Lyons. Nor was he unique. When Thomas M. Dent received permanent placement with the Census Bureau in 1902, it was Lyons again who wrote to thank the director.[87] And when Lafayette Hershaw earned a promotion in the Interior Department's GLO in 1911, the *Washington Bee* ran a front-page notice acknowledging the work of Hershaw's black Republican sponsors.[88] White party figures, too, could assist. John Edward Bruce, a Republican journalist, repeatedly turned to James Clarkson to secure federal clerkships, which served as rewards for Bruce's nationally known "Bruce Grit" columns.[89]

The patronage machine could also be set in motion to save the career of a civil service clerk. In 1902, William Jennifer was about to be dismissed from his clerkship when Theodore Roosevelt was alerted to his status as "the only Colored man in the Census bureau from Texas" by some concerned citizens.[90] Andrew Houston, appointed by Roosevelt as a "marshal" for the party in Texas, visited the Census office and stated that Jennifer was "a representative colored Republican of the state; that the Republicans all over the state know that he is in the office; that he is the only colored appointee remaining and they want him to stay."[91] James Clarkson and John Dancy, the D.C. recorder of deeds, wrote to Jennifer's supervisor to ask for his retention as well.[92] Black civil servants supported the Republican Party and effectively cashed in that support for job security.

Patronage and civil service could carry economic, social, and psychological costs. The middle-class men and women with Victorian sensibilities who rose through the civil service ranks often held a deep ambivalence toward poorer African Americans, limiting both the diversity of their ranks and their sympathy for others less fortunate. Elite visions of economic inde-

Laura E. Joiner, circa 1920s. Joiner was a clerk in the General Land Office of the Interior Department for four decades. An Iowa native, Joiner graduated from Wilberforce University in Ohio and earned a medical degree from Howard University Medical School. Joiner's career, as in her self-presentation in this photograph, spoke of a modern woman of ability, confidence, and ambition, attributes that surely helped to make her one of the few black women to work as a white-collar civil servant in the early twentieth century. (National Personnel Records Center, St. Louis, Mo.)

pendence, gender roles, and public behavior could be highly decorous and mentally imprisoning.[93] Indeed, a constrained, more male-dominated political sphere may have been one of the first "prices" African Americans paid for participation in civil administration in the late nineteenth century.[94] Calvin Chase, dogged defender of civil rights, was a supreme sexist, declaring that "women are uncertain, sentimental, and stubborn and you cannot reason with them."[95] He railed against the public employment of married women, such as in the District's schools. "If a married woman is going to fill her sphere in the home well," he explained, "she would hardly have the time or desire to continue as a teacher."[96] Black women did exert their presence powerfully and publicly, including in federal offices. Laura E. Joiner worked as a clerk in the Interior Department from 1890 to 1933 and spoke at meetings of the Bethel Literary and Historical Club. Even Calvin Chase's sister, Fannie, pulled the patronage strings to land a job in the GPO.[97] But these women were exceptions, and for the most part, patronage and white-collar civil service were men's work, undermining the breadth of black politics and the options available to black women.

Patronage was still a relationship of dependence, despite all of the work and ability it took to be deemed "worthy" of it. "Every colored office-holder, as you are doubtless aware, holds his appointment upon the recommendation of Senator Hanna," Ohio black Republican and journalist Ralph Tyler explained to Booker T. Washington in 1901. "I became perfectly disgusted with the professional colored politician and office holder, who danced every time Mr. Hanna cracked the whip," Tyler raged.[98] The patronage wheel kept turning, requiring obeisance, regardless of who participated. It was a system that was by no means restricted to black party members, but it was particularly burdensome on them, as the default position toward black people at the turn of the twentieth century was suspicion. Eligibility for patronage and livelihood was won only by extreme fidelity to the Republican Party and the establishment principles for which it stood.

Thus, capable, well-connected black clerks continued to earn good positions into the twentieth century, but it was all based on a fragile arrangement that relied on the inclusiveness of white bureaucrats, the "respectability" of black leaders, and, perhaps most important, the power of the Republican Party in Washington, D.C. Patronage had not been eliminated from the civil service system. Rather, it had been systematized, and maneuvering required knowledge of how the promotion system worked, whose letters of recommendation counted, and when jobs could be considered up for grabs. Swan Kendrick, Thomas H. R. Clarke, Thomas M. Dent, and so many black government clerks benefited not simply from political connections but from a network of white and black politicians who, under the watchful eye of Booker T. Washington, ensured that the civil service merit system advanced them as "representative Negroes."

Yet as the presidency of William Howard Taft began in March 1909, unsettling changes in Washington were underway. The Republican machine could protect its adherents, but black patronage was coming under greater scrutiny. Though the Taft administration would not inflict anything like the segregation and white supremacy that would distinguish Woodrow Wilson's presidency, racism was already rising in government offices by the end of the Roosevelt era. The way in which a racial regime that had benefited black employees was destroyed and replaced is the subject of the chapters that follow.

Personally, I didn't care much who got in the White House if only
W. H. Taft got out.
— Swan Kendrick to Ruby Moyse, March 10, 1913

Chapter Three

The Sensibilities of the People

Black Politics in Crisis

Egalitarianism in Washington was fading as Theodore Roosevelt began his second administration in March 1905. White Republicans
had begun to acknowledge the disconnect between the southern electorate, by then almost entirely white and Democratic, and the national prominence of black Republicans from the South. The result was a legitimation by
the party establishment of disfranchisement and a disparagement of black
southern politics, especially during William Howard Taft's presidency. In
response, black politicians and voters splintered: some tried to salvage the
Republican coalition, while others sought a place among Woodrow Wilson's progressive Democrats. Neither strategy brought much success, and
Taft's failed reelection campaign would bring a seemingly sudden end to
the broad-based black patronage machine.

By 1912, the coalition of black and white spoilsmen that had used patronage power to recover black politics from the ashes of Reconstruction
was already floundering. Republican spoilsman James Clarkson blamed the

Republicans' decline during the Taft administration, in part, on the party's disloyalty to African Americans. Its commitment to black citizenship, once indicated by its inclusion of black politicians, had been hollowed out into a dishonorable shell game. For all of the pain and struggle black Republicans had experienced after Reconstruction, the 1910s were worse. For Clarkson, the only way back to "public confidence and respect" was a "return to the principles of Lincoln" and a "full and final redemption of Lincoln's pledge to the Americans of the colored race, in both their political and their civil rights."[1] But Taft had no intention of such a redemption. His own suspicion of social policy and the erasure of the southern black electorate mixed with his desire to economize and shrink government administration. African Americans fit less and less well into twentieth-century Republican ideas about the proper role of government. Taft did not imagine a total abandonment of black patronage in Washington, yet his administration laid important groundwork for the Wilsonians' more specific attack on black government work.

Taft's Surrender

In July 1906, Secretary of War William Howard Taft added an ominous coda to the usual Republican condemnation of southern politics. Speaking before a white audience in Greensboro, North Carolina, Taft concluded his criticism of disfranchisement with an attack on the idea that patronage might offer compensation to black voters. "When all hope of choice by the people is abandoned and everything is given over to influencing a distant appointing power," he declared, "the result is not good for the men or the community."[2] Taft's ideology may have been anti-spoils, but the meaning of such words from the likely Republican presidential nominee in 1908 was broader: the Republican Party should not be in the business of propping up black civic life in the South.

Events in Brownsville, Texas, later that year disabused African Americans of any hope that the secretary's words were just political talk. In November, a few days after the voters had delivered another congressional majority to Republicans, Americans learned that Roosevelt had ordered Taft to dismiss, without trials or courts-martial, an entire regiment of black soldiers stationed in Brownsville. The soldiers, all but 3 of the 170 African Americans stationed at nearby Fort Brown, were discharged for their alleged role in a riot that had taken place on a hot summer evening in August.[3] African Americans all over the country exploded with resentment and anger at

Roosevelt's wholesale dismissal as well as his calculated hiding of the order until after the elections.[4]

Tuskegee was noticeably quiet about Brownsville, and black leaders in the capital began to seriously debate Booker T. Washington's relevance.[5] In March 1907, elite men, including civil servants Lafayette Hershaw, Thomas H. R. Clarke, Shelby Davidson, and William LePre Houston, spent a long evening toasting Washington's intellectual adversary, W. E. B. Du Bois, over oysters, lamb chops, ice cream, and cigars at Gray & Brother's Café on M Street.[6] At a Bethel Club meeting a week later, Clarke, the good Republican and long-serving employee of Tuskegee-backed registers of the Treasury, declared that the successors to abolitionists Frederick Douglass and John Mercer Langston were none other than Du Bois and William Monroe Trotter, both Harvard men who despised Tuskegee's limited horizons.[7]

Brownsville was not enough to create a national insurgency among black voters in 1908. Roosevelt still made occasional pronouncements in favor of civil rights, and he managed the black patronage machine carefully in the days leading up to the Republican National Convention.[8] Taft won the nomination easily, and in the general election, most voters, black or white, did not turn against the Republicans or Tuskegee. Despite growing elite criticism, Booker T. Washington still commanded huge audiences in the capital, and he remained at the head of the patronage network that many credited with helping them find work.[9]

Over the next four years, however, the dissidents would gain more traction. Taft did little to shore up the GOP's flagging reputation among African Americans during his presidency. Among his crimes were forswearing the use of patronage to win black southern votes and attempting to reduce the southern delegation at Republican conventions—an act designed to put nominating power in the hands of people with electoral power but that would have had the effect of disarming black Republicans from the South.[10] Though Taft would later abandon both of these plans, his public advocacy of them put black party members on notice that Taft was looking for a way out of the patronage game. Taft had pleased some by appointing Tuskegee-backed men, including Register of the Treasury James Napier, a wealthy black Tennessean and the son-in-law of John Mercer Langston.[11] But his administration had also diminished the register's role, a move seen as an assault on the place of African Americans in the civil administration.[12] What had always mitigated charges of tokenism was the actual power and prestige of the few black appointments. Taft seemed intent on undermining that power. In fact, from the earliest days of his administration, federal personnel managers were beginning to wonder privately if a racially mixed civil service was practicable, even in Washington.[13]

Taft made it clear that he would not challenge white southerners on executive appointments. He did make pious pronouncements about political equality, and he used a congressional recess to appoint Harvard Law School graduate William H. Lewis as an assistant attorney general, at that time the highest-level appointment of a black man in U.S. history.[14] Yet soon after the election, Taft declared that his appointments would take into account white preference. In a carefully composed speech in Atlanta that merged coded racial speech with civil service reform rhetoric, Taft said he recognized "the difficulty of making proper selections in a part of the country where the sensibilities of the people are different from those of one's own section."[15] Taft and his audience knew well that local "sensibilities" in the South meant obedience to the Democratic Party and white supremacy. The *Atlanta Constitution* hailed Taft's speech as that of a "great American."[16] The South Carolina General Assembly was so thrilled that it considered a concurrent resolution in appreciation of the speech.[17]

Taft quite intended his words to mean the imposition of a color bar in southern states as far as federal appointments were concerned. William D. Crum, whom Roosevelt had appointed collector of the Port of Charleston and had publicly defended against racist objections in 1902, was forced to surrender his position under Taft. Crum was quickly shipped off as the minister to Liberia, where he contracted a terminal case of malaria. Though he did not say so publicly, Booker T. Washington found Taft's treatment of Crum disrespectful and disturbing.[18] Taft also removed Thomas Richardson, who had served for thirty-three years as the postmaster in Port Gibson, Mississippi. Richardson was placed, by Taft's executive order, in a high-level clerkship in the Washington office of the fourth assistant postmaster general. Richardson was lucky enough to be pulled out of Mississippi, while other black federal officials in the state were left to run out their terms and be replaced by white officials.[19]

Actions in the South mattered everywhere. "Fully eighty per cent of the colored voters in the northern states are either southern-born or have many near relatives back in the South," Ralph W. Tyler told Taft's secretary. "This interest and sympathy [with black southerners] is responsible for the unpopularity in the North of the removal of practically every colored officeholder in the South."[20] Some charged that the president's southern policy was leaving black federal employees vulnerable in the once-secure offices of Washington. Revealing the connection that leaders made between pa-

tronage and civil service, Tyler recommended that the president either appoint African Americans in the South or balance the losses with northern
appointments to help stem the assault on black federal employees.[21] But,
again, Taft seemed little interested in compensating black politicians for his
southern policies, and the effect was a profound shake-up of the status quo
in the capital.

Taft made a more serious run than Roosevelt at reforming the way government personnel were managed. He ordered the first precise accounting
of federal employment, asking every single employee to fill out detailed
information cards (cards that now universally asked for race), and he pio-
neered the use of a federal budget to trim the nation's bureaucracy.[22] Taft
also furthered Roosevelt's efforts to enforce more deliberate quantitative
rating systems for employees. He established a new Commission on Economy and Efficiency, and his administrators worked to streamline personnel
practices.[23] In 1910, Taft promoted Charles A. Kram to head the office of
the auditor for the Post Office Department. Determined to cut down the
salary expenses of his office, Kram cut fifty-eight temporarily appointed
employees. Twenty more were forced to resign. Early in 1913, female employees reported that Kram ran his office like a "sweat shop," converting
salaried employees to pieceworkers and limiting annual leave. Kram's management style involved mechanizing as much work as he could and diminishing workers to machine feeders, thereby reducing the necessary skills
and salaries.[24]

Calls for reform and economizing within the administration seemed to
fall hardest on black employees. The NAACP reported, for example, that
Kram had specifically targeted black employees for reduction.[25] In the Bureau of Engraving and Printing, administrators froze the wages of female
employees, a large portion of whom were African American.[26] Under Taft,
the patronage network that had protected and promoted black clerks
seemed to be breaking down. Even those with the very best Republican
connections found it harder to maneuver. Treasury clerk Charles Cuney, a
nephew of the Texas Republican Norris Wright Cuney, had been personally
introduced to Taft's secretary by Tuskegeean Emmett J. Scott. In July 1911,
Cuney was looking for a job with a better chance for promotion, perhaps
in the office of the register of the Treasury.[27] This was a relatively routine
request for well-connected clerks, but Cuney encountered resistance. He
grew desperate after Taft failed to win reelection, and even though he was
willing to take a reduction in pay, Cuney did not get his transfer.[28]

Cuney's story seemed to fit into a developing pattern that differed from that of previous Republican administrations.[29] In 1911, the NAACP's journal, *The Crisis*, noted that despite, or because of, the obvious success of many African American government workers, racism in Washington was increasing under President Taft. "Once [the anti-Negro campaign] howled at and contended against Dirt and Poverty; Bad Manners and innate and eternal Inferiority," the magazine editorialized. "To-day it contends against human beings, even though they are clean and thrifty and polite and can demonstrate their ability."[30] In February 1912, *The Crisis* reported that discrimination had led black employees to consider forming a "National Association of Afro-American Classified Federal Employees," the first time black federal employees outside of the Post Office Department contemplated organizing against a Republican administration.[31] Indeed, Calvin Chase was profoundly disturbed by Taft's administration, urging Washingtonians in 1910 to be aware of "white Republicans who are doing everything in their power to degenerate colored Americans."[32] The government's diminishing egalitarianism within its own walls seemed to have an effect outside also, as reports of segregation and discrimination around the capital cropped up increasingly after Taft's election.[33]

Ultimately, Taft's declining enthusiasm for black patronage stemmed from Republicans' developing view of social and welfare policy. Taft was no more or less racist or patronage-oriented than Roosevelt. Both were racists in the simplest terms. However, where Roosevelt's personality and individualism had led to all kinds of contradictory passions, from Anglo-Saxon pride to black rights, civil service reform to party loyalty, Taft held fast to a judicial detachment and, perhaps unwittingly, placed himself at the forefront of the conservative backlash against progressive politics.[34] As progressives began to strike out for a more involved national government, Taft stood for a less expansive state and a weaker chief executive.[35] A retreat from the needs of black southerners aligned this aspect of Republican policy with the rest of the party's platform.

Taft did not transform suspicion of black politics into a deliberate attack on African American civil servants, however. Ideologically endangered, the old racial regime was not yet extinct, but by 1912, black Republicans had been forced to adopt a more compromising tone. Ralph Tyler and a host of other politicians, including James Napier, William Lewis, Henry Lincoln Johnson, and Whitefield McKinlay assisted in justifying Taft's southern policy during his reelection campaign.[36] Their memorandum to the president reflected Taft's drastically narrowed view of the government's obligation to African Americans. They did not ask that Republican presidents stand against massive southern disfranchisement. The fact remained that the Constitution did not prevent a limitation of the franchise, they admitted. "Good government is a series of compromises," explained the leaders. The first step was for African Americans to act as good Republicans and "not confine their attention solely to their own special problem."[37] Yet even these powerful leaders could not dress up what was a fundamentally conservative version of Republican ideology. Perhaps a change in party could offer better prospects.

Seeking an Alternative

In Boston, William Monroe Trotter was on the case. Trotter, editor of the militant *Boston Guardian*, was not impressed with Taft's reasoning and accused the GOP of colluding with Tuskegee to further disfranchisement. Trotter condemned Booker T. Washington's accommodationist politics and, from the old abolitionist stronghold of New England, made a career of throwing militant daggers at Bookerite gradualism. Washington and the Republicans, Trotter said, were selfish and vainglorious. They supported only their own men, black spoilsmen and political hacks who were spineless and self-involved.[38] The threat of an African American bolt from the GOP was real. Despite longstanding claims by Tuskegee that resistance came only from "a few soreheads in Washington and Boston," 1908 had seen the strongest opposition yet by black politicians against a Republican candidate.[39] As black leaders turned to the 1912 election, some viewed wearily another fight for relevance within the Republican Party.

Others, however, saw opportunity. Those African Americans who expected jobs and favors from Democrats in 1912 now seem foolish or unrealistic. But it was not a lack of realism as much as it was a lack of imagination that blinkered their views. They could not envision U.S. politics without patronage, and they assumed that the Democrats would have to include African Americans loyal to the party. In 1908, the *Washington Evening Star* had noted matter-of-factly that a victory for William Jennings Bryan would mean the arrival of black Democrats to the usual positions in the departments.[40] Certain traditions would have to be upheld, and waiting in the wings was a cohort of black Democrats and independents ready to broaden the patronage power beyond a Republican coalition.

Adam E. Patterson was representative of black Democrats who hoped to forge an alternative to the Republican machine in the early twentieth century. Born in the tiny town of Walthall, Mississippi, in 1876, Patterson

William Monroe Trotter. A graduate of Harvard College and the son of a black Democrat who had served in the first Cleveland administration, Trotter was an early opponent of Booker T. Washington and the Republican machine. Trotter viewed the Republican Party as unreliable at best and, at worst, collusive with forces trying to diminish black citizenship. From Stephen R. Fox, *The Guardian of Boston: William Monroe Trotter* (New York: Atheneum, 1970).

earned a law degree and joined the increasingly beleaguered black middle class. In 1896, he supported Bryan, who struck some black voters as a sincere populist.[41] In 1904, Patterson moved to Muskogee in the Oklahoma Territory and established himself as an attorney and real estate broker. A latter-day Exoduster, he had lit out for the territories from Mississippi with tens of thousands of other black southerners to seek his fortune.[42] The move to Oklahoma represented Patterson's search for independence from the constrained economic, social, and political life of a black southerner. Oklahoma real estate offered a new frontier for black Americans, a place where, Patterson said, they could "promote good government" by becoming financial "stockholders in the body politic."[43] By the 1910s, Patterson had established ties to the Oklahoma Democratic Party and would work for Wilson's election in 1912, hoping to become the kind of patronage broker to black Democrats that Judson Lyons had been to black Republicans.

Patterson was by no means the first African American to aspire to political power from outside the Republican Party. An alternative to the Republican machine had existed since the 1870s, especially in the North. Leaders like James Trotter (father of William Monroe), Archibald Grimké, C. H. J. Taylor, Alexander Walters, John Edward Bruce, and T. Thomas Fortune, all prominent black politicians, journalists, and clergymen, had at one time or another advocated a turn away from the party of Lincoln.[44] Though they found the Democratic Party inhospitable, these black activists also found the Republicans ineffectual, sometimes hapless, patronizing, and, often enough, duplicitous. The removal of federal troops from the South and the general cooling of northern, Republican interest in the rights and "uplift" of African Americans had made some black leaders fear for the future of black citizenship. When the Civil Rights Act of 1875 was declared unconstitutional by the Supreme Court in 1883 and was never replaced or reaffirmed by Republicans in Congress, these fears seemed justified.[45]

Even when it worked, the GOP's black and white coalition was based too often on personal favors and influence and not on more fundamental grounds of civil equality. Booker T. Washington's consolidation of the system under Theodore Roosevelt seemed to place black politics even further from independent thinkers and an aggressive push for equal rights. For some, such as *Washington Bee* editor Calvin Chase, independence would help black voters to spur a competition for their votes and, thereby, demand more from the parties: "It is not necessary for all the negroes to die the same death."[46] Chase also resented the way Tuskegee's control over black patronage under Roosevelt had narrowed black politics in general. The editor, whose financial problems occasionally sent him begging to Tuskegee, knew as well as any the difficulty of remaining independent. But he and many others believed that the Republican Party could no longer be the sole provider of civil rights protection. Black strivers like those working in federal offices had to struggle too hard to protect what they had rightfully earned.

The primary goal of the independents was political relevance, because without it, African Americans lost both rights and jobs.[47] Some leaders, like Du Bois, Fortune, and Grimké, came to independence through an intellectual journey away from both the policies and political strictures of Republican loyalty. In the 1880s, for example, Grimké began to favor the free trade and low tariff policies of the Democrats.[48] But for most, their support could be earned by either party through a role in the creation of party platforms and access to federal jobs.[49] "We do not propose to run this [Republican] paper for fun or for our health," explained the black editors of a Kansas newspaper in 1894. "We are in it for money and if the Republicans will not give us a share of their patronage, perhaps some other party will."[50]

Independents blamed black Republicans for the party's betrayals, too, especially the conservative "Race Men" of the Republican Party, from the first black governor in U.S. history, P. B. S. Pinchback of Louisiana, to Mississippi senator Blanche K. Bruce, to the most celebrated of black Republicans, Frederick Douglass. These men commanded the unswerving admiration and loyalty of most African Americans. But as the stalwarts left national political power by 1890, some began to raise the question of whether or not the Democrats were really any worse than the Republicans.[51] Grover Cleveland's two Democratic administrations had not been total disasters for all black leaders. He was willing to follow some of the norms established by Republican administrations, especially through appointments.[52]

Black politicians outside the South felt freer to join the Democratic column. The National Colored Democratic League (NCDL) was founded in 1892 to be a central element of the party of Jefferson and Jackson, as opposed to the black auxiliary they accused black Republicans of being. It was composed principally of northerners, such as James M. Trotter, James L. Curtis, and J. C. Matthews, who had been well-served by connections to powerful Democratic machines in cities like Boston and New York, and westerners, such as Patterson, J. Milton Turner, and C. H. J. Taylor, whose political landscapes had not been so drastically narrowed by the southern Democratic Party. These black voters and politicians attempted to answer the increasing ineffectualness of the Republicans with truly partisan retort.

Being a black Democrat was not easy. Historian John Hope Franklin recalls that his father, who referred to himself as a "Jeffersonian Demo-crat," was treated as an "anomaly" and an outsider in turn-of-the-twentieth-century black America.[53] The Democrats were the party of outspoken white supremacists like "Pitchfork" Ben Tillman and the "White Chief," James K. Vardaman. The violent annihilation of the Republicans and black voters in the South and the creation of an all-white southern electorate had been a Democratic project. Their willingness to do nearly anything to forge the United States into a "white man's country" was manifest in every election and in the daily lives of African Americans by the end of the 1880s.[54] If this pattern had been inchoate in Cleveland's first administration, by the 1890s, it was impossible to deny, and until Roosevelt's second administra-tion, black Democrats were an isolated few.

But Brownsville and Roosevelt's shrinking commitment to black equality reignited the independence and Democratic movements. Under Taft, the independents had built enough steam to make their case to black voters across the country. The new National Independent Political League (NIPL), organized in 1908 by William Monroe Trotter and Baptist minister J. Milton Waldron, declared that black loyalty in response to Republican failures had actually spawned contempt in white party leaders for "subservi-ent" black voters.[55] To NIPL organizers, hypocrisy was a crime worse than white supremacy. "Whatever may be said of Tillman, Vardaman, Heflin et al., they are not hypocrites and do not seek to use the Negro and then kick him out," asserted a group pamphlet.[56] Another independent, W. E. B. Du Bois, told readers in the NAACP's magazine that Tillman's speeches needed to be broadcast so that his meanness could be heard and then exor-cised. "Let us tell the truth, unpleasant though it be, and through the truth seek freedom."[57]

Pragmatism, without illusion, led black independents to the Democrats in 1912. "The Negro should awaken to the fact that politics have become the machine for economic rather than sentimental expression," they declared, "and that therefore, neither the Republican party nor any other party will ever give something for what it can get for nothing."[58] Without real partici-pation in the political system as voters and officeholders, black Americans were losing their last hope in America.

Even though politically independent African Americans were a minority in 1912, they were among America's most high profile and elite black citi-zens. Trotter, by dint of his Harvard education and successful Boston news-paper, belonged to elite circles of black and white Americans. NCDL presi-dent and AME Zion bishop Alexander Walters commanded the significant resources and reach of both the AME and the AME Zion churches for his Democratic league. Upon the urging of Walters, for example, Reverdy Ransom, editor of the influential *A.M.E. Review*, endorsed Wilson. As officers in the nascent NAACP as well, Walters and Trotter were able to convince secular leaders like Du Bois that the Democrats were worth an experimental black vote.[59] All that was left was for the Democratic candidate to be someone who could unite black Democrats and independents.

That the candidate turned out to be Woodrow Wilson might be surprising. "Tommy" Wilson was a white son of the South. He was born in Staunton, Virginia, in 1856 and spent his childhood consumed by the Civil War and Reconstruction in Augusta, Georgia, and Columbia, South Carolina. Neither of Wilson's parents were born southerners, but his father, a Presbyterian minister, was involved in secession and the Confederacy's fight for slavery. Other than four years at the College of New Jersey (now Princeton University), Wilson lived south of the Mason-Dixon Line into adulthood.[60] He never disavowed the South as his own homeland distinct from the rest of the United States, despite his strong patriotic nationalism and a deliberately muted regional accent. "It is all very well to talk of detachment of view, and of the effort to be national in spirit and purpose, but a boy never gets over his boyhood, and can never change those subtle influences which have become a part of him," Wilson told an appreciative crowd gathered to memorialize Robert E. Lee at the University of North Carolina in 1909. "So I am obliged to say again and again that the only place in the country, the only place in the world, where nothing has to be explained to me is the South."[61]

And yet Wilson did seem to be something apart from the typical southern Democrat. After earning a doctorate at Johns Hopkins University, eventually to make him the only U.S. president with a Ph.D., Wilson became a scholar of American political development and a northern academic. He taught at Bryn Mawr College, Wesleyan University, and Princeton before assuming the presidency of Princeton in 1902. Entering politics in 1910, Wilson earned renown as a progressive, anti-machine governor of New Jersey. Though unwilling to speak publicly to integrated audiences, he met privately with Waldron and Trotter in July 1912. He made verbal promises to them and assured Alexander Walters that "should I become President of the United States [black Americans] may count upon me for absolute fair dealing and for everything by which I could assist in advancing the interest of their race in the United States."[62] Woodrow Wilson would govern *all* Americans without prejudice, black Democrats and independents said, and

Woodrow Wilson, August 1912. Though he could be a passionate and spirited stump speaker, Wilson's public image in the presidential campaign was that of a learned and abstemious scholar. Often depicted in political cartoons in a cap and gown, he cut a careful contrast to the blustery Roosevelt and blubbery Taft, of course, but also to the sweaty Fire-Eaters in the southern wing of the Democratic Party. (Library of Congress)

they were ready to help put the Democrat from New Jersey in the White House.

Black Republicans, by far the majority even in 1912, reacted to the increasing stridency of black Democrats with a mixture of derision and dismissal that betrayed real defensiveness.[63] When civil servant William T. Ferguson, after daring to support Bryan in 1908, tried to return to the GOP, Ralph Tyler told a Taft aide to close the door on him. Political profligacy, claimed Tyler, was a reflection of other moral failings, including the most heinous of all sins for a black man. "You will possibly recall that this same Ferguson was dismissed from the Census office some time ago for making presents, and writing love letters to a white lady clerk," noted Tyler. "He is one leopard that has not changed his spots."[64] The NIPL's dream was a farce and its organization merely a "paper army." NIPL supporters were not actually independents at all but "Negro Democrats" who had opposed Taft since 1908. Most were, declared Tyler, part of a claque, a paid group of political gadflies. Tyler's advice to Taft was to simply ignore them, and he assured Taft that he and other black Republican leaders would deliver the president the votes for reelection in 1912.[65]

Facing a tough election campaign, Taft took the complaints of black independents seriously. In September 1910, he reached out to Oswald Garrison Villard, a white journalist and treasurer of the NAACP, to request a list of potential black advisors, "not merely of the office-seeking kind."[66] Taft also ordered the investigation of every incident of a black officeholder being dismissed. He understood he needed to keep African Americans in the Republican fold, and he was counting on black southern delegates at the Republican convention. When he removed leading black Republicans from office in the South, he worked within the patronage machine to find them new positions.[67] Taft's conservative principles indicated in nearly every way an abandonment of black politics, but as with civil service reform, principle and party tactics could easily diverge in an election year. Black patronage and partisanship were still very much a part of national politics in 1912.

The End of the Affair

Taft's concern over wavering black politicians grew dramatically with Theodore Roosevelt's entry into the 1912 presidential campaign. Incensed over what he viewed as Taft's abandonment of his progressive and conservationist legacy, Roosevelt challenged him for the Republican nomination.[68] As he had in 1908, Taft approached the 1912 Republican National Convention with his hand firmly on the tiller of patronage. When Cyrus F. Adams, a well-known Republican journalist in Chicago, resigned as assistant register of the Treasury to work full time on Taft's reelection campaign, the president directed Republican National Committee chairman Charles Hilles to "take care of Adams" and offer him a place in the party headquarters in New York.[69] Taft explained to Treasury secretary Franklin MacVeagh his desire to kill as many birds as possible with a few black patronage maneuvers: "What I want to do is to take Adams out of office and send him over to Hilles. Then I want to put in Adams' place a colored man from Arkansas to whom I have promised the position. Adams has been so long in his present place that if you could find another position anywhere in the Treasury for which his present duties have fitted him, I could lift the Civil Service rules and put him in. I wish you would give your attention to this problem and help me out."[70] Taft also managed to beat back an effort by Roosevelt supporters to force popular primaries, so that he was able to build loyal delegations loaded with federal employees whose jobs depended on him.[71]

Loyalty, as always, was to be rewarded with job security. In February 1912, for example, Census clerk Ocea Taylor and Oliver M. Randolph, a clerk in the office of the fourth assistant postmaster general, were found to be involved with a Republican newspaper, a violation of civil service rules.[72] According to Randolph, Ralph Tyler passed word from "parties higher up" that the two black clerks would not be "molested in any way."[73] Taylor and Randolph kept their jobs after department officials landed on the spurious reasoning that the men were not really guilty of political activity, because their work was for civil rights generally. "To the average negro the support of the Republican Party appears as an essential result of his race," explained Census director E. Dana Durand.[74] The Taft administration worked hard to take care of its most loyal soldiers.

Impassioned delegates for Roosevelt showed up in Chicago anyway. It was, said the New York Times, a "sullen, ugly, ill-tempered" convention.[75] For Roosevelt, the Republicans had abandoned "the people" in the four years since he had left office. Sounding a theme that would ultimately help to elect the Democrat, Woodrow Wilson, Roosevelt declared Taft's nomination indicative of the rottenness at the core of the Republican machine. It was a rottenness, Roosevelt knew, that many pinned on black politicians, as William Jennings Bryan did explicitly during the campaign.[76] Nevertheless, Taft's conservative and African American base held firm, and the convention stuck with him. Roosevelt bolted, taking with him a mixture of progressives and wealthy friends who soon formed the Progressive Party.[77]

Black delegates were torn. Whitefield McKinlay found that the vast majority of northern blacks were against Taft.[78] Though Ralph Tyler assured the president by telegram from Chicago that the "colored delegates will stand by you to the end," he later admitted to Roosevelt that the black delegates had acted against their own wishes. "Our sympathies and hopes were bound up with you," he confessed.[79] But Taft had let it be known that black government work was dependent upon his reelection, leaving black leaders with little choice. Mississippi leader Perry Howard left the convention hall with the Roosevelt delegates, but most stayed behind to watch Taft build a platform that was more muted than previous Republican platforms on civil rights.[80]

For black voters frustrated with the Republicans, 1912 presented a political crisis. They could not sit comfortably with Taft; and Roosevelt's new Progressive Party had alienated many at its convention by refusing to seat black delegations from the South.[81] Further, Roosevelt had declined to include in the party platform an antiracism plank written by W. E. B. Du Bois, sending Du Bois and other black progressives into the Democratic camp.[82] Roosevelt gambled that Taft's support for black delegates had lost him any hope of winning southern states in the election. Setting upon a strategy long rejected by Republican leaders, Roosevelt built a shadow Republican Party in the South made up of lily-white organizations. He declared southern black delegates to be illegitimate representatives of "rotten boroughs."[83] In the long run, Roosevelt's work undermined the ability of black Republicans to operate as representatives of the national party in the South — the so-called black and tan coalitions.

For his part, Taft had misjudged his popularity among black voters. He believed that Roosevelt had erred in his use of lily whites to gain an advantage in the South. He was right: Wilson carried every state in the South. But Taft was wrong that Roosevelt's strategy would send black votes his way. For Taft, it seemed insane for African Americans to turn away from the regular party with all of its historical and structural connections to black politics. "Those who are venal I suppose he will retain, as well as some crazy ones."[84] The majority of black voters appear to have disagreed and supported Roosevelt.[85] Taft was too weak, and the Democrats were too dangerous. Roosevelt had too much goodwill dating from his first administration, and his progressive politics attracted black voters who expected more from the federal government than Taft was willing to offer. Independent Archibald Grimké, for example, who had voted for Cleveland and worked for Democrats in Massachusetts, could not bring himself to vote for a southern Democrat and cast his lot with the Progressives.

Among federal employees, however, patronage could still pull votes. There is no way to know how black government workers voted, but it is likely that most stuck by the Republicans because Tuskegee did so and they were afraid of losing their connections and their jobs. Treasury clerk Thomas H. R. Clarke protested Roosevelt's third-party campaign in speeches all over Maryland and claimed to be offended by Roosevelt's seeking a third presidential term, though his second one by election. More likely, it was Clarke's position under Tuskegee lieutenant James Napier in the register's office that tied him to Taft and the GOP.[86]

The experience of Robert Smalls illustrated the refusal of many federal employees to abandon the Republicans. Though Republicans were allowing the Democratic senators of South Carolina to block his renomination for U.S. customs collector of the Port of Beaufort, Smalls had no plans to defect from the Republican Party.[87] Even as it became apparent that Republicans were listening less and less to its recommendations, Tuskegee stuck by the party because there was too much to lose for its now decade-old political machine. Indeed, because of the function of this black-white alliance, threats to Republican dominance were terribly dangerous. "I ask that every colored man in the North who has a vote to cast, would cast that vote for the regular republican party," Smalls wrote in September 1912, "and thus bury the democratic party so deep that there will not be seen even a bubble coming up from the spot where the burial took place."[88]

Calvin Chase was keenly aware of the importance of politics for the salaries in his community in Washington: "Democratic success means a sweeping out from under us our present foundation of political recognition," wrote Chase on the eve of the election. "It means, in all probability, permanent destruction of that foundation, for with the unjust adverse sentiment now existing against the race, even should the Republican party be restored to power at the end of four years, it is improbable that we would recover all we shall have lost under a Democratic administration."[89] Put plainly, "If Wilson wins Negro clerks lose."[90]

Wilson did win, of course, and he did so reportedly with about 100,000 black votes, the largest exodus to date of black adherents from the Republican Party.[91] For some it was a one-time protest vote. Pension Bureau clerk Ferdinand Lee had been born a slave and risen to become a Republican convention delegate from Virginia in the 1880s. He understood the stakes of supporting the wrong party, having lost his position in the Pension Bureau after Grover Cleveland's election in 1884 and again in 1892. But in 1912, Lee joined the independents.[92] Such political independence had roots as deep as black politics itself but was pushed to the fore in 1912 by the declining place of racial liberalism in the Republican Party. Some who worked for Wilson's election hoped that, at the very least, a divided black vote might multiply the pathways to uplift.[93]

As the reality of Democratic victory began to settle in, the Republican "black cabinet" gathered at Gray's one last time. Over a banquet of "four prime o'possums and a trunk full of delicious Tuskegee sweet potatoes" sent directly by Booker T. Washington, the male luminaries of Washington society, including Tyler, Chase, McKinlay, William Houston, and James Napier, put the tragic election out of their minds to revel in each other's company. But Chase was already wondering what would happen to this world. "Will such a galaxy of men be seen holding similar positions under the incoming administration? Will Mr. Wilson have the confidence in an alleged Negro Democracy that Mr. Taft and Col. Roosevelt had in their Black Cabinet?"[94]

Ralph Tyler did not want to wait to find out. Days after the election, he begged the lame-duck president, unsuccessfully, for appointment to Haiti. "One dream of my life has been that some day I might serve my country, my people, in the capacity of Minister to Haiti—the oldest Black Republic." Tyler had a premonition that the United States was no longer the best place to work in the nation's service.[95]

Part II

A NEW RACIAL REGIME, 1913–1917

After the inauguration of Mr. Wilson, the hungry brows will infest this city, the hay-seeds of the South will permeate the government departments and eye one another, and say to themselves: that is a good place that "nigger" holds. I can sit down like he does and draw his salary.

—W. Calvin Chase, *Washington Bee*, November 16, 1912

The fact that you attempt to keep these people down shows there is something in them you fear.

—Archibald Grimké, testimony before Congress, March 6, 1914

Chapter Four

Democratic Fair Play

The Wilson Administration in Republican Washington

Swan Kendrick was ebullient on March 10, 1913. He had spent the week soaking up all the fanfare that accompanied Woodrow Wilson's inauguration. He was elated by the presence of black women in the suffragette parade and by "the colored soldiers (National Guards) and high school cadets, in the inaugural parade." Howard University, too, had entered its students in the parade's college section. Black Washington was well represented in the city's most important political celebration, a reflection of both the prominence of African Americans in the capital and the new administration's desire to appear egalitarian. The politics of it all really mattered, Kendrick told Ruby Moyse. "Everybody who stays in Washington for ever so short a time gets saturated with it, and straightaway imagines everyone else is."[1] Middle-class clerks, supposedly rendered politically inert by civil service rules, were of course saturated like everybody else. "Washington is a city of officeholders and political changes perhaps mean more here than anywhere in the country, in spite of civil service rules."[2] He was hopeful that the Democratic president would breathe fresh life into black federal employment.

Kendrick, it turned out, had misjudged Wilson. The Democrats who arrived in March 1913 aimed at reforming government, demolishing the Republicans, and instituting a whites-only civic life. Such change did not merely reflect a new ruling party. The timing of Wilson's administration was crucial. The coeval expansion of progressive reform, white supremacy, and Democratic power in Washington all contributed to a permanent shift in the national racial regime, one in which many progressive reformers equated African American social mobility with political corruption and social disorder. Black politicians and civil servants operated under patronage rules long ago established by white politicians, and patronage and congressional privilege continued in the progressive state. Yet as Americans moved toward a political and administrative system that aspired to efficient and centralized bureaucracy, Wilsonians used progressive critiques of patronage to malign black Republicans as corrupt and to associate egalitarian politics with dirty politics. White Democrats figured black government workers and the unsegregated capital city as unhealthy vestiges of the nineteenth-century spoils system. Through this racialization of patronage, Wilsonians began to transform clean government into white government.

Progressive politics converged with white nationalism in Woodrow Wilson's Washington. White southerners in the Wilson administration, accustomed to dominating society in nearly every way, found Washington's racial circumstances confounding and deeply unsettling. The failure of Congress to formally segregate black and white people in the District of Columbia left racists open to encounters with black Americans on an equal basis. The city's proud black people walked the streets freely and spent money they earned in federal paychecks. White supremacists, haunted by memories of Reconstruction, saw a federal city out of control, a society nearly ruined by Republican rule and black power. A clean, progressive capital needed not only Democrats but white Democrats to function morally and efficiently. Woodrow Wilson's demands for good government provided the progressive frame for an administration he loaded with white supremacists. The result was toxic for African Americans in the nation's service.

The New Freedom

The 1912 presidential campaign had been about the search for social harmony in the face of modern capitalism, industrialization, urban corruption, and white ethnic diversity. Four candidates battled for the White House, two of whom were viewed as Republicans and incumbents (Taft and Roosevelt). Two relatively new parties were prominent (Progressive and Socialist), one of which stood for a total reordering of American society. In the end, the campaign became a contest between brands of progressive politics. Most American voters had come to believe that the United States was in need of major reform. Its politics seemed dirty and inefficient. Its economy was prone to collapse, its society to class division. And poor people in cities and on farms were too vulnerable to the upheavals and commodification of modern life. "America to-day is in a somber, soul-questioning mood," began Walter Weyl's 1912 call for progressive change, *The New Democracy*. "We are in a period of clamor, of bewilderment, of an almost tremulous unrest."[3] In a show of support for new answers, nearly a million people voted for the socialist Eugene Debs; the most conservative candidate, Republican William Howard Taft, came in third.[4]

The winner occupied the firmer but still progressive ground between these extremes. The division of the Republicans and the socialist insurgency certainly helped Wilson, whose popular vote was actually smaller than William Jennings Bryan's losing minority had been in 1908. Still, the 1910 midterm elections had seen major Democratic gains, including the capture of the House of Representatives for the first time in eighteen years.[5] Since the Civil War, the Democrats had shattered into an ill-fitting collective of gold bugs and silverites, Mugwumps and Populists, New York Tammanites and New Jersey anti-Tammanites, southern racists, Midwestern progressives, black refugees from the Republican Party, unionists from Pennsylvania and farmers from Alabama, Catholics from Chicago and Baptists from Georgia. Yet during Roosevelt's second administration, they began to come together around a profound mistrust of northeastern capitalists. Asking "Shall the people rule?," Bryan had tied the Republicans to big business during the 1908 campaign, laying the foundation for Wilson's victory in 1912.[6]

During the campaign, Wilson painted Taft and Roosevelt as incapable of truly democratic change. Not only were Republicans responsible for the corruption in the federal government, but even progressive Republicans held a patronizing view of Americans. Roosevelt's "New Nationalism" campaign, for all its concern with social welfare, concentrated power in the hands of a few northeastern experts with a disdain for average Americans. "I do very much fear the ideas back of Mr. Roosevelt," Wilson explained. "For those ideas were bred in the very company which has debauched and debased the Government of the United States." Corporate interests had separated "the people" from their government. "If we are to redeem the promises of America to mankind we must redeem the Government of the United States from private control," Wilson told voters.[7] Republicans, conservative or progressive, did not really want to listen to the majority of Americans.

In his campaign book, *The New Freedom*, Wilson argued that a functioning government was one in which all members worked in collaboration and an open discussion of ideas was guaranteed. He was seeking a "method of talk, of exchange of opinion, of parlay," Wilson said. Removing impediments to this "honest" talk, especially special and corporate interests, would allow leaders to speak effectively for the people and govern.[8] And speaking for "the people," in Wilson's opinion, was the job of great men who could not only articulate the people's desires but also lead them toward the best outcome for all Americans. He appeared to many, according to journalist A. Maurice Low, to be "a champion [of the people] rather than a political leader," for he "shared with them their aspirations and held the same ideals."[9] Championing was not the same thing as regulating. Experts were "smug" elitists who made decisions from far away; true leaders were merely humble shepherds deeply connected to the needs of their flock.[10]

Wilson imagined a strong government, but he located the source of that strength in decentralized federalism. The new president had long argued for an understanding of the Constitution and federal power that allowed for contending with "the exigencies and the new aspects of life" but always within the "legitimate extension" of federal power, an "extension which does not change the character of the Federal power but only its items—which does not make new kinds, but only new particulars of power."[11] With his emphasis on the difference between structures and "particulars," Wilson seemed to be far more respectful of traditional institutions, what Wilson called "habits," than Roosevelt. He did not want to change Americans himself, only their circumstances so that they might develop on their own into better people. As opposed to the inflexibility of Taft and the grandiosity of Roosevelt, Wilson spoke for many Americans' desire to restore harmony and unity against the social "fragmentation" of modern life, all the while cautiously guarding individuality and localism.[12]

In many ways, it was a strange and ambiguous brew, which, as journalist George Kibbe Turner noted in February 1913, cloaked Wilson and his plans for his administration in mystery. "It has been nearly thirty years since there has been such absence of information concerning the incoming national administration as exists today in the wisest centers of the political news in

Washington," Turner wrote in *McClure's Magazine*. Wilson, already famous as a leading scholar and university president, had made his political name as governor by fighting the old New Jersey Democratic machine and pushing a series of reforms, like anticorruption laws and utility regulation, through the state legislature in less than two years in office. But, wondered Turner, what would such progressive politics look like on the national level, when his opponents were not northeastern politicians but powerful and conservative southern Democrats? Would he retreat to the "stream of political generalities which glittered so brightly through the campaign"? Who was this "solitary, self-contained man"?[13]

One thing seemed clear: Woodrow Wilson's election did not bode well for African American civil servants. He was the first southern-born president since the Civil War. He was also the first Democratic president to enjoy undivided government in eighteen years. Moreover, in the area that concerned black civil servants most, departmental administration, Wilson was a committed reformer. He was, after all, a former vice president of the National Civil Service Reform League and the founder of the study of public administration in the United States. Not surprisingly, then, Wilson always advocated a nonpartisan bureaucracy. "Administration lies outside the proper sphere of *politics*," he wrote in his foundational article "The Study of Administration" in 1887.[14] The political ties that had protected black civil service were anathema to such managerialism.

Yet Wilson never insisted upon a civil service entirely cut off from the electorate, despite founding a field of study deeply concerned with the dichotomy of politics and administration. Politics, properly channeled, tied administration to the people and the ideas it served. "The ideal for us is a civil service cultured and self-sufficient enough to act with sense and vigor," he explained, "and yet so intimately connected with the popular thought, by means of elections and constant public counsel, as to find arbitrariness or class spirit quite out of the question."[15] There was no place for an autonomous civil service like that of Meiji Japan or Great Britain in the democratic United States, said Wilson, and nearly all American politicians shared this view.[16]

Patronage and congressional privilege continued to flourish in his administration.[17] Democrats were simply too hungry for jobs that they had been shut out of since 1897. Wilson agreed with Democratic operatives that his need for a united party would have to come before his desire for clean government. His presidential secretary, Joe Tumulty, had already become proficient at using the patronage stick to achieve progressive legislative victories as Wilson's secretary in New Jersey. Apparently sickened by the whole thing, Wilson fled to Bermuda after the election, leaving much of the dirty work to subordinates. Secretary of State William Jennings Bryan, whom Wilson referred to as a "spoilsman to the core," carried enormous political debts from three presidential campaigns, for example, and managed to purge most of the State Department of active Republicans.[18]

The replacement of Republican spoilsmen with Democratic ones was a major change for African Americans. And it is easy today to view Wilson's election in 1912 as a final blow to black civil service. Simply put, white Democrats did not have the kinds of personal and historical connections to African Americans as did white Republicans. Moreover, the justifications Republicans offered for their recent failures to stand up for black southerners, from states' rights to civil service reform to administrative efficiency, were strongly shared by the new Democratic president. Wilson's status as a progressive reformer in New Jersey presented a clear threat to the kind of political maneuvering that had preserved a space for black Republicans in Washington. Politicians, Wilson believed, needed to channel moral "virtue" into their service to Americans, and he did not see African Americans as fitting into a new ethic of clean politics. Finally, Wilson typically privileged concepts like neutrality and efficiency over ideals of justice, a practice that allowed him to stay above more troublesome issues like disfranchisement and segregation. All in all, it was unlikely that Wilson would direct his patronage managers to work hard for black job candidates.[19]

Nevertheless, black Democrats believed they had reason to hope for a renewal of black patronage under Wilson. Wilson's bowing to the patronage machine meant that African Americans who had campaigned for the president at least had a claim on the administration, one Wilson himself acknowledged.[20] Racism was nothing new in the White House. If the patronage machine could overcome the racism and "good government" reforms of other presidents, why should it necessarily be so different under a progressive Democrat? In fact, Wilson and many within his party were unsure of how to deal with black Democrats. As in most of Wilson's achievements, policy would come only after an extended period of negotiation among key players, in this case Wilson's administrators, black civil servants, and civil rights organizations.

A Model Capital City

Some Democrats placed black power at the center of their complaints about Republican rule in the capital. Campaign promises to segregate every part of Washington had brought Democratic audiences to their feet during the 1912 campaign, and during the next few legislative sessions, Democrats would try (and fail) repeatedly to segregate federal offices and the city's transportation system.[21] White supremacists hoped that Wilson and his new administration would establish racial order in a Republican city out of control. Order required not simply Democrats in federal offices but white Democrats.

Washington and its federal officeholders had long been emblematic of political corruption, especially since Reconstruction. The sectional reconciliation at the turn of the century had led to some agreement about the necessity of the Union and even the virtue of Lincoln, and most white Americans believed that Reconstruction had involved too great an imposition of federal power.[22] White southerners, however, saw more than a failed experiment: the Republican Congress that dominated the war's aftermath had led the nation morally astray. Wilson's own writing was an important source of this particular narrative. Lincoln had sought national unity; the Radical Republicans in Washington, free of any southern representation in Congress, had run roughshod over the Constitution and, Wilson wrote, put the South in the hands of "a vast 'laboring, landless, homeless class,' once slaves, now free, unpracticed in liberty, unschooled in self-control; never sobered by the discipline of self-support, never established in any habit of prudence; excited by freedom they did not understand, exalted by false hopes; bewildered and without leaders, and yet insolent and aggressive; sick of work, covetous of pleasure, — a host of dusky children untimely put out of school."[23] Black southerners, "children still," had been forced to turn the government over to "unscrupulous men" from the North who had "come on expedition for profit" and left behind "ruin."[24]

While Washington had served as a hopeful laboratory for Radical Republicans and African Americans, for Democrats it embodied everything that was wrong with Republican racial politics.[25] Early emancipation and early enfranchisement, vibrant black politics, assertive black laborers, wealthy and educated black families in close proximity to the nation's levers of power: it was all a terrible nightmare for white supremacists. And unlike the Reconstruction South, in the federal capital it was a nightmare from which they had not yet awoken.

Of course, racial politics was far from the only problem Democrats had with Republicans. The tariff, monopolies, and monetary reform were serious areas of disagreement. Even in the capital, Democrats complained more often about Republican corruption than explicit "Negro domination."

In its inaugural issue in 1906, the Hearst-owned *Washington Herald* promised to be "an honest newspaper and a clean newspaper." Positioning itself
against the rival Republican *Star*, the *Herald* "starts out clean and will be
kept clean."[26] The *Star* reflected a dirty kind of politics and patronage that
infected the city with corruption and dishonesty.

The Republican-dominated civil service became a symptom of the infection. When Mississippi senator John Sharp Williams noted that instead of
forced retirement plans in federal offices, elderly workers were "hang[ing]
like barnacles upon the very bottom of the ship," he was expressing the opinion of many Democrats that Republicans in Washington were suffused with
entitlement.[27] With a majority in the House and new strength in the Senate
after the 1910 elections, Democrats pushed through a bill limiting classified
employees to seven-year terms. Recognizing the bill for what it was, more
an attack on Republican officeholders than civil service reform, Taft vetoed
it. A month after Wilson's inauguration, the Democratic chairman of the
Senate Civil Service Committee, Atlee Pomerene of Ohio, opened hearings
to investigate alleged Republican favoritism in the merit-based civil service.
Though little came of the investigations, Democrats continued to paint the
civil administration as lousy with overpaid Republicans.[28]

In their efforts, race served as useful shorthand for the problems of Republican rule in Washington. For example, when Democratic congressman
William Borland of Missouri went on a campaign to increase the hours of
federal clerks in 1916 (an effort that would inspire the first federal employees union), he put a black face on civil service laziness and privilege. "On
the slackers we need waste no sympathy," he informed Congress. "I am told
that among the young negro couples it is customary for both the husband
and wife to take the civil-service examination and secure appointment, if
possible, in the same office. As they get to work late in the morning and go
home early in the afternoon, it is possible for them to keep house and raise
an interesting brood of pickaninnies while drawing two comfortable salaries from the Federal Government."[29]

Though the parties always charged each other with corruption, black Republicans were especially dogged by the accusation, as nearly every black
appointee was maligned by the label "merely political" or even by more
specific charges of corruption.[30] That the charges against black politicians
were occasionally true was more an indictment of politics at large than of
black politicians. Moreover, African Americans never had the autonomy or
power to cut deals among themselves only. When black politicians participated in dirty politics, they did so in league with white politicians. None-

theless, African Americans were regularly held apart from systemic problems. On the front page of that first edition, the *Washington Herald* ran a
lengthy description of South Carolina senator Ben Tillman's latest racist
logorrhea, a plan for the prevention of "a great race war" and "protection
of white women" by tracking every movement of black Americans through
government-issued passports, an updated and nationalized version of antebellum slave passes.[31] The message was clear: Republicans were still willing
to let African Americans run amok, and only the Democrats fully understood how to take control.[32]

Ben Tillman actually fancied himself a reformer. An advocate of national
progressive policies for laborers and farmers and moderate railroad regulation, Tillman was frequently a populist in economic policy as long as the
beneficiaries were white. And though his feverish racism seems out of place
in portrayals of progressive politics, Tillman was typical of southern politicians who sought reforms within the confined space of the white South. In
this way, he was not a "conservative." The same was true of Senator Hoke
Smith of Georgia, who had served in Cleveland's second administration,
and Mississippi senator John Sharp Williams, who, despite an aristocratic
mien, fit the easiest of the three into a progressive fold.[33]

Seeing Washington firsthand joined southern senators' race fears to other
concerns about urban disorder. The complaints Tillman, Smith, Williams,
and other Democrats voiced about Washington, loaded as they were with
racism, were also part of a transatlantic discourse about the decay of cities.
This turn-of-the-century conversation transformed longstanding Anglo-
American discomfort with urban living into an urgent pursuit of rational
and governmental "solutions" to the social problems of modern industrial
cities, from class conflict to child labor to crowded houses.[34]

Washington followed a pattern for cities that grew larger and more di-
verse at the end of the nineteenth century. Though not transformed by industry, to visitors and residents alike, the District seemed to be far more
chaotic and heterogeneous than it had been before the Civil War. While
many, including elite African Americans, reveled in the vibrant capital,
greater size brought greater problems. The government and its city raced
to meet the tasks of administering first war and then the country's massive
postwar industrial growth. The government and its need for labor expanded
at the same time that thousands of African Americans poured into the city
seeking work and shelter from the South's post-emancipation paroxysms.[35]

By the end of the century, numerous associations had sprung up to tackle
the problems of urban life in Washington. The Associated Charities, the

Civic Center, the Monday Evening Club, the Committee on the Improvement of Housing Conditions, and the Citizens' Child Labor Committee all studied and publicized the city's problems in order to drive philanthropic organizations and government toward new ways of viewing and improving city life. Previous eras had seen plenty of concern about poverty and crime, but the turn of the twentieth century was notable for reformers' belief that scientific and objective information brought out into the open could yield real and lasting change in the conditions and directions of people's lives. Though loaded with paternalism and moralistic judgment, city elites took seriously the way growth and poverty were undermining the wellbeing of the society as a whole.[36]

A model capital could serve as a beacon to other similarly afflicted cities, but politicians differed over what constituted ideal city life. In May 1914, a Senate subcommittee convened to consider legislation to clean up Washington's alleyways crowded mostly with poor, black families. Democrats were involved in these efforts, though always with some defined limits. Maryland senator John Walter Smith, who chaired the subcommittee, believed it was "the duty of the city to furnish proper sanitary conditions," a clear stand for the role of government. Yet he also argued against the government providing housing for those removed from the alleys.[37] John Sharp Williams was willing to think more comprehensively, offering legislative plans to turn Washington into a "'model territory'" by eradicating its slums, ending child labor, and improving its governance.[38] Theodore Roosevelt had also called for making Washington a "model city," much as Radical Republicans had done a generation earlier.[39] But the ideology behind Williams's model city was, of course, very different from the abolitionism and racial egalitarianism of mid-nineteenth-century Republican idealists.

Moral fears of urban chaos led many reformers in both parties away from broader democracy. Instead, they sought to inculcate orderliness and middle-class probity and inoculate the native white population against the city's potential poisons.[40] Those motivated by a Christian social gospel to serve the neediest did seek to address directly the struggles of African Americans. Yet even these more inclusive progressives, black and white, held disadvantaged people up against a civilizationist standard that frequently served to confirm people's worst fears about the rottenness of cities as much as it helped to delineate the need for change.[41] Journalist Jacob Riis's famed photography of New York slums, for example, simultaneously motivated Americans to make things better *and* labeled the people and places in those photographs as dangerous, inferior, and un-American.[42]

For white southerners looking at Washington, nothing symbolized that erosion of moral and community welfare better than the size and prominence of the capital's black population. "No matter where or when the scene may be in Washington," noted one senator's wife in 1901, "the ubiquitous negro colors it."[43] A report by the city health department in 1913 regarding smallpox, for example, displayed the fear among white Washingtonians that the color line was no protection from the city's non-white residents. Noting that the disease was more prevalent among African Americans, an official bulletin recommended that white city residents should "not believe themselves safe because smallpox is not yet prevalent amongst them." The problem in a city like Washington was that even residential segregation did not mean true separation. "The points of contact between the races are so numerous, through the public domestic service, through street cars, through public eating houses, possibly through places where beverages are sold, through washerwomen and through other services," said the city's health officer, that no one was safe from the disease black residents seemed to be breeding.[44] The belief that contact with African Americans, whose higher rates of poverty did often result in more sickness, could spread disease had long been a potent concern for white Americans, belying any pretense by white people that the color line held firm.

Thus, exposure to life in Washington could turn some senators, even those from states as rural as Mississippi, into urban progressives. To be sure, most southern Democrats showed little interest in urban reform, and D.C. was not suddenly home to the "teeming masses" of immigrants that so frightened old-line white Americans and inspired ground-level activists in other major cities. Yet Washington did have crowded slums in easy view of better-off citizens, and federal patronage resembled the local political machine of cities like Chicago and New York. Republicans, without input from white southerners, had long controlled the capital's governance and the management of its most important public institutions, the federal departments. Jobs went to Republicans in Washington the way they went to Tammanites in New York. It was exactly the "private processes of nomination by party managers" that Woodrow Wilson had warned against as a political scientist.[45]

In Washington, "dirty" politics brought not merely political corruption but racial mixing, which evoked in Democrats an especially strong desire for social control. The problem in Washington, declared one of the earliest citizen letters William Gibbs McAdoo received as Wilson's secretary of the Treasury, was that the city was not properly managing its population. "People generally blame the negro, but where there is efficient government there is generally a small rate of murder among the negroes," the writer noted. What Washington needed was strong colonial control over its black population. "There are nearly 800,000 negroes in Jamaica. Last year there were 8 murders in Jamaica, as against 30 in Washington." The problem was obvious: "The negro constitutes about one-quarter of the population of Washington, and contributes about one-half of the crimes."[46] As in the post-emancipation South, African Americans in Washington were not ready to handle the privileges Republicans bestowed upon them. The inevitable result was crime, corruption, and immorality. White supremacists hoped that Wilson would restore law and order in the nation's capital in the same way he had sought to destroy machine-ridden urban politics in Newark, New Jersey. Washington was the most national of all American stages, and taking control of African Americans there could help bring racial order to the country as a whole.

For Wilson, the key to cleaning up the city was harnessing the "natural instinct for organization" bestowed to Americans by their "Germanic" and "English" ancestors. While Wilson was not a "race thinker" on the order of Theodore Roosevelt, it is easy to find references to races of people—especially white races—in his writing.[47] What made the United States great, and what could once again make its cities great, was a "community" that understood its common traits, desires, and needs and could arrive at an understanding of the "general interest." Like other progressive social scientists, Wilson believed this general interest, sometimes called the common good, could be achieved only when the nation's best people crossed lines of "taste" to engage the people in the worst circumstances. Only then could interests be harmonized for the good of all.[48] "If you don't like dirt, if you don't like rooms that are not properly appointed, if you don't like stale air, if you don't like manners that are not like your own, then you have a wall built between you and the people who live where they can not keep their premises clean, where all the conditions of life exclude taste," Wilson wrote in a 1911 issue of the progressive journal American City.[49] Despite the seemingly benign nature of Wilson's abstractions, it is apparent that a healthy community in his thinking was one that brought the uglier features of modern industrial America into harmony with the nation's better nature, embodied by its Anglo-Saxon majority.[50] Though Wilson spoke warmly of eastern European immigrants and vetoed immigration restrictions, his concern for social harmony betrayed discomfort with both the heartlessness of industrial capitalism and the incivility of the ethnic poor it brought to

American cities — both of which needed to come under the influence of leaders imbued with an understanding of the common good.[51]

Cities at the turn of the twentieth century were suffering the same fate as the South had in the 1870s, according to Wilsonian thought. Political machines motivated by profit took advantage of the ignorance of "backward" peoples to pursue corrupt and unwholesome policies. The solution, Wilson explained, was building a moral government that could lead by legitimate example, as "redeemed" southern legislatures were presumably doing. Wilson applied this model to all who needed white stewardship. When considering the case of the Philippines under U.S. occupation nine years earlier, Wilson had argued that Americans must accept an imperative to influence and "impart to the peoples thus driven out upon the road of change." Filipinos had been thrust suddenly into modern life, and Americans needed to "teach them order and self-control in the midst of change; impart to them, if it be possible by contact and sympathy and example, the drill and habit of law and obedience which we long ago got out of the strenuous processes of English history."[52] The need for right-minded leaders always undergirded Wilson's faith in "the people." It was up to leaders to educate the masses on the necessity for reform for the good of all. "Our duty," Wilson declared in his first inaugural address, "is to cleanse, to reconsider, to restore, to correct the evil without impairing the good, to purify and humanize every process of our common life without weakening or sentimentalizing it."[53] Whether those masses were living in urban slums, in southern Black Belts, or on faraway islands mattered little.

Calls for racial segregation most clearly connected southern Democrats' ideas about law and order with those of urban progressives in Washington.[54] Segregation restored order by more means than merely separating white and black people. Segregation was also a method of managed contact, much as enslavement had been: a way of keeping African Americans close and available for service, and perhaps tutelage, but not too close or too empowered. "There is no opposition to colored men being messengers and laborers in this Department," explained one Post Office employee.[55] Constant interracial contact was acceptable, so long as black people were in a distinctly subordinate position. Indeed, even an explicitly racist bill to segregate the civil service made an exception for "messengers, janitors or porters."[56] The problem was that in Washington, African Americans had maintained a good deal of social, political, and economic prominence, even as segregationists were instituting white supremacy throughout the United States. Democrats promised to finally bring Washington into line with the rest of the country and, thereby, return the nation as a whole to the tranquillity of the past. Much like other "progressive" tools of reform, segregation was a new and modern technology for restoring an order that supposedly existed before modern life brought so much class and ethnic strife.[57]

D.C. socialite and social reformer Charlotte Hopkins illustrated the relationship between white progressives and segregation. Hopkins was involved in a number of black uplift projects, including a black settlement house and an alley reform effort led by J. Milton Waldron. While she appears to have put off efforts to enjoin her in more aggressive white supremacist activism, Hopkins accepted segregation in government offices as a way of bringing order and protecting white female workers. She saw no contradiction between her reform and uplift impulses and segregation. Such was the nature of white paternalism among most progressives. Some progressives did object to segregation. Charles Weller of the Playground and Recreation Association of America, for example, crusaded against Washington's urban slums but strongly urged Wilson not to segregate federal departments.[58] Yet by the 1910s, the subordination of African Americans in the cause of social uplift had been normalized. As Wilson put it toward the end of his tale of Reconstruction, the redemption of southern governments by white southerners had returned a "normal balance" to American life. Segregation and black disfranchisement were salubrious to the society as a whole. "It is marvelous what healing and oblivion peace has wrought, how the traces of Reconstruction have worn away."[59] The problem, of course, was that in 1913, no such "peace" had yet been brought to Washington.

Clean Government

The racist potential of progressive social thought was apparent in the anticorruption campaigns of Democrats. In 1912, the National Democratic Fair Play Association (NDFPA) was founded to draw attention to the various perfidies of Republican management of Washington. Shortly after the inauguration, the NDFPA sent the White House a top-to-bottom plan for building a white man's capital. In his fourth letter to Wilson, NDFPA officer John Adriaans called on the new president to turn his "attention to one of the largest unsolved problems pending before the American electorate; to-wit: the negro question."[60] A "Dear Madam" mass mailing, sent also to Wilson, begged its recipient to join the association to help "labor for the segregation of the races, the complete supremacy of the white race, and the purification of the institutions of a White Man's Country."[61]

The NDFPA publicized one of the earliest "reverse discrimination" arguments in American history by blaming the Republican Party for the relative absence of white southerners in Washington. The point was not simply
that Republicans had worked *for* black citizens. The party had been, since
Reconstruction, endeavoring to discriminate *against* white southern men.[62]
By employing black men and women in federal offices in Washington, white
southerners (that is, Democrats), morally and culturally disposed to be re-
volted by the very idea of sharing work space with black people, were kept
from enjoying political patronage and a federal paycheck.[63] By placing African Americans in federal offices, Republicans had made those places — and
those jobs — noxious to "Negrophobic" Democrats.

The NDFPA's name was a careful construction. First, it attempted to connect the group with the official Democratic Party, though there is no evidence that the Democratic National Committee officially sanctioned it.
More important, "fair play" was a phrase with a long history in civil service
reform, referring to removing arbitrary discrimination in the patronage system. It was the opposite of irrational and inefficient political favoritism,
also known as "spoils."[64] And like all civil service reformers, the NDFPA
proposed a thorough analysis of federal employment in order to reveal empirically its many failings. The problem was, these progressives maintained,
most people had no idea what really went on in Washington. "The civil service is in reality a big business and is in itself a study worthy of any man's
time," explained NDFPA president Ernest Martin.[65] Study would lead to reform, and indeed, a "Platform of the National Democratic Fair Play Association" forwarded to Wilson by Senator James Reed of Missouri included
general anticorruption reforms of the civil service as its first six resolutions
before turning to racial segregation. At a meeting that was ostensibly held
to expose the abuse of white women by black men in federal offices, one
speaker rose to emphasize the ineffectiveness of the Republicans in the
Indian Service. "Now that the Republicans are out of office, I hope that the
Democrats will make some much needed changes," the speaker said. "We
ought to have a clean new deal in the Indian Service."[66]

Anticorruption rhetoric that connected black Republicans with the
spoils system helped to delegitimize Republican and African American
administrators.[67] For example, in May 1913, Wilson's postmaster general,
Albert Burleson, aroused Republicans by demanding that fourth-class postmasters be chosen by competitive exams. In its coverage of the debate, the
New York Times noted that the most important fourth-class appointee cur-
rently under consideration in the Senate was Robert Smalls of South Caro-

SHALL THE NEGRO RULE?

Is a serious question with this Association. We contend that negroes are not legally entitled to vote, and this Association in October last filed a brief in suit 423 U. S. vs. Guinn & Beal, of Oklahoma, showing proofs of this contention. The Supreme Court has put the case over to the October term.

HOME RULE FOR THE DISTRICT OF COLUMBIA

Is also heartily indorsed by us. We dare to tell the President of the United States that he violates his party's platform when he appoints a non-resident to the purely local office of Recorder of Deeds.

THE NATIONAL DEMOCRATIC FAIR PLAY ASSOCIATION

Incorporated for the purpose of testing in the highest courts the negro's right to vote, and which is making a nation-wide fight on the question, has called

A MASS MEETING

To Be Held Under the Auspices of the Association at

Old Masonic Temple, Tuesday June 30th, 1914, at 8 o'Clock P. M.

To Oppose the Appointment of a Non-resident Black or White for the Office of

RECORDER OF DEEDS FOR THE DISTRICT OF COLUMBIA

We have invited the following gentlemen to address the assemblage, and many acceptances have been received at this writing:

The Hon. James K. Vardaman, Hon. Hoke Smith, Hon. J. Thomas Heflin, and the Presidents of All Citizens' Associations

Permanent headquarters have been established, and the fight has only just commenced. The only sources of revenue are from the sale of the Comprehensive and Convincing Brief, membership fees, and contributions.

EVERY BONA FIDE CITIZEN OF THE DISTRICT OF COLUMBIA

Is cordially invited to attend this great outpouring of indignant people—at the audacity of the proposed payment of a political deal at their expense. If it is impossible to be there, send in your application for membership. Active membership, $1.00; honorary, $10.00; life member, $50.00 upward; Contributing members, 25 cents monthly. Copies of "Adriaan's" brief, $1.00; synopsis "Adriaan's" brief, 25 cents. For further particulars call or address LORENZO G. WARFIELD, Secretary The National Democratic Fair Play Association, Washington, D. C.

The National Democratic Fair Play Association, Washington, D. C.

National Democratic Fair Play Association meeting notice, June 1914. The NDFPA's sensational appeal tied government reform to white supremacy, labeling black Republicans as both beneath and threatening to American democracy. After beating a steady drum for federal segregation in 1913, the NDFPA widened its war on African American citizenship by attacking the legitimacy of the Fourteenth and Fifteenth Amendments to the Constitution. Though the Supreme Court rejected the NDFPA's amicus brief in *Guinn v. United States* and struck down the grandfather clause, a tool of disfranchisement, in 1915, the conflation of racism and reform in American politics had a long-standing impact on Washington and the federal government. From *Washington Herald*, June 29, 1914.

lina.[68] A few months later, the administration was reportedly mulling plans to remove the recorder of deeds office from the patronage game. The current recorder, Henry Lincoln Johnson, a black Republican from Georgia appointed by Taft, would be replaced, according to the *Washington Post*, by someone "whose sole qualification shall be business experience and executive ability." The office, which employed "eleven white and eighteen colored copyists," would be reduced to just "the fifteen best copyists."[69] The NDFPA helped to turn black government workers into symbols of inefficiency and corruption.

Key personnel managers within the Wilson administration were connected to the NDFPA's campaign, though Wilson himself does not appear to have responded directly to the association. First Assistant Secretary of the Treasury John Skelton Williams, for example, was forwarded the letters the association wrote to Secretary McAdoo.[70] Williams would become a leading enemy of African American federal employees during Wilson's first term, as he brought to the classified civil service the racism and reform that swirled around Wilsonian Washington. Before Wilson appointed him to the Treasury Department, Williams had earned renown as a leading financier, railroad executive, and author on "fiscal questions." Wilson apparently believed Williams would be useful as he attempted to reform the nation's monetary system; in 1914, Wilson would promote him to the comptroller of the currency.[71] Whether he counted on Williams's other passion, white supremacy, playing a role in his executive branch is not as clear. Nonetheless, Williams's background and racism were representative of a pattern in Wilson's cabinet choices.

Williams believed in a mythic Old South where black people were happy in their manacles and white people were all cultured gentlemen and ladies. "Let me say that I am not one of those who would proclaim a new South," declared this relative of Martha Washington. If the war had not come, everything would have been grand, he explained. "Upon a proud, sensitive people, with grand ambitions and loving honor, living a life at home upon which poets love to linger — a life so far from us now that it seems as that of some distant, mystical, beautiful land seen faintly in our dreaming, that its echoes come to us as from an unseen shore beyond a soundless sea — the devastation of war swept like a sudden, overwhelming storm."[72]

It was a powerful story that, by the turn of the century, had come to form the central narrative in the white South's Lost Cause mythology.[73] The Civil War had wrenched the South from its happy idyll, the myth went, and the South's loss had led to the tragic events of Reconstruction. The rule of black men, white supremacists said, retarded southern culture, economy, and politics. It was only in the 1890s that the South had begun to recover from this difficulty, thanks to a "redemption" of power by white men. "As a capable servant, faithful and affectionate friend, docile and patient toiler, we can respect and even love [the Negro]," Williams asserted. "[But] as a ruler he is more consuming than fire, more destroying then the whirlwind, and we will not have him."[74] Even more impassioned and stultifying than Wilson's nationalist version, this all-consuming narrative left no room for any other vision of southern history and culture. Whereas Wilson was pleased to see active sectional and racial conflict die out, Williams imagined an ongoing battle.

Williams made no secret of his conviction that only through the suppression of black people would his South rise again. "The one thing on which the white people of the South of all creeds, classes, and parties are united, is the determination that, no matter what argument, or threat, or force may be used against them, the negro shall never again be trusted with political power in the South," Williams told a Nashville audience in 1892.[75] As a federal official two decades later, Williams remained adamant about the subordination of black Americans. Like many white supremacists, Williams updated his racism with pseudoscientific concerns about the decline of the white race and sexual intermingling.[76] Segregation had never been more necessary, he maintained. "There are many good mulatto citizens, but it is true indisputably that any mixture of the races makes a mongrel, and ultimately an inferior blend."[77] The District of Columbia, with its light-skinned black elite and its nonsegregated public spaces, had been mongrelized.

Williams was not the only mythologist of southern history in the Wilson administration. Daniel Calhoun Roper, a South Carolinian who served as Wilson's first assistant postmaster general, began his 1941 memoir with his earliest recollection: the "Tragic Era" of Reconstruction. Describing a group of federal soldiers marching past his home in 1872, Roper used his child's mind to perform the literary erasure essential to the white South's Reconstruction myths. The Confederacy's great cause in the Civil War, slavery, was gone. Gone too were the severe Black Codes and racist intransigencies that prompted congressional action during Radical Reconstruction. "Never before had I seen so many men with guns, nor could I comprehend the reason for them," Roper recalled. "South Carolina and the other Southern states," Roper's father explained to the young Daniel, "had been fighting for self-government since the surrender of Lee at Appomattox." Having lost, "they [since] had been governed by bayonets and the sword, by tyranny beyond the abuses of the slave trade." And what about the soldiers, the boy wondered? "'They're here to guard the election next Tuesday; to see that the Negroes vote for carpetbaggers.'" Roper concluded his memoir's opening with the lesson he took in that day. "I learned that I, together with my family and all the whites in our part of the country, lived under a black and fearful cloud. We had to fight for the sunshine of liberty."[78]

Several others in Wilson's cabinet were willing to join Roper and Williams in the fight for white liberty. Navy secretary Josephus Daniels had participated in the violent 1898 coup in Wilmington, North Carolina, that demolished one of the last municipal governments in the South that included both black and white officeholders. Daniels had helped incite the riot by using his newspaper, the *Raleigh News and Observer*, to publicize reports that black men were raping white women in Wilmington.[79] Attorney General James C. McReynolds, whom Wilson appointed to the Supreme

Court in 1914, was, according to one legal historian, "a notorious racist" and anti-Semite who had famously refused to be anywhere near another of Wilson's later nominees, Louis Brandeis.[80] McReynolds's replacement, Thomas W. Gregory, had delivered a speech in 1906 in which he explained that the Reconstruction-era Ku Klux Klan had served a noble cause. "If the reconstruction laws were unconstitutional, and wrong and vicious in theory, their practical application to the situation was even worse," the nation's top lawyer had declared.[81]

For Gregory, as for others in the cabinet, African Americans brought only corruption to American politics. Fittingly, Gregory quoted Wilson's *History of the American People* in support of his view that, given the circumstances, the KKK had no choice but, in Wilson's words, to "act only by private means, as a force outside of the government, hostile to it, proscribed by it, of whom opposition and bitter resistance was expected, and expected with defiance."[82] Finally, the man Wilson chose for postmaster general, head of the department with the most black employees nationally, was Texan Albert Burleson. During the campaign, Burleson had declared that the Democratic Party was the only political party that could be counted on to keep "the negro out not only of its own ranks but [also] out of the governmental affairs of the Southern States."[83]

Even Secretary of the Treasury William McAdoo, known for his railroad-tunnel building in New York, was a member of that city's Southern Society and held firm to his boyhood in central Georgia.[84] In July 1913, the *Star* reported that McAdoo's African American nursemaid, Adelaide Brown, visited the secretary at the Treasury Department and "carried [him] back to boyhood," when Brown's son had been McAdoo's closest friend. According to the *Star*, Brown mentioned that she frequently "interfered in their quarrels to punish her Henry for disrespect to his young master." All this, of course, came to an end after the war and, wrote the *Star*, when McAdoo's father saw his fortune "sadly crippled by that civil strife, he especially suffering through the devastation caused by the army of Gen. Sherman in his march to the sea."[85] Warm feelings for beloved "mammies" were common in the memories of white southern men, and they saw these allusions as signs of their friendliness and closeness with African Americans. McAdoo was clearly proud of this moment of embrace with Brown. This invocation of "good," "respectful," and "selfless" black women stood in opposition to more threatening women of the post-emancipation generation.[86] Whether consciously or not, McAdoo's "mammy" figure of his pastoral days in the Old South was useful for delegitimizing urban and assertive black women,

Woodrow Wilson and his cabinet, April 1913. Five of ten cabinet members hailed from the South, a proportion not seen since before the Civil War. *Clockwise from left*: William Gibbs McAdoo (Treasury), James C. McReynolds (attorney general), Josephus Daniels (Navy), David F. Houston (Agriculture), William B. Wilson (Labor), William C. Redfield (Commerce), Franklin K. Lane (Interior), Albert Burleson (postmaster general), Lindley Garrison (War), and William Jennings Bryan (State). (Library of Congress)

like those in the Bureau of Engraving and Printing who would soon give McAdoo headaches by refusing segregated lunch tables.[87] Altogether, the Wilson administration was more connected to the South and to a white supremacist vision of the United States than any since the Civil War. Or, as many put it in 1913, with Wilson as president, "the South is in the saddle."[88]

For these white southerners, as for the NDFPA, concerns about the social order mixed with a striking fear about the alchemy of race and sex in Washington. White people could be found suffering under "Negro supervision" everywhere, NDFPA officer Ernest Martin explained in April 1913. Black employees were crossing gender as well as color lines. "There are similar cases where white women are under negro heads," Martin said, "and it is for this reason that our great South, which represents one-third of the population of the country, one-third of its exports, and has about 6 per cent of the government positions is not better represented." Merit and sectional representation were certainly important for white southerners, but perceived threats

WOMEN'S WORK IN THE TREASURY.   COUNTING UNCLE SAM'S NEWLY PRINTED DOLLARS.
Every dollar and all the bonds issued by the Government have passed through the hands of these expert counters, who count and examine more than a million dollars a day with a celerity that is perfectly astonishing.   It is impossible to count the rapid movements of the fingers of any one of these women.   Each one will average counting 32,000 notes a day.   They do nothing but count all day long, week after week and year after year.   No one in the world has handled so many dollars as they.

"Women's Work in the Treasury," circa 1900. This photograph appeared in Mary Logan's *Thirty Years in Washington* in 1901. Logan was a D.C. socialite and the widow of Illinois senator John A. Logan, an early Republican and Union hero. The photograph was meant to capture the rise of female employment in lower-level clerical work in federal departments. It also, unwittingly, illustrates the mixing of black men among white women common at the time. From Mrs. John A. Logan, *Thirty Years in Washington, or Life and Scenes in Our National Capital* (Hartford, Conn.: A. D. Worthington and Co., 1901).

to white women gave special urgency to the civil service problem. "Do you think that you would want your sister or your wife working under a negro? Would you allow it?'" Martin bellowed.[89]

The presence of white female office workers became an important instrument in the effort to delegitimize black civil service. Women had been working in Washington's federal offices since 1862, but their numbers grew most significantly around the turn of the century.[90] Between 1870 and 1930, the percentage of clerical workers in the United States who were women grew from 2 percent to about 50 percent, reaching 90 percent in typing and stenographic jobs by 1920. No wonder Swan Kendrick saw the work as "not a man's work."[91] The vast majority of female clerical workers were young white women from middle-class families. Even if their wages equaled those of working-class men and women, their social origins and marital prospects were generally higher.[92] According to Victorian mores, such women changed office culture by inserting new rules of class and racial decorum. Lucian Thompson, a black laborer in the State, War, and Navy Building, explained that his long career in the government into the 1940s was dependent on his "hard work, keeping a stiff upper lip and leaving the white women in the office strictly alone."[93] The threat posed by black men was imaginary, but the fact that black men were increasingly in contact with middle-class white women in offices was not.

With the arrival of white southern Democrats, Washington was becoming more like other southern cities in the late nineteenth century, where white southerners developed a deep anxiety about interracial sex. Extreme moral vigilance against lascivious bosses and coworkers was essential to preserving the safety of all women in clerical offices.[94] But in post-emancipation America, the idea of white womanhood as the guardian of racial purity and supremacy held particular power. The vaunting of white womanhood while imagining every black man a sexual predator infused American racism with physical danger.[95] In May 1913, Ernest Martin wrote Charlotte Hopkins that offices with black and white workers led to "forced affiliations and compelled associations of the races," which were "antagonistic to every feeling of delicacy, purity, and morality, and it therefore follows that such a system is un-Democratic, un-American and un-Christian."[96]

This merging of proscribed Victorian femininity, race purity, and political and religious culture created a way of connecting cultural values about sex and gender to issues of political rights. Black men could not be allowed to exercise rights that would threaten the moral fiber of the community, as Republicans had done for decades. The NDFPA used stories of threatened white women in government departments to attack black officers. Both the *Washington Evening Star* and the *Washington Post* reported that Irene Monroe from Saratoga Springs, New York, had asked the association for protection because black employees in the recorder of deeds office had threatened her for exposing the "conditions which existed in the office."[97] The recorder, a position still held by Henry Lincoln Johnson, agreed to investigate Monroe's charges, and the association stated that it would continue to press Monroe's case by submitting affidavits to her senator, Democrat James O'Gorman. Johnson was forced to step down in June 1914, to be replaced by a white Democrat.[98]

Other stories made national news. The *New York Times* and *New York World* picked up a report that "A Woman From the South" employed in the Interior Department had written a letter to the NDFPA describing her abuse by two black men from whom she took dictation. She charged that one man was "drunk most of the time" and "blew his whisky fumes in my face." The *Times* also published a full copy of the letter. In it, the unnamed woman asserted that, as a southern lady and daughter of a "distinguished [Confederate] officer during the civil war," the indignities of working with, and especially for, "a dark-skinned, woolly-headed negro" were simply unbearable. The *World* reported that she had called him a "coal black, wooly headed nigger."[99]

White women participated in the public campaign for their protection. In August 1913, more than half the audience at an NDFPA rally was made up of women, as Mississippi senator James Vardaman told of white women taking orders from black men in government offices. Mary Walker, a suffragist and federal employee, demanded that white men fulfill their responsibilities of protecting white womanhood.[100] In December 1913, the women's department of the National Civic Federation began to investigate the working conditions of women in federal departments. Margaret and Ellen Wilson, daughter and wife of the president, participated in tours of federal buildings and made recommendations regarding improving the conditions of working women. While not explicitly racial, reports coming from these public investigations nonetheless helped to publicize the non-segregated nature of government offices.[101]

Duty to white women was a powerful force. Southern politicians in Washington, normally wary of imposing federal authority, could be moved to demand state action. Laws against "white slavery," the trafficking of women for sex, as well as other morals acts regulating drugs and alcohol were supported by rhetoric involving white fantasies of intoxicated black men preying on virginal white women. Legislation in Congress for racial segregation or the prevention of marriage between white and black Americans was nearly always introduced by congressmen who formed the "states' rights" cordon, which, for example, prevented any meaningful federal effort to stop lynching. Lynching was a states' rights issue, but prohibition and white slavery were not.[102]

Protecting white women involved a preservation of their "delicacy" through the manly exercise of Democratic politics. The fears *for* women in working offices, a sign of their increasing self-assertion, were equally fears *of* these women and undergirded attempts to "protect" them.[103] "Our women, generation after generation have endured willingly deadly pain and gone to the gates of death to give sons and daughters to the Republic," John Skelton

Williams told a meeting of bankers in 1913. "Having these splendid stories before us, surely it behooves us with our special responsibilities to be true to our obligations to aid loyally and patriotically in the work of keeping our standards high, our finance clean, our business methods honest; to make sure that we shall not permit internal decay and corruption to sap away the life of our Republic."[104] Once again the metaphor of clean government arose in Democratic discourse against Republicans and black men. Williams coupled it to metaphors of female domesticity.

In fact, white supremacists repeatedly connected Republican and black politics with immoral sex and social degeneration. "The establishment of Negro men over white women employees of the Treasury Dept. has in the minds of many thoughtful men & women long been a serious offense against the cleanness of our social life," Thomas Dixon Jr. told Woodrow Wilson. Dixon's white supremacist fantasy novel, *The Clansman*, provided the basis for D. W. Griffith's 1915 epic film *The Birth of a Nation*, for which Wilson held a private screening at the White House.[105] In that famous film, as in the speeches of white supremacists in Washington, black politicians' professional ambitions were dragged through the prurient imaginations of men like Williams and Dixon.

Such fictional tales had very real consequences. The campaign against Cyrus F. Adams indicated the seriousness with which some took the cause of white womanhood in the nation's service. Taft had placed Adams in a civil service position in Chicago's Customs House after the election, and the black Republican assumed he had escaped the Democratic housecleaning.[106] In July 1913, John Skelton Williams directed the chief clerk of the Treasury Department to investigate Adams's record. The clerk reported that, in 1911, Adams was rumored to have been involved with another employee in the office, a white woman named Violet McKee. Williams, with permission from Secretary of the Treasury McAdoo, ordered the collector of the Port of Chicago to demand an explanation from Adams for his "improper overtures" to the white woman.[107] Somehow Adams held on, but the incident reveals the moral and patriarchal ardor Williams drew from his role as a government administrator. Sexuality involving a white woman and a black man was presumed to be nonconsensual: Violet McKee, silent and placed on a pedestal, was the victim, Adams the unwanted aggressor. Williams was the righteous prosecutor.

WOODROW WILSON REMAINED ABOVE much of this racist fury. In part, Wilson's disconnect reflected his delegating management style. But it also grew out of his particular form of racism. Wilson viewed the hysterical blackphobia of white southern politicians as unseemly. The Lost Cause mythology exhibited little pull on him; he had always favored a restored Union over a resurgent Confederacy. He was as offended by the grotesque injustice of lynching as by all forms of mob violence. While Wilson could speak passionately about white southern heritage, viewed black people as inferior, and loved his "darky" jokes, he did not fill his speeches with racist diatribes like many southern Democrats. As a Mid-Atlantic governor, he did not have to rely on black scapegoats to get elected. During the presidential campaign, Wilson had pledged his "willingness and desire to deal with that race fairly and justly" and said little else afterward. Wilson diverged markedly from the stereotypical unreconstructed white southerner.[108]

Yet Wilson also thought little of destroying the structures that preserved African American equality if it served the welfare of other Americans. To achieve his aims of party unity and smooth government, Wilson brought into his administration Josephus Daniels, John Skelton Williams, and plenty of other politicians who, though more preoccupied by race, were useful to his agenda in other ways. Wilson claimed to care deeply for African Americans—indeed, he said, "I know myself, as a southern man, how sincerely the heart of the South desires the good of the Negro and the advancement of his race on all sound and sensible lines"—but his racism led him to view black political power as untenable.[109]

Aspiring Democrats

While white Democrats were formulating plans to whiten government, black Democrats were preparing for service to the nation. Writing to Secretary McAdoo a week after the inauguration, William Monroe Trotter explained, "My motive has been to lead the Colored voters to support the Democracy and get in return their willingness to accord equal rights to colored citizens of their own free will." And now, political payoff was expected. McAdoo had been a general in the election campaign, and therefore, Trotter felt, he should know "that Colored men worked hard and conscientiously, for the Democratic ticket with a burning desire to start an era of good feeling for our racial class with the party." Trotter signed his letter, "Yours for freedom."[110]

Trotter was not blind to the racism of Wilson's administration. He surely knew of Williams's reputation and would not have been surprised to learn of the pressure the NDFPA and other white supremacists within the Democratic Party were putting on Wilson. Rather, he thought in terms of competing interest groups, and he hoped that pressure from black Democrats on "friends" within the administration could hold back the zealous white supremacists and preserve a space for African Americans in the nation's workforce and its politics. He never imagined that white Democrats would do this of their own accord. But he planned to keep tabs on them, publicly and privately shaming them into honoring the rights of all American citizens.

If Trotter was the conscience of the black Democrats, Alexander Walters, a national leader of the AME Zion Church, was the operator, pulling the political strings necessary to placing black men and women on the government payroll. Walters had worked hard to turn thousands of black voters away from Taft and Roosevelt and had earned a national profile as, in the words of Josephus Daniels, "the ablest and most influential colored man in the party." Walters was expected to fill the vacuum in black politics left by the neutering of the Republican Tuskegee Machine.[111] Arriving in the capital from his home in New York with the rest of the victorious Democrats, Walters found himself momentarily in the sun, toasted by the District's leading black citizens. Walters's gamble on the Democrats appeared to pay off.[112]

Walters expected what every prominent supporter of presidential candidates expected: jobs for his allies. He sent McAdoo specific details on the states where the National Colored Democratic League had delivered strong African American support and the people who had helped to engineer those votes.[113] Some white Democrats, usually from the North, confirmed that Walters had been instrumental in the election and that African Americans should be recognized by the new administration. Robert Hudspeth, a Democratic national committeeman from New Jersey, seemed to understand the level of organization of the NCDL as well as the risks African Americans took in coming out for the Democrats.[114] In May, Hudspeth wrote Wilson's secretary Joe Tumulty a twelve-page letter listing the names and details of black men who were good Democrats and should receive presidential appointments. The list included Trotter, Walters, J. Milton Waldron, and Adam E. Patterson.[115]

John Sharp Williams had other ideas. White southerners held great power within the party and, thanks to seniority built by regional solidity, most of the senior positions in Congress.[116] They, too, felt they had a right to the spoils. Williams began his lobbying of McAdoo around the same time as Trotter and Walters did. On March 25, he wrote to recommend one of his friends, a Mississippi resident, for register of the Treasury. The register position required presidential appointment and "hitherto, in a perfectly illogical way," Williams noted, "[had] been left to some negro to fill. I have never seen any reason for it."[117] A few days later, McAdoo forwarded Williams's request on to the president, noting that Williams's recommendation "collides with the idea of continuing the policy of naming a negro."[118] In addition to blocking appointments to be made, southern senators targeted African Americans already serving in the government. Ben Tillman was not simply urging the appointment of white Democrats; he wanted the utter demolition of black government employment. "Do cut the negro's head off instanter," he told McAdoo, "and I will sleep easier." After forcing Robert Smalls from the office of collector of the Port of Beaufort, South Carolina, Tillman went after Smalls's deputy.[119]

Initially, it appeared that Williams and Tillman would get their wishes. In March, McAdoo declined an invitation from Milton Waldron to discuss what, exactly, black Americans would get from the Wilson administration.[120] Perhaps the secretary was hoping not to have to explain the forced resignation of the government's highest-ranking African American, Assistant Attorney General William H. Lewis, just two days after the inauguration. According to the *Washington Evening Star*, Lewis was asked either to tender his resignation or to have his position eliminated. "Lewis is a colored man," the paper added. "His appointment was entirely a political one."[121] Booker T. Washington noted in April that African Americans were already "beginning to feel disappointed" by the Wilson administration's replacement of black officeholders by white Democrats. Washington at least took some solace that "perhaps the colored people needed this lesson" in Democratic politics.[122] Trotter too saw that loyal African Americans were being shut out by the new president and began to write a steady stream of letters to McAdoo about injustices in the government. By June, the NCDL was warning Tumulty that it could not hold black voters in the party without some show of "the administration's appreciation of the colored voter."[123]

One black Democrat tried to explain the difficult position Wilson's lack of recognition was putting him in. "We are publicly and frequently charged with having sold the Race into slavery and told that we ought to be beaten to death with clubs and forever despised by the colored people," he told Tumulty.[124] Black Democrats had hoped to quell such sentiment with examples of black party members serving the administration in powerful, nationally prominent positions. No such appointments materialized. "We who have fought hard democratic battles, in the face of criticism and ostracism," wrote the Harlem Democrat Robert L. Waring, "now find ourselves without a leg upon which to stand, after our assertions in past campaigns, that the democratic party would be as liberal to us in Federal patronage as any other party has been."[125] These were among the few African Americans to whom Wilson actually responded, though usually in the form of a short apology and evasion. Writing to Waring, Wilson stated, "I am very sorry indeed that you should feel as you do about the course of the present administration. It has been doing everything that was possible in a difficult situation."[126]

In fact, the president did not immediately move to "cut off the negro's head." Despite Williams's lobbying for a white Mississippian, Wilson nominated a black Democrat, Adam Patterson of Oklahoma, to succeed James Napier as register of the Treasury. After all his hard work for the Democrats, Patterson was hungry for federal employment. He was as interested in power and status as he was in financial reward: he could carry on the tradition of Judson Lyons and Napier and other registers and make sure that black Americans, albeit Democrats, would be promoted in Washington. "If my appointment to this position carries with it the power to select my assistants you will be pleased indeed with the result of our work both as servants of the Government and of the Democratic party," he told McAdoo.[127]

Patterson came to the attention of the Wilson administration in the typical way, through his senator, the progressive Democrat Thomas P. Gore.[128] Gore, like John Sharp Williams, had hoped originally to have a white constituent appointed register of the Treasury. But when Wilson and McAdoo decided to follow tradition, Gore settled for offering a black Oklahoman, thus at least demonstrating his close connection to the president. No doubt a patronage appointment from Oklahoma was an attractive maneuver for the administration, since Oklahoma senator Robert Owen chaired the committee that would usher Wilson's banking reform bills through Congress.[129] In July 1913, with the backing of Hudspeth of the Democratic National Committee, the NCDL, and, most important, his senators, Adam Patterson became Wilson's first African American nominee for a presidential appointment.[130]

While African Americans of all parties were delighted by Patterson's nomination, most white southerners were outraged. "We all know this is a white man's government, and that negroes should have no part in its administration," a "plain citizen" wrote to Wilson from Little Rock, Arkansas. "There cannot be any obligation on a Democrat to appoint negroes to office, no matter how many Democratic speeches they may have made," the "citizen" explained.[131] James Vardaman spoke for the southern Democrats when he threatened to block Wilson's and the party's entire political agenda if the president tried to force through Patterson's nomination. Patronage was always a tricky game of balance between the president and Congress, and the party unity promoted by the spoils system required both racial and party loyalty. "The race question involved in this appointment is as Pikes Peak to the shrub-covered foothills," Vardaman declared. "I would rather see the tariff and the money legislation defeated than this nomination confirmed."[132] Vardaman and his colleagues from Georgia and South Carolina had vowed to their constituents that they would fight for white supremacy in Washington, and they were not about to waste party dominance in both houses of Congress and the White House.

Patterson bowed to the inevitable. When neither Gore nor Wilson spoke up in defense of his appointment, he withdrew his nomination on July 30. Three days later, Wilson nominated another Oklahoman, Gabe E. Parker. Parker, a Choctaw Indian, was confirmed easily.[133] Joe Tumulty said he had directed Patterson to "stick" and also claimed to have advised Wilson to fight for Patterson. Yet McAdoo's secretary, Byron Newton, applauded Patterson for being a "good soldier" and stepping aside in a pleasant way.[134] Patterson likely realized that Senate filibustering or some other parliamentary procedure would block his confirmation. Withdrawal could save his chances for another position in the administration. Surely, he was disappointed, he wrote McAdoo as he rode out of Washington, but "if a similar situation should arise one hundred times I would do the same thing each time with an added degree of pleasure."[135]

Black newspaper editors unanimously condemned Patterson. For having had anything to do with Democrats, Calvin Chase labeled Patterson "weak" and declared that he possessed a "child's mind, and a child's view of things" incapable of "comprehend[ing] such ideas as liberty, justice, humanity, self-respect, and common sense."[136] Another writer was most disturbed by Patterson's willingness to deny black citizens a man in public office. Patterson's withdrawal was not just a disservice to his own political career or a sign of his weakness but a crime against black America.[137] The presence of black men in responsible positions stood as reminders that people of African descent were supposed to be treated as citizens, and included in that citizenship was the right to participate in politics and earn a decent living in service to the state. In giving up on the system, Patterson was inviting Wilson to change the rules and write out black citizenship entirely.

All across the nation, Patterson's dismissal became the target of scathing editorials. The *Cleveland Gazette* declared the failed nomination a sign of the Democratic government's danger to African Americans everywhere in the country. "Good Lord! Scat! You 'Negro democrat,'" the paper sneered.[138] Farther west, the *Indianapolis Freeman* placed the fault for Patterson's withdrawal with the "rabid anti-Negro members of Congress." Wilson "had no chance to exhibit the Roosevelt tenacity."[139] Fred R. Moore's Tuskegee-supported *New York Age* chose not to leave the unassertive as blameless. Moore claimed to have never been taken in by Wilson's inclusive statements in 1912. The fact remained, he was forever "Southern in sympathy," and had so "passed under the yoke of Southern Negro hatred and intolerance with such silence and indifference as to indicate the whole nauseous business was good and pleasant to him."[140]

Patterson never found his way to any departmental office in Washington, settling instead into a law practice in Chicago. In 1916, as president of the largely defunct NCDL, he continued quixotically to connect his party service with the effort to land African Americans in government offices. "I want the Register of the Treasury and I want you to help me get it," he told McAdoo, who remained attentive to his fellow Democrat.[141] After Wilson's reelection, Patterson enlisted to fight in World War I and rose to major and judge advocate of the segregated Ninety-Second Division. After the war, he returned to legal work in Chicago and finally achieved some measure of public employment in 1923, becoming a city attorney. Patterson received the appointment from a Democratic mayor seeking to make inroads with black voters, a growing constituency in Chicago after the first great migration of African Americans from the South.[142] More than an affirmation of Patterson's long support of the national Democratic Party, the appointment reflected a newer form of twentieth-century urban politics in which black politicians parlayed the growing black municipal constituency into local power. In general, however, these politicians had great difficulty regaining the kind of national presence possible during the earlier Republican administrations — nor could they offer the broader social and economic mobility made possible by egalitarian government employment.[143]

Patterson's defeat served notice that even the most innocuous and traditional of African American appointments would fail. If Democrats wanted to argue that Woodrow Wilson's administration was almost entirely white because there were no black Democrats, Wilson and Patterson knew otherwise. Rather, the patronage machine for black appointees was deliberately dismantled. In his first term, Wilson made only one other attempt to appoint an African American to a federal position in Washington, the pro forma reappointment of Robert Terrell to a District municipal judgeship.[144] The famous black men of Washington's "black cabinet" were pushed out. Black Republican officeholders like James C. Napier and Whitefield McKinlay left positions that went to white Democrats.

These changes reflected a pronounced shift in presidential policy, one that would affect black federal workers all the way down the line. Some clerks ran for cover. Census clerk Ocea Taylor resigned just before Wilson arrived in Washington, and Oliver Randolph in the fourth assistant postmaster general's office managed a transfer to a post office in Newark, New Jersey.[145] The absence of black politicians in positions of responsibility would, declared Calvin Chase, create "a void detrimental to the advancement of the men and women in the ranks" in Washington and in the rest of the country. "For the Black Cabinet, here's ros[e]mary—that's for remembrance."[146]

Chase's editorial was prescient. Taft had appointed eighteen black men, including an assistant attorney general. Further back, Benjamin Harrison had made seventeen black appointments; McKinley had appointed twenty-two African Americans; Roosevelt had made twenty appointments; and even Democrat Grover Cleveland had fought his own party's congressional delegation for at least four appointments of black men. Between 1880 and 1920, fifty black men would serve as U.S. consuls around the world. The number serving at once had grown to as many as seventeen in 1905. Wilson did follow one precedent by appointing a black man, New York Democrat James L. Curtis, as minister to Liberia in 1915, and he retained some previously appointed black consuls usually serving in majority black countries. But these were hardly satisfying. "The only job [Wilson] will give one of us antediluvian charcoal misconceptions is a job in some ever infested country where a fellow has got just about one chance in fifty to live," rang the Bee. By 1920, only four black men held any kind of federal post: Robert Terrell and three consuls serving abroad.[147] This virtual disappearance of black appointees represented the first clear sign of a new racial regime in the American state. The undermining of ordinary civil servants would soon complete the transformation.

IN LATE JULY 1913, SWAN KENDRICK'S mind was wandering away from his work in the War Department. "I've had you on my mind all the morning," Kendrick swooned to Ruby Moyse. He hoped she would be able to "forgive the typewriter," but if only she could see all that he was ignoring to write her: "papers piled on my desk for reply, and the pages of my notebook full of 'pot-hooks' as yet untouched." Fortunately, "the commandment, 'Thou shalt not steal' does not apply to Government time and other folks' umbrellas, you know."[148] Kendrick's levity reflected the slowness with which black Washingtonians recognized the changes underway in federal offices. Woodrow Wilson moved uncertainly into the effort to rid Washington of black officeholders. In April 1913, Wilson gave tacit approval when Albert Burleson mentioned departmental segregation at a cabinet meeting, but the president issued no official policy then or ever.[149] As late as 1915, the *Star* was reporting that Wilson was still considering appointing a black Democrat to be recorder of deeds, a position he left vacant for two years rather than face the question of appointing a black or white man.[150] Wilson's participation in federal discrimination was so guarded that the African American leader Reverend Francis J. Grimké claimed that it was not until November 1914 that he was sure that Wilson supported racial segregation at all.[151]

In the absence of clear policy, discrimination in federal departments would proceed piecemeal and be met at every step by black protest and civil rights activism. Ideas about black politics, Reconstruction memories, theories of "scientific management," and democratic values were the lenses through which Wilsonians made determinations about who and what would be reformed. But for all of the ideology the Wilsonians brought with them to Washington, the regime they constructed was as much a response to the conditions they faced in the offices—from bureaucratic regulations to resistant workers and administrators—as it was a product of philosophy and racial fantasies. Campaign slogans were designed to articulate and simplify plans for administration; the reality of actual governance had a way of making things far more complicated.

Baby girl, I'm not trying to get rich before I come asking for you. I simply have a horror of being buried in Washington—not that I dislike the city, but the limitations. As soon as I can get fare and a few shekels, I see myself leaving.

—Swan Kendrick to Ruby Moyse, January 27, 1914

Chapter Five

Wilsonian Praxis

Racial Discrimination in a Progressive Administration

In September 1911, after a decade of clerking in the Census Bureau, George Harris Cox decided to make a final push toward finishing his medical degree. He received permission to work temporarily as a night watchman and began attending classes at Howard during the day.[1] It was the kind of opportunity that government work in Washington had afforded many ambitious young men. By March 1913, however, the burdens of pursuing an education while trying to hold a job overwhelmed him, and he returned to census work.[2] But the office was not as he had left it. The flexibility and relative egalitarianism had vanished. Segregated into the black section of the bureau, Cox was assigned to work he found to be largely meaningless. "The old clerks (colored) who have been in the office 10 and 16 years have had very little opportunity to do any field work," he told his supervisor in 1916.[3] More important, a promotion he had earned before his temporary absence was no longer available. Cox never completed his medical training, and into the 1930s, he labored without much responsibility and for little pay, despite being the bureau's "senior colored clerk."[4]

Stories like George Cox's reveal racial discrimination in practice. The image that predominates in memory and in many history books is one of Woodrow Wilson ordering a sweeping spatial reorganization of government work to separate black and white workers. He never did, and the reality was not so simple. A panoply of humiliations—separate bathrooms, segregated lunchrooms, and separations between white and black employees doing the same work—did appear in places like Cox's Census Bureau office. But the work of installing white supremacy across Washington's federal offices was less complete, more personal, often difficult to pin down. There was resistance, or at least negotiation, among workers and even between administrators.

And yet the results were even more devastating than a focus simply on physical separation could possibly convey. "Federal segregation" cannot capture what it meant for African Americans that the recorder of deeds for the District of Columbia was a white man for the first time in thirty-five years or that a clerk making $1,200 a year was suddenly reduced to a laborer at $500 a year. The cruelty of George Cox's circumstances was registered in his exhaustion, mental isolation, and loss of pay. Black clerks like Cox were not simply fired or separated out: they suffered the pain of reduced status and income in a system that no longer valued their work. Discrimination in the federal government after 1912 involved the erection of a ceiling above black employees that capped their economic and social mobility. Further, it was all inflicted by supposedly logical and progressive mechanisms of administrative reform. This was Wilsonian praxis: bureaucratic initiatives that overran personal ambition, party loyalty, or basic justice.

Adding to the complexity of organizing a bureaucracy according to race was the way in which the Wilson administration went about the work. The federal government, even in 1913, was a massive operation with layers of hierarchy that left room for great variation in office management. In its public explanations, the administration was neither candid nor consistent about segregation in part because there was little unanimity about how to deal with black employees. Even among the white supremacists of Wilson's cabinet, the degree of vitriol toward black Americans varied, and it is difficult to connect an executive's demands with a deputy's actions. Official orders are rarely extant in archives. Letters between administration officials refer to verbal conversations obliquely, and in one of the only letters between Treasury secretary William Gibbs McAdoo and President Wilson in which segregation was mentioned, McAdoo suggested that they meet privately.[5] A diary kept by Assistant Secretary of the Treasury Charles S.

Hamlin is a rare and brief record of key talks about race and segregation within the Treasury Department, which employed the most African Americans among the executive departments in Washington.[6] It reveals a lack of administrative clarity, multiple changes in direction, varying degrees of commitment, and sensitivity to protests among some administrators.

Wilson himself disclaimed any direct hand in departmental business. The president was focused on his legislative program in the year or so in which government administrators most aggressively imposed segregation, and his officials were free to work on their own most of the time. For example, McAdoo's invitation to Wilson to speak about segregation was written in September 1913, six months after the first reports of it began to appear in newspapers. Wilson said almost nothing about segregation, and he appears to have paid little attention to its details.[7] Nonetheless, Wilson did know that segregation was being pursued, and he did approve of it. In a letter to Oswald Garrison Villard, owner and editor of the *New York Evening Post* and a founding member of the NAACP, Wilson described segregation as a "departmental" affair for which he took no responsibility. Nevertheless, he "sincerely believe[d] it to be in [black people's] interest."[8] Wilson heartily approved of segregation in his government and the black inferiority the system implied. Once protests focused public attention on federal segregation, Wilson defended the practice.

Perhaps as a result of Wilson's refusal to initiate policy, segregation was inconsistently established in his government. Despite declarations that segregation was intended to enhance administrative efficiency, Wilsonian discrimination was not based upon an explicit set of policies and principles. Instead, the patronage demands of white Democrats, the howls of white supremacists, the needs of a modernizing governmental bureaucracy, and, indeed, the desire of some managers to feel they were being fair were forged into a racial discrimination that needed years to become institutionalized. The rising national wave of white supremacy did not easily or completely demolish a long-standing bulwark of black ambition, politics, and progress. Ultimately, what stands out about Wilsonian discrimination is the way in which it combined a determined and deliberate effort to subordinate black citizens with an ambiguous, negotiated process among bureaucrats and employees. Although progressives were interested in order, they rarely achieved something orderly.[9]

For all the messiness, a distinct change in climate accompanied the exit of powerful black politicians and their allies. Democrats eagerly dismissed the Republican machine, and blackness formed the most immediate indicator of Republican affiliation to the new administrators.[10] For example, Post Office Department clerk Thomas Richardson had been pulled from his postmastership of thirty-three years in Port Gibson, Mississippi, in 1908 as part of Taft's southern policy and compensated with an $1,800-a-year clerkship in the office of the fourth assistant postmaster general.[11] In April 1913, the chief clerk of the department noted that the reason for Richardson's placement in Washington and his salary "are unknown to the present officials." Richardson's work was deemed insufficient, and the sixty-four-year-old Mississippian was demoted from $1,800 to $1,000 a year. He was also placed in the Dead Letter Office, a well-known ghetto for demoted black clerks. Eventually, Richardson was transferred to Boston and then back to Mississippi, where, no longer eligible to be the boss, he worked as a minor postal clerk.[12] Segregation and demotion, both aimed at the results of black patronage, worked together to demolish black mobility in Washington.

Segregation

Some spaces in federal buildings were easier to segregate than others. Cafeterias in federal buildings were among the first places to be segregated by Wilson's administrators. Their social nature and lack of practical labor requirements made them opportune sites for taking a stand against "social equality." Postal worker Stephen Plummer reported to the NAACP the difficulties segregation caused for black workers. "If they patronize the lunch room, they are not allowed to go to the counter and buy food but must go to the kitchen door, where there is no one to wait upon them but the cook, and usually he is at the counter until all white employees have been served." Plummer added that the situation in the government lunchroom was actually worse than out on the street. "The lunch rooms in the neighborhood discriminate, but any colored man can go to the counter and buy what he wants and walk out, but here in the Post Office in a cafe run by the Government, a colored man can't even go to the counter."[13] Most brought their lunches and ate in segregated bathrooms or other out-of-the-way places where they could find some peace. Swan Kendrick preferred to go hungry, since there was no "place near the War Dept. where one can get anything fit to eat. I mean, of course, a 'Colored' one."[14]

From lunchrooms, humiliations spread out to other areas of government work. Lafayette Hershaw, a black government lawyer in the Interior Department and a founder of the NAACP, reported that most of the Post Office Department's black clerks had been placed in the Dead Letter Office and separated from white clerks by a row of lockers running down the center of the room.[15] Segregated bathrooms in the Government Printing Office forced black employees to walk around the enormous building to use the toilet. In addition, A. L. Tilghman noted the extra humiliation for women using a bathroom originally designed for men. The urinals in the "Colored Women's" restroom disgusted her and the other women in the GPO.[16]

Tilghman objected to her supervisors' explanation that segregation avoided problems between black and white workers. According to Tilghman, it created them. There had been no trouble until GPO officers began segregating workers. "Some of us have been there, ten, twelve, fifteen and some more than twenty years, and in each division and in different rooms where we might be detailed to work we sat about promiscuously in different chairs, where ever a vacant seat could be found." Now black women were being grouped together and separated from white workers. The women suffering these sudden indignities did not deserve them. "All these young ladies are nice, well behaved, intelligent, high and normal school graduates full of life and a good time." For Tilghman, the anger and despair these changes had engendered overwhelmed her. "There is much more I want to say, and have wanted to say for a long time, but when I sit down to write about this segregation, I find myself losing my temper when I think of all the years many of us have spent in the G.P.O. with the most cordial relations always existing between the two races."[17] But now, with Wilson, everything was different.

The Treasury Department soon earned the strongest reputation for segregation. It employed the most African Americans, all of whom came under the control of Assistant Secretary John Skelton Williams. On April 2, 1913, just a few days after being appointed, Williams toured the Bureau of Engraving and Printing, a large plant near the Capitol in which the nation's currency was made. About 15 percent of the bureau's workers were African American, and its 3,800 employees were a mix of skilled tradespeople and relatively low-paid laborers and minor clerks.[18] As he inspected the building's cramped and dirty workrooms, Williams "noted that young white women and colored women were working together side by side and opposite each other." He was sure "that this must go much against the grain of the white women."[19] In other rooms, white women could be found working close to black men. Shocked, Williams reportedly walked straight up to one worker and asked "in a loud tone whether it was not offensive to her to be so near a colored man."[20]

The BEP was overseen by bureau director Joseph Ralph. Born in Allegheny City, Pennsylvania, Ralph was raised in Joliet, Illinois, where, according to the *Washington Evening Star*, he developed his "western spirit of hustle" and "frank and open-handed manner." After some time as a steel-worker and union leader, the Republican patronage machine landed him several federal positions, from assistant postmaster in the House of Representatives to superintendent of construction at Ellis Island to the deputy collector of customs at the 1893 World's Fair in Chicago. During the Cleveland administration, he entered the civil service in the BEP. Roosevelt appointed him director in 1908, a position overseeing more than 10,000 employees and paying $5,000 a year. Ralph spent the next few years improving the BEP's machinery and management and designing a new, modern plant. Charlotte Hopkins told Ellen Wilson that Ralph's innovations were helping to make the "National Government" a "model employer."[21]

Williams saw room for improvement in Ralph's work. Though there was already a good deal of "grouping" according to race, there was no official order segregating black and white employees. As Williams discovered, in practice, white and black workers worked side-by-side throughout the building. The new assistant secretary wrote up an order for Ralph: "No white girl should be permitted to sit alongside of a colored man or woman on the same machine," even if "alongside" meant more than ten feet between them. An order officially segregating workers in a factory like the BEP was an innovation. Though business practices in the South usually meant that white and black people did not work together on an equal basis, it was not until 1915 that the South Carolina legislature passed a specific act barring workers "of different races to labor and work together within the same room" in textile factories.[22] Williams had his own ideas about how to make the federal government a model employer.

Though Ralph dutifully followed orders, he noted that Williams's visit to the bureau had "stirred up trouble."[23] Washington was still not a place in which segregation was an agreed-upon institution, even among white residents. Unwilling to "put in writing" his reply to Williams, Ralph elected to meet personally with him.[24] In their meeting, Ralph told Williams that the order was "unpracticable," particularly since no complaints by the workers themselves had been registered. Williams then withdrew the written order but gave a private, verbal order separating black women from white women. The NAACP soon confirmed that separate toilet and dressing rooms were officially in effect in the bureau and that workers had been "paired according to race."[25]

By the summer, Williams was looking beyond the BEP, noting to Secretary McAdoo that in the main Treasury Building, "up to this time the races have been using the same toilet rooms indiscriminately." Chief Clerk of the Treasury James L. Wilmeth, a Democrat from Arkansas, was ordered to arrange for "colored" bathrooms on the ground floor. Williams cared not that one men's and one women's bathroom on the ground floor for African Americans hardly equaled bathrooms throughout the building for white people. He also did not seem concerned that black workers would have to circumnavigate the five-story, five-acre Treasury Building to find a bathroom. But he did tell McAdoo that while white men had one toilet for every 107 employees, black men had one toilet per 204 employees. This apparently was supposed to be offset by the fact that black women had one toilet for every 66 employees, even if they were all in one bathroom on the ground floor.[26]

Williams's actions appear to have been inspired more by his own sensibilities than by any specific demands by white workers; there are no surviving complaints by white Treasury employees about sharing toilets with black coworkers. Indeed, one report from a black Treasury clerk to the NAACP in September 1913 noted that the white clerks were "quite as friendly as formerly and several have declared the lavatory matter infamous."[27] Nonetheless, Williams and other segregationists, including Wilson, always maintained that they were responding to the needs and desires of the majority of federal employees.[28]

SEGREGATION IN THE TREASURY DEPARTMENT would become more complicated and more recondite under John Skelton Williams's more liberal successor, Charles S. Hamlin. Assistant Secretary Hamlin would ultimately seek a compromise between the administration's desires to confine black workers and to appear progressive and fair. Hamlin discovered Williams's segregation work somewhat by accident. Williams had been promoted to comptroller of the currency, and on March 7, 1914, Ralph wrote Hamlin about a problem with the new BEP building set to open in a few days. Ralph had just discovered the new building's one key flaw: though designed by Franklin MacVeagh, Taft's secretary of the Treasury, to be "the most modern factory plant in the world," the new building lacked arrangements for the segregation of white and black workers.[29] "I find a very embarrassing situation due to the fact that, in planning the building, the necessity for separate toilet and dressing rooms for the colored employe[e]s was overlooked," Ralph told Hamlin. The director promised to "make proper arrangements" as soon as possible. In the short term, though, he was forced "to permit the commingling of the two races in the work and other rooms."[30] Ralph assumed that Hamlin knew of the process of segregation begun by his predecessor.

In fact, Ralph's letter set off a discussion within the office of the secretary of the Treasury. Hamlin, a Boston Democrat with several degrees from Harvard, opposed segregation and the most blatant forms of discrimination. According to his diary, he "advised" Ralph personally that there should not be any segregation, and on March 9, he prepared, but did not issue, an order barring segregation or discrimination "based upon color" in the Treasury Department. Hamlin sent the draft order to McAdoo, who was out of town. He also shared his plans with Second Assistant Secretary of the Treasury Byron Newton and McAdoo's personal secretary, George R. Cooksey, both of whom "warmly approved" of them.[31] Late in the afternoon on March 10, 1914, McAdoo and Hamlin met to discuss their response to Ralph. According to Hamlin, McAdoo "seemed distressed." When Hamlin suggested eliminating segregation completely, McAdoo replied "in a disparaging tone—that will cause opposition in the South." Hamlin assured McAdoo that the opposition would be short-lived and that "if segregation were permitted there would be continuous trouble which would last through the administration." Hamlin argued for an official policy statement against segregation to avoid a "great political issue for the future," but McAdoo promised only to consider Hamlin's recommendation.[32]

The question Ralph and Hamlin faced in the spring of 1914 was what to do with the new bureau building, so inconveniently designed by a liberal Republican. Though the old building did have separate dressing rooms, there was no mandatory segregation policy before 1913. "The blacks were very discreet as to use of common toilets and no complaint ever made," Ralph said.[33] Hamlin saw the difficulties of instituting segregation. What, for example, would be done with the "3 girls of mixed blood but to all appearances absolutely white who would have to be forced into the colored partition"? Hamlin imagined that they would "bitterly object" to being so grouped. Ralph told Hamlin that he hoped to follow through with Williams's order to segregate workrooms, but Hamlin dropped this plan. Further, he drew up five "general rules" by which Ralph should run his bureau. They were: "Justice to all; No notices in toilet rooms; No discrimination in promotions; No discrimination in work rooms; No partitions in dressing rooms." Ralph said he could operate under the rules.[34]

Wilson approved the rules and told McAdoo that they "were to be given to Ralph verbally." Hamlin added in his diary that as far as the rule against discrimination in workrooms went, "it was distinctly understood that the Director was given discretion in individual cases to arrange as far as possible, without open clash, so that individual dissatisfaction would be met by reassignment." Peace was to be valued over justice. The next week, Hamlin gave Ralph the secretary's verbal instructions. Hamlin noted that he "did not let him know the President also had approved them."[35] Wilson's distance was to be preserved.

In practice, Ralph and Hamlin's plan was to obscure segregation in the bureau, not to eliminate it. White employees would not work with black employees, but no signs announcing segregation would be allowed. Ralph told Hamlin that he could "quietly talk to some of the negro leaders and advise caution," thereby turning the racist objections of white workers into the concern of black employees. Ralph laid out for Hamlin precisely where segregation had been instituted or now made mandatory, listing the working circumstances for black employees division by division. In most cases, Ralph described arrangements that were tantamount to segregation but insisted that there was no segregation. For example, the Plate Printing Division consisted of "100 colored women working for white printer and 20 colored messengers. *No Segregation here*" (Hamlin's emphasis). In the trimming room, fifty women were working, forty of whom were black. In the postage stamp perforating room, there were "150 women of whom 40 are colored. Each machine requires 2 women. Of these, 30 machines are manned entirely by white girls and 10 machines by colored girls. There is no isolation however; are all near together."[36]

Thus, while Ralph was claiming a lack of segregation, Hamlin's notes reveal a racial geography in the BEP. White and black workers did mix, as in the Surface Printing Division, where black women were permitted to sit at worktables with white women. But the grouping by race existed in enough rooms of the bureau that black workers could recognize segregation instantly. In the Numbering Division, where printed money was completed, there were no black workers. The greatest concentration of black men was in the rag laundry, with the second largest number working as skilled laborers. All of the unclassified laborers, those lacking the protections of the civil service system, were African American. All of the men working in the stables were also black, except, notably, the foreman. Most black women were doing the very dirty work of plate printing, where skin diseases and irritations from fumes, regular hazards in the ink-flooded bureau, prevailed.[37]

Ralph worked out a way of more subtly separating white and black workers without using signs, which would, he thought, "remove the trouble." He had not put partitions in the dressing rooms, but he did arrange the lockers so that, simply by circumstances, there would be little mixing between black and white workers. And since all of the unskilled laborers were African American, their dressing room could be set apart based on job rather than on racial identification.[38] But the overlap was no accident. Ralph also added a shower to the dressing room in response to white workers' complaints about perspiring black laborers during the summer. The men were told to "pay more attention to bathing and frequent changes of clothing."[39] Ralph readily reinforced the racial hierarchy in the building by accusing black men of poor sanitary habits on the word of white employees. Overtly, Ralph's plan may have been to follow Hamlin's anti-segregation rules, but by the spring of 1914, the BEP bore all of the marks of subordination and white supremacy.

Charles Hamlin's primary goal appears to have been to keep everything quiet. He instructed Ralph to "turn his face away from segregation in work rooms, but to proceed very slowly and cautiously." Ralph was not to grant interviews regarding segregation and was to work toward "good feeling and harmony" among the workers. Ralph reported that he had "cautioned some of the colored people to be reasonably discreet" to prevent further objections by white employees — once again laying the burden for "good feeling" and "harmony" on the black workers. Ralph also told Hamlin that black women in one division had asked for separate dressing rooms. The lunch-room had been organized smoothly, with black workers "voluntarily" eating by themselves.[40]

In the end, the administration decided to remove segregation notices so long as black workers agreed to pretend they were still up and act accordingly. It was made clear to African Americans that it was "in their interest" to avoid arousing white racism.[41] Hamlin's desire for justice assumed his right to choose the terms of justice and was simply not of the same order as the affirmative action of Republican administrators. Whereas in 1914 Hamlin sought to work quietly behind the scenes to induce "harmony" by satisfying racists, Republicans had previously demanded that white and black employees work together.[42] Overall, Wilson's administrators made no such demands, even within departments with less segregation or fewer African Americans than Hamlin's Treasury offices. If departments differed in their level of discrimination, Wilson's appointees did not vary in their unwillingness to ensure equality.[43]

Segregated Careers

Along with segregation and all of the indignities it implied, there was something else in Wilsonian praxis: an attack on black ambition. If segregation had a patina of progressive and impersonal management practice, the discrimination against individual careers was startlingly personal. John Skelton Williams did not just want white and black workers in the BEP separated; he wanted to reduce the status of black federal employees in every way possible. Williams ordered Ralph not to recommend black workers for promotion and even changed the way African Americans were addressed by the department. "While ordinarily letters were addressed—'Sir' or 'Madam' and signed 'Respectfully yours,'" one Treasury official reported, under Williams, "when addressed to colored employees, the words Sir or Madam and the ending Respectfully yours—were omitted." Williams even had letters already drafted to black men and women rewritten to omit respectful salutations.[44]

Those who displayed the most ambition were especially targeted. Treasury clerk Thomas H. R. Clarke, for example, came under Williams's gaze during the summer of 1913. Clarke was an active Republican whose career had been helped along by important connections; he was well known and well paid. It was no coincidence that Clarke had always served in department offices run by powerful black Republicans, like Judson Lyons and James C. Napier. But he was also a permanent classified employee with all of the protections granted by the civil service system. Within a year of Williams's arrival, Clarke was demoted, transferred, and finally forced to resign.[45]

Service to the Republican Party had guaranteed Clarke job security. Prior to Wilson's inauguration, Clarke had been accused of violating civil service rules by campaigning in the 1912 federal election. The Civil Service Commission determined that Clarke had broken the rule with the best of intentions: in the "patriotic service" of "answering certain defamatory statements which had been circulated concerning the character of the President."[46] Importantly, Clarke worked for Taft, the keeper of the patronage keys. Clarke was told to "refrain from future violations of the law" but not reduced in pay or status. The case was closed.[47]

Clarke's political activity became an issue again, however, when Democrats took control of the Treasury Department a few months later. An accuser, C. E. Simmons, claimed that Clarke had been appointed over several better-qualified Democrats and, inaccurately, stated that Clarke had not passed the civil service examination.[48] Clarke threw himself at John Skelton Williams's feet: "I have advanced through the various grades by hard work, and the conscientious performance of duty," he wrote. "With a military and civil record without a blemish, I appeal to your impartial judgment in the matter."[49] But Clarke's high profile eventually proved too much for Democratic administrators. He had become an NAACP officer and worked with the national office in its investigations into segregation in federal offices.[50] In July 1914, Charles Hamlin demoted Clarke without cause and transferred him to the office of the auditor of the Post Office Department, under the direction of Charles Kram, a well-known racist. A month later, presumably long enough for him to catch the infamous auditor's drift, Clarke resigned.[51]

Well-connected, Clarke was one of the few federal workers who escaped successfully into Washington's black business enclave.[52] But when that economy collapsed in the 1930s, Clarke, by then sixty-seven years old, tried to return to the civil service. Like most Americans, he was looking for secure employment in the midst of the Great Depression. Leaving government work in 1914, he had missed the installation of a federal employee pension system in 1920. Though Clarke was denied reinstatement, Franklin Roosevelt appointed him deputy recorder of deeds in 1935, a job with a higher profile but fewer job protections.[53] Clarke's older brother David managed less well during Williams's tenure. Dismissed from his $1,000-a-year Treasury clerkship in June 1913, the elder man was reinstated as a laborer earning $660 a year and died two years later.[54]

Thomas Clarke was not simply the victim of a partisan purging. Some dismissed workers did accuse Wilson's managers of partisan actions, especially white Union veterans who had been assured permanent employment by Republicans.[55] But C. E. Simmons referred to Clarke as "the negro Clark," and an anonymous letter had informed administrators that Clarke was fighting to reverse segregation in the department, not just working for the Republican Party.[56] Clarke's "agitation" was explicitly racial, the letters charged, and so was the campaign to oust him. His political activity took on a new seriousness because it was indicative of a forceful black citizenship that was declared illegitimate by the Democrats in power. Similarly, Richard W. Thompson, a messenger in the Treasury Department and a Republican journalist, was transferred and reduced in pay after the National Democratic Fair Play Association targeted him.[57] Clarke and Thompson had stepped out of their proper places not simply as Republicans in a Democratic administration. They had violated the sanctity of white supremacy by earning a decent wage in the nation's service, by politicking against the Democratic Party, and, ultimately, by demanding equal treatment under the law.

Other administrators in Wilson's government were less direct than John Skelton Williams in their racism. They were subtler, slower to set policies, and ostensibly more dedicated to establishing "good government" practices.[58] In some ways, these tactics were more successful. The segregation that stuck in the BEP had started with Williams but, in the end, was more Hamlin's and Ralph's creation. Thomas Clarke chose to resign only when he found himself in the hands of Charles Kram in the office of the auditor of the Post Office Department. Kram was neither a Wilson appointee nor a southerner, but he explicitly connected segregation and effective office management. During the Taft administration, Kram had undertaken a massive reorganization scheme, with the president's blessing, that was designed to make the office more businesslike. While all of the employees suffered under this mechanization, Kram appears to have taken special interest in disrupting the work lives of black employees.

Kram was proud of his administrative innovations. In September 1913, NAACP national secretary May Childs Nerney informed Wilson that African Americans were almost always given the worst work areas in Kram's division.[59] Kram had set aside three rooms, an alcove, and a corner for black workers. The employees in these areas were all doing minor clerical work. The chief clerk asserted that Kram's reorganizing was undertaken for efficiency, not discrimination, and he noted that some rooms did contain both white and black workers.[60] Kram told Nerney that one group of black men forced to work separately were doing difficult work at which they were "more expert." They had been collected from throughout the department and set to work together in their own room. Kram also bragged to Nerney, who spoke to him undercover, that his new "tabulating system" easily allowed for racial segregation. Reporting to McAdoo on his segregation efforts, Kram explained, "All action that has been taken in the matter was upon my own initiative with a view to getting the best results."[61]

Kram's mixture of personal prejudices with claims of administrative "results" reveals the idiosyncratic inner workings of Progressive Era "scientific management." New bureaucracies, however "rational," were still administered by ordinary people.[62] In July 1914, Kram devised similar office reorganizations for the Post Office, Interior, and Commerce Departments, abolishing positions and producing demotions with little explanation offered to workers. The changes do not appear to have been motivated by segregation plans, and white workers were among those who lost jobs.[63] Yet as the *Washington Bee* noted, "Many deserving colored government employees [were] humiliated, maimed, or decapitated" by the changes, and Kram was "the most despised among all the miserable [Taft] 'holdovers.'" He could, the paper said, "display a greater variety of official scalps than any Democrat now in the government service."[64] Kram's bureaucratic structures supported white supremacy just as they supposedly furthered administrative efficiency.

The results could be disastrous for individual employees. Shelby Davidson, for example, was by far the most conspicuous black clerk in Kram's office, and he became one of the auditor's earliest victims. Davidson was an inventor whose contributions to government accounting systems won him a high salary and national respect. If anyone had contributed to the efficient, businesslike practices of the office, it was Davidson.[65] In July 1911, Davidson's career was advancing briskly. Until then, he said, he had never been the victim of discrimination. Kram, however, was already beginning his disruptions by refusing to endorse Davidson's promotion despite work that Kram admitted was excellent.[66]

Ultimately, Davidson's inventions and government service were lost behind the veil of racism. Under Kram, Davidson was removed twice to dimly lit offices while a white subordinate was made his supervisor. Privately, he concluded that this was happening "because I am a colored man and this is the crux of the whole situation."[67] In March 1912, health problems forced Davidson to take temporary leave. Kram assured him that his job would remain open until his health improved. A year later, perhaps emboldened by the white Democrats now in charge, Kram reneged on his promise and refused to reinstate Davidson. The department's most heralded black employee was pushed out. Davidson turned to practicing law and NAACP organizing, but his attempt to be reinstated a few years later suggests that life outside the government was less rewarding.[68]

"Buried in Washington"

The racism evident in the cases of Richard Thompson, Thomas Clarke, and Shelby Davidson appears to fit into a larger pattern, even if most black clerks did not have such dramatic forced resignations. Most commonly, it appeared as if their careers suddenly slowed down, like rivers reaching their muddy deltas. Barriers, inconveniences, and indignities cropped up that narrowed the promise of civil service employment for all African Americans. Treasury clerk and journalist John Paynter, who had been covering government employment in Washington for black newspapers since Roosevelt, told the *Washington Post* that black workers were being deliberately held back. "Instances of the advance of the negro to the more remunerative grades of Federal employ being willfully retarded are so numerous as to seem to establish an acceptable rule of action," Paynter reported. "The unrelenting opposition and ingenious scheming of prejudiced persons, unwisely clothed with the power of selection, seeks to restrict the employment of the negro to the grades of messenger, skilled laborer, and laborer." The scheme seemed most interested in keeping black men out of positions of responsibility, Paynter added, so that even promotions came with little increase in status.[69]

Under Wilson, black clerks were less likely to be promoted — and more likely to be demoted — than in previous administrations. An examination of the careers of 97 black civil servants between 1909 and 1916, from Taft's presidency through Wilson's first administration, shows that there were 66 promotions and 8 demotions/dismissals under Taft and 23 promotions and 35 demotions/dismissals under Wilson.[70] For the 49 black clerks making $1,000 a year or more in the selection, there were 48 promotions and 4 demotions between 1909 and 1912, while there were 11 promotions and 22 demotions or forced resignations between 1913 and 1916. The first year of the Wilson administration was particularly bloody, as 19 of the 22 black clerks who suffered direct demotions or dismissals did so before the end of December 1914.[71]

Some African American clerks were promoted during the Wilson administration. In my selection, 3 of the 49 black clerks earning $1,000 or more when Wilson took office received promotions during the first term.[72] The problem was, as Paynter suggested, segregation meant that employees could be promoted in pay but suffer a loss in status or responsibility that resulted in greatly attenuated careers. Some were promoted to racial isolation: Arthur Gray and Thomas Dent, who earned promotions in the 1910s, were segregated into their own corner in the Commerce Department's Division of Statistics and set to work on reports relevant to black America only. Separated out from the majority of the staff and the bureau's main work, these men were made to feel marginal, regardless of their pay.[73] Finally, only four of those ever promoted during Wilson's two terms were advanced beyond the $1,200 Class 1 clerkship. No black clerk was allowed to ascend to the uppermost supervisory positions (Class 4 clerk, $2,000 per year and up) within the civil service system.[74]

Government work in Washington lost its promise of mobility, and as promotions became rarer, it would seem increasingly natural to Washingtonians that black workers would predominate in the lower grades of the civil service.[75] While the demotions, dismissals, and forced resignations bear witness to discrimination, in some ways it was the lack of promotions that most indicated a change. Fenwick Bush, a skilled helper in the GPO, earned twenty-five cents per hour for thirteen years, before finally being swept up in the wartime raises in 1918. Clerks John H. Cook, Charles R. Douglass (son of Frederick Douglass), Charles E. Hall, and Robert A. Pelham Jr., among others, all went at least ten years without a salary increase. More telling was the career of Post Office clerk Robert Culley, who earned promotions in 1909, 1910, and 1911 but not another until the wholesale reclassifications of 1918. Lawrence Wooden, also a Post Office clerk, earned promotions every year between 1909 and 1914, then was summarily reduced without cause. The case for black women appears to have been even worse: Laura Joiner was held at her $1,000-a-year clerkship in the Interior Department from 1903 until 1921; Lucretia Mott Kelly, also of the Interior Department, went without a pay increase from 1893 until the inflationary reclassifications of 1919.[76] Though all government clerks complained of being underpaid, and increasingly so in the 1910s, black clerks in particular seem to have been held back.[77]

With the civil service no longer a secure bet, the risks associated with leaving Washington seemed more acceptable for smart and ambitious African Americans. "As I see it, the chances for advancement to anything like what both of us want, in clerical work, are absolutely negligible," Swan Kendrick told his new bride, Ruby. Nearly everybody seemed to be waiting to move up, and "add to this the fact that I have no influential friends (especially during this administration), and the fact that I am not white, and you see just what my chances are for ever getting more than I am now making." That reality made the War Department a dead end, even though Kendrick had not experienced the kind of racism seen in other departments. "You wouldn't be satisfied with that, even if I were, which is unthinkable," he declared. The Kendricks would have to move on to somewhere else where they could "live a more complete and independent, and therefore a more satisfactory life. I know it's going to be hard to do it."[78]

William Jennifer discovered just how hard it could be to leave Washington. Using his Howard University education, the civil service exam, and his connections to the Republican Party, he had left Milford, Texas, behind in 1900. Over the next dozen years, white and black Republicans, from Theodore Roosevelt to Booker T. Washington, stepped in to make sure he held on to his job and earned more money and status.[79] Shortly after Wilson took office, Jennifer was told that another promotion, to $1,200, was in the works. His coworkers, Robert A. Pelham Jr. and Charles E. Hall, were already earning $1,200 a year. Jennifer noted that there was a ceiling in the office on pay for black clerks at $1,200, and he appears to have been correct. Pelham and Hall had been held at $1,200 for a decade, despite being highly valued clerks.[80]

Jennifer's money did not materialize. Repeated attempts to ingratiate himself with the new administration failed, and it seemed that Jennifer would never receive the promised raise. After fourteen years of working his way up the civil service ladder, everything just seemed to grind down. "My life is wrecked unless you are merciful and come to the rescue," he told the Census Bureau director.[81] The director made no move. Jennifer decided to stick it out and continued, with Hall, to conduct pioneering work on statistical data about African Americans.

Their work brought them new status briefly. Hall's team was the first to gather evidence of a significant black migration north and to tie it to labor issues. Workers were being drained from the South, leading to "possible if not probable change in industrial conditions in many communities North and South."[82] Hall and Jennifer were lent to the Labor Department to gather the data necessary to justify a dedicated division for studying the migration. Jennifer was finally promoted to $1,200 a year.[83] But when the work with the Labor Department ran out, Hall and Jennifer were left to dangle without pay. Hall was desperate to return to the Census Bureau, "having about exhausted my personal financial resources and those of my friends who were fit subjects for a *touch*." He preferred not to beg, but "neither [did he] wish to be forced to go out in the street some dark night with a sand-bag."[84]

Reinstatement to the Census Bureau did not come easily for either man, as the wheels of bureaucracy turned slowly. Jennifer believed he was the victim of a racist conspiracy when a Kafkaesque apportionment tangle required that he prove that he was from Texas — from which he had originally been appointed — despite the fact that he had, by government appointment, spent the previous decade and a half in Washington.[85] Hall and Jennifer did get reinstated, back into their segregated division under Robert Pelham Jr. In 1918, they were selected to return to the Department of Labor in the newly established Division of Negro Economics (the fruition of Hall's recommendation two years earlier). At the end of their service, both were returned to the Census Bureau.[86]

Jennifer had had enough, however, and decided to seek calmer seas outside of government work altogether. They did not exist. Using connections he had made working with the Department of Labor in Michigan, he sought employment in Detroit. Nonfederal work, it turned out, was no better for African Americans, and he could not find a place to establish his family. Stuck as a low-paid apartment residential manager in Detroit with his family still in Washington, he sought reinstatement in the new Republican administration in 1921. Despite increasingly "dire" circumstances, he was denied reinstatement then, and denied again in 1934 and 1937. In his final effort, the once important and nationally recognized Census Bureau clerk was willing to do just about any kind of work or, as he put it, land in "any port in a storm." Two years later, Jennifer died.[87]

IN ADDITION TO REDUCTIONS AND SEPARATIONS, growing suspiciousness and a willingness to entertain racist accusations also marked this era of deteriorating working conditions for black employees. In 1929, almost ten years after messenger Bernard Quiller resigned from the Library of Congress, his supervisor still remembered that Quiller's ambition in the 1910s had irritated a white assistant librarian. She found Quiller to be "impudent," a word African Americans recognized as signaling a black person's refusal to play the hapless subordinate.[88] Even Swan Kendrick, whose status actually rose during the Wilson administration, was accosted by a white building guard in the War Department's washroom. The guard insisted that Kendrick was forbidden to use the washroom.[89] The flood of racism finally reached Kendrick directly, and he resigned.

Yet as Kendrick's struggles to support his family outside of Washington would soon reveal, economic limitation became the most enduring legacy of segregation. When black federal employees were demoted or fired, they suffered greater harm than their white colleagues because they had nowhere else to go. No other industries in the United States offered as much opportunity to black men and women with education and middle-class aspirations. "Conditions are so deplorable in this city that there is nothing for our girls and boys to do after graduation," explained Calvin Chase in 1916. "The avenue for a livelihood is closed against them in places where they can earn a decent living."[90] Wilsonian discrimination constituted the state-sanctioned restriction of one of the last remaining pathways to social and economic stability still open to African Americans in the early twentieth century.

The combination of bureaucratic blustering and subtle discrimination, exemplified by the practices of Treasury officials, obfuscated the reality of discrimination in federal departments. Joseph Ralph and Charles Hamlin's discussions about segregation in the BEP, for example, were not public information—indeed, most historians have not seen them—because Ralph and Hamlin were seeking to avoid exposing anything (including protests) that might undermine their status as meritocratic and modern managers and the administration's larger status as democratic and just. But in Hamlin's diary, we can see the ways in which Treasury officials both fostered racial discrimination and hid it behind public denial and well-wishing for black employees. They maintained that segregation was not official policy, and in places where it may have *appeared* to be practiced, it was only for the good of black employees themselves.[91]

Federal employees working in Washington witnessed the color line being drawn across their working lives. "Whether an order is 'formal' or not, if the authority behind it is mighty enough to demand observance the effect and result are the same as if some one in authority had the temerity to sign it and thus make it 'formal,'" Ralph Tyler explained to *Star* readers.[92] A process that had taken decades in the South took less than five years in Washington, thanks, no doubt, to the momentum sweeping up from the South. Most black Americans had always lived separately from white people, and the indignities that accompanied the end of Reconstruction, the redemption, and the passage of segregation laws were part of a very long history of white supremacy and racial inequality. But black federal government workers insisted that their story was different. This notion of a change, of an overthrowing of a long-standing system of opportunity, was central to the protests that soon brought the nation's attention to Wilsonian discrimination.

Suppose that I were building a great piece of powerful machinery, and suppose that I would so awkwardly and unskillfully assemble the parts of it that every time one part tried to move it would be interfered with by the others, and the whole thing would buckle up and be checked. Liberty for the several parts would consist in the best possible assembling and adjustment of them all, would it not?
—Woodrow Wilson, *The New Freedom*, 1912

Chapter Six

Resistance and Friction

Challenging and Justifying Wilsonian Praxis

The changes in federal buildings that white Treasury officials viewed as fairly subtle were not at all minor to black workers and civil rights activists. African Americans and their allies went beyond such humiliation to more fundamental questions of citizenship. "There [can] be no freedom, no respect from others, and no equality of citizenship under segregation of the races," William Monroe Trotter told Woodrow Wilson in November 1913, "especially when applied to but one of the many racial elements in the government employ."[1] A fully integrated civil service, with black men and women working at all levels, was an unambiguous, concrete representation of equal participation in the laws and government of the United States. The symbolic and civic nature of federal employment made segregation in Washington a representative threat to black citizenship, and it sparked resistance and a national movement.

News of federal segregation spread quickly through a well-developed network of black newspapers in the spring and summer of 1913. The *Pittsburgh Courier* and the *Chicago Defender* sounded alarms all over the country. They joined Calvin Chase's *Washington Bee*, which had been publishing news of segregation in federal offices since Wilson's inauguration. In the fall, some liberal white editors, especially Rolfe Cobleigh of the *Congregationalist and Christian World*, picked up the story.[2] The obfuscation that became a hallmark of Wilsonian praxis accomplished its goal of making protests more complicated, but the reports began leaking out almost immediately. Ralph Tyler, a black Republican still serving as auditor for the Navy Department, was one of the first to take the reports seriously and voice his objection to racial segregation in May letters to the *Bee* and to the president directly.[3] By the summer, black leaders were moved to action. They joined the workers' efforts already underway to establish a broad resistance movement to Wilsonian praxis.

By resistance, I mean the ways in which black civil servants and their allies acted to protect their dignity, their rights, their jobs, and all aspects of autonomy, personhood, and citizenship that came under attack by white supremacists.[4] Importantly, this was a resistance whose goal was to stave off change — to "protect" against the crippling of black mobility — more than to create it. Clerks, in particular, were a relatively conservative lot. What they wanted was the right to work, live, and aspire to a more comfortable and prosperous future. In fact, they were little different from white workers, plenty of whom chafed under managerial "rationalization" that threatened their autonomy in the federal bureaucracy.[5] Many black clerks lived under middle-class proscriptions and surveillance that precluded overt protest. The toll that "holding in" frustration took can be seen in the weariness of clerks under Wilson. In 1920, for example, Treasury clerk Edward Scott was forced to ask for a leave of absence after working "seven years and a half in the Division of Bookkeeping and Warrants faithfully and conscientiously at the lowest salary for clerks in the division without advancement and with little or no hope for advancement now."[6] Yet part of the story of resisting federal discrimination was the subtle radicalization of a group of middle-class strivers. As their aspirations were made illegitimate or unrealizable by the national state, they became increasingly engaged with civil rights activism.

The historical record reveals myriad attempts by activists and federal employees to resist white supremacy. Two main groupings emerge, however. First, there was the "routine" or "hidden" resistance of black federal workers themselves, many of whom felt too vulnerable to participate in public activism.[7] The subordinates' actions, left generally unseen or unintelligible by superiors, included self-preserving assertions like quitting, complaining to civil rights leaders, secretly passing information to the press, racial passing, being "difficult," and perhaps even stealing and slowdowns. No doubt, there were also other methods of voicing personhood and frustration less legible in the historical record, from disengagement to physical catharsis to private and intimate confession.[8]

In most cases, employees' resistance consisted of desperate attempts to save their jobs in Washington. Though largely a battle of attrition, such work constituted resistance because black men and women refused to simply give up their livelihoods and their places in the government in the face of discrimination. Some reached out to the NAACP, turning the District of Columbia branch into an office for handling the grievances of federal employees. Their greatest asset was Archibald Grimké, president of the local branch, who used connections within the federal government to advocate on behalf of employees needing work or those who had already been segregated, demoted, or dismissed. Grimké recognized that abandonment by both political parties left African Americans with few strings to pull within the federal government.

In addition to this worker resistance, there was a very public and collective movement led mostly by private citizens who had the means to protest openly. This group included white and black civil rights activists. Their efforts helped to catalyze and consolidate the NAACP into the era's most prominent rights organization. Early on, the NAACP and William Monroe Trotter's National Independent Political League ran competing but complementary movements against federal segregation. They were part of a developing civil rights movement newly reconfigured around secular, nonpartisan interest groups in order to meet the challenges of the new racial regime. In the absence of the more structured Republican machine, they held rallies, organized petitions, wrote letters to the president and cabinet members, and based their demands that black Americans be treated as equal citizens on the terms of the U.S. Constitution.[9]

Civil rights activists turned back some of the most egregious indignities of federal discrimination by forcing administrators to disclaim overt racism. The broader movement, which Trotter articulated as a battle for black citizenship, was largely a campaign of speeches and letters. African American civil servants had very little electoral or legal power to actually end discrimination. But civil rights activists could expose the changes. As a result of public attention, whites-only signs were taken down and, despite proposed bills, Congress did not pass any laws segregating federal offices.

The actions of activists and civil servants forced Wilson and Secretary of the Treasury William McAdoo to answer difficult questions about federal discrimination, though their answers often succeeded in obfuscating persistent discrimination.

Wilsonians' public justifications for their actions were critical to the changing place and power of African Americans within the twentieth-century American state. No one here was as important as Woodrow Wilson himself. At last, the elusive chief executive came clearly into the picture of federal discrimination when he explained the work of his subordinates in the terms of his progressive politics. Wilson had always maintained that the goals of his administration were fairness and efficiency, and, in response to protests, he proclaimed segregation to be an act of managerial best practice. The president's reply mattered so much because, as he spoke, negotiated praxis became theory: segregation and discrimination were *necessary* for modern government.[10] The issue was not one of politics or rights. His managers, he said, were seeking only to "prevent any kind of friction between the white employees and the Negro employees."[11] Wilsonians, therefore, could simultaneously deny and defend segregation. "There is no 'segregation issue' in the Treasury Department," McAdoo declared. "There has been an effort in the Department to remove the causes of complaint and irritation where white women have been forced unnecessarily to sit at desks with colored men," but this was all done to aid black employees. "Compulsion of this sort creates friction and race prejudice."[12]

Those in the administration sought to delegitimize public objections to segregation by marking any protest by employees as both insubordinate and fallacious. They veiled their racism with anodyne claims of neutrality and meritocracy, a process that social theorist Pierre Bourdieu has labeled "euphemization."[13] Black workers who rejected the civil service's image as an objective, rational bureaucracy with no particular racial agenda were "impudent" or downright crazy. If African Americans were disproportionately in the lower ranks of government service, Wilsonians insisted, this said more about people of African descent than about their employer. African Americans and some allies never accepted this argument, of course, but the vast majority of white Americans did not question it. In this way, federal discrimination, including administrators' explanations of it, played its part in the national institutionalization of white supremacy in the United States. False meritocracies can transform socially constructed hierarchies into natural expectations.

Resisting from Within

By the summer of 1913, black government workers were feeling the ground shake beneath them. "Conditions have grown and are growing steadily worse," Treasury clerk Andrew Hilyer told Archibald Grimké in December 1913. The first African American graduate of the University of Minnesota and a Howard-educated lawyer, Hilyer was an accountant with nearly thirty years of government experience by the time Wilson took office. Segregation, he declared, "is elimination — death to us! It will make us pariahs — social and economic outcasts in our own country!"[14] Hilyer's outcry indicated the expectations of many black civil servants that federal employment should make them better off than African Americans elsewhere in the United States, most of whom already lived and worked in segregated spaces. It also reflected the degree to which black civil servants saw segregation and discrimination as not merely humiliation but an attack on status and livelihood.

Some black workers took collective action. Working-class black women were more likely to act explicitly against workplace discrimination in Washington than were more elite black men.[15] In April 1913, for example, Bureau of Engraving and Printing workers Maggie Keys, Rosebud Murraye, and Bertha Saunders refused the order to sit at the "colored tables."[16] Charlotte Hopkins, the well-known white social reformer, told Murraye to give up the protest. "Why will you go where you are not wanted?" she reportedly asked. "Do you know that the Democrats are in power? If you people will go along and behave yourselves, and stay away, we may let you hold your places."[17] Bureau director Joseph Ralph described Murraye's response to Hopkins's patronizing threats as "impertinent" and "insolent." She was soon fired. The rest of the black women in the BEP refused to eat in a lunchroom "where our food choked us" and turned to eating in the waiting room outside the "colored women's" toilets.[18]

Government employees were also among the 20,000 names on an antisegregation petition that Trotter presented to Wilson in November 1913. Postal workers in Cincinnati sent a protest letter to Postmaster General Albert Burleson.[19] Those in Washington attended mass meetings and contributed financially to the NIPL and the NAACP. Elite government employees like Hilyer, Thomas H. R. Clarke, Lafayette Hershaw, and Swan Kendrick would become the core of the D.C. branch of the NAACP.[20] They provided what little data they could about the discrimination and segregation being instituted in department offices.

Simply reporting information was a form of protest that came with great risk. "I get this information from Mr. Moses Walker who is a clerk in that office," Clarke wrote NAACP official Jessie Redmon Fauset in a detailed letter about segregation in the Treasury Department. Walker, Clarke reported, "had the courage to face John Skelton Williams and denounce segregation — however, I do not think it would be wise to use his name. He is now trying to get transferred to Chicago and publicity might hurt him."[21] A November note from another federal employee reflected a similar concern about the safety of those who dared to share information. "Please withhold my name as I am employed in the Gov't Service," read a letter to Oswald Garrison Villard. The writer provided more details about segregation in the dressing rooms, including information most likely about the standoff between Rosebud Murraye and BEP officials. Murraye and the other women were "complaining bitterly," and an "old time Negro Mammy" counseled the young women to accept segregation, telling them they "'done better got satisfied wit' dis 'rangement an' be glad dese w'ite folks lettin' you earn your bread and butter.'"[22] The writer's inclusion of the older woman's admonishment of Murraye is a reminder that collective action is not the same as universal or unanimous action. Young upstarts like Murraye faced enormous pressure to keep quiet from an older generation that remembered all too well the days before freedom and government employment.

Indeed, most black federal employees did not sign petitions and were not activists, lawyers, or founders of the NAACP. They were men and women whose frustrations with racism were expressed in individual encounters and attempts to maintain some personal respect. These workers often undertook smaller-scale acts of resistance. Raymond Fisher, for example, was working as a helper in the Government Printing Office when Wilson took office. By 1914, his supporting congressmen were gone, and he was demoted on June 20. Writing to his supervisor, Fisher appealed to his record of competence, a kind of resistance supposedly supported by meritocratic management. "I have always been congratulated upon my work," he wrote the new public printer Cornelius Ford. Ford had taken over for the racial egalitarian Samuel B. Donnelly and had quickly segregated the GPO.[23] His record rendered meaningless, Fisher pleaded for leniency, being a young man with several dependents, but this line led nowhere too. He was eventually forced to leave federal employment, and by 1930 he had moved to Boston and was working as a railroad porter.[24]

Quitting was a form of resistance and an important indicator of the degree to which the circumstances of black federal employment had changed. Up until 1913, government work was an extremely attractive employment

option for African Americans, especially for those with education. Few oc-
cupations provided decently paid, white-collar work; and no other line of
work was as clear an expression of one's active citizenship and place in the
democratic nation. But the benefits were declining. Swan Kendrick, for example, began to dream of alternative careers by the summer after Wilson's
inauguration. "As soon as the fall advances somewhat I am going to take up
another cause—Electrical Engineering," he reported to Moyse. "I really believe that's my 'calling.'" This was no sudden flight of fancy. Kendrick had
studied mathematics in college, but "there came the thought that a 'colored'
engineer is usually a sort of square peg trying to get into the round hole
of American life." Nor was Kendrick thinking only of a career change. He
took up Spanish and began to send away for information about businesses
abroad. Kendrick's frustration with the United States led to mythical fan-
tasizing about other places. "And now what about the color line in South
America? There isn't any," he declared triumphantly. "In a word, I want the
opportunity for self-realization. . . . If I fall, let it be my failure, not blame it
on the 'white folks.'"[25] Exiting on one's own terms preserved an individual's
right to refuse subordination.[26]

The cost of leaving government work for the racist American job market was decreasing as government salaries fell and promotions disappeared.
"Reductions of more than 55 per cent of my salary in less than a year necessarily demand a rearrangement of all my plans and my mode of life," GPO
employee John A. Davis informed his supervisor.[27] Demoted from a clerk
making $1,200 a year to a laborer at $500 a year, Davis began to see his plight
as one of deliberate discrimination, a direct attack on his manhood. "The
reputation, which I have been able to acquire and maintain at considerable
sacrifice of time and effort," Davis wrote his superior in May 1913, "is to me
(foolish as it may appear to those in higher stations of life) a source of personal pride, a possession of which I am very jealous and which is possessed
at a value in my estimation, ranking above the loss of salary—though the
last, to a man having a family of small children to rear, is serious enough."[28]
In 1917, he resigned.

Many, like Davis, tied together civil and economic rights in their pleas
for justice. A right to decent pay inhered in African Americans' sense of
their rights as citizens in the early twentieth century. These appeals need
not explicitly refer to citizenship to indicate their speaker's sense that his
or her political rights, that the Constitution itself, guaranteed a "right to the
fruits of one's labor."[29] Explaining personal financial struggles was a particu-

lar form of appeal: it resisted the increasing racism and rationalization in the state bureaucracy by demanding recognition of one's humanity. When Theophilus Houston was threatened with the loss of his Post Office clerkship, he confessed that he was teetering on disaster. Hounded by a debt to a man who had "never known the pinch of poverty," Houston pleaded "for mercy since to separate me from the Post Office now would entail much suffering upon my mother and the rest of my family."[30] When John Rattley lost his $1,200-a-year clerkship in the Pension Bureau in 1913, NIPL leader J. Milton Waldron told his superior the separation would cause problems for Rattley's family: "Rattley is not only without property and money," Waldron appealed, "but he and two of his children are living with a married daughter of his and making all kinds of sacrifices in order to keep her from losing the little home she and her husband (who has been out of work for many months) are trying to buy."[31] After three years of unemployment, Rattley managed to take advantage of wartime labor needs and was hired as an assistant messenger in the War Department earning $720 a year—a significant step down from his $1,200 clerkship.

Clearly frustrated, Rattley refused to accept disrespect. In the summer of 1921, a white clerk named Wheeler, not wanting more work, refused to accept a group of files Rattley was delivering. Wheeler waved Rattley away, telling him to "shut up." Rattley replied, "I'll talk to you as long as I like." The two were separated by another worker. Rattley testified that Wheeler was rude on a regular basis, but it was Rattley whom the white clerks labeled a problem: "He makes himself very obnoxious by his general attitude, as though he was looking for trouble. Some of the ladies of the Division have objected to him bringing work to their desks on that account." None who gave depositions referred to Rattley by name, simply calling him "the colored man" or the "colored messenger," though they all saw him regularly. And while every deposition stated that the white clerk had unnecessarily lost his temper, one concluded, "I think the colored man was entirely at fault."[32] What the white workers saw as troublemaking was more likely an expression of both Rattley's frustration and his pride.

Others sought to avoid racial designation entirely: "passing" was a form of resistance because it mocked white purity and represented a refusal to be an object of racism.[33] In her memoir, the white-skinned but black-identified Mary Church Terrell described being set to work in a segregated office in the Census Bureau as a typist during World War I. There, she witnessed the outing of women passing as white:

I saw a woman who I knew had been working in another section of the Bureau, come into our large room carrying her hat, her umbrella and purse. . . . In a few minutes another woman was ushered into a room and given a seat. And this was repeated half a dozen times. . . . They were colored women so fair that they had been assigned to sections set aside exclusively for white women. By fair means or foul their racial identity had been disclosed to somebody "higher up," who was opposed to allowing women of two races to work in the same room. Suddenly on that beautiful spring afternoon somebody pounced upon those fair colored women, snatched them from the places to which their ability and their personal appearance caused them to be assigned, and removed them to the room to which "they belonged."[34]

Though black critics condemned race deniers as traitors, light-skinned African Americans often succeeded in passing as white in Washington. The journey from "home" to federal work in Washington could be a deracinating experience in so many liberating ways.

Passing grew more common as racism hardened in the city and drew a thicker color line between black Washingtonians. In February 1915, a "'fair-haired, blue-eyed octoroon'" clearly enjoyed ruffling Florida congressman Frank Clark, who had recently introduced a bill in Congress to segregate Washington's streetcars: "'You need not think you will be able to escape me, as I can go into any gathering in churches, theaters, or anywhere else you go.'" In terror, Clark sought reassurance from the White House. A color hierarchy in Washington had always existed in some form or another, but with the advent of aggressive segregation, skin tone became an even more powerful agent of privilege.[35]

Another form of passing, or performing an identity that might provide more personal safety, was claiming to be a member of Wilson's constituency. "I am one of the colored men who has given service to the Democratic Party," wrote William T. Ferguson to McAdoo in 1915. Ferguson had tried to align with Taft in 1912 but been rejected for his past Democratic support. Ferguson massaged away this aspect of his history. "I was the first man of color to offer organized support to the party," he claimed, hoping that this supposed loyalty would lead to a civil service promotion. "I just want to be placed as a clerk at $1200.00 per annum by *Executive order*. I am clerk at $720.00 per annum in the Patent Office."[36] Ferguson's hope was unrealistic but not impossible. Executive orders were signed for civil servants regularly, and Wilson did so 332 times in his first term—though not for Ferguson.[37]

Resistance is not the same as overcoming, of course. Civil servants who struggled against the subordination of Wilsonian praxis did not hold off the installation of racism in government offices. Indeed, some of their non-aggressive forms of resistance, like quitting and passing, helped to institutionalize a racial hierarchy that delegitimized African American white-collar government work. "To give up a lucrative position simply because everything is not as smooth as we would like," wrote Calvin Chase in September 1913, "is to display a false pride and to perpetuate an injustice and hardship on those who are dependent upon us."[38] Facing an indomitable force backed by majoritarian and moralistic justifications, most black federal employees could act only to preserve their individual autonomy and personhood. Andrew Hilyer was wrong: segregation was not "death" to black government workers. Most resisted *and* adjusted to find ways to live with a new regime of racism.

For all of its weakness and failures, resistance to white supremacy did accomplish at least two broader goals. First, the protests and assertions of people like Rosebud Murraye and John Rattley had some success at piercing the veneer of "fairness" that Wilsonians tried to spread over federal segregation. Charles S. Hamlin's machinations, McAdoo's denials, and Wilson's defensiveness were all products of an incipient, if unsympathetic, awareness that black workers were being victimized. White progressives who objected to segregation in the pages of *The New Republic, The Independent*, and *The Nation* needed to be prodded to stand for a liberalism that included African American rights and equality. Black people said "no" often enough that those who *could* hear them sometimes did. Second, their objections and the information they provided sparked the NAACP and the early civil rights movement. Black civil servants turned first to party politics to address their problems, but when they found little support there, they moved increasingly to collective organizations outside of politics to safeguard and demand their rights.

Party Men

Black Democrats were among the first outside the government to respond to federal segregation. Leaders of the National Colored Democratic League believed throughout Wilson's first term that they should have special access to the president. They had supported his campaign, and they expected to gain from his election. When the new president began replacing black Republicans in executive appointments with white Democrats instead of black party members, names of whom were forwarded to Wilson through the Democratic machinery, members of the NCDL worried. In their home districts, league leader James L. Curtis told William McAdoo, they were being pummeled for their apparent foolishness. As late as the summer of 1914, Curtis was promising that his fellow Democrats could "present an organized militant adjunct to the white supporters of the administration," but they needed help.[39] Despite Curtis's eventual appointment as minister to Liberia, black Democrats never received enough from the administration to remain supportive. Indeed, their greater investment led to greater disappointment and early awareness that Wilsonian praxis was an attack on black government work, mobility, politics, and citizenship.

By August 1913, Robert N. Wood, president of the United Colored Democracy of the State of New York, decided he could no longer worry just about executive appointments. Wood tried to assure Wilson that equality of citizenship need not overturn the long-established convention that black and white people could never be socially equal.[40] He also sought to remind Wilson that government work was about more than political equality: it was a bulwark against impoverishment. "We resent [segregation], not at all because we're particularly anxious to eat in the same room or use the same soap and towels that white people use," he explained, "but because we see in the separation of the races in the matter of soup and soap the beginning of a movement to deprive the colored man entirely of soup and soap, to eliminate him wholly from the Civil Service of the United States." Racial discrimination was a part of federal employment in the past, Wood noted. But with Republicans in charge, "there was always recourse to the proper authorities." Instead, Wilson's administration was encouraging the eclipse of black government work entirely.[41]

Wood connected the treatment of black federal workers to the larger reign of terror being inflicted on black Americans and laid responsibility for both at the feet of the president. Noting that Americans and even the foreign press were waiting for Wilson to do something about lynching, Wood attempted to appeal to the high moral authority of the office Wilson occupied. "As Chief Magistrate you cannot refuse to hear our side of the case, even if your own personal sympathies should lean rather toward the other," Wood declared, adding with some sarcasm, "If some innocent colored man should be pulled off a train and lynched—a fate which a traveling secretary of the YMCA, barely escaped two years ago in a village in Georgia—we should not consider it your duty to ask Congress to provide an appropriation for the relief of his family." Black Americans asked only that Wilson extend the same progressive impulses to black citizens as he was doing to the white ones.[42] Joe Tumulty deemed Wood important enough in 1913 to recommend that the president read "the whole of" Wood's letter as he passed it up to him. That Wilson probably saw Wood's letter that first summer of his presidency is significant, because its perspicuity undermines Wilson's feigned ignorance of discrimination within his administration. Moreover, Wood wrote as a friend and ally, offering Wilson the opportunity to do better. Wilson's failures were not those of a completely disconnected or credulous national leader: they were a conscious betrayal.

Other black Democrats, often those outside the more liberal Democratic strongholds of New York and Boston, were less candid with the president. Their hesitancy may have actually provided Wilson with some of the political cover he claimed to have as the segregation controversy wore on. Bishop Alexander Walters reportedly told Wilson that he and other black Americans actually supported segregation, and although NAACP secretary May Childs Nerney doubted the claim, the controversy resulted in Walters's resignation from the NAACP.[43] The continuing efforts of Walters, Adam Patterson, and others to secure presidential appointments through Wilson's second term suggested that at least some African Americans were willing to overlook the administration's perfidies either to gain employment or to support an administration that was, in other ways, a progressive force for reform.[44]

But most could not overlook the changes in Washington. Far away in Boston, William Monroe Trotter was the first among Wilson's black supporters to openly question the administration on segregation. His shift from supporting Wilson to protesting the new administration was particularly swift. Letters praising Wilson and McAdoo in March 1913 were followed by questions about segregation and presidential appointments in May. Using his Washington contacts, Trotter tried to keep tabs on the situation in the capital. But details were hard to come by, and Trotter treaded lightly initially, passing along a newspaper article to McAdoo about alleged segregation. In July, Trotter wrote again expressing his "hope" that "color segregations reported to have been made by your assistant secretaries" were not true.[45]

By August, Trotter was sure that a revolt was necessary. "Segregation untenable, morally, politically[.] indignation [among] colored rising. nationally[,] supporters of wilson must oppose or be ruined," read Trotter's August 15 telegram to Joe Tumulty.[46] Federal segregation constituted a national regime of white supremacy. Members of Trotter's NIPL, "supporters of the National Democratic ticket," found "themselves under the manly though painful necessity" of forwarding their dissent to the president directly.[47] Objections to the Wilsonian regime would, in fact, frequently be articulated in terms of "manliness" and "manhood" by elite leaders as well as by federal workers. Political relevance — as for many white men — was considered manful, especially with a suffrage system that excluded women. Disfranchisement had long been figured by black men as emasculation, and federal discrimination constituted yet another attack on the potency of their citizenship.[48]

Trotter met with Wilson at the White House on November 6, 1913, ostensibly to present an antisegregation petition with the signatures of 20,000 people in thirty-eight states. Standing with Trotter was a delegation of supporters from Philadelphia, Chicago, Washington, New York, and Boston, including Ida B. Wells-Barnett, the nationally recognized reform journalist. Wells-Barnett and Trotter had come together through mutual alienation from the less militant NAACP and would remain allies for many years.[49] Trotter's carefully prepared statement focused only on segregation as a symbol of inequality between citizens. "No citizen who is barred because of the prejudice of another citizen can be his equal in citizenship," he explained. "By subjecting the former to the latter's prejudice, the Government denies equality." Trotter attempted to educate Wilson to the lie in the "separate but equal" doctrine suggested by the Supreme Court's *Plessy v. Ferguson* decision in 1896. The problem with segregating one group of people, Trotter said, was that it created a hierarchy of citizens, unacceptable in a republic based on the equality of all men. Trotter reminded Wilson that black Americans were citizens who, by definition, could not be subjected to discrimination by their own democracy. Acceptance of such "insulting, humiliating, unjust, intolerable, and hostile" treatment would require acceptance of innate inferiority. And African Americans most certainly did not consider themselves inferior to white Americans, declared Trotter.[50]

Wilson's response was a mix of defensiveness and denial. He claimed no interest within the administration in treating black workers unfairly. The president did not deny that new "arrangements" had been made in the Treasury, but he assured Trotter that "Secretary McAdoo honestly thought [they] would be acceptable to everybody." McAdoo had received numerous protests against the "arrangements," and he surely knew they were not acceptable to "everybody." Wilson promised that he was doing everything he could. "There are these difficulties of which we must be patient and tolerant," he explained in a patronizing tone. "We have to accept them as facts, no matter how much we may deplore them in their moral and social consequences." "Facts" were the progressive reformers' calling card, and Wilson's way of dealing with Trotter was to insist that segregation was empirically fair—a technique that could both disarm protests and burnish Wilson's image as an enlightened liberal. Wilson then ended, paradoxically, with a categorical denial: "There is no policy on the part of the administration looking to segregation."[51]

Wells-Barnett sensed Wilson's obstinate inability to sympathize with black Americans. "I have found by experience that the only way by which we could even convince our best friends who can't see how we suffer would be to suffer, you would think, a black or brown face, as we do, and then they would see this democracy in a new light."[52] It is doubtful that Wilson's imagination could follow Wells-Barnett's object lesson in empathy, but Trotter, nonetheless, believed the meeting had gone well. The president had appeared to listen to their pleas, and Trotter counted this an achievement for the NIPL.[53]

In fact, declining public support for his efforts, the apparent continuation of segregation, and silence from Wilson in response to his subsequent communications soon indicated that Trotter had accomplished little that fall. He proudly described his encounter with the president at a mass meeting at the Nineteenth Street Baptist Church the next evening, but leaving the church, Swan Kendrick could only sigh, "Whether anything will come of it or not no one knows, except, perhaps, the president."[54] Both the administration and the increasingly preeminent NAACP overwhelmed Trotter's underfunded and overextended NIPL. Trotter's well-publicized meeting with the president was a triumphant but fleeting moment.[55]

New Patrons

Trotter's bravery and stridency did bolster a changing racial consciousness among civil servants. In the absence of Republican egalitarianism and Democratic patronage, black federal workers now began to peel away their investment in the American party system: affiliation with the Republican Party had brought less and less security and mobility, and Wilson's Democratic Party was failing to live up to the promises made during the campaign. In looking beyond parties for political action, African Americans were not alone. This era saw the rise of interest groups as replacements to more vibrant parties. The most powerful of these groups formed a new point of contact between citizens and government and influenced government policy.[56] In many cases, these new interest groups were organized along lines of gender, class, and racial identity, as women, workers, African Americans, and so on sought, with varying degrees of success, influence that the political system had long denied them. For federal employees so dependent on the political patronage system for jobs and status, this was a dramatic change of affiliations.

Black clerks had little opportunity to join one important interest group, the nation's growing labor movement. Though unions were just beginning to gain state recognition under Wilson, federal clerks outside of the Post Office Department did not have a union of their own until 1917, when the National Federation of Federal Employees (NFFE), affiliated with the American Federation of Labor, was founded.[57] Before the creation of the NFFE, only skilled craftspeople were unionized, usually in locals founded by their counterparts outside government. White-collar clerks and unskilled laborers remained unorganized.[58] Moreover, most white-led unions that admitted African Americans segregated their locals, further alienating black workers. Black clerks did join the federal employees union, even though the NFFE local in the District of Columbia actively discouraged African American membership. In 1919, African American workers established a separate branch, Local No. 71, but there is little extant information of that branch's activities, nor is there any record of the NFFE protesting racial segregation or discrimination in federal departments.[59] Finally, some elite black Washingtonians shared an antiunion ideology that combined racial distrust with a Republican, capitalist ethos. Unions, wrote J. C. Cunningham in the *Bee*, "think that only members of the union [usually white workers] are entitled to earn a decent living." Ultimately, black union activity in Washington was negligible before the 1930s.[60]

Unable to organize along class lines, some workers sought to combat racism directly for the first time. Simply put, they joined "the movement."[61] In May 1912, Lafayette McNeill Jr. had complained to his superiors about "low-grade work" and scarce promotions for "certain workers" but did not mention race.[62] In January 1914, however, he forwarded his letters to a local NAACP official.[63] Similarly, in March 1913, customs officer Victor P. Thomas addressed his frustrations to W. E. B. Du Bois: "It is my belief that if I were not a colored man, with a colored man's chances in such matters, my chance for retention would be excellent."[64] Though Du Bois had publicly supported Wilson, he was not a political player in the way that Booker T. Washington or other black Republicans had been. Instead, Du Bois was a civil rights leader, a founder of the NAACP, outside of the constraints of party politics.

The NAACP provided an outlet for political and civic demands that political parties no longer would. For Swan Kendrick, helping to organize the NAACP in the capital provided an opportunity not necessarily to be a "race leader" but to have a public voice: "What I do want is, the consciousness that my life has been worth something; that I have really had some connection with the great movements of my time; that I have not been a cipher, as it were; that I have not simply moved forward with the world, but have helped it to move," Kendrick said. He spent evenings attending mass meetings, listening to papers at black debating clubs, and distributing copies of *The Crisis* to a growing subscribers' list in Washington. "I hate to be always bringing up this question of color, yet the thing can't be overlooked," Kendrick told Ruby Moyse. "We must have organization and education, and I want to help do a little of both."[65]

The National Association for the Advancement of Colored People

In 1913, the four-year-old NAACP was not yet the premier civil rights organization it would become at midcentury. Unsure of its own organizational structure, the relationships between white and black members, and the strength of its opposition to Tuskegee, the NAACP was still an inchoate entity. At the start, its involvement in the segregation controversy was little different from that of Trotter's NIPL. Key members of the NAACP, including Oswald Garrison Villard and W. E. B. Du Bois, had supported Wilson in the presidential election. And like Trotter, they were shaken from their allegiance in the spring of 1913 by reports of employee discrimination and racial segregation.[66] Yet unlike in Trotter's case, the opportunities of the segregation fight would produce lasting power, stability, and prestige for the NAACP.

The NAACP was founded at a series of meetings between 1908 and 1910 as a civil rights organization made up of white and black progressives increasingly out of step with Booker T. Washington's uplift gradualism.[67] Nonpartisan, secular, and integrationist, the NAACP was intended to take on questions of citizenship rights, racist legislation in Congress, lynching, and segregation in federal offices. By 1917, there were fifty local branches doing this work around the country. For many, the association was defined by its major publication, *The Crisis*, and by the words of its editor. Du Bois's literary fervor, bourgeois aestheticism, black pride, and uncompromising politics boosted *The Crisis* to a circulation of 22,500 in 1912, making it the most important civil rights publication in the nation.[68]

The events of 1913 animated the association and offered it new organizational opportunities. From the beginning, there was a sense, especially among its white board members, that federal segregation provided an opening for the NAACP to assert its importance. Federal segregation was just the striking abrogation of citizens' rights that they needed to bring publicity to their organization. "This is the most important thing that has been before us for years," Mary White Ovington explained to fellow board member Joel Spingarn in July, just as news of federal segregation was spreading outside Washington. "We have a loyal group in Washington who are willing to sacrifice their personal comfort and to give of their financial means for our support. I want to work with them."[69]

National secretary May Childs Nerney also underlined the auspiciousness of the moment. "The Washington people had backbone enough to act independently in the face of the most outrageous appeals to race prejudice and in a way colored people have never done before. This in a city like Washington is doubly significant since some of the most active members have endangered their positions." If the NAACP did not act, it would have difficulty drawing black Americans into the organization. "The colored press is watching and all our branches are watching, and no branch in the future will have the courage to do anything but trim and listen to self-constituted leaders."[70] Like so many white progressives, Nerney proposed to show people in need what expert leadership looked like. The idea that black Americans were, for the first time, aroused to fight for their rights was a useful fiction for an organization looking for people to lead.

More than any other single officer, Nerney would exert the most influence over the NAACP's antisegregation efforts in Washington. She made important decisions about when to act and on what information. Early on, for example, Nerney noted that segregation of bathrooms in federal offices was probably not enough of an issue to make an NAACP campaign tenable.[71] Frustrated with the lack of specific, verifiable information about segregation in federal offices, Nerney disguised herself as a friend of segregation and toured the Treasury Department in September 1913. Her written report, which the NAACP sent to cabinet secretaries, supporters, and newspapers around the country, represented an important breakthrough for the association.[72]

Nerney, whom historian David Levering Lewis describes as a "hot-tempered, former librarian," was careful to maintain the reputation the NAACP sought as a reasonable, interracial body of progressive citizens.[73] She and the board worked hard to appear less confrontational than Trotter.

For example, it was the white members who made direct contact with administration officials. As a wealthy white friend of Wilson and of Tumulty, Villard managed to hold a meeting with the president without generating Trotter's kind of controversy. The NAACP's white leaders were certainly liberal progressives with a far greater dedication to black equality than most white Americans. Many could even be called radical in their support for socialism, world peace, and labor rights. Yet few considered themselves anything less than well-bred leaders, statesmen of a republic of ideals that they fully expected to bring into reality through reason and enlightened political advocacy. In this way, they differed little from Woodrow Wilson.[74]

Maintaining this "reasonable" position required some careful grooming by NAACP officials, black and white. Most important, the association sought to align only with the most reputable of victims, a cautiousness that shaped their campaign as a whole. For the most part, the NAACP focused on segregation and chose not to address larger structural issues of working conditions or wages.[75] It sought cases of good, "clean" people under a demonstrably unfair attack. In the case of Rosebud Murraye's protest against segregated lunch tables, for example, Thomas H. R. Clarke reported to Nerney that most in the BEP believed Murraye's trouble to be the result of the young woman's "militancy," prompting concern within the NAACP about Murraye's character.[76] "From all the information I can gather Rosebud Murray[e]'s case would not be a good one to follow up," Lafayette Hershaw confirmed.[77] "If there is anything that I could personally do for Miss Murraye," Nerney lamented, "I would gladly do it, but I have heard from a variety of sources that this is not a good case."[78] This would not be the first or last time the NAACP could be described as failing to take up a case because of concerns about the character of those involved.[79]

Despite its guardedness, the NAACP held well-organized rallies, published Nerney's report, wrote eloquent open letters to the Wilson administration, and sent out "Dear Friend" letters to its members, encouraging them to write to their governmental representatives. While Trotter was superb at drawing dramatic attention to segregation, he was limited by his radical reputation and by the regional reach of his newspaper. The fully national NAACP, with the powerful voice of *The Crisis*, could draw on support from around the country and make the case to the entire nation that federal segregation mattered. NAACP officials focused on symbolism. "This mistaken action of the Federal Government will be cited as the warrant for new racial outrages," the NAACP charged. "Wherever there are men who rob the Negroes of their votes, who exploit and degrade and insult and lynch those whom they call their inferior," Washington would be the new model.[80] The organization's appeal bore some results.

Between August 1913 and December 1914, Wilson received nearly 200 letters opposing segregation from twenty-six states across the country. "Mr. President, just imagine yourself a Negro working in one of these Departments," wrote Paul Bolin of New York City. "I ask, could you do your best work; could you have the right respect for yourself; could you consider yourself really and truly a man if you had to do your work behind a screen simply because you were identified with the Negro Race?"[81] H. M. Beard of Oak Park, Illinois, reminded Wilson, "We as the white Race expect much of them, claiming that they should be intelligent, should be of good character, be thrifty, and respectable citizens living in peace." But with segregation and other systems of discrimination, Beard continued, "we as individuals, as states, and now as a nation try to crush their manhood, their self-respect, and close the doors of employment and industry to them, and make them to feel that their citizenship counts for naught."[82] Federal segregation, this writer noted, elevated racism to the level of national practice.

Mass meetings in cities from Boston to Chicago to Tacoma supplemented the epistolary campaign. Such meetings took the form of revivals. Black churches repeatedly served as sites of protest against discrimination. Indeed, churches were more than mere theaters for staging protests. Their longstanding capacities to connect people, teach organizing techniques, and demand respect for divinely created humanity made them powerful sources of inspiration and resistance. In Washington, D.C., church meetings were especially important. "Washington people can't vote, you know," Swan Kendrick reminded his fiancée, "and the mass meeting is the only means we have of letting public men, congressmen, etc., know what we think about things."[83]

The largest "monster" meeting was held on October 27, 1913, at the Metropolitan AME Church on M Street NW. The site of Frederick Douglass's funeral service, the Metropolitan was one of the most prominent African Methodist Episcopal churches in the country, placing the event firmly under the aegis of the city's African American elite.[84] The Metropolitan's red brick Gothic building was filled beyond its maximum—the Bee generously estimated that 4,000 people were able to make it inside with another 8,000 forced to stand outside. Inside, the crowd heard some of the city's most prominent white and black citizens, including Justice Wendell Stafford of the District Supreme Court, former U.S. senator from New

Metropolitan AME Church, circa 1899. The leading church among Washington's black elite, the Metropolitan was the site of the capital's largest mass meeting to protest segregation in federal offices in 1913. The church still stands on M Street, nestled among the District's ubiquitous office buildings. (Library of Congress)

Hampshire Henry W. Blair, Archibald Grimké, and Reverend Walter H. Brooks of the African American Nineteenth Street Baptist Church.[85]

In the defining speech of the evening, Oswald Garrison Villard spoke of matters greater than federal segregation. His very name announced the association's reengagement of the abolitionist crusade, the last century's great civil rights campaign. White progressives were returning to take responsibility for black Americans and stand for the previous generation's achievements, now almost totally vitiated by the resurgent rebels. Flyers handed out at the meeting included the lyrics to the "Battle Hymn of the Republic," and Villard explicitly connected the new movement with the fight for black freedom in the Civil War. "The great struggle which convulsed the United States was, in its simplest terms, nothing else than the attempt of the aristocracy of cotton and land to create two classes of human beings in this country, slave and the free," he told the cramped audience. Villard was in high voice, quite deliberately reminding many of his grandfather, William Lloyd Garrison. "Let a precedent [like segregation] be established, and who shall say what outcome will be, to what lengths despotic officials will take their way by means of discrimination, intimidation, by above-board or underhand methods?" he warned.[86]

At stake was the possibility of an all-out race war, Villard explained. African Americans would not take re-enslavement lightly. "I have personally been appealed to by high authority to do my best to keep the colored people in 'cool and just equipoise,'" Villard reported. "It is beyond me to influence them in this direction, but I would not if I could."[87] Dipping into the same well of imagination from which Ben Tillman and James Vardaman drew, Villard pictured an angry black beast lurking on the fringes of American society. But for Villard, it was segregation that disturbed the very order and harmony that Wilsonians claimed it preserved.

Fear of black people let loose hobbled the NAACP's ability to find concrete means of addressing the needs of workers. After an antisegregation meeting in Boston on October 20, 1913, Alfred Hussey "came away disappointed," he told Villard. "Like you, I come of a shiny abolition ancestry, and never have I felt for our black brothers anything but the utmost goodwill." But, when it came to segregation, he admitted, "Frankly, I do not see the way out." Hussey was hoping for a specific way to advance the cause and thought that Villard had failed to offer one. "As I see it, in this gathering, you had a magnificent opportunity; and to speak plainly, you failed to measure up to it. What these people need is what I went there for, — a specific program! And what did we get? Your words were brilliant, but inflammatory." And in the end, they were just words.[88]

Indeed, the NAACP proved a poor patron for the preservation of black equality. At times courageous and righteous, the national organization was nonetheless incapable of repairing black workers' linkages to political power. For all of his appeals to abolitionism, Villard could not reach into the innards of government departments and affect government personnel management the way the Radical Republicans had done almost two generations earlier. Interest group politics could not replace party politics in promoting the demands of government workers. This was especially true when white progressives, who had long fought to replace political machines with efficient bureaucracies, dominated the group. Ultimately, Villard and Wilson were cut from similar cloth: both were invested more in their own notions of fairness than in any realistic sense of the way in which power operated in America.

Archibald Grimké

Black civil servants were not nearly as dependent on their activist allies as the allies themselves imagined—nor were they on the verge of igniting an all-out race war. Instead, black Washingtonians worked to maintain their role in the national government far more quietly and in ways that more closely resembled the previous regime: they found those people who *could* actually affect personnel management, and they turned those people into useful advocates. Most settled on a former slave and Harvard Law School graduate named Archibald Grimké. The president of the D.C. branch of the NAACP and an accomplished patronage broker, Grimké presaged the kind of local, urban clientage managers that dominated black politics after World War I. Yet contrary to the image of such machine politicians as corrupt, Grimké was a principled defender of black citizenship and economic rights.[89]

Grimké had lived most of his adult life in Boston, except for a sojourn in the Dominican Republic in the 1890s. Real estate investments and frequent trips to visit his brother Francis, pastor of the Fifteenth Street Church, had installed Grimké in Washington semi-permanently after his return to the United States. As head of fund-raising for the NAACP, he earned the trust of various sectors of middle-class black Washington, including the many federal employees who joined the local D.C. branch in 1913.[90] Grimké's diplomatic and conservative demeanor made him an easy fit with the national board, and Villard may also have considered the agreeable Grimké a useful counterweight to the more independent Du Bois.[91] He maintained near constant contact with the national board and helped to give Nerney a strong hand in branch activities.

Grimké recognized the fundamental importance of employment and decent pay. Echoing the workers themselves, he connected workers' civil rights with their economic rights to a decent and dignified livelihood. Grimké's longstanding materialism was reflected in his decision to become a Bryan Democrat almost thirty years earlier. Attracted to William Jennings

Archibald Grimké, circa 1919. Grimké was born in slavery in South Carolina in 1849. His white aunts, the famed abolitionist Grimké sisters, ensured that he and his brother Francis attended Lincoln University in Pennsylvania after emancipation. Archibald then graduated from Harvard Law School and went on to a career in law and Democratic politics. A statesman with experience in national politics and international diplomacy, he became an effective local advocate for black civil servants in Washington. (Manuscript Division, Moorland-Spingarn Research Center, Howard University)

Bryan's populist war against "the money power," Grimké saw that in the United States, the disadvantaged were too often black and the wealthy too often white. The battle for racial uplift became an economic one when Reconstruction failed to redistribute the wealth away from a small monopoly of white former masters.[92] For Grimké, the denial of decent pay in the nation's service by white Democrats was just one more example of the southern master class undermining black Americans.

In the Dominican Republic, Grimké also developed strong feelings about the virtue of a racially integrated society. Appointed by Grover Cleveland, Grimké served as the U.S. consul in Santo Domingo from 1894 to 1898. There, Grimké sampled both a society run by people of color and a government reeling under imperialist pressures and internal corruption. While the Dominican Republic was hardly a place free of racism and white domination, for Grimké, living there pointed to the great potential of a society in which black and white people were equal participants in civic life.[93]

If nothing else, Grimké's experience as a diplomat gave him an understanding for how to deal with government officials at the highest level, and he gained a reputation for his discretion. On March 11, 1914, Grimké visited Assistant Secretary Charles Hamlin at the Treasury Department. The purpose was to leave a letter for Secretary McAdoo requesting a cessation of segregation.[94] It is likely that Grimké wanted to size up the new administrator and fellow Bostonian, perhaps aware that Hamlin's views of African Americans were more liberal than those of his predecessor, John Skelton Williams. In the years following that meeting, Hamlin would become Grimké's major contact within the administration, even after Hamlin moved on to the Federal Reserve Board in the fall of 1914. Grimké sent Hamlin what amounted to laundry lists of complaints and grievances, which Hamlin claimed to receive "with great pleasure."[95]

In June 1914, for example, Grimké contacted Hamlin regarding Samuel A. Browne, Charles M. Butler, and William L. D. Wilkinson, postal clerks at Station F of the Washington City Post Office. All three had been suddenly reduced to "senior substitutes" because their positions were "abolished," meaning that their permanent civil service jobs had ceased to exist.[96] Wilkinson had been appointed as a mail distributor in 1887 and had risen to Class 1 clerk, earning $1,200 a year. Butler had been appointed in 1907 and had received promotions in 1908, 1909, 1911, 1912, and 1913, when he finally earned $1,100 a year.[97]

Grimké's letter to Hamlin was typical in its appeal to material needs.

White clerks had been told to seek new orders from the central office, but the three black clerks had heard nothing. "They are men of families, who would be made to suffer severely should their bread winners come to grief at the hands of the Government."[98] Grimké used very similar language in other cases, emphasizing employees' long careers with high ratings, their desires to be treated fairly on the job, and those depending on their government salaries.[99] Emblematic of the reduced status of black government work, Grimké's advocacy was only partially successful. Hamlin contacted First Assistant Postmaster Roper and seems to have been helpful in securing reappointments. But Wilkinson and Butler were both reduced to $800 a year, and Browne, whose pay was probably reduced as well, was stuck working for a superintendent who still was not giving him a "square deal."[100]

Despite the limitations, black workers began to see value in both Grimké and the NAACP. Those who were unsure of the nonpartisan, secular organization began to come around. Mabel Phillips was a typical applicant for a government laborer job who, in 1915, had yet to make any connection to the NAACP. When she passed the civil service exam for a skilled laborer position but was unable to gain employment, despite her high score, Phillips went to her pastor for help. The Reverend A. C. Garner took Phillips down to the BEP, carrying with him a note from Grimké. "I saw Director Ralph," Phillips recounted. "He read the note, rang an electric bell, his secretary appeared and he directed him to take me to the appointment clerk." Eight days later, Phillips began work. "I now realize that I am under great obligation to the NAACP and to you personally Mr. Grimké. I thank you heartily and expect to join the association that is helping so wonderfully to aid those who have no influence to be fairly treated," she wrote a few days later. "I never knew the value of such an organization until now."[101] In this slow and individual way, Grimké spread the influence of the NAACP.[102]

For many, Grimké and the local NAACP stepped into the space once occupied by congressmen and the Republican Party. By the 1910s, much of the black population of Washington was native to the city, descendants of men and women who had literally walked off slave plantations in the 1860s for a better life in the nation's service. But the District had no representative municipal government or elected leaders, and the old racial regime of political patronage had collapsed. As Walter Hawkins, a postal worker from Anacostia, told Joel Spingarn in the summer of 1915, the NAACP was giving these people a renewed, if still limited, voice. "Generally the will of a Senator or Representative has meant much in behalf of individual clerks of my acquaintance who have had grievances," Hawkins wrote, "but living in the

District, I have no Senator or member of Congress to whom I can appeal as a constituent." Instead, he explained, he needed the NAACP to help him gain "a fuller measure of justice."[103]

In March 1914, Grimké was forced to break his practice of working behind the scenes. The House Select Committee on Reform in the Civil Service was considering legislation for the "segregation of clerks and employees in the Civil Service." Made up of two bills proposed by James Aswell of Louisiana and Charles Edwards of Georgia, it would legally force the separation of black and white employees in all government offices.[104] The committee hearings were not well advertised, and the only citizens invited to speak were members of the National Democratic Fair Play Association, who brought with them white women's accounts of having been preyed on by black civil servants. Much of the hearing, particularly the speeches of Aswell and Edwards, amounted to a lengthy discourse on the danger posed by African Americans and the necessity of white rule as a form of civil service reform. Charts testified to the large number of African Americans working in the service. Aswell explained that his bill would "relieve the white man in the public service from the intolerable humiliation of being compelled, in order to earn his daily bread, to work side by side with an objectionable people, the continuation of which practice must result in irreparable injury to both races and ultimately destroy the efficiency of the public service."[105] Grimké heard about the hearing by accident and rushed over to make a statement. He would be the only African American to testify before Congress regarding segregation in the civil service.[106]

Grimké eschewed theoretical questions of constitutionality and focused his remarks around the material concerns of the workers themselves. "What I want is a human feeling toward these people," he declared. He spoke about humiliation and the danger of allowing one class to rule another. His metaphor was not one of freedom and citizenship but of capital and labor: "The industrial workers say capital can not rule them, and so it will be as between the races," Grimké explained, echoing Villard's earlier threat. White rule would necessarily lead to trouble, because black Americans could never be held down securely. Instead, Grimké suggested economic enfranchisement. Why not let the best black Americans rise?, he asked. If they rose, they were likely to side with those in power. "Capital always gets hold of the able workman and makes it of interest to him and shows him he is a part of the vested interests of the country." Black clerks were the best men, Grimké declared. There was no reason to hold them down. But Grimké touched the deepest core of white racism when he glimpsed fear. Representative Martin

Dies of Texas admitted, "I do not want to live to see the negro race a part of the ruling class."[107]

The bill went down to defeat, despite the feelings of Dies and the other southern Democrats on the committee. But Grimké needed help. As in the years before Wilson's election, legislative influence required political friends. Representative Martin Madden of Illinois also deserved credit for the defeat of the segregation bill. An old-time Republican egalitarian, Madden had black constituents, for in Chicago black men could actually vote. Faced with an increasingly black district in the city's South Side, Madden used his position and power in Congress in the old way to help African Americans obtain government jobs. He also fought racist legislation in Congress. Madden was the only committee member to offer Grimké verbal support, and he played a key role in ensuring that federal segregation was never enshrined in legislation.[108]

Madden was unusual. For the most part, national legislators who had electoral reasons for supporting black politics after 1913 were extremely rare. Instead, black government workers, once loyal and active partisans, were forced to seek help outside of mainstream politics. Archibald Grimké's quiet advocacy represented a form of resistance to the new regime, but as with other forms, it was resistance only. Those whom Grimké helped to gain or keep jobs worked in the civil service's supporting staff and did not rise to the level of well-paid, white-collar clerks. They could not pierce the ceiling erected by federal discrimination to keep black men and women in a subordinate status in the nation's service. Woodrow Wilson's government no longer offered a promise of mobility to hardworking black Americans.

Friction

Two years after his election, Wilson was no longer the mystery George Kibbe Turner had wondered about in *McClure's* in February 1913. Most of Wilson's signature legislative achievements were already behind him, from tariff reform to the income tax to the creation of the Federal Reserve to a new antitrust act, and he had taken firm leadership of both the Democratic Party and progressive politics. Those who had rallied to Theodore Roosevelt and the Bull Moose Party in 1912 would soon line up behind Wilson's domestic agenda and his refusal to plunge the United States into the European war in 1914.[109] Oswald Garrison Villard's disappointment notwithstanding, the administration had weathered almost eighteen months of protest against its racial policies with its white liberal support largely intact. Whites-only signs came and went and Archibald Grimké saved careers here and there, but segregation and discrimination continued. The president had no intention of yielding to the demands of civil rights activists.

It is curious, then, that on November 12, 1914, almost a year to the day after their first meeting, Wilson agreed to a second meeting with William Monroe Trotter. In their previous encounter, Wilson had urged Trotter, Ida B. Wells-Barnett, and the rest of their delegation to be "patient and tolerant," but since that time, he had given African Americans little reason to be either. Why Wilson gave Trotter another chance to make his case is unclear. It was likely the result of a confluence of factors: Wilson's managers, especially Joe Tumulty, were aware of Trotter's support during the campaign and may have felt that he deserved the meeting. For his part, Wilson believed sincerely that he had good answers for Trotter's questions. In his mind, he held no particular animus toward African Americans.[110] Any report to the contrary was the result of a misunderstanding. Segregation was a just and fair solution to a problem created by Republicans, who had irresponsibly integrated federal workplaces for political reasons. Wilson probably hoped to put the matter to rest.

Wilson was also caught in a moment of weakness. Having spent the summer watching Bright's disease destroy his wife's kidneys and finally take her life in August, he was emotionally exhausted. "What am I to do?" Wilson had sighed in the moments after her death. Wilson confided to his advisor Edward M. House that he felt unable to handle the presidency, a complaint he reiterated to House later that fall. The outbreak of war in Europe compounded the pressures. The dual strain of war and personal loss combined with declining health brought lasting change to the president. Friends and neutral observers alike noted the intensification of Wilson's already rigid bearing in this period.[111]

For his part, Trotter had also had a difficult year. Allies like Alexander Walters and J. Milton Waldron had resigned from the NIPL by the end of 1913. And despite the transformation of a tiny letter-writing campaign into a national outcry, the movement against federal discrimination had made little progress.[112] In May 1914, the Civil Service Commission began requiring photographs with job applications. While the photographs served only to speed a process already accomplished by interviews and questions about education — a Howard University degree was far more definitive than skin tone could ever be — there was no question that the new rule did not bode well for black applicants. Finally, on top of the task of fighting white supremacy came competition with the better-funded and larger NAACP.[113]

The second meeting with the president, then, was a stroke of good fortune not just for the movement but also for Trotter's relevance in it.

The result was a confrontation that revealed just how difficult it could be to penetrate the fundamental racism of Woodrow Wilson. It would also help to set the terms on which white supremacy would be justified in national government for decades afterward. Wilson was clearly uncomfortable with Trotter. The brilliant and demanding civil rights leader understood Wilson far better than Wilson did him. All too aware of Wilson's refusal to see him as an equal, Trotter nonetheless demanded to be heard. He pushed Wilson hard to live up to the principles of American democracy and the "New Freedom." But Wilson's response, a grumpy and patronizing reiteration of his pledge to run a just and well-managed government, revealed his inability to grasp Trotter's forceful rights claims. The two men faced each other from different planes.

Trotter spoke first. He reminded Wilson that segregation meant "there could be no freedom, no respect from others, and no equality of citizenship," because segregation "constitutes inferiority of status." Wilson had not fulfilled his promise to him and other black Democrats to deal fairly with black Americans. Trotter spoke powerfully and steadily. He elevated what Wilson saw as a question of public administration to one of American citizenship and liberty. Segregation in Washington was distinct from segregation elsewhere. If African Americans could be "segregated and thus humiliated by the national government at the national capital," Trotter said, "the foundation of the whole fabric of their citizenship is unsettled." Hoping to provoke his liberal sympathies, Trotter cut to the marrow of Wilson's progressive politics: "Have you a 'new freedom' for white Americans and a new slavery for your Afro-American fellow citizens?" Joe Tumulty later told Villard that the speech "was one of the most eloquent he had ever heard."[114]

Wilson's answer revealed the toll that the last year had taken on him. His famous patrician demeanor and didactic tone were largely absent. He sounded exasperated and tired, falling back awkwardly upon platitudes. Narrowing Trotter's demands for equality, he imagined Trotter as merely representing one of the many interest groups within American politics that he had long found loathsome. "If the colored people made a mistake in voting for me, they ought to correct it and vote against me," Wilson declared. Immediately, however, he tacked in a different direction: "I don't want politics brought into it at all, because I think it lowers the whole level of the thing." Conveniently, Wilson suddenly favored an absolute barrier between politics and administration. Segregation was simply a managerial matter, an essential but nonpartisan ingredient of democratic government. Wrapping himself in the cloak of a morality higher than politics, Wilson played victim. He talked of the burden he felt in the White House. "God knows that any man that would seek the presidency of the United States is fool for his pains," he moaned. "The burden is all but intolerable, and the things I have to do are just as much as a human spirit can carry."[115]

Trotter's blackness unnerved Wilson. The assertive Trotter calling out the incomplete vision at the heart of the "New Freedom" was a nightmare. Though his mental state probably made his "angry black man" fantasy all the more vivid, Wilson nonetheless would never have had a way of processing Trotter's outrage. Wilson's meeting with Trotter revealed the way in which his "democratic universalism" applied only to white people.[116] To the extent that Wilson dealt with inequality between white and black Americans at all, he explained it away as the result of inherited and backward traits rather than of any disparity in power or privilege. In his cooler moments, Wilson saw such "lesser" peoples as candidates for tutelage, but he could react with anger when his generosity was not accepted.[117]

Gathering himself, Wilson returned to his usual well-wishing talking points on "race relations," a kind of cold speech that disclosed Wilson's assumption that black people were something other than real Americans.[118] Firm in the belief that Anglo-Saxons were the shepherds of the United States (and indeed of all humanity), he spoke as if welcoming a visiting group of foreigners. "The American people, as a whole," he promised Trotter, "sincerely desire and wish to support, in every way they can, the advancement of the Negro race in America." White prejudices, Wilson instructed, take a long time to pass, "and we must treat this thing with a recognition of its difficulties." This was Wilson's practical voice, a kind of dispassionate manner that he used to explain ideas and plans that he deemed useful or convenient. It was simply "unwise" to expect prejudices to vanish overnight, and, therefore, it would be rash not to obey the wishes of white workers. For if things moved too quickly, "friction between the white employees and the Negro employees" would be the inevitable result. "We are all practical men," Wilson declared, invoking his manly and progressive empiricism. "We know that there is a point at which there is apt to be friction, and that is in the intercourse between the two races. . . . We must strip this thing of sentiment and look at the facts." Federal administrators had no intention of being unjust, Wilson explained; "they have intended to remedy what they regarded as creating the possibility of friction, which they did not want ever to exist."[119]

Wilson's repeated use of the word "friction" was meaningful. It was an appeal to the kind of civil service reform he had long advocated, though now merged with a racist disregard for African Americans.[120] In 1887, Wilson had proposed a rational "study of administration" that sought the means to "destroy all wearing friction" in the management of government.[121] On both sides of the Atlantic, mechanical metaphors became standard in progressives' discussions of institutions and bureaucracies, reflecting their hope that scientific management might bring order and harmony to the chaos of industrial capitalism.[122] Friction, explained bureaucracy's famous interrogator, Max Weber, was the enemy of efficient management.[123] "Precision, speed, unambiguity, knowledge of the files, continuity, discretion, unity, strict subordination, reduction of friction and of material and personal costs—these are raised to the optimum point in the strictly bureaucratic administration." Further, in language that echoed Wilson's frustration with the inefficient chumminess of patronage, Weber wrote that "work organized by collegiate bodies (not colleges, but collegial administration), on the other hand, causes friction and delay and requires compromises between colliding interests and views."[124] Progressives clung to notions of dissolving "friction" and promoting bureaucratic efficiency as essential to government reform. Walter Weyl argued that progressive government could even "regulate business as to prevent or lessen waste, internal friction, [and] inter-business friction." To Wilson's policy muse, Louis Brandeis, "efficiency is the hope of democracy."[125]

In the mouths of segregationists, this discourse turned white and black workers into mere "colliding interests" with segregation as the neutral solvent rather than an act of discrimination. "Race friction" as a concept erased the individuality of the people involved, even as those who talked of it varied in their sympathy for African Americans (nearly everyone in the period, black or white, used the term).[126] Government efficiency, as Weber explained, was a profoundly impersonal matter, and the mechanical metaphor necessarily dehumanized human relations, reducing racism to an inevitable function of circumstances. It had a discursive power that insisted upon, indeed naturalized, the belief that black and white people could not be expected to get along as equals. It was this ability to further a racist assumption while also promoting a progressive agenda that gave that specific word so much power for Wilsonians. William McAdoo told Oswald Garrison Villard that segregation in the Treasury Department was intended to rid the department of "friction."[127] Navy secretary Josephus Daniels explained that black sailors were restricted to mess duty "to avoid friction between the races."[128] Further back, Albert Burleson had charged in 1911 that the integrated District of Columbia Board of Education had resulted in "friction and misunderstanding."[129]

Nor was "friction" used exclusively to refer to government. In 1909, *The Dial* noted that two new books, *Race Questions, Provincialisms, and Other American Problems* by Harvard professor Josiah Royce and *Studies in the American Race Problem* by Alfred Stone, had shown that "the last few years have seen an increasing accentuation of race-friction in many parts of the world." Royce sought a way in which "the white man and the negro" might "learn to live with a minimum of friction." Notably, Stone, a Mississippi gentleman planter, had taken time to criticize Roosevelt's support of black politics. In 1914, University of Pittsburgh philosophy professor John Moffatt Mecklin titled his analysis of race in America *Democracy and Race Friction*.[130] "Friction" was every place black and white Americans were.

Facing Trotter, "friction" was thus a useful metaphor for Wilson. Eliminating friction meant rising above "collegial interests" to see administration as merely a matter of moving parts that could be made to move more smoothly. When Trotter tried to make apparent the human toll of racial discrimination, Wilson retreated to bureaucratic speak, with its comforting assurances that anything that increased efficiency was in the interest of all Americans. "Efficiency is the difference between wealth and poverty, fame and obscurity, power and weakness, health and disease, growth and death, hope and despair," wrote one "expert" in a November 1914 issue of *The Independent*. "Efficiency makes kings of us all."[131]

This creed was integral to Wilson's approach to government. In a message to Congress, the president declared that the nation's tariff system had gotten so out of hand that "nothing is normal, nothing is obliged to stand the tests of efficiency and economy."[132] When Josephus Daniels sought to bring greater democracy and meritocracy, as well as racial segregation, to the Navy Department, Wilson praised Daniels's efforts to ensure that "efficiency runs into every well-considered detail of personnel and method."[133] Wilson's message to McAdoo that the nation's port collectors could not dole out deputy appointments as political spoils insisted that "the object of the provision is efficiency and only efficiency."[134] His Agriculture Department, Wilson announced, was "seeking to assist as never before to make farming an efficient business."[135] And the new Federal Reserve System, he said, would "make our prosperity not only stable but free to have an unimpeded momentum."[136] Every Wilsonian cause—from tariff reduction to civil service management to rural credits to monetary reform—carried the virtue of efficiency. As president of the United States and an articulate spokesman for administrative reform, Wilson made a powerful case for ignoring the demands of black Americans in the service of efficient government.

Perhaps most important, Wilson's call for smooth administration depicted Trotter as the radical activist demanding drastic change. It was Trotter, not the Wilsonians, who was trying to imagine a new kind of government management. It was African Americans, not southern Democrats, who were creating "friction" by moving too quickly to alter the terms of American citizenship. Such a formulation performed a powerful erasure: suddenly fifty years of competent and peaceful black government service had never happened. Wilson leaped from the "unwise" empowerment of slaves in the 1860s to the "unwise" equality Trotter was demanding. Whatever Wilson's beliefs about the potential for human evolution and the possibility of uplift, black Americans were no more ready for full citizenship in 1914 than they had been after the Civil War. "Practical men" knew this, even if Trotter did not.

Despite Wilson's refusal to recognize the terms of his appeal, Trotter persisted. Over the last year, the extent of discrimination had become clearer, and Trotter now wanted an answer not only for the humiliation of segregation but for employees whose government careers had been confined or ended entirely. This kind of discrimination belied Wilson's assurances of fairness, said Trotter. But Wilson snapped back to the question of segregation and laid the blame for any discrimination on black Americans themselves. The sensitivity of black Americans was the real problem. They had started the trouble with their objections to segregation: "If you take it as humiliation, which it is not intended as, and sow the seed of that impression all over the country, why the consequences will be very serious," warned Wilson. "But if you should take it in the spirit in which I have presented it to you, it wouldn't have serious consequences."[137] Trotter resented Wilson's paternalism: "We are not here as wards. We are not here as dependents. We are not here looking for charity or help," he informed the president. "We are here as full-fledged American citizens, vouchsafed equality of citizenship by the federal Constitution."[138] If Wilson wanted to talk management, Trotter had moved on to fundamental rights and equality.

Wilson lost his composure. "Your tone, sir, offends me," he scolded. Pushed back on his heels, Trotter apologized. "I am pleading for simple justice," he said. Searching for a way to ease the tension, he claimed "responsibility for the whole matter." Wilson was not to be mollified. He accused Trotter of attempting to blackmail him, returning to Trotter's suggestion that segregation was making it difficult for black voters to support the Democrats. "When you call upon an officer and say that you can't get certain votes if you don't do certain things, that is the kind of course which ought never to be attempted," Wilson speciously declared, knowing better than anyone, of course, that that was precisely how American politics worked.[139] But accusing a black politician of corruption was a useful counter to accusations that a democratically elected president was not serving "all the people." Corruption had justified disfranchisement, and now it demanded a white man's national administration. The meeting was over.

As he stepped out of the Oval Office, Trotter was met by reporters. Contrary to Tumulty's wishes, Trotter took the chance to make his case to the nation. "[Wilson's] statement that segregation was intended to prevent racial friction is not supported by the facts," he declared. "It was not until the present Administration came in that segregation was drastically introduced." For a brief moment, Trotter had gotten the better of Wilson: he had finally overcome a year's worth of denials and dissembling, and the president appeared small and not up to the task of ensuring the rights of Americans. "It does not seem obviously appropriate for the President of the United States to complain of the 'intolerable burden' of his own office to negroes who daily suffer burdens more intolerable, who come to the President with real grievances due to the President's own inaction in a moral crisis," said *The New Republic*.[140] In an editorial entitled "Friction," *The Independent* agreed with Trotter that Wilson's concerns with friction were unwarranted: "The heads of the bureaus could control it if they cared to," rang the Christian progressive journal. "Those that made friction could be dismissed." Indeed, it was Wilsonian praxis that was causing the problem: "There will be 'friction' and there ought to be friction, if any race, black, yellow, or brown, is humiliated and insulted by the Government."[141]

Charles Hamlin thought Wilson had made a mistake. The president, Hamlin recorded in his diary, did not really know the facts and said far more than was necessary. Hamlin believed his innovations had made it unnecessary for Wilson to justify segregation, an interesting refusal to accept Wilson's desire to do so. Trotter, Hamlin told McAdoo, was really just after "political notoriety." Wilson, too, was said to have regretted having been forced to speak on Trotter's terms. Recounting the story to Franklin Roosevelt many years later, Josephus Daniels said Wilson believed he had erred. "'I lost my temper and played the fool,'" Daniels recalled him saying; "'I raised that incident into an issue that will be hard to down.'"[142]

The morning after the meeting, the front page of the *New York Times* told of Wilson's support of segregation.[143] Despite a year's worth of publicity about the segregation controversy, the conservative *Times* declared this to be something of a revelation. Speaking before his congregation of black Washingtonians on Thanksgiving Day, Reverend Francis J. Grimké thanked Trotter for revealing where Wilson stood. "He was so constantly dodging the issue, pretending at times that he did not know that there was segregation, and succeeding in so mystifying the matter that even some very good white people, and good friends of ours, still felt that the thing was done, but not with his approval," Grimké explained. "Now, however, the truth has at last come out."[144]

Trotter received a warrior's praise from a black press that often maligned him as overly militant and irrational. "Somehow I can't help but admire Monroe Trotter's fighting spirit," wrote Roscoe C. Bruce in his weekly column in the *Bee*.[145] Calvin Chase reprinted articles from around the country praising Trotter. Adding his own praise, Chase addressed the issue of Trotter's demeanor before the president. "We have known instances where colored men and women have been persecuted for being 'sassy niggers,' when the head and front of the entire offense, if there were any, consisted of a determination to live down lies, free from the encroachment of scandal and gossip." Of course Wilson was deserving of respect, and Trotter would have no excuse for treating the president unfairly. However, asserted Chase, "this does not mean that the spokesman should have been obsequious, wobbling, apologetic, mealy-mouthed, fawning, and unmanly; and we are satisfied that this cannot be shown." Whatever Trotter's manner, Chase concluded, his cause was just and pure.[146]

Trotter was aware that if Wilson's claim that he had been victimized were to dominate news reports, the meaning of his having fully admitted his support for segregation would be lost. A meeting the following Sunday at the Second Baptist Church in northwest Washington gave Trotter another chance to tell his story. Before a crowd of 2,000 in the church's Gothic Revival sanctuary, Trotter stood for five minutes of "deafening" applause. Taking the pulpit, Trotter spoke for over an hour. He took special pains to deny any attempt to insult Wilson. Noting that two years earlier, Wilson had happily received a delegation of black politicians and pledged his support for their cause, Trotter claimed that this time Wilson had behaved very differently.[147]

In fact, Trotter's concern was warranted, and his triumph was fleeting. The well-meaning and liberal Wilson overwhelmed by an aggressive black man would be the meeting's lasting image. The *Washington Evening Star*

THE NEW FREEDOM FOR THE NEGRO.

"The New Freedom—For the Negro." This political cartoon appeared in the *New York Tribune* in response to Woodrow Wilson and William Monroe Trotter's dramatic encounter in November 1914. The meeting helped to clarify Wilson's support for segregation and to bring national attention to racial discrimination in his administration. From *New York Tribune*, November 14, 1914.

chose to emphasize the offense, reporting secondhand that "the President is known to have said in effect that the spokesman's manner was offensive beyond his previous experience in the White House."[148] Julius Rosenwald, the millionaire owner of Sears, Roebuck & Co. and a financial backer of Booker T. Washington, spoke for many white liberals when he expressed his unhappiness with Trotter. Rosenwald had previously written to Wilson encouraging him to halt segregation, but now he wanted Wilson to know that he considered Trotter a "notoriety seeker, whose methods are dismaying to the conservative members of his race."[149] Other white respondents were less generous. In a letter to the *Los Angeles Times* that she forwarded on to Wilson, Mary S. Smith supported the president "for refusing to allow a committee of insolent negroes to dictate to him how he should run the office of a great country."[150] Claude Stotts, secretary of the chamber of commerce in Hot Springs, Arkansas, took the opportunity to "commend" John Skelton Williams, whom Trotter had named in his statement, for implementing segregation in the Treasury. Stotts, like Wilson, read black men demanding equality as a physical threat. Trotter and his delegation were not politicians or citizens; they were a "gang of negroes" whose "insulting and uncalled for manner" revealed "that the more you educate a negro the smarter he thinks he is, and the meaner he gets."[151] The encounter with Trotter had given racists something about which they could both cheer and grouse.

Trotter had African American detractors as well, though civil rights activists A. Philip Randolph and J. Franklin Patterson insisted that those repudiating Trotter were in the minority. In some, the meeting stirred fears of a white backlash against African Americans. Referring to the meeting as an "odium heaped upon the race," one writer told Wilson he hoped that the president's "good will and wishes for my race" were not "marred by the attitude of Mr. Trotter."[152] Salem Whitney of Philadelphia was "forced to admit" to Wilson that "by a lamentable loss of self-control, [Trotter] defeated the object of the committee and injured the Negro's cause at the capital and abroad."[153] Howard University professor Kelly Miller supported Trotter's position but noted that "in the intensity of his ardor he has been so violently denunciatory and so bitterly intolerant as to alienate the sympathy and cooperation of the radical spirits of his own race."[154] White people who felt victimized by black people, African Americans had learned long ago, were to be feared.

Some saw a chance to bolster their own positions. District of Columbia municipal court judge Robert Terrell—the only presidentially appointed black judge in the United States between 1901 and 1932—forwarded to Tumulty a newspaper article expressing disappointment in Trotter. Charles W. Anderson, the collector of customs at the Port of New York who had gained his appointment under Taft and managed to hold on for a year under Wilson, went out of his way to cut short Trotter's publicity tour after the meeting.[155] Carefully spreading word that Trotter was seeking to "commercialize" his meeting with Wilson, Anderson managed to undermine support for an already scheduled and advertised meeting in New York City. Anderson alerted Tumulty to his efforts and passed along both an advertisement for Trotter's speech in the *New York Amsterdam News* and an announcement of its cancellation.[156] Writing to his sponsor, Booker T. Washington, Anderson explained his handiwork: "It won't hurt to have 'our friend' [Wilson] know that we are able to serve this connection."[157] Another of Washington's lieutenants, Robert Russa Moton, also wrote to Wilson to express his disapproval of Trotter's "conduct." For his part, Washington confessed to a friend that he approved of Trotter's mission but not of Trotter himself and did not write directly to Wilson because he wished to be left out of the matter entirely.[158]

Trotter's meeting with Wilson in November 1914 was the high point for the segregation protests and for Trotter's career as an agitator for civil rights. He would continue to confront federal segregation and other forms of racism into the 1930s, still occasionally staking out territory well ahead of his fellow activists. Nevertheless, Trotter's life from 1915 on revolved mostly around his newspaper in Boston, which he ran with his wife, Deenie, until her death from influenza in 1918. Trotter lost the national place he had earned, first through his battles with Booker T. Washington and then through the segregation protests. The rising leader of black America, Du Bois, was no longer a friend, and the more powerful, and more compromising, NAACP occupied the stage in the civil rights theater. Trotter slowly faded into the background. Some still read the *Guardian*, which continued to demand a better America. But its editor was left to walk the streets of Boston alone, feeling lost in a city in which he knew many. Marginalized but still restless, Trotter could not seem to ease into a comfortable old age. On April 7, 1934, his sixty-second birthday, Trotter took his own life by jumping to the street from the roof of his three-story building.[159]

IN THOSE FIRST YEARS OF THE WILSON ADMINISTRATION, white supremacists achieved two major victories: they vanquished the Republican patronage machine that had been so crucial for black mobility, and they established federal discrimination as a progressive reform for the whole nation. Wilson successfully connected white supremacy to the progressive and moral imperative of efficiency, and efficient administration continued to serve as a justification for discrimination by bureaucracies and by the state in general. The packaging of tales of "racial friction" in consistent rhetoric helped to embed a belief in American culture and politics that black and white Americans sharing space was necessarily a combustible circumstance — one to be avoided at almost any cost.[160]

There were plenty of indications of Wilson's rhetorical success over the next few years. For example, NAACP board member Joel Spingarn advocated segregated army camps for the training of black officers during World War I because doing so would offer more opportunities for promotion of black soldiers — the same justification McAdoo had offered for separate divisions within government departments. And black soldiers at the segregated officer training camp in Des Moines, Iowa, were told by their white officer that it was up to them to keep racial peace: "It should be well known to all colored officers and men that no useful purpose is served by such acts as will cause the 'color question' to be raised," read the infamous Bulletin No. 35. "Attend quietly and faithfully to your duties, and don't go where your presence is not desired."[161] The *Milwaukee Free Press* credited Wilson's "endorsement of the segregation principle" for a slew of residential segregation laws in American cities, from Baltimore to St. Louis.[162]

Moreover, after accomplishing only a few short-term goals, like the removal of "whites-only" signs in the Treasury Department, the NAACP staged fewer protests against segregation. For the next decade, Archibald Grimké would continue his quiet work on behalf of individual government employees. But he worked largely alone. By early 1915, in fact, the NAACP's national campaign against federal segregation had essentially ground to a halt.[163] In January 1916, the national board of the NAACP declared the struggle for federal workers over. The board wired Wilson and McAdoo that the NAACP's annual meeting was pleased by "the report that segregation of colored employees in federal departments at Washington has been checked" and "urged" Wilson to "put an entire stop to this injustice."[164] But it was clear that the president was not to be baited into a genuine debate over segregation. Wilson's ability to paint his second meeting with Trotter as an attack weakened the movement, and most Americans had accepted Wilson's version of history: what Trotter wanted was impossible. At the same time, the NAACP had launched an antilynching campaign, which diverted the national office's time, energy, and finances. That campaign focused on legislative reform, which could be done more quietly in Washington, and lynching was a wrong most Americans recognized as such. Finally, war in Europe began to occupy everybody's mind.[165]

In addition to a confluence of circumstances, the change in the NAACP's tactics also indicated the inability of the association's white members to fight facets of American racism they, in fact, accepted. Lynching and disfranchisement were gross injustices, but they did not entail daily physical proximity with black people. Prejudice ran more deeply through the nation than most NAACP officials wanted to admit. Apologizing to Archibald Grimké for being unable to speak at a protest rally, Boston attorney and NAACP member Albert Pillsbury confessed that even white egalitarians were not fully behind the antisegregation cause. "Would Villard himself invite negroes, though gentlemen and scholars, to his house or his clubs, or invoke general association with them exactly as though they were white men? No, he would not. He could not." The power of social convention was overwhelming, Pillsbury declared. "If we attempted any such thing we should be in trouble with our friends, our wives and even our *cooks* and it would not be long before we too should be socially ostracized." And the infection of social prejudice afflicted even the most active liberals. "[Moorfield] Storey, at the head for the NAACP[,] is making antisegregation speeches and presiding at antisegregation meetings while condoning, by his own public example, one of the worst cases of segregation both morally and practically, by remaining a member of the [whites-only] American Bar Association."[166] It was one thing to fight for citizenship rights, and another to fight for true equality. For the women and men who were steadily watching their jobs slip away, the national board of the NAACP offered little remedy.

By the end of Wilson's first term, racism was institutionalized enough within federal offices that decreased protests actually reflected an expectation, including among black workers, that the offices would be segregated. For African Americans, the 1916 election involved a far more conventional campaign than in 1912. Wilson's reelection was closely contested by Charles Evans Hughes, a Supreme Court justice and former governor of New York, but black Democrats were demoralized by four years of Wilsonian racism, and black Republicans had been reduced again to a predictably loyal but scaled-down part of the Republican coalition.[167]

News coverage of segregation slowed after 1915, even as reports of discrimination continued to arrive at NAACP offices. In January 1917, a building supervisor distributed a poll to the secretaries of the State, War, and Navy Departments—all occupying one building at 17th Street and Pennsylvania Avenue NW—asking whether they believed it reasonable "to ask the chief clerk of each office in the building to request colored employees as a matter of courtesy not to use the toilet rooms previously set aside for use by white people, and the white people also as a matter of courtesy, not to use the toilets set apart for the colored people." Apparently, in August 1916 an order was issued to establish "white" and "colored" toilets in the building, but the order had been rescinded. Repeated requests, the letter said, had inspired polling of the secretaries.[168]

Toward the end of 1915, Calvin Chase tried to sum up what the progressive fervor of Wilson's first term had brought African Americans: "Out of the Democratic victories in 1912 thousands of colored Americans have been discriminated against, and told that the black must respect the white; that cultured and educated colored Americans must not sit at the same desk with the white man; that our colored young ladies of the Bureau of Engraving and Printing use separate everything." Though "God saw the injustice" and removed John Skelton Williams from personnel management, there was much more work to be done. "God will come again, and he will not leave the next time until he removes every hindrance [to] Negro progress and civilization."[169] African Americans would have to struggle a long time, not only for the removal of segregation in government offices but for the next revolution in the state's racial regime.

Part III

REPUBLICANS IN THE NEW REGIME,
1918–1929

To live in a country where there is no hope of rising in the public service through education, through character, and conduct is to be "a man without a country."
—William H. Lewis to Calvin Coolidge, August 8, 1924

Chapter Seven

Creating Normalcy

Washington after Wilson

On May 30, 1922, the Lincoln Memorial in Washington, D.C., was officially dedicated. Gleaming white, the enormous neoclassical marble temple housed a larger-than-life statue of Abraham Lincoln, seated, with huge hands to symbolize the generosity he insisted upon and the bigness of his message. Stretching up to the ceiling along the inner walls were the words of Lincoln's Gettysburg Address, his pithy paean to American democracy, union, and sacrifice. It was supposed to be a moment of national pride and sectional reconciliation: "Emancipation was a means to the great end—maintained union and nationality," said President Warren G. Harding. To illustrate the unifying meaning, the temple's thirty-six columns represented all of the states of Lincoln's United States, and above them, forty-eight ornaments represented the Union's members in 1922.[1]

Yet Republicans also sought to own the day: an event to honor a Republican president was chaired by another Republican president, William Howard Taft, and the keynote address was delivered by the Republican Harding. Former president Wilson had wired earlier in the day that he

Tuskegee principal Robert Russa Moton speaking at the dedication of the Lincoln Memorial, May 30, 1922. It is no accident that Moton appears to stand so entirely alone against a white backdrop in this photograph. Despite the return of Republican rule in Washington and the occasion of honoring the "Great Emancipator," distinguished black guests at the event were segregated out of sight behind white attendees. The betrayal signaled that the national Republican Party no longer held much interest in even symbolic pronouncements of egalitarianism in the nation's capital. (Library of Congress)

would be unable to attend.[2] It should have been a triumphant moment for African Americans too. Robert Russa Moton, who succeeded Booker T. Washington as principal of the Tuskegee Institute and as black doyen of the GOP, was invited to eulogize the martyr to black freedom and citizenship. Indeed, African Americans were just as delighted as Taft and Harding that the White House and Congress were again under Republican control. The last eight years of Democratic rule had been far worse for them.

But black dignitaries invited to attend the dedication—important and well-known Republicans like Whitefield McKinlay, Emmett J. Scott, Perry Howard, and Mrs. Emanuel Hewlett—discovered a nasty surprise when they arrived: the opening of a monument to the Great Emancipator was a segregated event. Shelby Davidson reported that the African American guests were seated on a platform behind the white guests and roped off. Guarding them were "marines who were distasteful, discourteous, and abusive even to swearing in the presence of our colored women."[3] Outraged, many simply left. The *Washington Post* reported the next day that the event had gone off with "no mishaps," but for African Americans, the takeaway was entirely different.[4] The South was still " 'in the saddle,' " said the *Chicago Defender*. For the *Washington Tribune*, the dedication offered a "full realization" of Harding's invocation to the NAACP that "colored men should fall in behind the leadership."[5]

The 1920s were the years in which black civil servants were forced to construct different, less hopeful careers in the new racial regime. For some, it was a realization that citizenship for African Americans did not come with the right to play an important role in the civil administration, a sort of delayed end to the dreams of the Reconstruction era. For most, it meant that whatever luster and mobility that had once come with being a part of a democratic state apparatus was lost, leaving behind a fixed racial and working-class identity with little opportunity for rising. This is not to say that black Washingtonians lost their ambition or their brains, their diversity or their style. What they lost was the hope that they could be different from black Americans elsewhere and the expectation that *their* United States was still interested in seeing them succeed. Changes in how the American state interacted with its own black workers played a dramatic role in the changing identity of black Washingtonians and, indeed, of black citizens throughout the United States.

Fighting Black Citizens

When the United States entered World War I in late 1917, African Americans around the country and in Washington hoped that supporting and fighting for the country in war would prove their loyalty and usefulness to the nation. They might come out with a stronger claim on the rights and privileges of American citizenship.[6] Though hotly contested in black homes and communities, Wilson's progressive framing of the war led most black Americans, in the words of W. E. B. Du Bois, to "close ranks" and stand "shoulder to shoulder with [their] white fellow citizens and the allied nations that are fighting for democracy."[7] Nearly 300,000 black men responded to draft calls in the summer and fall of 1917. A higher proportion of them were actually inducted, thanks to racist selective service practices, fewer friends in high places, and less refined evasion strategies. Yet the vast majority of black soldiers were not given the chance to fire guns at the enemy. "No colored man, however able or ambitious, may look to being anything other than a servant in the Navy," Swan Kendrick protested to Secretary of the Navy Josephus Daniels on behalf of the NAACP.[8] As in his government, black men were laborers in Woodrow Wilson's military, there to support and serve white Americans in their service to the nation. When Wilson saw to it that the famed black military hero Charles Young was denied a commission, the hope that black Americans would be able to prove their valor in war quickly began to fade.[9]

In Washington, African Americans could at least look with pride at the black National Guardsmen assigned to keep the capital safe, and many were heartened by the elevation of Booker T. Washington's former assistant Emmett J. Scott to a prominent position in the War Department as a representative of black America—and organizer of its loyalty.[10] Several black civil servants were promoted to work in Scott's division, and even Ralph Tyler returned to government employment as a war correspondent under Scott and the Committee for Public Information. Tyler sent home reports of the valiant fighting by African American combat soldiers and revealed the crucial work of black laborers.[11] Black civil servants were also experiencing some relief from Wilsonian discrimination, as positions opened up to meet the wartime government's administrative needs and salaries rose to counter wartime inflation.[12] "Everybody is trying for a Government job now," noted the *Washington Bee*. "Wives are leaving home and husbands have already left home for the purpose of assisting Uncle Sam for pay."[13] Indeed, among the 82 black federal employees examined for this study who held positions in 1917, 32 received raises during the war.

In the end, however, most of the wartime gains were in proportion to the general expansion of government labor, and African Americans did not pick up any ground on white employees. Most new hires were into subclerical positions, the number of white employees grew at the same rate, and pay raises were negated by spiraling inflation.[14] The establishment of a Division of Negro Economics in 1918 appeared to represent the federal government taking an interest in African Americans, but much like Emmett Scott's position, the purpose was really to ensure and monitor black loyalty to the war effort.[15] Indeed, Scott's all-black division was the apotheosis of federal segregation, and his position within the War Department was largely symbolic. Once the war was over and Scott's division was closed, several black clerks who had moved to his office were not permitted to return to their previous positions in other federal departments.[16]

Four days of racial violence in the District of Columbia in July 1919 dramatized the disappointments of the Wilson years.[17] Weeks of rumors about threatening Negroes spilling out of the city's crowded alleyways — some, supposedly, to rape white women — made all black Washingtonians, regardless of class and status, targets for arrest or harassment by the city's police.[18] That the city contained roughly 100,000 more people than it did before the war strained further the capital's resources for social control. On hot summer nights, thousands roamed the streets with little more to do than get drunk. When the riot began on July 18, after yet another report in the papers of an attack on a white woman by two black youths, white soldiers and sailors as well as civilians combed the District looking for black people to beat up or lynch. A military force of 2,000 men and a terrible rainstorm helped to end the rioting finally on Tuesday, July 22. Seven people were dead; more than 100 went home injured.[19]

The 1919 riot made Washington common in some ways. It had become a typical American city with seething racial tensions. A city once free of racial violence joined twenty-five other cities, from Omaha to Chicago to Philadelphia, that experienced race riots that summer. James Weldon Johnson called it the "Red Summer" for both the blood spilled and the charges that anarchists were behind the trouble.[20] But the violence in Washington was distinguished from other urban race riots by the force with which black people fought back, by the extensive involvement of federal officials to end the violence, by the belief that many of the white rioters were only temporary residents, and by the power and organization of the city's black leadership in preventing further bloodshed.[21] Respectable Washington was shocked by the "murderous race antagonism," said the *Washington Evening Star.* "Every time the white mob runs amuck against the negroes, the latter grow more bitter in their defensive and retaliatory measures." What the paper called a "vicious circle" represented a drag on "progress toward solution of a problem that continues to plague the American people and to shame them in the eyes of the world."[22]

Black Washingtonians connected discrimination in federal offices, the violence, and the lost hope for a "colored man's paradise." They were keenly aware of the national importance of racial discrimination in their city.[23] Washington, D.C., was the nation's city, and federal discrimination was national discrimination. It was the realization that the nation's city could be just like any other in America that called into question the aspirations of

black Washingtonians. The only hope left was that Republicans might return to power and protect Washington against the national wave of white
supremacy.

Grand Old Party, Redux

In July 1920, 1,200 black Republicans gathered at Riverview Park overlook-
ing the Potomac to salute the party's nomination of Senator Warren G.
Harding of Ohio for president of the United States. The days when Washington's Republicans crossed the color line were gone, but there was something fitting about black Washingtonians gathering separately to herald the
departure of Woodrow Wilson. They found even more to celebrate in the
nominee's acceptance speech: "I believe the Negro citizens of America
should be guaranteed the enjoyment of all their rights, that they have earned
the full measure of citizenship bestowed, that their sacrifices in blood on
the battlefields of the Republic have entitled them to all of freedom and
opportunity, all of sympathy and aid that the American spirit of fairness
and justice demands."[24] Rumors circulated by Democrats that Harding had
"Negro blood" only endeared him to African Americans.[25] A few months
later, Harding rode his "return to normalcy" campaign to a landslide victory over another Ohioan, Democratic governor James M. Cox. It was a
bad economy, labor unrest, and Woodrow Wilson's stubbornness over the
League of Nations — not their white supremacy — that had snuffed out the
Democrats' political capital.

That they had been mostly marginalized from the campaign did not
keep African Americans from witnessing Harding's arrival at the White
House in March 1921 with a cautious hopefulness.[26] In April, NAACP official James Weldon Johnson delivered to Harding a list of the organization's
demands for racial reconciliation in post-Wilson America, which he titled
a "memorandum."[27] The semantics mattered: Johnson, who had already
met with Harding more times than he had ever met with Wilson, was passing along neither an "open letter" nor a plea but a communication between
colleagues. In fact, it could even have been seen as a directive from a constituency that still placed itself at the party's foundation.[28] Though Johnson worried about Harding's capacity to sympathize with black Americans,
Harding did tell Congress a few days later that the legislative body should
take the necessary steps to "wipe the stain of barbaric lynching from the
banners of a free and orderly, representative democracy," and he proposed

renewing the effort to organize a national race commission that Wilson had scuttled.[29]

Government copyist Irene Monroe shared the expectation of black civil servants that the return of Republicans would mean diminished sympathy for racism. Eight years earlier, Monroe had been a star in the theatrical hysteria staged by the National Democratic Fair Play Association in its campaign to whiten federal offices. Monroe had told newspaper reporters that she was a victim of black men who preyed on white women in the office of the recorder of deeds for the District of Columbia. Wilson had solved the problem by appointing a white man to the recorder position. When Harding appointed an African American recorder, Arthur Froe, Monroe feared for her job and had friends in Congress maneuver to safeguard her against retribution. "I certainly hope nothing will arise which might disturb her position in your office," Representative Julius Kahn, a California Republican, warned Froe. Monroe left nothing to chance, ingratiating herself with Froe, despite her earlier professed terror of black men.[30]

Monroe need not have worried. The winds of sympathy had not changed direction with the return of Republican rule, and if anything, white Republicans were looking for ways to distance themselves from racial liberalism. Indeed, with the advent of woman suffrage, some in the party grew concerned that white women would eschew the GOP because of its association with black politicians.[31] Despite Harding's egalitarian acceptance speech, the 1920 Republican National Convention had seen, for the first time, the seating of lily-white delegations, and Tuskegee principal Robert Russa Moton had found the candidate to be woefully uninformed about black politics.[32] Government lawyer Lafayette Hershaw saw more clearly than most that a rollback of Wilsonian racism was unlikely. "It was evident to me at the Chicago Convention of 1920 that we were not to expect relief from segregation through the coming to power of the Republican Party," he later told James Weldon Johnson.[33]

Harding soon made it clear that the resurgent Republicans would not restore the party's legacy of strong egalitarianism. In a speech on race in Birmingham, Alabama, in October 1921, the president did promise black southerners full "economic and political rights as . . . American citizen[s]." He even suggested that white southerners needed the contributions of African Americans, that black southerners ought to be more than "mere political adjunct[s]," and that "the race problem" was no longer simply a sectional concern. But whatever inclusiveness these words implied was undermined by Harding's insistence that white southerners had a "superior under-standing" of the "Negro problem," as he railed against the threat of "social equality" and "racial amalgamation." Taking a stand against the most suc-cessful tool black southerners had against discrimination, migration, Hard-ing declared that African Americans ought to stay in the South. Black and white Americans should embrace "natural segregations" and "take the time to read and ponder" the work of eugenicist Lothrop Stoddard, the president said.[34]

Harding's speech was a careful attempt to balance egalitarianism and progressive white supremacy, but at its heart lay the president's overriding interest in sectional reconciliation and bolstering his rising reputation among white southerners.[35] Though the *Washington Bee* was glad Hard-ing had broached the subject, the *Washington Tribune*, soon to overtake the *Bee* as the capital's leading black weekly, declared that the speech "reads the colored man out of the Republican party and flaunts the red flag of 'social equality.'"[36] The *New York Times* agreed with the *Tribune* about the speech's main thrust, noting that the white members of the Birmingham audience had clambered to shake the president's hand: "There are many who do not agree with him as to political equality, but what he said about the impossibility of 'social equality' more than offset anything he said on the other lines."[37] Harding later regretted even bothering to address the issue. "I doubt now myself if it were worth while to have made the effort," he confessed to a friend a few months later. Harding had hoped the speech would appease "the negro politicians" by delivering on promises made dur-ing the campaign. But, the president groused, "the negroes are very hard to please."[38]

It was true that words were not enough for black Americans, especially in the wake of World War I and the Red Summer. They demanded that Con-gress act on Harding's call for action on lynching. With a strong Republi-can majority in the Senate during the 1921–23 session and a growing black voting constituency in the North, there was renewed hope for passing Rep-resentative Leonidas Dyer's antilynching bill. As the bill passed the House and arrived in the Senate, Julia West Hamilton, daughter of a black govern-ment worker and a rising leader among the city's "New Negro" women, led a silent parade through the streets of Washington to match similar anti-lynching events elsewhere in the country. But it was to no avail. Republi-can senators delayed and then crumbled, unwilling to overcome their own doubts about the bill's constitutionality and Democratic senators' maneu-verings to quash the bill. In fact, noted the *Tribune* in September 1922, the

Republican-controlled Congress failed to pass a single one of the nineteen bills aimed at supporting black Americans.[39]

Further, Republicans failed to take strong action to improve conditions in Haiti. In 1915, Wilson had invaded the small Caribbean nation after a series of revolutions there threatened American strategic and commercial interests on the island. The occupation was marked by the marines' vicious abuse of Haitians, whom Wilson and his military officials viewed as racially inferior. The NAACP had helped Republicans turn the occupation into an issue during the 1920 campaign, and in 1921 and 1922, congressional investigations revealed terrible abuses. But neither Harding nor Congress questioned the occupation itself, which dragged on for another decade.[40]

In fact, the return of Republican rule in 1921 revealed the way in which the new racial regime crossed party lines. Though Harding and Coolidge did appoint a total of fourteen black men to federal offices, they did not turn back the clock to the days of the Republican patronage machine. Six appointments were again for long-serving consuls in mostly black nations. Robert Terrell was reappointed and then, upon his death in 1928, succeeded by another black lawyer, James Cobb. Harding nominated black stalwart Henry Lincoln Johnson for recorder of deeds in the District of Columbia. When Johnson proved too vulnerable to accusations of corruption, Harding offered the unimpeachable Froe. Operatives like Perry Howard of Mississippi, Walter Cohen of Louisiana, and Charles W. Anderson of New York were given appointments, and here and there a job paying more than $3,000 went to a black man. Two black men were appointed to lead the Division of Conciliation, the successor to the Division of Negro Economics, between 1921 and 1929, but this was a position specifically created for African Americans with almost no bearing on the functioning of the government in Washington.[41] As the *Tribune* explained, these were largely "special clerkships" that did not require the party to publicly endorse an administrative role for black Americans by putting candidates through Senate confirmation. Register of the Treasury and auditor for the Navy Department, positions both held by black Republicans before Wilson, went to white men.[42]

As in the case of his Birmingham speech, Harding responded to black frustration over his appointments with indignation. He dismissed "the restlessness on the part of Negro citizens about matters of federal patronage," telling journalist Nahum Brascher that "it [was] not possible to meet all the demands for patronage from the various elements, which make up our citizenship." Further, he reinforced Taft's southern policy. "I do not intend to add to the irritation [in the South] by the appointment of Negroes to federal offices there," he told Brascher. "I believe with all my heart that there is no possible chance of a Republican Party in the southern states except through white leadership."[43]

Harding's sudden death in the summer of 1923 brought Calvin Coolidge to the White House but not much improvement for African Americans. Though Coolidge was a Bostonian with a "record of fairness and justice," he offered little more than his stricken predecessor.[44] Over NAACP protests, he elevated a paragon of lily-white Republicanism, Virginia congressman C. Bascom Slemp, to his personal secretary. Slemp was master of a white Republican machine in Virginia that managed to keep him in Congress in the Democratic stronghold for fifteen years and that distributed the spoils of national party victory into the 1930s. Slemp was a classic party spoilsman, and while he did occasionally promote black Virginians for federal positions, he was deeply invested in building a white Republican Party in the South.[45]

During the 1924 campaign, former assistant attorney general William H. Lewis warned Coolidge that the Republican brand was in serious trouble among African Americans. "Can colored voters be particularly enthusiastic for the success of the Republican Party when its success means nothing to them?" Lewis asked the president. "You expect the colored people to be good citizens, to be a decent, God-fearing, law-abiding people; they need the same incentives as other people." Lewis noted that the migrations of hundreds of thousands of black southerners to northern states like Illinois, Michigan, Ohio, and New York meant that more African Americans had the vote every day. Demands for representation within the administration were not just idle talk.[46] After the social programs for the Republican National Convention in Cleveland were segregated, loyal Republican and former civil servant William Houston wondered to his son Charles Hamilton Houston if the two well-known men in Washington should split their votes and give the family two shots at political relevance.[47]

Coolidge won the election handily. Corruption scandals involving Harding's administration—most famously the Teapot Dome case in which Secretary of the Interior Albert Fall personally benefited from the sale of strategic oil reserves—were effectively put aside by Harding's death and Coolidge's ability to pin everything on Fall.[48] Rising living standards, a bustling economy, and Coolidge's careful and distinctly modern public relations management convinced a majority of Americans that all was well in the United States.[49] A team of capable and conservative administrators, including Herbert Hoover (Commerce), Andrew Mellon (Treasury), and

Charles Evans Hughes (State) deftly kept up the tone Harding had set in 1921: America had returned to "normalcy."

Normalcy was a fiction that a rapacious business community, an inert government, and a buoyant, inward-facing mass culture were somehow "normal." Few white Americans, including Coolidge, paid much attention to the spectacular terrorism of a resurgent Ku Klux Klan or the fact that most black Americans and many white Americans were not benefiting from the strong economy.[50] Coolidge was more sympathetic to individual African Americans than Wilson had been — he counted William Lewis, a fellow Amherst alumnus, among his friends — but as president, he failed to imagine any role for the federal government in the improvement of black life.[51]

"The national outlook for the Negro in politics at this time is dark," concluded the *Tribune* shortly after Coolidge's inauguration in 1925. "Scenes in Washington now are different from those of four years ago when colored Republicans believed that the late President Harding would surpass all former Republican presidents in his recognition of them by appointments to offices requiring the advice and consent of the Senate." The Republicans' disconnect was felt in the streets and offices of the capital. "It was believed that he would abolish segregation in the Government departments, dismiss from the service Democratic officeholders who were responsible for conditions under the Wilson administration, and enforce the Fourteenth and Fifteenth amendments to the Federal Constitution as well as the Eighteenth." For the hopeful, the paper declared, "the last four years, however, proved disappointing," and though Coolidge "was an enigma," he did not seem to have plans to do any better.[52]

Ultimately, Coolidge, like Harding, accepted the Wilsonian standard that efficiency in government required segregation and a suppression of black aspiration beneath the demands of white supremacists.[53] Black Republicans could no longer be a voice for black America. Accusations of corruption, frequent even before Wilson, stuck to black southern politicians better as real constituencies and definable achievements shrank. And with the party, if not Coolidge himself, still dogged by the Harding scandals, white Republicans were eager to distance themselves from "rotten" politicians.

The case of Republican National committeeman Perry Howard offered the Coolidge administration an opportunity to prove its purity. Howard was the head of the Republican Party of Mississippi. As a black leader of a state political party without electoral portfolio, Howard was really a national politician. His job was to throw the Mississippi state delegation behind the "right" candidate at the national convention and then dole out the patronage spoils he acquired in doing so. Much like urban "race men" in northern cities like Chicago and New York, Howard's political life revolved around small favors and individual racial representation. Reviled by black activists and politicians for his accommodationism, Howard nonetheless remained an important figure in black politics.

Under the banner of nonpartisan, anti-spoils activism, Coolidge's Justice Department went after Howard. The aggressive good government hawk, Assistant Attorney General Mabel Walker Willebrandt, developed an airtight case that Howard was in the business of selling federal appointments, generally postmasterships, to white Mississippians. Shut out of the patronage business for most of the period between the Civil War and the Great Depression, southern Democrats were usually forced to seek the help of black Republicans for federal appointments.[54] Willebrandt went after Howard with all of the doggedness of a brilliant prosecutor.

Willebrandt and the Coolidge administration did not count on the ways in which Howard was useful to white southerners. When Howard's case went to trial in late 1928, the image of a white woman accusing a black man of anything should have led to one result.[55] But to Willebrandt's complete shock, Howard walked, stopping only to thank the good people of Mississippi before hopping a train back to Washington. And then he did it again in 1929, after President Hoover encouraged Willebrandt to retry Howard in his own effort to aid the lily-white Republicans in Mississippi. There was only one thing southern Democrats feared more than black Republicans, and that was white Republicans who might actually crack the solid South. As the Mississippi press explained after the acquittal, those white Democrats in the jury box chose the national devil they knew over the devil who might actually pose a threat at the state level. Howard remained the head of the Mississippi Republican National Committee until 1960, despite not residing in the state after 1921. But he never again wielded much national patronage power. After Hoover fired him from his position in the Justice Department, he settled into a private law practice in Washington.[56]

The prosecution of Perry Howard revealed that the South and its black Republicans had become politically meaningless to the national Republican Party. Howard may well have been corrupt, but he had been an important player in Republican politics at one time. However, things had changed. In 1912, in response to William Taft's lock on southern delegations through patronage machines, Theodore Roosevelt had put the energy into building an insurgent, lily-white Republican Party in the South. That he ultimately polled better than Taft undermined the power of the conventional Republican machine. Black Republican committeemen like Howard, Walter Cohen, and Henry Lincoln Johnson lost the ability to hold their state-level party influence over the heads of white Republicans. The 1916 election saw black-oriented civil rights issues drop out of party platforms and the speeches of party standard bearers. The fading of egalitarianism that had begun in the 1870s finally led to a total disappearance of black issues from national politics. Black delegations to the 1920 and 1924 conventions were no longer given priority over lily-white delegations or regarded with much seriousness. Finally, Perry Howard's prosecution at the hands of a Republican U.S. attorney confirmed for many the essential corruption of black politics, providing justification for jettisoning it once and for all.[57]

The demolition of the black Republican machine made any reversal of Wilsonian racism impossible. Black Republicans continued to operate in northern cities that benefited from the migration of 1.5 million black southerners during and after World War I.[58] They even gained some political representation: in 1928, the South Side of Chicago sent conservative businessman Oscar DePriest to Congress as the first black representative since George White of North Carolina left office in 1901. But intensely local machines operating from contained, majority-minority districts had little to offer the mass of black voters who supported them. These were patronage machines similar to the one that had once operated for federal employees, but the jobs secured were not of the same order as clerical positions in the national government. Virtually all of the beneficiaries of spoils in Chicago were janitors and letter carriers with little opportunity for promotion.[59] These were respectable jobs, to be sure, but they did not offer the kind of status and economic mobility once promised by federal civil service in Washington. Without a strong voice in national politics, black northerners ghettoized into districts in southern Chicago and northern Manhattan struggled to turn the franchise into material advancement.[60]

Black Government Work after Wilson

Inside federal offices, the shrinking of black Republicanism was manifest in the experiences of black civil servants. In December 1919, Census Bureau clerk Charles E. Hall was placed in charge of all of the black employees in the Agricultural Statistics Division. The chief statistician for the division deemed Hall "an unusually capable colored man" with superior education and "excellent judgment." Indeed, division head William L. Austin "congratulated" himself for placing Hall in a position of responsibility.[61] But despite his promotions and exceptional reputation, Hall was painfully aware of his segregated and circumscribed status as well as of the general decline of black federal employment in Washington.

In March 1921, Hall asked the new Republican secretary of Commerce, Herbert Hoover, to end Wilsonian segregation. A year earlier, chief clerk T. J. Fitzgerald had ordered Hall to "instruct the colored lady clerks" to use a separate toilet. The order "seriously disturbed the morale of the clerks, most of whom are cultured and highly educated," Hall told Hoover. Hall had refused the verbal order and demanded a written one before he would deliver any instructions. "After several days of turmoil and unsuccessful subterranean efforts to force me to issue the order, the matter was dropped." Nevertheless, Hall acknowledged a disturbing pattern that was now beginning to affect his own career prospects: "Possibly I would not call this matter to your attention, but promotion to a vacancy in my division was recently denied me, regardless of the fact that I had been recommended by the Division and other chiefs who have an intimate knowledge of my work and capabilities."[62] Hall was so dismayed he began making arrangements to leave the bureau, despite the return of Republican rule.

Outgoing Census Bureau director Samuel L. Rogers explained in near perfect Wilsonian-speak the circumstances that had given rise to Hall's complaint. Neither race nor party had anything to do with it. According to Rogers, the large staff necessary for the Fourteenth Census had created a number of administrative problems, especially in one of the bureau's larger buildings. "For administrative and other reasons it was desirable that the clerks should be grouped, as far as possible, according to the work upon which they were employed, and it was found necessary to group the colored employees in certain wings," Rogers explained. "In making this grouping by wings, we naturally supposed that the employees would utilize the most convenient toilets, but it was found that they did not, and a great deal of time was lost by persons going from one end of the building to another for this purpose." The order had been given verbally because this was deemed best for a "request of this nature." The problem, the director explained, was that without specific orders, black employees were irrational—they did not do the "natural" thing. In the end, the director stated, the policy was largely a success. "It certainly led to less friction."[63] The words and phrases were by now familiar: "administrative and other reasons," "necessary," "naturally," "efficient," and, of course, "friction." They did not leave with Wilson.

Hoover was even more dedicated to scientific management philosophy than the former president, and the results were similar for black employ-ees.[64] According to Hoover, for example, Commerce clerk Joseph McDuffie was "a colored" who had "conducted himself as to avoid friction with the white people associated with him in the statistical work."[65] The extent of the segregation in the Census Bureau was illustrated by the fact that nearly all black Census employees worked in what was known as "Pelham's sec-tion," after their supervisor Robert Pelham Jr., who retired in 1929 as the highest paid black clerk in the Commerce Department.[66] Hall did not fol-low through on his threat to quit. He continued to do excellent statistical work, though supervisors claimed he was "sometimes difficult to handle" and known to make statements "derogatory to the Census Bureau and its work." Although he continued to supervise all "Negro statistics," the much-lauded clerk never rose above junior administrative assistant. In 1938, Hall reached mandatory retirement age and was forced out, despite appeals by William Austin, by then Census director, to President Roosevelt.[67]

Pelham's and Hall's supervisory roles and the prominence of their small cadre of black clerks were unusual. African American civil servants did not generally move up into the clerical ranks after the 1910s.[68] The work that black Washingtonians did do in the 1920s was essential to the country, but much of the prestige and uplift were gone. As one officer in the Bureau of Engraving and Printing explained, "I have no objections to employing [Negroes] in skilled positions, but this is a Southern city and the white workers would object."[69] Black women continued to clean the desks of white workers; black men continued to shovel coal on mail trains. Govern-ment Printing Office messenger John Davis, once a well-paid clerk, spent the 1920s "running errands and doing light manual tasks with some respon-sibility; carrying important documents from one office to another; attend-ing the door and private office of the chief of the division."[70] In 1925, Cen-sus officials "recommended that eleven colored persons be appointed on a piece-rate basis to paste labels on portfolios and tie strings in the holds of portfolios." The reason was clear: using temporary black workers was cheap.[71]

Pension Bureau employee David Lane wrote in 1921 that he could liter-ally quantify how much money the Wilson administration had cost him: "I was the victim of the former administration to the extent of a loss of about $1,400, on account of an unjust reduction in salary from Class 3 ($1,600) to Class 4 ($1,400)."[72] Lane, who had earned a bachelor's degree and a medi-cal degree from Howard University, had appealed his reduction in 1913 "for the good of the service," attempting to point out the lie of the usual justifi-

cation for reductions. "My reduction does not appear to have been necessary for the good of the service, as I have always been punctual in my attendance and have not abused the privilege known as 'sick leave.'" Moreover,
Lane had added, "I have not been an active partisan," by which he meant
Republican activity. Indeed, Lane had actually earned the endorsement of
Secretary of the Navy Josephus Daniels, a fellow North Carolinian, who
stepped in to make sure that Lane would not be dismissed entirely.[73] After
the war, Lane was promoted to medical examiner in the Pension Bureau,
likely because the segregated state needed him to deal with pension claims
for black veterans.

Edward Arnold, Lane's Pension colleague, was less successful. In 1922,
Arnold explained to a superior that he had been reduced "under the previous administration," but he had not been reinstated under the new one,
despite the return of his party. Letters from his New Jersey congressional
delegation, including Senator Joseph Frelinghuysen and Congressmen
Charles Fowler and Ernest Ackerman, all Republicans, expressed the same
concern. Like many black clerks, Arnold had seen his salary reduced in 1914
without explanation; his record since his appointment in 1891 had indicated
an efficient and able clerk. Arnold had accepted the demotion as part of
the political game, and his record contains little correspondence until 1921,
when he assumed he would have a better chance at an appeal. But the rules
of the game had changed. Pension administrators determined that Arnold
did not merit a restoration of his status.[74] Lane, Arnold, and many others
had held out hope that the racism of the Wilson administration was only a
function of Democratic rule. Not only did discrimination continue, but as
implied by the staying power of words like "friction" and "efficiency," the
theory that Wilson had articulated to justify his praxis was now institutionalized.

Any claims of unfairness in government administration continued to be
illegitimate even after the Democrats left power. In 1922, John M. Botts,
a Post Office clerk, requested that he be considered for promotion. His
supervisors decided that he did not merit the promotion. This was routine
enough. But Botts went a step further, implying that his inability to earn
the promotion was the result of racial discrimination. Indeed, like many
black employees, Botts's career had stalled after 1912. "I seriously question
the advisability of eternally putting forward my best efforts in attempting
to attain perfection," Botts said, "if some clerks of the official section are
forever barred from the possibility of reaching this special grade."[75] Botts's
allegations, passed up the chain of command by his supervisor, raised an

alarm. "I consider this part of your letter serious enough," wrote the D.C. postmaster, "to warrant my calling upon you for a written explanation in detail of the veiled charge of discrimination and either prove it or retract."[76] Such a demand from a white employer to a black employee amounted to a gagging. Botts saw the writing on the wall and withdrew his allegation: "It is not compulsory that I remain in the postal service forever," he tried to explain. "I could resign if I saw fit and pursue a career more eminently fitted to my temperamental inclinations and my ambition and determination."[77] Botts was temporizing. There were very few career moves for black men with such inclinations, and he remained at the City Post Office until he reached the mandatory retirement age.

Charging discrimination in the 1920s could doom even the best-connected clerks. Joseph Murray, a clerk in the General Land Office, had also gone without a promotion for most of Wilson's presidency. In May 1923, Murray visited his old friend Theodore Roosevelt Jr. for help. Roosevelt, the assistant secretary of the Navy (a Roosevelt rite), explained to the assistant secretary of the Interior that Murray's father had been a servant in the White House during his father's presidency.[78] Surely, a letter from the son of a Republican president would help. But Murray had a bad reputation. "His services have not been entirely satisfactory," explained GLO commissioner William Spry, "largely because of the fact that his mind apparently dwells upon the condition of his race in comparison to the white race." Spry, a former Utah governor, had discovered that Murray was "quite an agitator on the question of equality and kindred subjects." The commissioner noted that Murray's supervisor would be glad to be rid of the troublemaker but decided he could "probably get as much work out of Murray as anyone else." Still, Spry concluded snidely, he would be happy to send Murray over to the Navy Department.[79]

Unlike John Botts, Murray refused to back away from his accusations. His proof, Murray said, was that he had been assigned to work designated for messengers and laborers, not for clerks of his rank. Such persistent allegations of racial discrimination made his position in the GLO unsustainable, according to Spry.[80] Even a letter from President Harding's personal secretary, Judson Welliver, that identified Murray as "a person of excellent standing and considerable influence among the colored community" was not enough. Murray had also accused his superiors of ignoring a gambling racket in the GLO. Welliver pointed out that gambling was known to be rife in Washington offices, and if Murray was wrong, "the case may be a truly remarkable one."[81] Nonetheless, Spry was finished with Murray. "The fact remains that Murray has been more or less of a trouble maker and has tried to stir up racial animosities," he declared. "Murray's connection with this office must be terminated if the morale of the division in which he is employed is to be maintained."[82] Murray was dismissed.

The government's supposed managerial rationalism, while still incomplete and constantly under negotiation even after Wilson, nonetheless provided a powerful discourse of race blindness. Under Harding and Coolidge, departmental officials regularly denied any segregation or racial discrimination, much as they had under Wilson.[83] Though dozens of cases like Murray's had ended favorably for black employees before the 1910s, the new racial regime in Washington invalidated accusations of unfairness. Meanwhile, the now-standard notations of color on all personnel records testified to systematized racism, as did the "Negro corners" in nearly every department. In 1924, the *Tribune* noted that the standardization pursued by the new Personnel Classification Board, supposedly an achievement of scientific management, deliberately discriminated against charwomen, messengers, and laborers, the positions held most often by African Americans.[84] But black employees who pointed out the injustice in this bureaucratic ethic were dangerous not only to the offices in which they worked but to the entire edifice of a good government.

Government managers believed segregation—with the resulting ceiling above black careers—to be a natural and efficient system for the management of the "Negro problem." Discrimination implied something that was unfair and was aimed at a specific class of people; government segregation was in the best interests of everyone. In 1927, Interior Department officials argued that segregation would allow for the promotion of black division heads, the same argument Wilsonians had made, because such an elevation would not result in African Americans supervising white workers. "I want no feeling that there was any so-called segregation intended in the changes complained of, because such a feeling would militate against efficiency, the only purpose contemplated for the change," Interior Secretary Hubert Work told the *Star*.[85] Treasury Secretary Andrew Mellon told James Weldon Johnson in 1928 that there was "no grouping of employees by reason of color" in the Treasury, but a different imperative led to what appeared to be racial segregation: "It so happens that the separation of certain colored men and white women employees in separate rooms has resulted in placing the five colored employees in a separate room, but it will be obvious to you that this separation on the basis of sex is more pleasant for both groups and this was the reason for the separation."[86]

Physical separation was actually beside the point. It was the collapse of career opportunities and economic mobility that really signaled the new racial regime to black Washingtonians. Requesting a promotion in 1923, for example, Thomas Hutchins acknowledged the special circumstances affecting promotions of black Census clerks. "I know that all of us cannot be promoted at once," he told his supervisor, but he wondered if his years of being underpaid might push him up the list.[87] His senator, in recommending him for promotion in 1924, noted that he was "a clerk in the colored group of the Bureau." The reply confirmed Hutchins's suspicions. "Mr. Hutchins is a good, faithful employee," explained his supervisor. "It has not been possible, however, to recognize him by promotion to $1200 because of the few vacancies that occur in that grade, and the more pressing needs of the Bureau to take care of persons with special qualifications who are likely to leave us in the event they do not receive promotions."[88] Hutchins had no special qualifications, but more important, everyone knew that a college-educated black Arkansan like Hutchins had few options elsewhere.

A younger man than Hutchins, Pierre Davis Jr. learned about the limitations the hard way. Having fallen out of favor with Robert Pelham Jr., he left the Bureau in 1925 to seek better prospects in Connecticut. A bachelor of science degree from Howard University and years of teaching math and science were surely formidable credentials.[89] Four years later, he was forced to admit that "I was unsuccessful in locating a vacancy there for a colored man, and had to return to Washington after a few months."[90] Years of campaigning, including appeals to President Hoover's personal secretary, resulted in a temporary appointment. By 1931, with the nation sinking to the bottom of the Great Depression, Davis was out of work with a family "practically destitute."[91]

Fellow Census clerk Herbert F. McGirt decided to go home to Camden, South Carolina. Like Davis, McGirt was of a newer generation of black men, and he was not as dedicated to the promise of national service. Brought to Washington as part of a huge cohort of temporary clerks to labor on the Fourteenth Census in 1920, McGirt had worked previously as a hotel bellman, messenger, switchboard operator, and, briefly, a Pullman Porter. He had too much ambition for the limitations of federal employment after Wilson. Called away because of family illness, McGirt told a supervisor, "Sooner or later I would have been compelled to leave the Department anyway in order to take up the work for which I have been trying to prepare myself, and I know that you would not condemn a man for desiring to better his condition, since my position at the Bureau offered me no inducement whatsoever." "There never seemed to be any material recognition of my efforts," he added. "A man desires to advance sometime." McGirt appreciated the kindness and "evident desire to treat a man as a man" of his direct supervisor, but the system itself was no longer built for a black man with ambition.[92] His felt experience matched the statistics. Although the Department of Labor announced triumphantly in 1928 that the numbers of black federal employees had skyrocketed since 1910, most of the gains had been made during the war. More important, nearly all new positions were in lower-wage, non-clerical positions, such as janitors and messengers.[93]

The devaluation of government work for African Americans occurred alongside a more general deterioration of government employment.[94] "The relative position of the Government employees in Washington has declined more than that of any other class of which we have record," wrote economist Paul Douglas in his 1930 study of real wages. The advantages of government work over private employment in terms of hours and pay were gone by the mid-1920s.[95] The Labor Department's *Monthly Labor Review* reported that most government employees were not able to support their families on one civil servant's wages.[96] Dramatic declines in real wages for government workers in Washington between 1914 and 1920 militated against much of the prosperity of the following decade. Moreover, in the first half of the 1920s, real wages of working-class Americans actually declined. Despite the era's reputation for consistent, across-the-board affluence, 40 percent of Americans were poor, and even those who earned clerk salaries were still struggling to maintain housing and decent diets.[97] Thus, not only were fewer African Americans gaining upper-level positions in government, but those who did stay on experienced decreasing value in their wages.

Swan Kendrick left government work in 1921 to try finally to make it on his own as a dairy farmer. By January 1922, life on his New Jersey farm was miserable. "The daily, monotonous grind, the discomforts, the isolation," as well as the cold — which Kendrick found could literally freeze the ink in his pen — made life hard, as did the burden of the land debt.[98] Ruby Kendrick, now his wife, was forced to find work at a school in Pennsylvania, and Swan managed the farm and their children alone. "We are getting along bravely here," he told Ruby. "It takes me just all day to feed and dress them and keep them buttoned and unbuttoned." The days were long, but he assured Ruby that they were doing all right. "Are we downhearted? — NO!"[99] But it all took its toll. Six months later, Kendrick was hospitalized with an infection he contracted from his own livestock. He died in September 1923.[100]

Those in positions below white-collar clerks were tied more tightly to the deteriorating federal workplace. In 1921, the *Washington Tribune* ran a six-part series on the hardships of laboring in the BEP, a rare investigative report on the work lives of typical black federal employees. "The relief looked for under the Harding administration has not been forthcoming," the paper said. Declaring work in the BEP comparable to "peonage," the *Tribune* revealed that huge numbers of government employees were not earning "a living wage."[101] Working conditions were terrible: temperatures within the building were stifling, and bosses ruled with fear, "keeping a vague uneasiness in the breast of every employee." The lack of a board of personnel meant that "nothing or no one safeguard[s] the rights of employees."[102] Attempting to subvert Wilsonian management philosophy, the paper asserted that "adequate pay" was in fact necessary for "efficiency" and "economy."[103] The only hope for the BEP workers "chained to their positions" was the *Tribune's* exposé. "In thousands of homes and offices, we record a protest against discrimination," rang the last report. "To the bureaucrats of the system, we serve this summons and this indictment: In the name of the employees you have treated unfairly, we charge you with discrimination. In the name of those you have dismissed thru trickery and the use of questionable methods, we class you as conspirators."[104] The *Tribune's* thorough and strident investigation was more than the NAACP or any government union did for BEP employees in the early twentieth century. Seventy years later, the bureau was still known as a "plantation" that discriminated against black employees.[105]

African Americans continued to be profoundly disturbed by discrimination in federal offices.[106] Nannie Helen Burroughs and her National Wage Earners Association pressed the Personnel Classification Board on the low wages of charwomen and messengers.[107] In 1925, fifty "prominent business, professional and political men from various parts of the country," including Census clerk Charles E. Hall, met with Coolidge to protest the ongoing discrimination in his administration. AME Church leader John R. Hawkins told the president, "We come today to call your attention to what we feel to be a violation of the principles of just government." Discrimination against African Americans in the civil service, both segregation and the refusal to hire and promote, stood for general racial discrimination "in the administration of law and the application of the rules and regulations enforced in the management and directions of the affairs of State."[108] Gone was an appeal as Republicans: black activists were now looking directly at the white supremacy apparent in the broad administration of the nation's government. And they never stopped protesting.[109]

Out of the Office

The suppression of black civil servants in lower level positions was illustrative of the triumph of white supremacy in Washington more generally in the 1920s.[110] When the Senate restaurant was closed to African Americans and a black woman was barred from the Senate Ladies' Gallery in 1917, government administrators reinforced inequality in the capital city.[111] "Can you not see by this that the segregation, which has existed in the several Departments of the Government, is gradually spreading on and on until, if allowed to continue, it will touch the sacred shrines of the home?" asked the *Tribune* in 1924.[112] When delegates from the National Association of Colored Women walked out of the Washington Auditorium to protest segregation at the International Council of Women's music festival a year later, the *Tribune* laid the blame for the kerfuffle at the feet of Coolidge. Because the president had failed to make an affirmative statement against federal segregation, "there is a feeling that the National Government approves or does not condemn segregation," the *Tribune* said. "Consequently, the Negro is forced to move as a gregarious herd in the departments of government, in residential sections and most of the public amusements."[113] Federal segregation was capital segregation.

The connection between federal policy and home life was literal in Washington, where federal space and personal recreation space overlapped. In the absence of a national segregation policy, the connection had left Washington racially integrated long after other places below the Mason-Dixon Line had been segregated. But in 1921, Harding appointed a white North Carolinian, Colonel Clarence Osborne Sherrill of the Army Corps of Engineers, as superintendent of public buildings and grounds. The position put him in charge of all public areas in Washington, including the city's 483 public parks, and gave him enormous power to shape where and how Washingtonians gathered, played, and relaxed. Sherrill was an avid segregationist.[114] It was he who directed the seating arrangements at the dedication of the Lincoln Memorial. A month before the dedication, Sherrill had posted "whites-only" and "colored-only" signs in picnic areas in Rock Creek Park.[115] Shelby Davidson and Archibald Grimké successfully lobbied to have the signs removed, but Sherrill had already made sure that the city golf course, tennis courts, and bathing beach along the Tidal Basin were closed to black residents.[116]

The bathing beach question aroused black Washingtonians like no other had since Wilson's administrators began segregating federal offices a decade

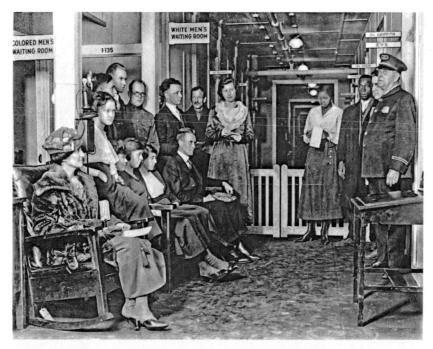

Federal employees at a Public Health Service dispensary for government workers, circa 1920. Despite the established color line, this is one of the only extant images of segregation signs in a federal building in Washington. After 1912, most government buildings operated under a code of separation that did not require such labels. (Library of Congress)

earlier. For those without the means to escape to vacation homes, bathing beaches were essential oases in the sweltering summer city in the days before air-conditioning. Nonetheless, black city leaders dug in and refused to accept the Harding administration's offer to build a separate "colored bathing beach." "This will be but the entering wedge for more jim crowism in the Capital of the nation and with the stamp of the Federal Government upon it," warned the *Tribune* in January 1923.[117] Responding to the protest, Secretary of War John W. Weeks, a Boston Republican, put the plans to build separate facilities on hold in August, leaving black Washingtonians without beach facilities for another summer.[118]

Black leaders were stunned the following spring when Weeks announced that, in addition to a separate golf course, the government again planned to build a separate beach, this one on the opposite bank of the Tidal Basin from the white beach. "This action on the part of Secretary Weeks is one of the boldest attempts ever made by a cabinet officer to put the stamp of Government approval on race segregation," the *Tribune* said.[119] Black

Tidal Basin bathing beach, 1922. Washington's bathing beaches were essential sites of recreation and cooling off for District residents before air-conditioning. Nonetheless, black Washingtonians refused to accept second-tier and segregated bathing facilities, and shortly after this photograph was taken, all Washingtonians lost access to the bathing beach. Congress chose to close it down rather than continue racially integrated leisure space in the city. (Library of Congress)

leaders fought the new plan, and another summer passed without swimming facilities for Washington's 110,000 black residents.[120] They gained a strange ally in the Senate when Thomas Walsh, a Democrat from Montana, removed money for all beach facilities, reportedly declaring that "the establishment in the most conspicuous place about the entire Basin of a bathing beach for the colored population" constituted a "desecration" of the Tidal Basin. The congressman's stand devastated city residents, who faced record heat during the following summer. Left without a bathing beach, everyone sought refuge in the city's fountains, where, much to the dismay of Texas congressman Thomas Blanton, black and white children frolicked together.[121]

By the mid-1920s, the capital's segregation took on an air of timeless normalcy, and most black Washingtonians were forced to settle into the new racial regime.[122] Black residents rejoiced in 1921 at the opening of Suburban Gardens in the Deanwood section, for example, but the blacks-only amusement park further institutionalized the capital's segregated leisure life.[123] In 1922, the Washington Board of Trade and a number of neighborhood citizens' associations aligned to ensure that local branches of the city library would be segregated. At Griffith Stadium, black and white baseball fans now cheered the Washington Senators from separate bleachers. Black golfers resigned themselves to the segregated golf course. In December 1925, Colonel Sherrill left to assume duties as city manager in Cincinnati, Ohio, and his replacement, Major Ulysses S. Grant III, pursued plans to build segregated swimming pools in District parks.[124]

City and federal officials continued to maintain that black people in Washington did not know how to get along with white people without causing problems. "Every time the Negro forces himself or is forced by others into places where the white race does not welcome him he injures the Negro race by offending the white race," said Georgia congressman William Chester Lankford on the floor of the House of Representatives. "I believe the Negroes teach their children here to be as offensive to the whites as possible." The reason was clear: despite all of the changes in the last decade, the capital was still not segregated enough. "On street cars, on railway trains, and in passenger waiting rooms, where the two races are forced to occupy the same seats and sit side by side, there is built up a race hatred that will eventually make the Negro bitterly hated by the white race, and which hatred will go far toward the destruction of the Negro race."[125] It always seemed to surprise white segregationists when African Americans failed to be grateful for these expressions of concern.

Some white Washingtonians took things into their own hands. In April 1923, the *Tribune* reported that "citizens associations" were cropping up to enforce racial covenants in the District's residential sections. The associations vowed to prevent the sale of property to black families. Because of Washington's long history of integration—and the remaining affluence of some of its black elite—their campaign of residential segregation required more than simply extending covenants over already-white neighborhoods. Black families needed to be forced out. On the 1700 block of S Street in northwest Washington, for example, a sale to Mrs. Helen Curtis was blocked by the local citizens association and a District judge. Even still, the association had to deal with Emmett J. Scott, Arthur Froe, and a host of other black professionals, who already occupied elegant townhomes on the block. The city's talented black lawyers mobilized when white homeowners tried to block or revoke sales, but unlike twenty years earlier, they made little headway in the courts.[126] In 1926, the Supreme Court ruled in Helen Curtis's case (*Corrigan and Curtis v. Buckley*) that racial covenants were enforceable in the District of Columbia.[127]

Not satisfied to leave things to the law, some segregationists chose terrorism. In November 1923, hundreds of white homeowners, apparently led by a group of government clerks in the North Washington Citizens Association, stormed the Bloomingdale section just southeast of Howard University to intimidate black homeowners in the neighborhood. Of course, such mob action was not uncommon in the United States, especially in northern cities after the Great Migration, but they were particularly jarring in the nation's capital. "Is the Capital of this great nation to be the leader in making the Constitution a scrap of paper as regards home ownership?" wondered the *Tribune*.[128]

Some black Washingtonians did not give up the exceptional mantle easily, and, of course, black life in the city carried on. "Famed for its beautiful women, aristocracy and exclusiveness," Washington, declared journalist Geraldyn Dismond, was "the cynosure of these colored United States."[129] Cultural clubs still met, often presided over by federal employees; families bought homes; a tiny minority of rich, light-skinned families continued to live courtly lives.[130] Economically, race-conscious investment seemed to have real potential in the District. Black businessmen held regular parades to trumpet their enterprises, and in 1921, the *Tribune* proudly announced that the U Street corridor boasted 125 black-owned businesses. Two years later, the black-controlled Prudential Bank opened on U Street.[131]

But for less sanguine observers, it was all a veneer. "The dignity of one's family background doesn't keep a fellow who's penniless from getting hungry," reminded bohemian poet Langston Hughes.[132] In fact, black Washingtonians seemed to have less capital than in earlier days. In 1922, the Department of Labor reported that the total savings of black savings bank depositors in Washington had decreased by 718 percent.[133] For all of the hope on U Street, the *Tribune* imagined what people would say about a "city with a population of [109,000] with one bank, one shoe store, no furniture store, a handful of grocery stores, no hardware stores, no clothing stores, no department stores."[134] Washington had lineage, but it was increasingly lacking in prospects. "We have but precious few enterprises, not only here in Washington, but throughout the country; and cannot begin to absorb all the graduates from the Washington schools."[135] The future looked bleak.

By the middle of the decade, even the once-vaunted black public schools were beginning to suffer from congressional neglect. Nothing symbolized the danger Congress posed to African Americans in Washington better than the placement of rabidly racist Mississippi senator James K. Vardaman on the Senate District Committee. Budgets began to dry up as Democrats blocked funding to black Washington, and Republicans, increasingly the party of fiscal conservatism, no longer fought back. Further, revelations in a dramatic court case that school administrators and parents had given a European amateur race scientist, Herman Moens, access to black schoolchildren to take nude photographs sullied the school system's reputation.[136] Dunbar High School, the successor to the M Street School, still produced stellar graduates, like Swan and Ruby Kendrick's accomplished children, Martha, Charlotte, and Webster. But the gleam had worn off.[137]

Moreover, declining mobility had ossified Washington's elite. Better-off African Americans sought isolation more often than racial unity, preferring to ignore the contrapuntal seediness on Seventh Street captured in 1923 by Jean Toomer in his modernist novel *Cane*. The novelist and social critic Waldo Frank, a friend of Toomer's, thought elite black Washingtonians had been made utterly "neurotic" by their declining status but unending desire to stay above the benighted masses.[138] The instability led some to turn inward and disengage with more complicated issues of being black in a white supremacist capital. Referring to the elite's escapist frivolity, the narrator of Edward Christopher Williams's 1920s Washington novel remarks, "My mind went back to [James Weldon] Johnson's haggard face, and the Dyer Anti-Lynching Bill, being slowly strangled to death, strangled to death to the sound of jazz music played by a dozen orchestras, while hundreds and hundreds of educated, refined, prosperous colored people danced themselves haggard and lame between Wednesday night and Sunday morning!"[139]

Washington was not a major recipient of southern migrants like Chicago, New York, Cleveland, or Detroit after World War I.[140] First, it was not *so* northern — it was not a place where black people could vote, and the same white southerners making life miserable farther south seemed to be running the city even after Wilson left. Second, increased demands for labor during the war dropped off sharply in 1919, and the demand was never in the kind of industrial work that offered decent wages to people with limited education. Thus, while Washington gained about 37,000 black residents between 1910 and 1930, African Americans as a percentage of the city's total population actually shrank, from about one-third in 1900 to 25 percent during the war to 27 percent in 1930. The black population in Washington would not constitute more than a third of the city again until 1950.[141]

The pages of the *Washington Evening Star* began to reflect both the declining black proportion and the national abandonment of racial liberalism during the Wilson era. The paper continued to report on black life, but the tenor of its racial politics changed. Once a complex but sturdy fount of Republican egalitarianism just below the Mason-Dixon Line, the *Star* leaped upon the sectional reconciliation bandwagon in the 1910s. Toward the end of Wilson's first term, the paper ceased hammering disfranchisement in the South in its editorials about Democrats. Suddenly, the Democrats were the legitimate representatives of the entire South.[142] Moreover, the paper began to favor "home rule" in federal appointments affecting the District, to the deliberate detriment of black politicians escaping the South. As Wilson considered applicants for the recorder of deeds position vacated by Henry Lincoln Johnson, the paper advocated strongly for a local man but assumed without protest that the new recorder would be white.[143] The shift could have reflected the power of the Democrats in the *Star*'s hometown, but the paper did not snap back with the return of the Republicans. Except for a single protest against lynching while the Dyer Bill was under consideration, the editorial page fell silent on issues of black politics, equality, and citizenship.[144]

BY 1928, LANGSTON HUGHES preferred Harlem, "where people are not so ostentatiously proud of themselves, and where one's family background is not of such great concern."[145] Washington did play a role in the black arts renaissance of the 1920s. Poet Georgia Douglas Johnson's home, purchased with the earnings of her federal appointee husband, Henry Lincoln

Johnson, was a haven for writers and artists. But postwar Washington was not where rising black men and women wanted to be. Howard University provided an education and connections, but Chicago, New York, and Paris were the desired and often actual homes of the New Negro. The list of people who left the District in the 1910s and 1920s is as remarkable as those who visited Johnson's Saturday night salons.[146] Hughes, Toomer, Rudolph Fisher, Marita Bonner, and Richard Bruce Nugent all departed in the decade following World War I. The underappreciated truth that Washington played a role in the so-called Harlem Renaissance should not obscure another truth, that D.C. was no longer black America's capital.

The federal equal employment program—whether consciously so or not—suggests that the governmental sector is not merely the instrument for induction of change, "the vanguard of equality," but the means of change itself.

—Samuel Krislov, *The Negro in Federal Employment*, 1967

Epilogue

At 3 P.M. on August 8, 1925, Imperial Wizard Hiram Evans led 35,000 members of the Ku Klux Klan down Pennsylvania Avenue in downtown Washington. An estimated 200,000 people watched without protest—many cheered.[1] The hateful but orderly parade of white-robed men and women in the nation's capital was a stunning image at the time and one that has become common in history books that document American white supremacy. Indeed, twentieth-century Washington often served as ceremonial ground upon which to make a statement about a group's national agenda.[2] What is less often noted is that Washington was and is a local place, too, and it was one African Americans had long considered their home. Certainly the federal government was what drew them there, and many were aware of their presence on a national stage, but D.C. was still, first and foremost, home. Klansmen marching proudly and unmasked through the streets brought almost unbearable tension to black Washingtonians, especially since they seemed to arrive along with segregated swimming pools, restrictive covenants, reduced funding for black schools, neighbors' distrust, and political cowardice.

The destruction of a legitimate role for black politics eroded the possibility that black Republicans might be effective representatives of black America. As the stalwart Republican generation began to pass away in the mid- and late 1920s, a new one emerged. Equally hardworking, this group of men and women was shaped by federal segregation, the disappointments following World War I, and the rise of a Republican regime that had no political or ideological connection to abolitionism or Radical Republicanism. Whereas the previous generation had funneled its racial consciousness into Republican politics and U.S. citizenship, the new one founded its identity upon black pride, transnational connections to people of color, and opposition to rigid white hate. The NAACP, the National Urban League, and briefly Garveyism replaced mainstream politics as guardians of civil rights. But these outside interest groups could not reach into federal offices the way political patronage could. It is also clear that for many African Americans in this latter generation, hard work, family, northern migration, and economic survival dominated their lives in a nation that offered them even less than it had a generation earlier.

But party politics was never forgotten entirely. In 1936, for the first time, a majority of African Americans who could vote cast ballots for the Democratic presidential candidate, Franklin Delano Roosevelt. Roosevelt, prodded by Eleanor Roosevelt and some urban northern Democrats, had begun to loosen the grip of white southerners on the national party's racial policies. By the mid-1930s, black Americans were benefiting from some New Deal programs, especially in the North.[3] Yet the roots of the move were deeper than the Great Depression and FDR's enormous popularity among black Americans. The new ties to an evolving Democratic Party also reflected the profound disappointment that accompanied Republicans' refusal to act against white supremacy in the 1920s.

Segregation and discrimination in federal employment persisted, however. In June 1941, labor leader A. Philip Randolph agreed to abort a march on Washington in exchange for Roosevelt's Executive Order 8802, which prohibited discrimination in federal agencies. But in 1942, the newly established Fair Employment Practices Committee (FEPC) found that the order was being applied unevenly or in bad faith. Personnel management continued to be extremely decentralized, especially as the administration sought to meet wartime labor needs.[4] The temptation to keep quiet out of fear of being labeled a troublemaker was still powerful in federal offices, and the FEPC was not up to the task of monitoring black labor in the enormous war effort. Though the 1940s hinted at a new shift in racial regimes, the federal government remained a model for managerial white supremacy until the 1960s. "The colored people of Washington have never recovered from the blow that struck them in the time of Woodrow Wilson," concluded a national report on segregation in Washington in 1948. "The example set by the government has been one of exclusion and segregation in menial jobs."[5] Discrimination in Washington was never merely another example of southern Jim Crow: it was evidence of the white supremacy at the heart of the nation.

Notes

ABBREVIATIONS

AGC   Archibald Grimké Collection, Moorland-Spingarn Research Center,
           Howard University, Washington, D.C.
BEPGCF   Central Correspondence Files, Bureau of Engraving and Printing,
           General Correspondence Files, 1913–1939, RG 318, National Archives
           and Records Administration, College Park, Md.
CEHP   Charles E. Hall Papers, collection maintained by archivist Rodney A.
           Ross, National Archives Building, Washington, D.C.
CHD   Charles Hamlin Diary, box 2, vol. 2, reel 1, Charles S. Hamlin Papers,
           Manuscript Division, Library of Congress, Washington, D.C.
GRDTDA   General Records of the Department of the Treasury, Division
           of Appointments, RG 56, National Archives and Records
           Administration, College Park, Md.
JSWP   John Skelton Williams Papers, Accession #10040, 10040-a, Special
           Collections, University of Virginia Library, Charlottesville, Va.
KBFP   Kendrick-Brooks Family Papers, Manuscript Division, Library of
           Congress, Washington, D.C.
LC   Library of Congress, Washington, D.C.
MSRC   Moorland-Spingarn Research Center, Howard University, Washington,
           D.C.
NAB   National Archives Building, Washington, D.C.
NARA   National Archives and Records Administration, College Park, Md.
NYT   *New York Times*
OGVP   Oswald Garrison Villard Papers, MS Am 1323, Houghton Library,
           Harvard University, Cambridge, Mass.
PF NPRC   Personnel File, National Personnel Records Center, St. Louis, Mo.
PWW   *The Papers of Woodrow Wilson*, 69 vols., edited by Arthur S. Link
           (Princeton: Princeton University Press, 1966–).
RNAACP   Records of the National Association for the Advancement of Colored
           People, Manuscript Division, Library of Congress, Washington, D.C.
RWPP   Records of the Woodrow Wilson Papers Project, Manuscripts Division,
           Department of Rare Books and Special Collections, Princeton
           University Library, Princeton, N.J.
WB   *Washington Bee*
WES   *Washington Evening Star*
WGMP   William Gibbs McAdoo Papers, Manuscript Division, Library of
           Congress, Washington, D.C.

WHTP	William Howard Taft Papers, Manuscript Division, Library of Congress, Washington, D.C.
WLHFP	William LePre Houston Family Papers, Manuscript Division, Library of Congress, Washington, D.C.
WP	*Washington Post*
WT	*Washington Tribune*
WWP	Woodrow Wilson Papers, Manuscript Division, Library of Congress, Washington, D.C.

NOTE ON SOURCES

Though much of the primary research for this book was conducted in traditional libraries, archives, and newspaper collections, the quest for information on African American civil servants was less straightforward. I have collected the personnel files for about 120 federal employees, mostly African American clerks, who worked in the District of Columbia in the first quarter of the twentieth century. This is both fewer than I would have liked and more than I imagined I could ever obtain. The National Personnel Records Center in St. Louis, Missouri, contains the files of nearly every nonmilitary employee who has ever worked for the federal government. But the NPRC serves mostly as a warehouse, responding to specific file requests by federal investigators conducting background checks and by employees' descendants seeking information about relatives. To access personnel files, one must have individual names. There is no way to request all the files for a particular department or division, and there is certainly no way to request all the files of African American federal employees from a particular time. From a published directory of black Washingtonians, *Sherman's Directory*, I was able to produce a list of about 350 black clerks working in Washington in 1912. Archivists at the NPRC were able to recover personnel files for about one-third of the list.

Personnel files are not carefully processed archival collections. They are musty, fragile folders containing random form letters, inscrutable efficiency cards, partially completed applications, short letters of complaint or criticism, chronological lists of salary changes, and the like. Spinning a person's history out of these many threads is tricky work, usually involving piecing together several one-sentence letters. This is why my depth of knowledge about individual figures varies dramatically and why citations to my text are sometimes confusing lists of names and dates. This is what it is to build narrative out of bureaucratic paperwork.

Civil service personnel records are not diaries or personal papers. They are files kept *on* employees, not *by* employees, which means the people I write about had no ability to determine what did and did not end up in their files. Even information sheets completed by employees themselves were filtered through the disciplining nature of bureaucratic forms. The data one gets are based on the blanks on the form. There were cases of civil servants fighting against this discipline: Laura Joiner, for example, replied "So called" in response to the question, "If colored, so state." Others left the line blank or lied. Where possible, I have cross-referenced information with other sources, from personal papers to newspapers to census records. Nevertheless, I have always been aware of the ways in which my understanding of a person's record is a function of a certain context and style of paperwork. I read them with and against the grain to get as close as possible to the experience of working in Washington at the turn of the twentieth century.

INTRODUCTION

1. William Jennifer to William Harris, July 31, 1914, William Jennifer, PF NPRC.

2. The most often cited works on federal segregation in Washington are Hayes, "Negro Federal Government Worker," and Green, *Secret City*. Others generally branch off of these works. See Wolgemuth, "Woodrow Wilson and Federal Segregation"; Blumenthal, "Woodrow Wilson and the Race Question"; Meier and Rudwick, "Rise of Segregation"; Weiss, "Negro and the New Freedom"; Sosna, "South in the Saddle"; Williamson, *Crucible of Race*, 364–95; King, *Separate and Unequal*; and Patler, *Jim Crow*.

3. E. Lewis, *In Their Own Interests*, 92.

4. William Leuchtenburg's invitation to historians twenty-five years ago to analyze the state's role in the lives of Americans has not yet been fully answered. For what constitutes "the state," I have followed recent scholars' expansion of Max Weber's classic definition as the concentration of physical force to mean the enormous apparatus of power that governs, regulates, and institutionalizes violence, property, and society in a recognized space. Leuchtenburg, "Pertinence of Political History"; Balogh, "State of the State," 458. On the necessity of merging scholarship on politics and labor, see Katznelson, "'Bourgeois' Dimension." On defining the state, see Margaret Levi, "The State of the Study of the State," in Katznelson and Milner, *Political Science*, 40.

5. For more on the state and the legitimation of constructed social hierarchies, see Bourdieu, Wacquant, and Farage, "Rethinking the State"; Franke, "Becoming a Citizen," 254–55; and Canaday, *Straight State*, 4.

6. Historians—from sympathetic biographers to younger, more critical scholars—have all acknowledged Wilson's white supremacy. Even Arthur Link, whose admiration for Wilson approached something beyond historiographical objectivity, never denied that Wilson "remained throughout his life largely a southerner on the race question." Whether or not Link thought this somehow made him less culpable is not totally clear, and the fact that for Link black people were not "southerners" is meaningful. Nonetheless, even Link found Wilson's view of African Americans hard to admire. Most historians also agree that Wilson's racism manifested itself in an "indifference" as president, an indifference that was surely harmful but not aggressively so. Segregation in the federal government, these historians conclude, was Wilson's responsibility but only because he was the boss and did nothing to stop it. Yet there are logical elisions in these analyses of Wilson and racism, and questions remain: Are there degrees of indifference? Nearly all of Wilson's predecessors, in thought and action, can be described as "indifferent" to the suffering of African Americans on the whole. Was Wilson *especially* indifferent? If Wilson is ultimately responsible because he was the boss, how exactly did the vectors of responsibility point to him? A. Link, "Negro as a Factor," 87; Cooper, *Woodrow Wilson*, 11; Clements, *Woodrow Wilson*, 97–101; Manela, *Wilsonian Moment*, 27.

7. The works of historians Gary Gerstle and Michael McGerr stand as important exceptions to the disconnect between racism and progressive politics, and political

scientist Stephen Skowronek has argued that Wilson's liberalism and racism share important intellectual roots. Gerstle, "Race and Nation in the Thought and Politics of Woodrow Wilson," in Cooper, *Reconsidering Woodrow Wilson*, 93–123; McGerr, *Fierce Discontent*, 182–217; Skowronek, "Reassociation."

8. Political scientists Desmond King and Rogers Smith, for example, have argued powerfully that the American state underwent a change of "racial orders" from the egalitarian possibilities of Reconstruction to the "racial bureaucracy" of the early twentieth century. This notion of "racial orders," similar to what I have called "regimes," is very useful because it suggests a crucial connection between racism and American political development during the Wilson era. Nonetheless, the work of political scientists lacks the *longue durée* and deep sense of experience to adequately explain a shift in "orders" or "regimes." King and Smith, "Racial Orders"; King, "Racial Bureaucracy." See also King, "Strong or Weak State?"; and King and Tuck, "De-Centering the South."

9. For bureaucratic reform and the progressive state, see Shefter, *Political Parties*, 76.

10. Recent work on public employees has just begun to address a void in political and labor history, though not yet for African Americans in this period. See McCartin, "Bringing the State's Workers In"; Rubio, *There's Always Work*; and Cahill, *Federal Fathers*.

11. Masur, *Example for All the Land*.

12. In 1883, the year the United States Civil Service Commission was established, 620 black men and women were working in Washington's federal offices. By 1912, there were more than 1,800. The proportion of federal employees working in Washington who were black kept pace with the increase in the size of federal government offices in this period and, in fact, increased slightly. Given the relentless attack on African Americans after Reconstruction, this is a remarkable statistic. King, *Separate and Unequal*, 39–51; Van Riper, *History of the United States Civil Service*, 161–62; Sherman's Directory, 388–407; Hayes, "Negro Federal Government Worker," 34; U.S. Bureau of the Census, *Statistical History*, 1102.

13. For black politics and the Republican Party after Reconstruction, see De Santis, *Republicans Face the Southern Question*; Sherman, *Republican Party*; Walton, *Black Republicans*; Casdorph, *Republicans, Negroes, and Progressives*; Wang, *Trial of Democracy*; Valelly, *Two Reconstructions*; and Materson, *For the Freedom of Her Race*.

14. On black organizing outside mainstream national parties, see Hahn, *Nation under Our Feet*; Gilmore, *Defying Dixie*; Sullivan, *Lift Every Voice*; Tuck, *We Ain't What We Ought To Be*; and Alexander, *Army of Lions*. The key role that government salaries played in supporting the intellectual and cultural activities of this privileged class can be seen in Gaines, *Uplifting the Race*, and Moss, *American Negro Academy*.

15. On the history of civil service reform, see Van Riper, *History of the United States Civil Service*; Hoogenboom, *Outlawing the Spoils*; Keller, *Affairs of State*; and Skowronek, *Building a New American State*.

16. For the meaning of Reconstruction in history, see Woodward, *Strange Career*, 105; and Foner, *Reconstruction*, xvii–xviii. For the standing model of this version of Reconstruction from the period, see Dunning, *Reconstruction*.

17. Despite the general dismissal of patronage as a dirty game of a few brokers, Robert K. Merton and Harold Lasswell noted decades ago that patronage could be

a link between citizens, the state, and economic and social well-being. Merton, *Social Theory*; Lasswell, *Politics*; Margaret Levi, "The State of the Study of the State," in Katznelson and Milner, *Political Science*, 46; Finegold, *Experts and Politicians*, 10–11.

18. Katznelson, *Black Men*, 66; Bates, *Pullman Porters*, 55–57.

19. Goluboff, "'Won't You Please Help Me,'" 781.

20. The complex combining of factors, from labor trends to racism, that I am describing here is part of what historian Thomas Holt has called "the levels problem," or "the problem of establishing the continuity between behavioral explanations sited at the individual level of the human experience and those at the level of society and social forces." Race is "made" by more than just hate. Holt, "Marking," 7.

CHAPTER 1

1. Capt. A. E. Pinanski to E. D. Morgan, July 26, 1918, box 8, folder 8, KBFP.

2. Swan M. Kendrick to Ruby Moyse, July 17, 1913, box 3, folder 1, ibid. On Kendrick's affiliations, see "Statement From Family," box 7, folder 7, ibid.

3. Swan M. Kendrick to Ruby Moyse, May 10, 1913, box 5, folder 2, and June 23, 1914, box 3, folder 6, ibid.

4. Kendrick and Moyse's epistolary love affair went on for five years, during which Swan wrote twice a week of his smallest affairs and his biggest dreams. These are just a few of them: Kendrick to Moyse, June 23, 1914; December 3, 1912, box 2, folder 6; October 30, 1913, box 5, folder 2; April 7, 1913, box 2, folder 9; all in ibid.

5. Ibid., July 8, 1914, box 5, folder 4.

6. Ibid., February 1, 1913, box 5, folder 2.

7. Gillette, *Between Justice and Beauty*, 12, 74; Smith, *Washington at Home*, 11; Lois Horton, "Days of Jubilee: Black Migration during the Civil War and Reconstruction," in Cary, *Washington Odyssey*, 65.

8. Smith, *Washington at Home*, 12; Lessoff, *Nation and Its City*, 9; D. Lewis, *District of Columbia*, 71–74; Green, *Washington*, 187–204.

9. Glassie, "Victorian Homes," 342; John W. Hall, "Capital, Beauty City," *WES*, November 15, 1908, sec. 8, p. 3; Jacob, *Capital Elites*, 108.

10. Low, "Washington."

11. Foltz, *Federal Civil Service*, 168–69.

12. "Pay of the Clerks," *WES*, December 20, 1906, 6; Mayers, *Federal Service*, 4.

13. "Washington During Recess," *WES*, June 8, 1908, 6.

14. Abbott, *Political Terrain*, 79, 100–101.

15. Low, "Washington," 771, 774.

16. Green, *Washington*, 80; Lessoff, *Nation and Its City*, 19; West quoted in "Taft Is Criticized," *WES*, February 26, 1911, 2.

17. U.S. Bureau of the Census, *Bulletin 94*, table 45, p. 64; Belle C. La Follette, "Colored Folk of Washington," *La Follette's Magazine*, August 5, 1911, 10–11, republished in Unger, "Belle La Follette."

18. As historian James Henretta has explained, "[Social mobility] is designed to measure how well an individual, an ethnic group, or a sexual caste performs in relation to another." Henretta, "Study of Social Mobility," 29.

19. The *Washington Bee* had a national profile, and papers such as the *Indianapolis Freeman*, *Pittsburgh Courier*, and *Chicago Defender* kept regular tabs on the District's politics and society. Chase, "'Shelling the Citadel,'" 373. For examples in papers beyond D.C., see E. H. Brooks, "Washington," *Pittsburgh Courier*, April 15, 1911, 5; R. W. Thompson, "Affairs in Washington," *Chicago Defender*, June 15, 1912, 5; and "Glad Hand Given Bert Williams," *Chicago Defender*, March 9, 1912, 1.

20. R. W. Thompson, "Dr. Booker T. Washington Speaks," *WB*, May 15, 1909, 1.

21. For the leisure practices of black Washingtonians in the early twentieth century, see McQuirter, "Claiming the City." For studies of black urban communities elsewhere in this period, see E. Lewis, *In Their Own Interests*; T. Reed, *Not Alms*; Greenwood, *Bittersweet Legacy*; Baldwin, *Chicago's New Negroes*; and Goings and Mohl, *New African American Urban History*.

22. In the much smaller cities of the old confederacy, blacks made up a larger proportion of the population. African Americans in Atlanta, Norfolk, Richmond, and Memphis held a larger share, but the total black populations there were significantly smaller than Washington's. None of these cities ranked in the top fifteen largest U.S. cities in 1900. (D.C. was fifteenth that year.) New Orleans and Baltimore had the next largest black populations and were the only other southern cities in the top fifteen, but neither approached Washington's 31 percent of the total. U.S. Bureau of the Census, *Historical Census Statistics*.

23. "Rejoice at Freedom; Negroes Celebrate District Emancipation Edict," *WES*, April 19, 1910, 13.

24. McQuirter, "Claiming the City," 24; "Race Discrimination: Reported at Theatre and Church," *WB*, March 29, 1913, 1; "False Alarm," *WB*, June 25, 1898, 4.

25. The club's name was short for Music-Social-Literary. Moss, *American Negro Academy*, 268–69; Jacqueline M. Moore, *Leading the Race*, 16; Gatewood, *Aristocrats of Color*, 48.

26. "National Meetings a Menace," *WT*, September 13, 1924, 6. For secret societies as key organizing and training institutions for black men, see Kantrowitz, "'Intended for the Better Government,'" 1002; and D. White, *Too Heavy a Load*, 27.

27. Jacqueline M. Moore, *Leading the Race*, 70. On churches as institutions for "mobilization," see Frederick C. Harris, "Religious Institutions and African American Political Mobilization," in Paul E. Peterson, *Classifying by Race*, 279.

28. For Blanche K. Bruce's stunning career and family history, see Graham, *Senator and the Socialite*; Gatewood, *Aristocrats of Color*, 38; and Green, *Washington*, 101–31.

29. Terrell, "Society among the Colored People"; La Follette, "Colored Folk of Washington," 10–11.

30. Masur, *Example for All the Land*, 54; Dabney, "History of Schools for Negroes."

31. Green, *Washington*, 116; Robinson, "M Street High School," 119; Jacqueline M. Moore, *Leading the Race*, 118.

32. Dunbar, "Negro Society in Washington."

33. Lessoff, *Nation and Its City*, 40; Foner, *Reconstruction*, 372; Horton, "Days of Jubilee," 67, 72; Masur, *Example for All the Land*, 7–8.

34. Foner, *Reconstruction*, 279; Woodruff, *American Congo*, 3. For more on labor and

peonage in the South after emancipation, see Goluboff, "'Won't You Please Help Me'";
Daniel, *Shadow of Slavery*; and Mandle, *Roots of Black Poverty*.

35. H. Clark, "Public Career," 112–15.

36. Abbott, *Political Terrain*, 74–75; Hayes, "Negro Federal Government Worker,"
123, 42 (n. 16). The *Bee* noted that after McKinley, the police department itself seemed
more welcoming to black officers. "Our Chief of Police and the Negro," *WB*, August 17,
1901, 4.

37. *WB*, May 22, 1909, 4; Harley, "Black Women," 63.

38. Mintz, "Historical Ethnography," 236, 239; T. Jones, "Alley Homes"; Weller, *Neglected Neighbors*; "Against the Negro," *WB*, September 19, 1891, 2.

39. Velma Davis quoted in Elizabeth Clark-Lewis, "'For a Real Better Life': Voices
of African American Women Migrants, 1900–1930," in Cary, *Washington Odyssey*, 99.

40. Green, *Secret City*, 126; "Color Line Drawn; Mr. Heflin Wants 'Jim Crow' Law on
Cars Here," *WP*, February 23, 1908, 6; "Jim Crow Bill Set Aside," *WES*, February 22, 1915,
2. Chapin Brinsmade to Archibald Grimké, July 8, 1914, box 39-25, folder 500, AGC.

41. "Washington," *WES*, September 14, 1907, 4.

42. *WES*, July 26, 1888, 2.

43. "Sambo" was a minstrel trickster character created in 1905 by William Marriner
and distributed by *McClure's Magazine*. The comic ran for ten years, though it was
never as ubiquitous as later iterations like Pat Sullivan's *Felix the Cat*. In other words,
the *Star's* choice to run the comic was a deliberate endorsement of the humorousness
of the racist caricature, a choice that plenty of major papers did not make. I. Gordon,
Comic Strips, 67–73.

44. For other statements against disfranchisement and racist violence, see these
articles in the *WES*: "Sentimental Statesmenship," January 5, 1901, 4; "Texas Democrats
and Negroes," November 4, 1901, 4; "The Maryland Suffrage," February 9, 1908, 6; "The
'Other Side' of Lynching," August 20, 1904, 4; and "The South's Shame," August 17,
1904, 1.

45. "The Dinner in the Campaign," *WES*, November 9, 1901, 4; "The Atlanta Mob,"
WES, September 24, 1906, 4. On the riot, see Godshalk, *Veiled Visions*.

46. In 1910, Calvin Chase, himself an attorney, remarked that the courts in D.C.
treated black lawyers well. "The Negro Attorney," *WB*, May 21, 1910, 4. The son of Recorder of Deeds John Dancy recalled that Armond Scott, a prominent D.C. lawyer,
had fled Wilmington, North Carolina, around the same time as his father. Dancy, *Sand
against the Wind*, 70.

47. "The Civil Rights Law: Mr. Hewlett Makes a Test," *WB*, November 5, 1887, 2.

48. Lambert responded by closing up her lunchroom permanently. "No Negro
Wanted," *WB*, March 9, 1907, 5; "Deprived of Lunch Room," *WES*, April 3, 1907, 11.

49. "Messrs. Vernon and Houston," *WB*, May 22, 1909, 1; "Negro Diners Cause
Trouble," *Washington Herald*, May 15, 1909, 2.

50. "Senator Defends Negro and Secures Acquittal," *Atlanta Constitution*, April 24,
1909, 5.

51. "Senator Defends Negro," *Washington Herald*, April 24, 1909, 14.

52. "Officer Watts Fined," *WB*, May 22, 1909, 1.

53. Masur, *Example for All the Land*, 97.

54. Solomon Johnson to William Windom, May 26, 1881, entry 213, box 2, Personnel Folders of Notable Treasury Employees, GRDTDA; memo to Treasury Department, date unknown, ibid. William Cooper Nell was appointed as a postal clerk in Boston in 1863, and John W. Curry became the first black postal worker in Washington, D.C., in 1868. Rubio, *There's Always Work*, 20; Hayes, "Negro Federal Government Worker," 25; King, *Separate and Unequal*, 45–46.

55. In his study of clerks in Philadelphia, Jerome Bjelopera noted that "unlike the white clerical workforce, its African American counterpart did not show a high degree of feminization by 1920." Bjelopera, *City of Clerks*, 28; Aron, *Ladies and Gentlemen*, 34, 100; Kocka, *White Collar Workers*, 143, 147; Jacqueline M. Moore, *Leading the Race*, 152; Rung, *Servants of the State*, 14.

56. Swan M. Kendrick to Ruby Moyse, October 30, 1913, box 5, folder 2, KBFP.

57. Foltz, *Federal Civil Service*, 105; Fish, *Civil Service*, 229.

58. Harley, "Black Women," 65.

59. Thomas M. Dent to Director of Census, application June 26, 1899, Thomas M. Dent, PF NPRC; Walton, *Black Republicans*, 51.

60. George H. Cox to Director of Census, May 20, 1899 [received], George H. Cox, PF NPRC.

61. Foltz, *Federal Civil Service*, v, 229.

62. For more on the rise of female workers in federal departments, see Aron, *Ladies and Gentleman*.

63. Lucretia Mott Kelly to Henry M. Teller, August 4, 1882; Annuity Claim of Lucretia Mott Kelly, December 2, 1921; both in Lucretia Mott Kelly, PF NPRC.

64. For a discussion of the difficulty of enacting labor regulations in the United States in the Progressive Era, see Skocpol, *Protecting Soldiers and Mothers*, 248–310. For the vulnerability of the working classes in this period, see Painter, *Standing at Armageddon*; and Spero, "Employer and Employee," 182.

65. Clark, Craig, and Wilson, *History of Public Sector Pensions*, 165; "Fifty Years in U.S. Service; Miss Emma R. Graves of Treasury Department is 82 Years Old," *WES*, April 11, 1914, 4.

66. The threat of forced retirement for older employees, in fact, led to the first permanent organization of federal workers in 1900, the United States Civil Service Retirement Association. Aron, *Ladies and Gentlemen*, 159.

67. John Elfreth Watkins Jr., "Draw Good Salaries; Several Thousand Colored Men in Uncle Sam's Employ," *WES*, November 6, 1897, 21.

68. Number based on records compiled by the Tuskegee Institute.

69. For the discriminatory use of a race-neutral framework, see Mack, "Law, Society, Identity," 380; and Omori, "Race-Neutral Individualism." For the ways in which an ethic of race-blindness could actually lead to blindness to discrimination, see Cuba's color-blind doctrine of the same era. Helg, *Our Rightful Share*; De La Fuente, *Nation for All*.

70. Watkins, "Draw Good Salaries," 21.

71. The 2,785 number did not include Navy Yard workers. In 1907, there were about 25,000 federal workers in D.C., with some 13,000 working in white-collar positions

(about 10,000 classified at the clerical grade). In 1912, Monroe Work estimated the number of black employees outside of D.C. to be about 12,000. U.S. Bureau of the Census, *Bulletin 94*, table 45, p. 64; Work, *Negro Year Book, 1912*, 71–72.

72. "A Worthy Promotion," *WB*, November 1, 1902, 1.

73. That Washington itself was a special destination was illustrated by the fact that while black professional, technical, and scientific appointees made up just 0.3 percent of black employees outside the District, they made up 1.5 percent in Washington. In general, black workers in D.C. were slightly more likely to hold white-collar positions than out in the field. All of these numbers were small, of course, but they constituted an important portion of educated black Americans, and they spoke to the concentration in Washington. U.S. Bureau of the Census, *Bulletin 94*, table 45, p. 64.

74. Jesse J. Porter to Bureau of Engraving and Printing Director, April 2, 1907, Jesse J. Porter, PF NPRC. Steven Mintz has determined that although most came from nearby states, in "1910, 56.2 percent of the District's black population had been born elsewhere." Mintz, "Historical Ethnography," 237.

75. Civil servants were appointed from specific states in order to follow apportionment rules set out by the 1883 Pendleton Act. Of all D.C. workers, white and black, 50 percent came from the South Atlantic portion of the United States, which included Delaware, Maryland, D.C., Virginia, West Virginia, the Carolinas, Georgia, and Florida. U.S. Bureau of the Census, *Bulletin 94*, table 90, p. 139.

76. "Public Men and Things," *WB*, October 15, 1910, 1.

77. Lyman Gage to Thomas H. R. Clarke, February 9, 1901; Thomas H. R. Clarke Employee Questionnaire, January 14, 1901; Hosea B. Moulton to Lyman Gage, March 19, 1901; all in Thomas H. R. Clarke, PF NPRC.

78. Division of Appointments Chief to Robert A. Pelham, February 1, 1929, Robert A. Pelham, PF NPRC; Simmons, *Men of Mark*, 1023.

79. Robert A. Pelham, Personal Information Sheet, Department of Commerce and Labor, June 30, 1904, Robert A. Pelham, PF NPRC. For Pelham and the American Negro Academy, see Moss, *American Negro Academy*, 222–24.

80. Swan M. Kendrick to Ruby Moyse, July 2, 1912, box 2, folder 6, KBFP.

81. McNeil, *Groundwork*, 19, 24–25; John Tweedale to William L. Houston, July 3, 1891, and May 11, 1893, box 17, folder 1, WLHFP.

82. "Congressional Lyceum," *WB*, May 13, 1899, 5; "Messrs. Vernon and Houston," 1; John Dancy to William L. Houston, January 29, 1909, box 10, folder 5, WLHFP; Robert H. Terrell to William L. Houston, April 6, 1906, box 10, folder 3, WLHFP.

83. McNeil, *Groundwork*, 31.

84. Ibid., 49; Marshall quoted in ibid., 3.

85. "Colored Army Officer," *WB*, May 19, 1917, 1; "Messenger for War Department Dies," *WES*, April 21, 1928, in John A. Davis, PF NPRC.

86. Post Office Department Auditor to Assistant Secretary Andrew, December 9, 1911, Shelby Davidson, PF NPRC; "Shelby Davidson," box MS 83-1228, folder 1, Shelby Davidson Papers, MSRC; Fouché, *Black Inventors*, 125–76.

87. L. Walker, "Struggles and Attempts," 174–75.

88. Green, *Washington*, 130.

89. Harley, "Black Women," 59.

90. "Negroes Not Wanted," *WB*, February 23, 1901, 1; "One Victim of Race Riot," *WP*, December 17, 1910, 11; Lessoff, *Nation and Its City*, 195.

91. Masur, *Example for All the Land*, 194; Lessoff, *Nation and Its City*, 101–29.

92. While women made up about 30 percent of all white government workers, fewer than 25 percent of black workers were women. U.S. Bureau of the Census, *Bulletin 94*, table 45, p. 64.

93. Harley, "For the Good of Family and Race," 340–41; Harley, "Black Women," 62–63, 67. For the work of most black women in D.C., see Clark-Lewis, *Living In, Living Out*.

94. In 1890, 20 percent of African Americans lived in urban areas. That number would rise to 49 percent in 1940. Clark-Lewis, "'This Work Had a End,'" 199; U.S. Bureau of the Census, *Social and Economic Status*, table 6, p. 14.

95. Gillette, *Between Justice and Beauty*, 78–79.

96. Mallalieu, "Washington Alley"; Gillette, *Between Justice and Beauty*, 116.

97. Borchert, *Alley Life*; Harrison, *Congress*, 130; T. Jones, "Alley Homes," 68–69; Riis, "Housing Problem," 163.

98. U.S. Bureau of the Census, *Bulletin 94*, table 45, p. 64. A 1911 article in the *Star* estimated the cost of living for a family of four in Washington to be about $2,000 a year. Many government clerks were living quite well on less money, and the article's bias was in favor of raising salaries for civil servants. "Pay of the Clerks: Commission at Work to Ascertain the Average Salary; Cost of Living Today," *WES*, September 21, 1911, 4.

99. Clerical grades in the federal government that denoted white-collar workers would be changed several times between the 1840s and 1920s. At the turn of the twentieth century, minor clerk grades were denoted by letters, from A to E, and regular clerical grades began at 1. Baruch, *Position-Classification*, 6, 18.

100. Friedman and Schwartz, *Monetary History of the United States*, 91, 135, 189; Jacobs, *Pocketbook Politics*, 15; Rauchway, "High Cost of Living."

101. Capers F. Rogers to James L. Wilmeth, February 1, 1913, Capers F. Rogers, PF NPRC.

102. Leupp, *How to Prepare*, 105; Baruch, *Position-Classification*, 34.

103. "Health of Clerks Suffers," *WES*, January 25, 1908, 9.

104. "Government Office Conditions," *Civil Service Advocate*, February 1914, 918–19.

105. "Noise in Offices Fatigues Workers," *WES*, December 30, 1913, 11.

106. "A Clerk" to Dear Sir, July 16, 1912; W. H. Hathaway to Mrs. T. N. McLaughlin, May 20, 1912; both in box 3, Charlotte Hopkins Papers, LC.

107. "Government Slavery," *WB*, November 6, 1909, 4; "No Increase for Women; Director Ralph Sees No Chance for $2 Scale of Wages," *WES*, April 2, 1909, 2.

108. Rung, *Servants of the State*, 35, 39; H. Walker, "Period Prior to the World War," 71.

109. "Jim Crow Air," *WB*, March 7, 1908, 5.

110. Robert E. Coleman to Hon. Charles Neill, December 20, 1910 [received], entry 21, box 1, Correspondence Regarding Job Applications, 1905–1919, Records of the Department of Commerce and Labor, RG 257, NARA; G. W. W. Hangar to George C. Havenner, January 6, 1911, ibid.

111. *WB*, December 30, 1882, 2; "Our Public Printer," *WB*, May 26, 1894, 2; *WB*, November 19, 1898, 4; "Government Printing Office," *WB*, March 25, 1911, 4.

112. Ernest J. Dillon to F. A. Vanderlip, July 6, 1898, entry 208, box 1, Correspondence of the Appointments Division, 1874–1912, GRDTDA.

113. Two letters I came across asked the recipient to "settle a bet." Division of Appointments Chief to John Z. Crook, July 15, 1904, ibid.; Fred S. Hazard to Ellis H. Roberts, September 14, 1905, entry 208, ibid.; Lewis H. Blair to Secretary of the Treasury, October 25, 1910, entry 207, box 6, Appointment Division, Misc. Correspondence, Office Files, 1910–1912, ibid.

114. Hall, originally from Illinois, was appointed to a permanent clerkship in the Census Bureau in 1900 and quickly earned promotion. He eventually produced groundbreaking statistical studies of black America, but he encountered racial barriers all along the way. Efficiency Report, Charles E. Hall, May 15, 1911, CEHP. For more on Hall's statistical work, see F. Wilson, *Segregated Scholars*, 131.

115. Charles E. Hall to John W. Langley, January 22, 1903, CEHP.

116. Memorandum, Census Bureau, Appointment Division, October 24, 1904, ibid.

117. Unsigned [most likely Census Director S. N. D. North] to Senator Albert Jarvis Hopkins, March 16, 1907, ibid.

118. "Washington and Its Inter-Lopers," *WB*, August 17, 1901, 4.

119. "Public Men And Things," *WB*, November 5, 1910, 1.

120. Williams wrote his novel in 1925–26. E. Williams, *When Washington Was in Vogue*, 48.

121. Twain and Warner, *Gilded Age*. For more on Washington's white elite society in the late nineteenth century, see Low, "Society in Washington"; and Jacob, *Capital Elites*.

122. Dunbar, "Negro Society in Washington."

123. Kathleen Ann Clark, *Defining Moments*, 141.

124. J. Logan, *Thirty Years in Washington*, 521.

125. Gaines, *Uplifting the Race*, 118.

126. Swan M. Kendrick to Ruby Moyse, September 27, 1915, box 4, folder 5, KBFP.

127. Terrell, "Society among the Colored People," 152. Political scientist Adolph Reed has noted that one important result of disfranchisement was the loss of a political voice that required much less capital than patronage, a parade, or even a newspaper. A. Reed, "Study of Black Politics," 108. For more on elite black Americans and their relations to poorer people, see Gaines, *Uplifting the Race*; Higginbotham, *Righteous Discontent*.

128. Gilmore, *Gender and Jim Crow*, 21; Hale, *Making Whiteness*, 137.

129. "No Rest for the Negro," *WB*, May 2, 1891, 2.

130. Belle C. La Follette, "The Color Line," *La Follette's Magazine*, August 23, 1913, 3.

131. Bruce, *Archibald Grimké*, 80.

132. Harley, "For the Good of Family," 340–41; Clark-Lewis, *Living In, Living Out*, 128. See also Clark-Lewis, "'This Work Had a End,'" 199; and Harley, "Black Women," 74.

133. Weiner, "Class Structure," 979; Litwack, *Trouble in Mind*, 114–16, 121; Terrell, "Society among the Colored People," 152; Kenzer, *Enterprising Southerners*, 9–34. See also U.S. Bureau of the Census, *Social and Economic Status*, table 96, p. 137.

134. U.S. Bureau of the Census, *Statistical History*, 168; Kocka, *White Collar Workers*, 176.

135. Merritt O. Chance to Civil Service Commission, March 20, 1915, Henry Hood, PF NPRC; Thirteenth Census of the United States, 1910, District of Columbia, E.D. 57; Twelfth Census of the United States, 1900, District of Columbia, E.D. 57; both available at http://www.ancestry.com.

136. The Hoods' single-income family was unusual not only among African Americans but also among most Americans in general at the turn of the twentieth century. J. Jones, *Labor of Love*, 112. For more on the occupational status of black women in this period, see Harley, "When Your Work Is Not Who You Are"; and Blumin, *Emergence of the Middle Class*, 290.

137. Swan M. Kendrick to Ruby Moyse, August 8, 1912, box 2, folder 6, KBFP.

138. Jacqueline M. Moore, *Leading the Race*, 132–33.

139. Sources like Monroe Work's *Negro Year Book*, a Tuskegee Institute publication, counted blacks in departmental service in 1912 at over 2,800 with gross yearly earnings of $1,263,985. Those working outside Washington earned another $7 million. Similar figures appeared each year in Work's publication, though the numbers were often rough and unreliable, since it was politically advantageous for Tuskegee and the Republican Party to exaggerate their patronage power. Work, *Negro Year Book, 1912*, 71–72; Woodruff, *American Congo*, 30; Daniel, *Shadow of Slavery*, 11.

140. Swan M. Kendrick to Ruby Moyse, July 30, 1914, box 5, folder 4, KBFP; Kocka, *White Collar Workers*, 130; Benson, *Counter Cultures*, 271; Hale, *Making Whiteness*, 125, 205; Baldwin, *Chicago's New Negroes*.

141. On consumption as "symbolic capital," see Scott Schaffer, "Hegemony and the Habitus," 38; Veblen, *Theory of the Leisure Class*; and Bourdieu, *Distinction*.

142. Jackson Lears describes how the supposedly moralistic Victorian views of consumption gained elasticity as one went up the class scale. Lears, *Rebirth of a Nation*, 78.

143. James L. Wilmeth to Saks and Company, June 6, 1913, Edward L. Scott, PF NPRC.

144. Historian Margaret Rung has noted that the American system, at least early on, was loaded with "humanity." Rung, *Servants of the State*, 20.

145. Thomas H. R. Clarke to Charles Lyman, March 23, 1901, Thomas H. R. Clarke, PF NPRC; "Several Suits for Divorce," *WP*, April 24, 1901, 10; Mrs. Lucille P. Clarke to Lyman Gage, May 31, 1901, Thomas H. R. Clarke, PF NPRC. On black Washingtonians' frequent use of divorce courts, see Penningroth, "African American Divorce."

146. Richard W. Tompkins to E. P. Seeds, November 6, 1902, Richard W. Tompkins, PF NPRC.

147. Less famous civil servants were also on the board, such as Jerome A. Johnson. Johnson had been a Treasury clerk since 1869 and, by 1888, was able to invest some of his $1,400 salary. Jerome A. Johnson, PF NPRC.

148. Charles R. Douglass et al. to Theodore Roosevelt, June 17, 1903, Richard W. Tompkins, PF NPRC; M. Sammye Miller, "Early Venture in Black Capitalism," 362–63; "The Capital Savings Bank," *WB*, January 24, 1903, 1; Jacqueline M. Moore, *Leading the Race*, 138–39; Schweninger, *Black Property Owners*, 222; Fitzpatrick and Goodwin, *Guide to Black Washington*, 213–14.

149. Aron, *Ladies and Gentlemen*, 23. For civil service employees owning property in Washington, D.C., see Borchert, *Alley Life*, 37.

150. Smith, *Washington at Home*, 12; Mitchell, *Righteous Propagation*, 150; U.S. Bureau of the Census, *Social and Economic Status*, table 96, p. 137; U.S. Bureau of the Census, "Historical Census."

151. Schweninger, *Black Property Owners*, 203–4.

152. Mitchell, *Righteous Propagation*, 142–44, 148; Lears, *Rebirth of a Nation*, 78.

153. More specifically, the concentration was north of O Street, south of W Street, and bounded on the east and west by 16th Street and New Jersey Avenue, respectively. For a map of Washington, D.C., showing the homes of black government workers, see E. Yellin, "In the Nation's Service," 52.

154. Marcia M. Greenlee, "Shaw: Heart of Black Washington," in Smith, *Washington at Home*, 120.

155. Linda Wheeler, "Dupont Circle: Fashionable In-Town Address," in Smith, *Washington at Home*, 113–14; Ronald M. Johnson, "LeDroit Park: Premier Black Community," in Smith, *Washington at Home*, 143–44.

156. In 1966, the area was officially named Shaw, after the school district of Shaw Junior High School. Greenlee, "Shaw," 119.

157. Fitzpatrick, "Shaw," 9; Greenlee, "Shaw," 121.

158. Fitzpatrick, "Shaw," 57; Jacqueline M. Moore, *Leading the Race*, 136; H. Cohen, *Duke Ellington's America*, 12–13.

CHAPTER 2

1. Foner, *Reconstruction*, 105–6.

2. Saville, *Work of Reconstruction*, 167; Richard M. Valelly, "National Parties and Racial Disenfranchisement," in Paul E. Peterson, *Classifying by Race*, 210–11; Walton, *Black Republicans*, 22.

3. Dailey, *Before Jim Crow*, 4; Perman, *Struggle for Mastery*, 37–38.

4. Douglass quoted in McPherson, "Grant or Greeley?," 50; Judson W. Lyons to Albert W. Washington, August 21, 1899, series 1, reel 7, William McKinley Papers, LC.

5. A. H. Holt to Walter Evans, March 27, 1884, William H. Haynes, PF NPRC.

6. "'Spoilsmen,'" *WP*, March 17, 1897, 6. The *Bee* reprinted portions of the *Post*'s editorial approvingly in its edition: "'Spoilsmen,'" *WB*, March 20, 1897, 4.

7. Stephen Skowronek has demonstrated the continued power of political patronage long after the creation of the competitive civil service and well into the twentieth century. Skowronek, *Building a New American State*, 191–92, 194.

8. Lyons to Washington, August 21, 1899.

9. Fish, "Lincoln and the Patronage," 56–57; Fish, *Civil Service*, 171.

10. Donald, *Lincoln Reconsidered*, 174; Foner, *Fiery Trial*, 193; Silberman, *Cages of Reason*, 250.

11. The 1883 Pendleton Act outlawed "mandatory" assessment, meaning that patronage recipients still "voluntarily" paid back to the party. Johnson and Libecap, *Federal Civil Service System*, 4; Skowronek, *Building a New American State*, 66.

12. Callcott, *Negro in Maryland*, 71.

13. "They Say," *WB*, November 19, 1892, 2.

14. L. White, *Republican Era*, 197.

15. Historians have sometimes called these years the second phase of black suffrage, when constitutional disfranchisement had yet to be imposed and black southerners who could withstand other forms of voter manipulation were still part of the electorate. Perman, *Struggle for Mastery*, 10–11.

16. Shaffer, *After the Glory*, 119.

17. Ibid., 120–31; Russell L. Johnson, "'Great Injustice.'" See also Theda Skocpol, "African Americans in U.S. Social Policy," in Paul E. Peterson, *Classifying by Race*, 131, 137.

18. McMurry, "Bureau of Pensions," 343–44.

19. Skowronek, *Building a New American State*, 66; Rung, *Servants of the State*, 12.

20. Hahn, *Nation under Our Feet*, 385.

21. James T. Moore, "Black Militancy," 172.

22. Dailey, *Before Jim Crow*, 67; revenue collector quoted in Hahn, *Nation under Our Feet*, 384.

23. Dailey, *Before Jim Crow*, 68, 141; Mark Wahlgren Summers, *Rum, Romanism*, 248. For the decline of fusionism in North Carolina and Louisiana, see Gilmore, *Gender and Jim Crow*, 119–46; and Perman, *Struggle for Mastery*, 124–72.

24. Dailey, *Before Jim Crow*, 57.

25. Hathorn, "C. Bascom Slemp," 248.

26. Wang, *Trial of Democracy*, 232.

27. Lynch, *Facts of Reconstruction*, 249–50, 280. For Cleveland's relationship with black Democrats, see C. H. J. Taylor to Grover Cleveland, November 28, 1884, series 2, reel 2, and March 30, 1888, series 3, reel 120, Grover Cleveland Papers, LC.

28. "The Government Printing Office," *WB*, July 21, 1888, 2; Fish, *Civil Service*, 222; Sproat, "*Best Men*," 265–66.

29. E. L. Godkin, "The Negro's Claim to Office," *The Nation*, August 1, 1867, 90–91; Fish, *Civil Service*, 222; Socolofsky and Spetter, *Presidency of Benjamin Harrison*, 32; Sproat, "*Best Men*," 258, 268.

30. Fish, *Civil Service*, 226. On Clarkson's career as a patronage impresario, see Skowronek, *Building a New American State*, 75; "Genl J. S. Clarkson in the South," *WB*, May 2, 1891, 3; and Cuney-Hare, *Norris Wright Cuney*, iii–xv.

31. Gatewood, "Theodore Roosevelt," 49; McMillen, *Dark Journey*, 61.

32. Socolofsky and Spetter, *Presidency of Benjamin Harrison*, 34, 38–39; Van Riper, *History of the United States Civil Service*, 228; Skowronek, *Building a New American State*, 75.

33. "Against the Negro," *WB*, September 19, 1891, 2.

34. Kousser, *Shaping of Southern Politics*, 21–22; Wang, *Trial of Democracy*, xvii–xviii, 233, 244, 257–61; Perman, *Struggle for Mastery*, 43–45; Socolofsky and Spetter, *Presidency of Benjamin Harrison*, 60.

35. For example, John R. Lynch told George Cortelyou that the sure way to deliver Maryland votes was to appoint a black surgeon to an army post in the state. Cortelyou undermined the threat by suggesting that the appointment would actually be better after the election. John R. Lynch to George B. Cortelyou, August 22, 1904, and September 13, 1904, both enclosed in George B. Cortelyou to Theodore Roosevelt, December 13, 1904, series 1, reel 47, Theodore Roosevelt Papers, LC.

36. Kousser, *Shaping of Southern Politics*, 38, 224; Valelly, "National Parties and Racial Disenfranchisement," 189–92.

37. Casdorph, *Republicans, Negroes, and Progressives*, 11, 55–56, 111; McMillen, *Dark Journey*, 58; Sherman, *Republican Party*, 19–20, 119–120; Walton, *Black Republicans*, 43–46, 170–76; Hahn, *Nation under Our Feet*, 385–87. For more on black party leaders in the South, see some of the underappreciated state-level studies produced before 1980, such as Callcott, *Negro in Maryland*; Bunie, *Negro in Virginia*; Lamon, *Black Tennesseans*; Holt, *Black Over White*.

38. "Call a Halt Mr. Director," *WB*, March 23, 1907, 1. Nominating power could be double-edged, of course, and black Republicans were expected to toe the correct line as carefully as any party operative. For example, the powerful head of the Texas Republicans, Norris Wright Cuney, lost control of his delegation when he failed to back McKinley in 1896. Still, Cuney was replaced by another black Republican. Casdorph, "Norris Wright Cuney," 461–63. See also Tera W. Hunter's introduction to Cuney-Hare, *Norris Wright Cuney*, xxii–xxiv.

39. "The Week in Society," *WB*, March 6, 1897, 5; "The Inaugural Banquet," *WB*, March 13, 1897, 5; "The Afro-American Press," *WB*, March 13, 1897, 4.

40. Lears, *Rebirth of a Nation*, 13; Perman, *Struggle for Mastery*, 118–19; Blight, *Race and Reunion*, 351–52; Valelly, *Two Reconstructions*, 131–34, 138; Painter, *Standing at Armageddon*, 146–47; Feimster, *Southern Horrors*, 223; "The Week in Society," *WB*, March 12, 1898, 5; "False Patriotism," *WB*, March 19, 1898, 4.

41. Holt, *Black Over White*, 218.

42. "Colored Solons: Afro-Americans Who Have Served in Congress," *WES*, February 8, 1890, 7; G. Reid, "Four in Black," 230.

43. Thomas M. Dent, PF NPRC; Walton, *Black Republicans*, 51; Harlan, *Booker T. Washington Papers*, 4:122.

44. Bacote, "Negro Officeholders," 225, 232–33.

45. Dancy was recommended by North Carolina's outgoing Republican senator, J. C. Pritchard. "At the White House; Dancy of North Carolina to Succeed Cheatham," *WES*, December 19, 1901, 1; Harlan, *Wizard of Tuskegee*, 17–18.

46. Dancy, *Sand against the Wind*, 60, 74.

47. Judson W. Lyons to George B. Cortelyou, August 22, 1899, series 1, reel 7, William McKinley Papers, LC.

48. P. D. Barker to Charles D. Hilles, June 29, 1912, file 190, reel 372, WHTP.

49. The *Bee* noted that Roosevelt reappointed McKinley appointee Judson Lyons because of Lyons's power over southern delegates at the Republican National Convention. "Roosevelt in 1904," *WB*, March 15, 1902, 1.

50. Henry P. Cheatham to George B. Cortelyou, October 8, 1900, series 1, reel 13, William McKinley Papers, LC.

51. Theda Skocpol, "Bringing the State Back In: Strategies of Analysis in Current Research," in Evans, Rueschemeyer, and Skocpol, *Bringing the State Back In*, 9.

52. As a crusading civil service commissioner in the 1890s, a young Theodore Roosevelt declared that as far as "discrimination on the ground of color" went, "there is no provision of the law or rules allowing the Commission to take cognizance of discrimination exercised for this reason." However, he recommended that such cases be inves-

tigated and that the president be notified of them. Theodore Roosevelt to the Civil Service Commission, January 24, 1894, in Morison, *Letters of Theodore Roosevelt*, 1:352–57.

53. Mayers, *Federal Service*, 20–22, 145–48.

54. U.S. Bureau of the Census, *Bulletin 94*, table 90, p. 139.

55. Fish, *Civil Service*, 224, 228; Census Director to Rep. A. J. Hopkins, January 26, 1900, CEHP.

56. The Pendleton Civil Service Reform Act of 1883 was named for Democratic senator "Gentleman George" Pendleton of Ohio, who was widely presumed to have bought his Senate seat. The text, however, was mostly written by longtime Republican reformer Dorman Eaton. Mark Wahlgren Summers, *Rum, Romanism*, 111; Skowronek, *Building a New American State*, 64; Mosher, *Basic Documents*, 47.

57. Rung, *Servants of the State*, 6–10; Skowronek, *Building a New American State*, 47. See also Butler, *Critical Americans*, 191–200; and Hoogenboom, *Outlawing the Spoils*.

58. Leupp, *How to Prepare*, 325–50; Foltz, *Federal Civil Service*, 45; Kaufman, "Growth of the Federal Personnel System," 40–43.

59. Silberman, *Cages of Reason*, 260.

60. Ben Franklin Caldwell to Henry T. Brian, April 24, 1908, Raymond Fisher, PF NPRC; Jesse Overstreet to Samuel B. Donnelly, January 21, 1909, ibid.

61. J. R. Burton to Binger Hermann, September 20, 1902, Charles Barker, PF NPRC; Charles Curtis to Binger Hermann, September 25, 1902, ibid.

62. The Civil Service Commission itself was understaffed and held no real power over dismissals or tenure, and numerous administrative loopholes and workarounds were maintained, such as abolishing old positions and creating new ones, reinstating former employees, and executive orders. Fish, *Civil Service*, 238; Skowronek, *Building a New American State*, 81; Mayers, *Federal Service*, 52, 465; Silberman, *Cages of Reason*, 259; Rung, *Servants of the State*, 34; H. Walker, "Period Prior to the World War," 68.

63. Fish, *Civil Service*, 229; Mayers, *Federal Service*, 72.

64. Chief Clerk to Division of Appointments Secretary of the Treasury, February 8, 1904, Maria Johnson, PF NPRC.

65. Spero, "Employer and Employee," 182.

66. John A. Davis, PF NPRC.

67. Swan M. Kendrick to Ruby Moyse, January 26, 1916, box 5, folder 7, KBFP.

68. Mayers, *Federal Service*, 148.

69. Swan M. Kendrick to Ruby Moyse, February 5, 1916, box 4, folder 8, KBFP.

70. Karen Haltunnen notes that manipulation became increasingly important as impersonal management practices became standard in modern business in the late nineteenth century. Halttunen, *Confidence Men*, 206–10.

71. Roosevelt, "Object Lesson"; Fish, *Civil Service*, 236.

72. Shefter, "Party and Patronage," 413; Heclo, *Government of Strangers*, 49; Silberman, *Cages of Reason*, 231–32; Mosher, *Democracy and the Public Service*, 67.

73. Harlan, *Wizard of Tuskegee*, 351.

74. Roosevelt's narrowing of the patronage was pitched as a race-neutral reform, though one can easily see in it the beginning of a removal of Republican interest in forcing the race issue in the South. Gatewood, "Theodore Roosevelt," 50.

75. "The Southern Politician," *WB*, November 23, 1901, 4; Morris, *Theodore Rex*, 39;

Scheiner, "President Theodore Roosevelt," 172; Justesen, *Broken Brotherhood*, 98–99; Norrell, *Up from History*, 238–39; Harlan, *Making of a Black Leader*, 261; Harlan, *Wizard of Tuskegee*, 8, 28.

76. Casdorph, *Republicans, Negroes, and Progressives*, 5; Gatewood, "William D. Crum."

77. Booker T. Washington, "Atlanta Exposition Address," in Harlan, *Booker T. Washington Papers*, 3:583–87.

78. Harlan, *Making of a Black Leader*, 254, 262.

79. Booker T. Washington to James S. Clarkson, September 15, 1902, series 1, reel 29, Theodore Roosevelt Papers, LC. Clarkson forwarded the letter directly to the White House. James Clarkson to William Loeb Jr., September 16, 1902, ibid. "Mr. Roosevelt and the Colored Voter," *WB*, November 15, 1902, 1; "The President Acts: The Enemies of the Negro Removed," *WB*, November 15, 1902, 1.

80. Emmett J. Scott to Charles D. Hilles, July 8, 1910, file 1928, reel 423, WHTP.

81. Chase, "'Honey for Friends,'" 108–83. See also Thornbrough, "American Negro Newspapers," 472.

82. Booker T. Washington to Philander Chase Knox, October 24, 1901, in Harlan, *Booker T. Washington Papers*, 6:266–67.

83. Theodore Roosevelt to V. H. Metcalf, January 26, 1905, William S. Fuller, PF NPRC; Executive Order of the President, January 6, 1905, ibid.

84. Gerstle, *American Crucible*, 13–43, 62–64; Painter, *History of White People*, 245–50.

85. Mayers, *Federal Service*, 161; Skowronek, *Politics Presidents Make*, 10, 234; Silberman, *Cages of Reason*, 275; Theodore Roosevelt to James Adgar Smyth, November 26, 1902, in Morison, *Letters of Theodore Roosevelt*, 3:383–85; Dyer, *Theodore Roosevelt*, 91–92, 96–98; Theodore Roosevelt to Albion W. Tourgée, November 8, 1901, in Morison, *Letters of Theodore Roosevelt*, 3:190–91; Morris, *Theodore Rex*, 52–58.

86. Lyman Gage to Thomas H. R. Clarke, February 9, 1901; Thomas H. R. Clarke Employee Questionnaire, January 14, 1901; Joseph C. Sibley to M. E. Ailes, June 19, 1902; Judson W. Lyons to Secretary of the Treasury, June 30, 1902; Judson W. Lyons to J. H. Edwards, January 16, 1906; J. H. Edwards to Charles Lyman, May 31, 1906; Committee on Personnel to Division of Appointments, November 16, 1906; all in Thomas H. R. Clarke, PF NPRC.

87. Judson W. Lyons to W. R. Merriam, July 1, 1902, Thomas M. Dent, PF NPRC.

88. "Auditor Tyler," *WB*, November 4, 1911, 1.

89. Crowder, *John Edward Bruce*, 70–73.

90. W. H. Love, L. M. Ferguson, and O. W. Dudley to Theodore Roosevelt, April 24, 1902, William Jennifer, PF NPRC.

91. Memorandum to Director of the Census, May 23, 1902, William Jennifer, PF NPRC.

92. James S. Clarkson to S. N. D. North, May 20, 1903, William Jennifer, PF NPRC; John Dancy to William R. Merriam, June 18, 1902, ibid.

93. Higginbotham, *Righteous Discontent*, 14; Gaines, *Uplifting the Race*, 209–33.

94. Brown, "Negotiating and Transforming"; A. Reed Jr., "Study of Black Politics," 111.

95. "The Election," *WB*, November 11, 1916, 4.

96. "Parents' League and Married Teachers," *WB*, May 1, 1920, 1.

97. Laura Joiner, PF NPRC; "Bethel Literary," *WB*, March 2, 1907, 1; Fannie Chase, PF NPRC.

98. Ralph Tyler to Booker T. Washington, December 1, 1901, series 1, reel 22, Theodore Roosevelt Papers, LC; Booker T. Washington to Theodore Roosevelt, December 8, 1901, ibid.

CHAPTER 3

1. Cuney-Hare, *Norris Wright Cuney*, xii–xiv.

2. "The Solidity of the South; A Significant Speech by Secretary Taft," *WES*, July 10, 1906, 8.

3. The most recent evidence suggests that none of the soldiers were involved in any shootings that night. D. Lewis, *W. E. B. Du Bois*, 651 (n. 65); Gaines, *Uplifting the Race*, 63–64; Thornbrough, "Brownsville Episode," 470. For a detailed narrative of Roosevelt's decision, see Morris, *Theodore Rex*, 462–73.

4. Calvin Chase, "Open Letter," *WB*, December 29, 1906, 1; Thornbrough, "Brownsville Episode," 471, 473. Louis Harlan credits Brownsville with pushing T. Thomas Fortune and other former Tuskegee allies away from Roosevelt and Washington. Harlan, *Wizard of Tuskegee*, 320.

5. Thornbrough, "Brownsville Episode," 473; Gaines, *Uplifting the Race*, 63.

6. "Dr. Du Bois Honored," *WB*, March 2, 1907, 5.

7. "Second Baptist," *WB*, March 9, 1907, 5.

8. Sherman, *Republican Party*, 68–70; "At the White House: Colored Man Appointed Auditor," *WES*, April 11, 1907, 2; "May Aid Gov. Hughes," *WES*, April 17, 1907, 1; *WES*, March 20, 1908, 6.

9. Washington spoke to a crowd of 3,000 at the elite-led Metropolitan AME Church in March 1908. "Booker T. Washington," *WB*, March 28, 1908, 1.

10. "Taft to the South; No More Appointments to Get Convention Votes," *WES*, January 16, 1909, section 1, p. 5; Casdorph, *Republicans, Negroes, and Progressives*, 6–7.

11. Taft's administrators had also labored to ensure that Napier's predecessor, William T. Vernon, a black Republican from Kansas, had a soft landing into a decent position back home, though Vernon's falling out with Tuskegee doomed any such efforts. Horace H. Lurton to William Howard Taft, March 14, 1910; R. F. Boyd, MD, to William Howard Taft, October 13, 1910; Charles Curtis to William Howard Taft, September 16, 1910; Charles Curtis to Charles D. Norton, September 28, 1910; all in file 2563, reel 342, WHTP.

12. "Register of the Treasury," *WB*, March 18, 1911, 1.

13. William Steuart to R. N. Pindell Jr., December 9, 1909, CEHP.

14. Roosevelt had earlier appointed Lewis U.S. district attorney in Boston. "Wm. H. Lewis to Accept Recess Appointment," *WES*, March 20, 1911, 10; Omori, "Race-Neutral Individualism," 39–40.

15. William H. Taft, "The Winning of the South, Delivered January 15, 1909," in Burton, *Collected Works*, 2:177; "Taft to the South," 5.

16. "Mr. Taft Gives Definite Promise," *Atlanta Constitution*, January 17, 1909, A4.

17. State of South Carolina, General Assembly, *Concurrent Resolution H. 561*, 403–4.

18. "Caste and Anti-Caste," *The Nation*, December 4, 1902, 436; "Right of Negroes to Hold Office," *The Independent*, December 4, 1902, 2855–56; "Dr. Crum Resigns His Post," *WES*, March 2, 1909, 10; Harlan, *Wizard of Tuskegee*, 19–24, 338; Gatewood, "William D. Crum," 318–19; Memorandum to White House Files, April 13, 1912, file 2452, reel 431, WHTP. Crum returned to the United States to die in 1915. "Public Men and Things," *WB*, November 6, 1915, 2.

19. The transfer required an order from Taft because postmasters were appointees, not members of the civil service, and could not simply be moved to a clerkship in an executive department. Richardson, a Republican, had not managed to hold onto his postmastership under the Democratic administrations of Grover Cleveland, but he had otherwise served continuously since the 1870s. William Howard Taft to Executive Order 1388, July 31, 1911; M. O. Chance to Postmaster General, April 19, 1913; Frank Hitchcock to Memorandum, August 12, 1911; all in Thomas Richardson, PF NPRC; McMillen, *Dark Journey*, 63.

20. Ralph W. Tyler to Charles D. Hilles, August 17, 1911, file 190, reel 372, WHTP.

21. Ibid.

22. "Puzzle over Queries," *WES*, August 10, 1909, 4; Logan, "Taft's Program of Economy Approved by Business Kings," *WP*, January 1, 1911, 13; "Taft Is Criticized," *WES*, February 26, 1911, 2; Skowronek, *Building a New American State*, 163.

23. Franklin MacVeagh to Charles D. Hilles, August 24, 1911, file 424, reel 1955, WHTP; Rung, *Servants of the State*, 31; Skowronek, *Building a New American State*, 189.

24. "End Treasury Jobs," *WP*, December 24, 1911, 1; "Postal Employe[e]s Dismissed," *WP*, August 28, 1912, 4; "P.O. Clerks in Revolt; Women Organize to Expose Auditor's 'Sweat Shop,'" *WP*, January 8, 1913, 3.

25. May Childs Nerney to Woodrow Wilson, September 30, 1913, box 129, RWPP.

26. "No Increase for Women; Director Ralph Sees No Chance for $2 Scale of Wages," *WES*, April 2, 1909, 2; "Politics in Shake-Up," *WES*, June 29, 1909, 1; "Government Slavery," *WB*, November 6, 1909, 4.

27. Emmett J. Scott to Charles D. Hilles, July 8, 1910; Charles Cuney to Charles D. Hilles, July 27, 1911; Post Office Department Auditor to Assistant Secretary of the Treasury, August 5, 1911; all in file 1928, reel 423, WHTP.

28. J. C. Napier to Charles D. Hilles, August 28, 1911; Charles Cuney to Charles D. Hilles, November 16, 1912; Charles Cuney to Charles D. Hilles, December 6, 1912; all in ibid.

29. Some scholars have found that black civil service overall declined after 1908. Sherman, *Republican Party*, 68; King, *Separate and Unequal*, 7, 47.

30. "Civil Service," *The Crisis*, May 1911, 21.

31. "Along the Color Line — Political," *The Crisis*, February 1912, 141.

32. "Don't Be Deceived," *WB*, November 19, 1910, 4.

33. "The Jew and the Negro," *WB*, March 5, 1910, 4; "Happy Land," *WB*, March 12, 1910, 4; "An Open Letter," *WB*, May 28, 1910, 1; "Negroes Attack Taft," *WES*, July 20, 1910, 16.

34. Gould, *William Howard Taft*, 131, xiii.

35. Addressing a petition demanding antilynching legislation from a cohort of black

civil rights organizations, Taft explained, "I cannot send a special message to Congress, and ask Congress to do what it has no power to do." William Howard Taft to White House Memorandum, May 31, 1911, file 1568, reel 418, WHTP; Anderson, *William Howard Taft*, 94.

36. Ralph W. Tyler to William Howard Taft, February 9, 1912, file 190, reel 372, WHTP.

37. Ralph W. Tyler et al., "Memorandum to the President," February 9, 1912, ibid.

38. Waldron and Harkless, *Political Situation*, 25; Fox, *Guardian of Boston*, 146.

39. Booker T. Washington to Theodore Roosevelt, January 24, 1903, series 1, reel 32, Theodore Roosevelt Papers, LC.

40. "Mr. Bryan and the Negro," *WES*, September 29, 1908, 6.

41. Adam E. Patterson to Woodrow Wilson, July 30, 1913, *PWW*, 28:97–98. According to Bryan biographer Michael Kazin, Bryan had even been willing to work with anti-Tuskegee blacks in the North. Kazin, *Godly Hero*, 93.

42. About 100,000 black southerners moved to Oklahoma between 1890 and 1910. William G. McAdoo to Woodrow Wilson, July 18, 1913, entry 228, box 155, General Records of the Department of the Treasury, Records Relating to Presidential Appointments and Commissions, RG 56, NARA; Adam E. Patterson to William G. McAdoo, January 11, 1915, box 129, WGMP; W. Cohen, *At Freedom's Edge*, 252, 254–56.

43. Patterson and Guy, *Homeseeker's Guide*, 23.

44. Meier, "Negro and the Democratic Party." See also Fortune, *Black and White*, 112–30; Bacote, "Negro Proscriptions"; Materson, *For the Freedom of Her Race*, 50–51; Goldstein, "Race Politics," 90–102; Lamon, *Black Tennesseans*, 52; Woods, "C. H. J. Taylor"; Hahn, *Nation under Our Feet*, 387; and Crowder, *John Edward Bruce*, 50.

45. Hahn, *Nation under Our Feet*, 323; Luker, *Social Gospel in Black and White*, 71.

46. "A Division of the Negro Vote," *WB*, March 11, 1899, 4; "The Political Boss," *WB*, July 12, 1902, 1.

47. De Santis, "Negro Dissatisfaction," 152.

48. Bruce, *Archibald Grimké*, 57.

49. Waldron and Harkless, *Political Situation*, 10.

50. The Kansas People's Party did in fact reward black supporters with jobs. *Parsons Blade* quoted in Chafe, "Negro and Populism," 413.

51. Painter, *Exodusters*, 27; Hahn, *Nation under Our Feet*, 387; Woods, "C. H. J. Taylor," 126–27.

52. C. H. J. Taylor to Grover Cleveland, September 8, 1893, series 3, reel 137, Grover Cleveland Papers, LC. For more on Cleveland and black patronage, see Meier, "Negro and the Democratic Party," 175; Woods, "C. H. J. Taylor"; Grossman, *Democratic Party*, 141; Grossman, "Democrats and Blacks," 143.

53. Franklin, *Mirror to America*, 37. As one former Tuskegeean wrote Democratic party leader William McAdoo, "I need not tell you what it has meant and still means to a colored man to espouse the cause of democracy especially as it applies to National politics." Peter Jay Smith to William G. McAdoo, June 28, 1913, box 106, WGMP.

54. Kantrowitz, *Ben Tillman*, 253–56; Painter, *Exodusters*, 134; Litwack, *Trouble in Mind*, 224; Brundage, *Lynching*, 170; Hahn, *Nation under Our Feet*, 367.

55. The NIPL was a spin-off of the Negro-American Political League, formed by

Trotter, Waldron, and Alexander Walters in June 1908. Fox, *Guardian of Boston*, 162; "Colored Men Revolt," *WP*, June 15, 1908, 2; Waldron and Harkless, *Political Situation*, 11.

56. Waldron and Harkless, *Political Situation*, 16.

57. "The Truth," *The Crisis*, April 1911, 21.

58. Waldron and Harkless, *Political Situation*, 25.

59. James L. Curtis, long-standing Democrat from New York, explained to Secretary of the Treasury William G. McAdoo in July 1914 how he and Walters had oriented the AME churches away from their usual Republicanism in 1912. James L. Curtis to William G. McAdoo, July 17, 1914, box 119, WGMP; G. Miller, "'This Worldly Mission,'" 367; D. Lewis, *W. E. B. Du Bois*, 424; Du Bois, "My Impressions"; "The Election," *The Crisis*, December 1912, 75–76.

60. Biographies of Wilson abound. The two I have found most useful are Cooper, *Woodrow Wilson*, and Thompson, *Woodrow Wilson*.

61. Cooper, *Woodrow Wilson*, 23–25; Woodrow Wilson, "An Address on Robert E. Lee at the University of North Carolina," January 19, 1909, in *PWW*, 18:631.

62. Wilson's words were promulgated by Oswald Garrison Villard. Two years later, Wilson recalled his promise in letters to Mississippi senator John Sharp Williams and Speaker of the House Champ Clark. A. Link, "Negro as a Factor," 91–92; Fox, *Guardian of Boston*, 167; D. Lewis, *W. E. B. Du Bois*, 423; Oswald Garrison Villard to R. H. Leavell, August 15, 1912, container 2221, OGVP; Woodrow Wilson to John Sharp Williams, April 2, 1914, box 1, John Sharp Williams Papers, LC; Woodrow Wilson to Champ Clark, May 4, 1914, box 150, RWPP.

63. Disloyalty had always invited vicious rebukes. Writing to Booker T. Washington in 1899, T. Thomas Fortune, himself an occasional independent, declared: "C. H. J. Taylor is dead. I have no rhetorical flowers to place on his grave, as I am no hypocrite and he was an unmitigated nuisance and disturbance and all the rest of it." Timothy Thomas Fortune to Booker T. Washington, June 1, 1899, in Harlan, *Booker T. Washington Papers*, 5:122.

64. In case Taft missed the hint, the reference to Thomas Dixon's vicious morality play against "Negro rule" and interracial sex would hit the mark. He was right about one thing: Ferguson claimed to be a Democrat in March 1913 when he wrote to Treasury Secretary William McAdoo for a job. Ralph W. Tyler to Rudolph Forster, November 29, 1910, file 190, reel 372, WHTP.

65. Ralph W. Tyler to Charles D. Hilles, June 24, 1911, ibid.; Dr. J. W. McDowell to William Howard Taft, April 1, 1911, ibid.

66. Villard's list included Du Bois, the novelist Charles Chestnut, philosopher and Howard University professor Kelly Miller, and Interior Department lawyer Lafayette Hershaw. All were political independents known for outspokenness. Villard tried to make Taft see the future: "So far as Mr. Washington's position is concerned, I can assure you that the opposition to him among his own people increases steadily." Oswald Garrison Villard to Charles D. Norton, September 20, 1910, ibid.

67. Handwritten memorandum dated October 4 on Fred Moore's letter to Charles D. Norton, September 30, 1910, ibid.; Postmaster General Hitchcock responded on October 24: Frank Hitchcock to William Howard Taft, October 24, 1910, ibid.

68. Morris, *Colonel Roosevelt*, 170.

69. Justesen, *Broken Brotherhood*, 40; Cyrus F. Adams, PF NPRC; William Howard Taft to Charles D. Hilles, August 3, 1912, file 1575, reel 419, WHTP.

70. William Howard Taft to Franklin MacVeagh, August 20, 1912, file 1575, reel 419, WHTP.

71. Needham, "William Howard Taft," 230, 302; "Political Activity in the Presidential Campaign."

72. H. A. Hesse and G. W. Hall to U.S. Civil Service Commission, February 9, 1912, Ocea Taylor, PF NPRC. The same letter appears in Randolph's file: Oliver Randolph, PF NPRC. J. C. Black to Commerce and Labor Secretary, March 14, 1912, Ocea Taylor, PF NPRC; Acting Chief of Appointment Division to Acting Secretary, September 26, 1912, Ocea Taylor, PF NPRC; "Puts Ban on Politics," *WP*, February 8, 1912, 3; "Would Classify District Clerks," *Washington Herald*, February 8, 1912, 3.

73. Statement of Oliver Randolph, February 9, 1912, Oliver Randolph, PF NPRC.

74. E. Dana Durand to Secretary of Commerce and Labor, March 19, 1912, Ocea Taylor, PF NPRC. For Randolph's defense, which, in part, matches verbatim that of Durand, see Chief Clerk to United States Civil Service Commission, August 6, 1912, Oliver Randolph, PF NPRC.

75. "An Ill-Tempered Convention," *NYT*, June 19, 1912, 2.

76. Accusations that Roosevelt operatives were trying to bribe black delegates only confirmed for many white Americans the corrupting influence of African Americans in politics. "Roosevelt Speaks to a Great Throng," *NYT*, June 18, 1912, 4; Sherman, *Republican Party*, 103; "More Negroes Tell of Bribe Offers," *NYT*, June 18, 1912, 1; Needham, "William Howard Taft," 232, 309.

77. Painter, *Standing at Armageddon*, 267-68.

78. Whitefield McKinlay to Robert Smalls, June 28, 1912, box 3, reel 2, Carter G. Woodson Collection of Negro Papers and Related Documents, LC.

79. Ralph W. Tyler to William Howard Taft, June 21, 1912, file 1965, reel 424, WHTP; Ralph W. Tyler to Theodore Roosevelt, March 25, 1913, series 1, reel 170, Theodore Roosevelt Papers, LC.

80. Sherman, *Republican Party*, 104.

81. "Beveridge Takes Lindsey's Place; Roosevelt Refused to Yield on Negro Delegates," *WP*, August 6, 1912, 1; Chace, *1912*, 163.

82. Cooper, *Warrior and the Priest*, 210.

83. Gary Gerstle notes that it was with some "agonizing" that Roosevelt aligned the Progressive Party with the lily whites. Gerstle, *American Crucible*, 75-79; Sherman, *Republican Party*, 108-9.

84. Taft to Hilles, August 3, 1912.

85. According to August Meier, a slight majority of black voters supported Roosevelt, while the rest were split between Wilson and Taft. Meier, *Negro Thought*, 188; Hiller, "Race Politics," 181-82.

86. Thomas H. R. Clarke to J. C. Napier, June 25, 1913, Thomas H. R. Clarke, PF NPRC.

87. Robert Smalls to Whitefield McKinlay, June 27, 1912, box 3, reel 2, Carter G.

Woodson Collection of Negro Papers and Related Documents, LC; Edward A. Miller Jr., *Gullah Statesman*, 241; Billingsley, *Yearning to Breathe Free*, 162–64.

88. Robert Smalls to Whitefield McKinlay, September 12, 1912, box 3, reel 2, Carter G. Woodson Collection of Negro Papers and Related Documents, LC.

89. "The Last Word," *WB*, November 2, 1912, 4.

90. *WB*, November 2, 1912, 4.

91. "The Election," 75–76; Hiller, "Race Politics," 174; D. Lewis, *W. E. B. Du Bois*, 424.

92. Ferdinand Lee, PF NPRC.

93. James L. Curtis to William G. McAdoo, July 17, 1914, box 119, WGMP; W. E. B. Du Bois, "The Republicans and the Black Voter," *The Nation*, June 5, 1920, 757; "The Last Word in Politics," *The Crisis*, November 1912, 29.

94. "Black Cabinet," *WB*, November 30, 1912, 1; "The Black Cabinet," *WB*, November 30, 1912, 4.

95. Ralph W. Tyler to Carmi A. Thompson, November 7, 1912, file 1965, reel 424, WHTP.

CHAPTER 4

1. Swan M. Kendrick to Ruby Moyse, March 10, 1913, box 2, folder 8, KBFP.

2. Ibid., November 4, 1914, box 3, folder 9.

3. Weyl, *New Democracy*, 1.

4. A. Link, *Woodrow Wilson*, 22–24; Chace, *1912*, 238.

5. A. Link, *Woodrow Wilson*, 6–13, 24; Cooper, *Woodrow Wilson*, 173–76.

6. Sarasohn, *Party of Reform*, 9, 20–21; Witcover, *Party of the People*, 296–97.

7. Wilson, "A Campaign Address in Cleveland," October 11, 1912, in *PWW*, 25:406; Wilson, "A Campaign Address in Chicago," October 10, 1912, in ibid., 25:402.

8. Chace, *1912*, 196; W. Wilson, *New Freedom*, 90–91.

9. Low, *Woodrow Wilson*, 30.

10. W. Wilson, *New Freedom*, 60.

11. W. Wilson, "States and the Federal Government," 698.

12. Bimes and Skowronek, "Woodrow Wilson's Critique," 48; Skowronek, "Reassociation," 393. For the notions of harmony and unity in Wilsonian progressive politics, see Rodgers, *Contested Truths*, 169; Thorsen, *Political Thought*, 188–89; and Cooper, *Warrior and the Priest*, 125.

13. Turner, "What Wilson Is Up Against," 148, 156–60. For Wilson's record as governor, see Cooper, *Woodrow Wilson*, 134–35.

14. W. Wilson, "Study of Administration." For more on Wilson and his scholarship on administration, see Arthur S. Link, "Woodrow Wilson and the Study of Administration," in A. Link, *Higher Realism*, 40–42; Rabin and Bowman, *Politics and Administration*, 3–4; and Skowronek, *Building a New American State*, 195.

15. W. Wilson, "Study of Administration," 210, 217.

16. Thorsen, *Political Thought*, 128–30; Rabin and Bowman, *Politics and Administration*, 3; Silberman, *Cages of Reason*, 230; Heclo, *Government of Strangers*, 49.

17. Wilson's presidency did see the establishment of a federal employees union, an

eight-hour workday for female workers, and a pension system through the Federal Employees Retirement Act of 1920, but these were passed more as wartime measures than as a fulfillment of Wilson's program. Rung, *Servants of the State*, 31; Shefter, *Political Parties*, 78; Van Riper, *History of the United States Civil Service*, 260–61, 276–77.

18. Cooper, *Woodrow Wilson*, 133, 215; Wilson on Bryan quoted in ibid., 279; Van Riper, *History of the United States Civil Service*, 230–38; Arthur S. Link, "Woodrow Wilson and the Democratic Party," in A. Link, *Higher Realism*, 63–64.

19. Though these words appeared all over Wilson's writings, the best example is probably W. Wilson, "Democracy and Efficiency." For Wilson's support of federalism and "local opinion," see W. Wilson, "States and the Federal Government." For neutrality over justice, see Thorsen, *Political Thought*, 130–31. John M. Jordan notes that Wilson was far more interested in notions of moral virtue than many of his social scientist peers, and in fact, progressive ideas about "efficiency" were incredibly vague. Jordan, *Machine-Age Ideology*, 26, 37; Mosher, *Democracy and the Public Service*, 71.

20. Woodrow Wilson to John Sharp Williams, April 2, 1914, box 1, John Sharp Williams Papers, LC.

21. "Keep Races Separate; Carlin's Dictum, at Wilson Rally, Wins Cheers; Wants District Race Law," *WP*, October 19, 1912, 3. See H.R. 1710, 63rd Cong., 1st sess., April 7, 1913; H.R. 9675, 63rd Cong., 2nd sess., December 2, 1913; H.R. 10150, 63rd Cong., 2nd sess., December 9, 1913; and S. 4941, 63rd Cong., 2nd sess., March 18, 1914. Copies of the legislation can be found in the AGC.

22. For the evolution of Abraham Lincoln's reputation, see M. Peterson, *Lincoln*, 38–50. For the meaning of Reconstruction in history, see Woodward, *Strange Career*, 105; and Foner, *Reconstruction*, xvii–xviii. For a model of this version of Reconstruction from the period, see Dunning, *Reconstruction*.

23. W. Wilson, "Reconstruction," 6.

24. Ibid., 11. For more elaboration, see W. Wilson, *History of the American People*, 46–52.

25. Masur, *Example for All the Land*, 237.

26. "The Herald: A Forward," *Washington Herald*, October 8, 1906, 6.

27. Williams quoted in "Rates U.S. Clerks; Senator Williams Adds Tests to Five-Year Terms; Would Oust 'Dead Timber,'" *WP*, June 14, 1912, 1; "A Thought from President Woodrow Wilson's Book 'The New Freedom,'" *Civil Service Advocate*, November 1913, 863–64; "The President and the Clerks," *WES*, February 8, 1914, 4.

28. "Pomerene to Ask Civil Service Inquiry by Congress Tomorrow," *Washington Times*, April 30, 1913, 1. Even well into the Wilson administration, Democrats refused to acknowledge a need for raising the pay of clerks, furthering the notion that the government was filled with overpaid Republicans. "Pay Issue Holds Floor in Senate," *WES*, January 23, 1917, 1; "Threat to Thwart Salary Increases," *WES*, February 28, 1917, 1.

29. Borland explicitly connected the hours problem with "the old political system" of patronage. Borland's racial comments were inserted into the *Congressional Record* and not delivered on the House floor, but the *Bee* published them and the NAACP wrote to government departments demanding data to show that Borland's comments were nonsense. "Extension of Remarks of Hon. William P. Borland," 53 *Congressional Record* 416 (1916), appendix, p. 417; "Favoritism," *WB*, March 11, 1916, 6. Attorney James C.

Waters conducted the NAACP's investigation. James C. Waters Jr. to Secretary of Commerce, April 1, 1916, entry 6, box 68, General Correspondence, General Records of the Department of Commerce Office of the Secretary, RG 40, NARA; "Federal Employes Organize Union," *WES*, April 8, 1916, section 1, p. 4.

30. "The Negro His Own Enemy," *WB*, March 5, 1898, 4; "Vernon Is to Be Register," *WES*, January 13, 1906, 1.

31. "Passport for Blacks," *Washington Herald*, October 8, 1906, 1.

32. For examples of Republicans being blamed for Washington's problems, see "Race Issue in Senate; Naming of a Colored Man as Recorder to Be Opposed," *WP*, June 21, 1914, 4; and "Debate Civil Service: Senators Discuss Charges after Overman Urges Probe," *WP*, May 2, 1913, 4.

33. Historian Stephen Kantrowitz has noted that the fact that the term "progressive" could be applied to both Ben Tillman and W. E. B. Du Bois reveals the "limited explanatory value" of the term itself. Nevertheless, I think it is important to avoid simply separating out white supremacists from streams of thought that were, at the time, labeled as "progressive"—just as it is essential to locate Du Bois, Ida B. Wells, and other black progressives within them. We do not have to resolve the messiness of progressive politics to talk about what they meant to people at the time. Kantrowitz, *Ben Tillman*, 264–68; Turner, "What Wilson Is Up Against," 162; Sarasohn, *Party of Reform*, 30, 184; A. Scott, "Progressive Wind," 54, 57–58; Blum, *Joe Tumulty*, 89. For general overviews of southern progressivism, see W. Link, *Paradox*; and Kirby, *Darkness at the Dawning*. For the problem of delineating something called "progressivism," see Rodgers, "In Search of Progressivism."

34. Rodgers, "Age of Social Politics," 250–59; Boyer, *Urban Masses*, 279; Wiebe, *Search for Order*, 153–54; Rodgers, *Atlantic Crossings*, 182.

35. Hays, "Changing Political Structure." For changes in turn-of-the-twentieth-century Washington, see Lessoff, *Nation and Its City*.

36. Harrison, *Congress*, 129; Jordan, *Machine-Age Ideology*, 25, 54.

37. U.S. Congress, Senate Committee on the District of Columbia, *Hearing on Inhabited Alleys*, 8, 13.

38. Harrison, *Congress*, 128–29.

39. "The National Capital should be a model city," Roosevelt had declared in his introduction to Weller, *Neglected Neighbors*, 1.

40. Mark Wahlgren Summers, *Rum, Romanism*, 23; Lears, *Rebirth of a Nation*, 310.

41. Boyer, *Urban Masses*, 279–80. For the role of Christian reformers in city reform in this period, see Luker, *Social Gospel*, 159–90.

42. Riis, *How the Other Half Lives*.

43. J. Logan, *Thirty Years in Washington*, 521.

44. "Wilson Will Bare Arm to Vaccination Knife; Wife and Daughters Already Have Undergone the Ordeal," *WES*, March 26, 1913, 3. For the history of black urbanites as sources of infection, see Wailoo, *Dying in the City of Blues*, 14–19; and S. Roberts, *Infectious Fear*, esp. chapter 6.

45. W. Wilson, "States and the Federal Government," 701.

46. R. S. McClure to William G. McAdoo, April 7, 1913, box 98, WGMP.

47. Wilson, in the same paragraph, slips between discussing the United States' "Ger-

manic" ancestors and the "English" colonists who founded the nation. They seem to be one and the same in his thinking. W. Wilson, "Need of Citizenship Organization," 265. For the ways in which nineteenth-century Americans conflated and contrasted "English," "German," "Anglo-Saxon," and "Teuton" inconsistently and conveniently, see Painter, *History of White People*, 159, 166–68, 201–2, 250.

48. McCormick, *Party Period*, 284.

49. W. Wilson, "Need of Citizenship Organization," 266.

50. Wilson's textbook on the development of government, for example, specifically excluded non-white people from any relevant role in the growth of American democracy. W. Wilson, *State*, 1–2. For more on Anglo-Saxonism and the "instinct" to organize in American imperialism, see Kramer, "Empires," 1332.

51. For Wilson and European immigration, see Gerstle, *American Crucible*, 96.

52. W. Wilson, "Democracy and Efficiency," 297–98.

53. Boyer, *Urban Masses*, 254–55; Rodgers, *Contested Truths*, 179–87; Thorsen, *Political Thought*, 61–62; John M. Mulder, "'Gospel of Order': Woodrow Wilson's Religion and Politics," in Cooper and Neu, *Wilson Era*, 236. For more on the connections between progressive politics and the U.S. colonial state in the Philippines, see Abinales, "Progressive-Machine Conflict"; Manela, *Wilsonian Moment*, 25; and Woodrow Wilson, "Inaugural Address," March 4, 1913, in *PWW*, 27:149–50.

54. McGerr, *Fierce Discontent*, 182–217.

55. Unsigned to NAACP, May 29, 1913 (stamped October 20, 1913), Part I: C403, RNAACP.

56. "Separation of Races Is Provided in Bill; Measure Introduced in House Proposes Segregation in Cars and Departments," *WES*, July 15, 1913, 7.

57. Cell, *Highest Stage*, 18; Hale, *Making Whiteness*, 93.

58. Weller, *Neglected Neighbors*; Charles Weller to Woodrow Wilson, August 29, 1913, box 125, RWPP.

59. W. Wilson, "Reconstruction," 13.

60. Very little can be found on the officers of the NDFPA. The *Herald*, no friend to black Republicans, suspected that the association was merely a cover for Democratic spoilsmen. A letter in an African American federal employee's personnel file carries a letterhead with Adriaans's name, over the line "Attorney and Counselor." That Adriaans wrote a letter himself to help a client collect a $5.75 debt suggests that Adriaans was a small-time lawyer. By 1928, Adriaans was disbarred and had lost an appeal in the Supreme Court for revocation of his disbarment. An investigation by the *Washington Herald* claimed to reveal that the NDFPA was far smaller than implied by its letterhead and that most of the officers were found to be small-time politicians and petty government office seekers. The association would officially make itself permanent in 1913 under Ernest Martin of Missouri. It is not clear why Adriaans was not made an officer. Joseph P. Annin, "Spoilsmen Are Wearing Mask of Civil Service," *Washington Herald*, May 14, 1913, 1; John H. Adriaans to Woodrow Wilson, March 31, 1913, box 107, RWPP; John H. Adriaans to Postmaster, August 4, 1905, Philip Shippen, PF NPRC; In re Disbarment of Adriaans, 278 U.S. 568 (1928); Joseph P. Annin, "'Guardians' of Civil Service Want Positions," *Washington Herald*, May 15, 1913, 1; "Organizes in States; Society

for Race Segregation Also Elects Its Officers," *WP*, April 26, 1913, 11; Green, *Washington*, 222–23.

61. National Democratic Fair Play Association to "Madam," May 9, 1913, file 152A, reel 230, WWP.

62. Many thanks to Kevin Kruse for our conversation about "reverse discrimination" in this context.

63. "White Bosses Is Plea," *WP*, April 24, 1913, 4; Adriaans to Wilson, March 31, 1913.

64. Historian Leslie Butler suggests that the term had some purchase even for racial justice immediately after the Civil War. Butler, *Critical Americans*, 102–3.

65. "Pushing Their Plans," *WP*, April 25, 1913, 2.

66. "White Woman Took a Negro's Dictation," *New York World*, May 2, 1913; article found in Navy File, reel 62, Josephus Daniels Papers, LC. Platform of National Democratic Fair Play Association, ,attached to James A. Reed to Joseph P. Tumulty, May 8, 1913, file 2B, reel 161, WWP.

67. This white supremacist argument was not new during the Wilson administration. In 1909, the *Herald* had reported that naval officers were not receiving their wages on time, "largely because so many of its competent and especially trained clerks have resigned or sought transfer to other offices owing to the fact that the head of the office is a colored politician from Cincinnati, Ohio," meaning Ralph W. Tyler. "Demoralization" aside, the paper said, the real problem was one of government efficiency. "The Trouble in an Auditor's Office," *Washington Herald*, January 27, 1909, 6.

68. "Resent Burleson's Plan," *NYT*, May 9, 1913, 2.

69. "Deeds Office Reform: President Wilson Considering Change of Radical Nature," *WP*, October 15, 1913, 4.

70. A letter from the association to McAdoo was forwarded further down the line in the administration by Williams, according to a handwritten note attached to it. National Democratic Fair Play Association to William G. McAdoo, May 11, 1913, Richard W. Thompson, PF NPRC.

71. "Names Five to Senate; Wilson Places John Skelton Williams in Treasury," *WP*, March 14, 1913, 1; Abby Gunn Baker, "New Officials in the Treasury Department, Their Families and Home Life in the Capital," *WP*, May 25, 1913, R3.

72. John Skelton Williams, "The Credit of the South," Commercial Club, Nashville, Tenn., May 24, 1892, box 84, JSWP; Tyler, *Men of Mark*, 1:415.

73. Hale, *Making Whiteness*, 49–50; Woodward, *Origins of the New South*, 155–57; Blight, *Race and Reunion*, 255–91. For the ritual and organizational patterns of the Lost Causers, see Foster, *Ghosts of the Confederacy*.

74. John Skelton Williams, "Credit of the South."

75. Ibid.

76. Degler, *In Search of Human Nature*; Painter, *History of White People*, 245–66.

77. John Skelton Williams, "Solving a Problem; Facing a Peril," Southern Society of New York, New York, N.Y., December 9, 1914, box 85, JSWP.

78. Roper, *Fifty Years of Public Life*, 3–4.

79. Gilmore, *Gender and Jim Crow*, 83; Painter, "'Social Equality.'"

80. Klarman, *From Jim Crow*, 115; Urofsky, *Louis D. Brandeis*, 388.

81. Gregory, *Reconstruction*, 7–8. For more on Gregory's role in the Wilson administration, see Capozzola, *Uncle Sam Wants You*, 120.

82. Gregory, *Reconstruction*, 11.

83. "T. R. Can't Fool South on Negro," *WP*, August 3, 1912, 3.

84. The New York Southern Society was established in 1886 as a social club for expatriate white southerners. For more on the society, see Samuel Lonsdale Schaffer, "New South Nation," 98–164.

85. Broesamle, *William Gibbs McAdoo*, 4–6; "M'Adoo Carried Back to Boyhood; Colored 'Mammy' Presents Photos of Secretary's Mother and Father; Daughter Bears Gift from Old Georgia Home; Incidents of Many a Year Ago Recalled in Chat at the Treasury," *WES*, July 20, 1913, 8.

86. For "mammies" and the southern racial landscape, see Feimster, *Southern Horrors*, 166; Hale, *Making Whiteness*, 113; and J. Johnson, "'Ye Gave Them a Stone.'"

87. "Bureau of Engraving and Printing," *WB*, May 3, 1913, 1. For the supposed "threat" of urban black women, see Carby, "Policing the Black Woman's Body."

88. Wilson's most famous cabinet member, Secretary of State William Jennings Bryan, was relatively removed from racial controversies. His department had few black employees, and in general, he seems to have ignored them. Kazin, *Godly Hero*, 227, 230. For more on southerners in Wilson's administration, see "The South Is in the Saddle," *WB*, September 13, 1913, 4; Villard, "President and the Segregation," 806; Sosna, "South in the Saddle"; and Samuel Lonsdale Schaffer, "New South Nation," 196–214.

89. "Pushing Their Plans," 2.

90. For the rise of women in government clerical work, see Aron, *Ladies and Gentlemen*, 3.

91. Hedstrom, "Beyond Feminisation," 145, 148; Davies, *Woman's Place*, 79; Swan M. Kendrick to Ruby Moyse, October 30, 1913, box 5, folder 2, KBFP.

92. Rotella, *From Home to Office*, 175; Aron, *Ladies and Gentlemen*, 19; Aron, "'To Barter Their Souls,'" 49.

93. Thompson quoted in Hayes, "Negro Federal Government Worker," 29.

94. Aron, *Ladies and Gentlemen*, 166.

95. Carby, "Policing the Black Woman's Body," 747; Hodes, *White Women*, 147.

96. Ernest D. Martin to Charlotte Hopkins, May 28, 1913, box 2, Charlotte Hopkins Papers, LC.

97. "Dreads Negro Clerks: Miss Monroe Asks Protection in Recorder of Deed's Office," *WP*, May 11, 1913, 7; "Alleged Threat Called to O'Gorman's Attention; Is Told of Complaint of Woman Clerk against Colored Employe of Government," *WES*, May 12, 1913, 2.

98. After the office had been vacant for two years after Johnson's resignation, Wilson appointed John F. Costello, a white Democrat, in June 1916. Interestingly, President Harding reappointed Henry Lincoln Johnson as recorder in 1921, but his nomination was blocked in the Senate out of deference for Johnson's senator, Tom Watson. "Demands Protection for Young Woman," *Washington Times*, May 13, 1913, 1; "Inquiry on Race Row: Recorder of Deeds Promises Investigation of Office," *WP*, May 13, 1913, 16; "Race Issue in Senate," 4; "Race Issue Looms Big; Hot Fight Is Likely over New District Deed Recorder," *WP*, June 30, 1914, 2; "John F. Costello Confirmed," *WES*,

July 11, 1916, 9; "Costello as Recorder; President Breaks Precedent by Naming White Democrat," *WP*, June 9, 1916, 12; "Negro Politicians Striving for Office," *WP*, April 28, 1929, M6.

99. "White Woman Tells of Negro Authority," *NYT*, May 4, 1913, 13; "White Woman Took a Negro's Dictation."

100. "Discuss Segregation of Races," *WES*, May 10, 1913, 8; "Women Take Up Race Topic: Demand Segregation and Other Reforms in Civil Service," *WP*, May 10, 1913, 2.

101. Joseph E. Ralph to Isabella L. Hagner, June 26, 1913, box 3, Charlotte Hopkins Papers, LC; Joseph E. Ralph to Charlotte Hopkins, July 10, 1913, ibid.; Joseph E. Ralph to Mrs. Archibald [Charlotte] Hopkins, July 29, 1913, entry 12-A1, box 6, BEPGCF; "'Spugs' in Big Rally; Society Leaders Are to Outline Campaign This Evening," *WP*, December 6, 1913, 2; "Bureau of Engraving and Printing," 1; "See U.S. Money Made; Mrs. Wilson and Mrs. Hopkins Visit Bureau of Engraving," *WP*, April 3, 1913, 5.

102. Holden-Smith, "Lynching," 45, 61; U.S. Congress, House Committee on the District of Columbia, *Intermarriage of White and Negro Races*; U.S. Congress, House Select Committee on Reform in the Civil Service, *Hearing on Segregation of Clerks*.

103. Holden-Smith, "Lynching," 60; Hall, *Revolt against Chivalry*, 154–55. For more on the relationship between assertive white women and racial violence by white men, see Hall, "'Mind That Burns,'" 328–49; and MacLean, "White Women."

104. John Skelton Williams, "Aroused Thought, Advancing Needs and Our Financial Emancipation," Annual Convention of the Maryland Bankers' Association, Blue Mountain, Md., June 26, 1913, box 84, JSWP.

105. Thomas Dixon Jr. to Woodrow Wilson, July 27, 1913, in *PWW*, 28:89; Gilmore, "One of the Meanest Books." Dixon held a few private screenings of the film in Washington. "'The Birth of a Nation,'" *The Crisis*, June 1915, 69–71; Benbow, "Birth of a Quotation," 519–20.

106. Cyrus F. Adams to Charles D. Hilles, February 27, 1913; Cyrus F. Adams to James F. Curtis, February 28, 1913; Assistant Secretary of the Treasury to Collector of Customs, March 1, 1913, all in Cyrus F. Adams, PF NPRC; Franklin MacVeagh to William Howard Taft, March 3, 1913; Cyrus F. Adams to William Howard Taft, January 8, 1913, both in file 1575, reel 419, WHTP.

107. John Skelton Williams to Collector of Customs, August 1, 1913, file 1575, reel 419, WHTP. Workers in the office reported that they had seen McKee and Adams together outside the office and that McKee's family had complained to Treasury authorities, though nothing official appeared in Adams's record. Chief Clerk to John Skelton Williams, July 26, 1913, ibid.; John Skelton Williams to William McAdoo, July 28, 1913, ibid.

108. Capozzola, *Uncle Sam Wants You*, 117–18; *PWW*, 21:390–91; Cooper, *Woodrow Wilson*, 11, 204–5; Woodrow Wilson quoted in *Trenton Evening Times*, July 31, 1912, reproduced in *PWW*, 24:574; Gary Gerstle, "Race and Nation in the Thought and Politics of Woodrow Wilson," in Cooper, *Reconsidering Woodrow Wilson*, 93–96; Gaughan, "Woodrow Wilson"; A. Link, "Woodrow Wilson," 10–11.

109. For an incisive analysis of the relationship between twentieth-century liberalism and Wilson's racism, see Skowronek, "Reassociation"; and Woodrow Wilson, "Remarks on the Race Question," December 15, 1914, in *PWW*, 31:464–65.

110. Wm. Monroe Trotter to William G. McAdoo, March 12, 1913, box 97, WGMP.

111. Josephus Daniels to William H. Osborne, September 19, 1913, box 563, reel 62, Josephus Daniels Papers, LC; Walters, *My Life and Work*, 177; George Mason Miller, "'This Worldly Mission,'" 367. Louis Harlan notes that Booker T. Washington's regular contact with the White House came to an end with Wilson's arrival. Harlan, *Booker T. Washington Papers*, 12:xvii.

112. "Banquet Walters," *WB*, March 8, 1913, 1; Trotter to McAdoo, March 12, 1913; Meier, "Negro and the Democratic Party," 191.

113. "At Counter for Pie; National Colored Democratic League Gets Busy," *WES*, March 11, 1913, 11; Alexander Walters to William G. McAdoo, March 10, 1913, box 97, WGMP.

114. Robert S. Hudspeth to Woodrow Wilson, October 7, 1914, box 124, WGMP.

115. Robert S. Hudspeth to Joseph P. Tumulty, May 6, 1913, box 112, RWPP.

116. "The South in Congress," *WES*, December 7, 1915, 6; Abrams, "Woodrow Wilson and the Southern Congressmen," 418–19.

117. John Sharp Williams to William G. McAdoo, March 25, 1913, file 41F, reel 185, WWP.

118. William G. McAdoo to Woodrow Wilson, March 31, 1913, box 517, WGMP.

119. Benjamin R. Tillman to William G. McAdoo, June 23, 1913, box 102, ibid.

120. J. Milton Waldron to William G. McAdoo, March 12, 1913, box 97; William G. McAdoo to J. Milton Waldron, March 20, 1913, box 478-1, vol. 1; both in ibid.

121. "Resignation Is Accepted: Assistant Attorney General Lewis Evades Official Elimination," *WES*, March 10, 1913, 8; Harlan, *Wizard of Tuskegee*, 406.

122. Booker T. Washington to Franklin MacVeagh, April 17, 1913, in Harlan, *Booker T. Washington Papers*, 12:168–69.

123. Wm. Monroe Trotter to William G. McAdoo, March 15, 1913, entry 207, box 7, Appointment Division, Misc. Correspondence, Office Files, 1912–1913, GRDTDA; Wm. Monroe Trotter to William G. McAdoo, May 8, 1913, box 100, WGMP; Peter J. Smith to Joseph P. Tumulty, June 16, 1913, box 115, RWPP.

124. Smith to Tumulty, June 16, 1913.

125. Robert Lewis Waring to Woodrow Wilson, May 26, 1914, in *PWW*, 30:491.

126. Woodrow Wilson to Robert Lewis Waring, June 1, 1914, in ibid., 493.

127. Adam E. Patterson to William G. McAdoo, July 15, 1914, box 118, WGMP.

128. Woodrow Wilson to William G. McAdoo, June 27, 1913, box 517, WGMP; Billington, *Thomas P. Gore*, 2, 10.

129. William G. McAdoo to Woodrow Wilson, July 18, 1913, in *PWW*, 28:40–41. Months later, McAdoo reminded Gore of Wilson's desire to appoint an African American and Gore's nomination of Patterson. Wilson read McAdoo's letter and approved his view of the events. William McAdoo to Thomas P. Gore, October 10, 1913, box 129, RWPP; Woodrow Wilson to William McAdoo, October 9, 1913, box 129, RWPP; Alexander Walters to A. H. Underdown, May 1, 1913, entry 228, box 155, General Records of the Department of the Treasury, Records Relating to Presidential Appointments and Commissions, RG 56, NARA; Abrams, "Woodrow Wilson," 419.

130. William G. McAdoo to Woodrow Wilson, July 18, 1913, entry 228, box 155, General Records of the Department of the Treasury, Records Relating to Presidential Appointments and Commissions, RG 56, NARA.

131. Jonathan Kellogg to Woodrow Wilson, July 28, 1913, ibid. For others, see Patterson's appointment file in Treasury Department Records, "Patterson, Adam E.," ibid. For more description of the outrage, see Villard, "President and the Segregation," 801; and Osborn, "Woodrow Wilson," 484.

132. "Revolt on Patterson; Vardaman Leads Fight for White Treasury Register," *WP*, July 27, 1913, 1; "War on 'Favorites': Wilson's Choice for Governor of Hawaii Stirs Critics; Patterson Opposed, Too," *WP*, July 26, 1913, 1.

133. Adam E. Patterson to Woodrow Wilson, July 30, 1913, in *PWW*, 28:97–98; "Drops Negro as Candidate," *NYT*, August 3, 1913, C4; "New Treasury Officials Sworn In," *NYT*, October 2, 1913, 7.

134. Tumulty spoke to Oswald Garrison Villard of the NAACP. Oswald Garrison Villard to Frank J. Garrison, July 31, 1913, container 1464, OGVP; Byron Newton to Adam E. Patterson, August 18, 1913, box 479-2, p. 427, WGMP.

135. Adam E. Patterson to William G. McAdoo, August 10, 1913, box 104, WGMP.

136. "Adam E. Patterson," *WB*, August 9, 1913, 4.

137. William Wilson, "Letter to the Editor: Patterson Document: A Bitter Pill — Vardaman and His Policy," *WB*, August 16, 1913, 1.

138. "What the Democratic Presidential 'Victory' Means to Our People in Washington, D.C. and the Entire Country — An Outrage!," *Cleveland Gazette*, July 26, 1913, 1.

139. "Gabe E. Parker Nominated for Register of the Treasury," *Indianapolis Freeman*, August 9, 1913, 4.

140. "President Wilson Knuckles Close to the South," *New York Age*, August 14, 1913, 4.

141. Adam E. Patterson to William G. McAdoo, November 18, 1916, box 169, WGMP. McAdoo corresponded with Patterson about getting him an appointment through most of his time as Wilson's Treasury secretary. William G. McAdoo to Col. W. H. Osborn, March 28, 1914, box 114; William G. McAdoo to T. W. Gregory, February 13, 1915, box 132; William G. McAdoo to Thomas P. Gore, March 1, 1915, box 133; William G. McAdoo to Adam E. Patterson, July 28, 1916, box 491-1, vol. 38; all in ibid.

142. James, "Robert Russa Moton," 237; Chad L. Williams, *Torchbearers of Democracy*, 322–23; Arthur G. Froe to C. Bascom Slemp, November 15, 1923, box 93, reel 63, Calvin Coolidge Papers, LC.

143. Kilson, "Political Change in the Negro Ghetto"; Bates, *Pullman Porters*, 55–57; Katznelson, *Black Men*, 66. See also Gosnell, *Negro Politicians*.

144. Terrell had the overwhelming support of black and white lawyers in the District. In a separate case, it appears that a black man was accidentally allowed to become head of the Customs Office in Brunswick, Georgia. An angry letter from a congressman in July led McAdoo to appoint a white collector immediately. Charles G. Edwards to William G. McAdoo, July 1, 1913; J. G. Weatherly to William G. McAdoo, July 2, 1913; both in box 102, WGMP.

145. Taylor went to work for the sociologist Thomas Jesse Jones in his study of black schools in the South, a study nominally sponsored by the Bureau of Education in the Interior Department but administered and funded by a private foundation, the Phelps-Stokes Fund. Taylor's federal personnel record ends in 1913, but the *Washington Post* listed him as part of Jones's staff within the Interior Department. In fact, Jones and

Taylor were employed by the fund, not by the Interior Department. According to the *Washington Tribune*, Oliver Randolph briefly held an appointment as an assistant attorney general in Newark under Harding but by 1925 was no longer a government employee. Ocea Taylor to Director of Census, January 31, 1913, Ocea Taylor, PF NPRC; Thomas Jesse Jones to Charlotte Hopkins, March 22, 1913, box 1, Charlotte Hopkins Papers, LC; "Departmental Notes of Interest to Uncle Sam's Army of Employees," *WP*, March 8, 1914, ES3; T. Jones, *Negro Education*, xiii; Patti McGill Peterson, "Colonialism and Education," 155. For Randolph's transfer to Newark: Chief Clerk to Fidelity and Casualty Company of New York, March 9, 1920, Oliver Randolph, PF NPRC; "Office Seekers Getting Little Encouragement," *WT*, April 18, 1925, 1.

146. "The Black Cabinet," *WB*, April 12, 1913, 4.

147. Wilson did appoint Emmett Scott as a temporary federal liaison to African Americans during World War I, but the position was symbolic and very short-term. See schedules in Hiller, "Race Politics," 25, 130–32; as well as Hayes, "Negro Federal Government Worker," 557; R. Logan, *Betrayal*, 60; H. Johnson, *Negro under Wilson*, 12–13; Blakely, "Black U.S. Consuls," 11–12; Plummer, *Haiti*, 190; Wolgemuth, "Woodrow Wilson's Appointment Policy," 465–68; and "Public Men and Things," *WB*, November 6, 1915, 2.

148. Swan M. Kendrick to Ruby Moyse, July 31, 1913, box 3, folder 1, KBFP.

149. Secretary of the Navy Josephus Daniels recorded in his diary that Burleson raised the issue of segregation at a cabinet meeting on April 11, 1913. Interestingly, Daniels says that Secretary of the Treasury William McAdoo believed that segregation of Treasury clerks would be unworkable. "From the Diary of Josephus Daniels, April 11, 1913," in *PWW*, 27:290–91; Daniels and Cronon, *Cabinet Diaries*, 32–33; Cooper, *Woodrow Wilson*, 205.

150. "Recorder of Deeds Problem Unsolved," *WES*, April 21, 1915, 1.

151. Grimké, *Excerpts from a Thanksgiving Sermon*, 4.

CHAPTER 5

1. George H. Cox to Voler V. Viles, September 20, 1911, George H. Cox, PF NPRC.

2. George H. Cox, March 6, 1913; George H. Cox to William L. Austin, June 1, 1914; both in ibid.

3. George H. Cox to William L. Austin, July 18, 1916, ibid.

4. George H. Cox to Sam. L. Rogers, June 13, 1918; George H. Cox Employment Card; both in ibid.

5. William G. McAdoo to Woodrow Wilson, September 30, 1913, box 517, WGMP.

6. Records for the Postal Service, the next greatest employer of black federal employees in Washington, were apparently lost in a series of fires, so the Treasury Department will be the focus of my discussion of segregation. The Post Office Department employed more African Americans nationally, but the Treasury dominated within the District.

7. The two instances implicating Wilson's involvement in segregation do not involve a clear administrative order. In April 1913, Wilson gave only tacit approval when Postmaster General Albert Burleson declared his plans to segregate the Post Office Depart-

ment. The second incident is hearsay: This tale says the Georgia-born first lady Ellen Axson Wilson ordered her husband to segregate the government in the name of her white ladyhood. Yet there is no evidence that Ellen Wilson was either offended by what she saw in federal offices or that she mentioned it to her husband. When, in November 1914, Wilson defended segregation in an explosive meeting with William Monroe Trotter, Hamlin recorded in his diary that Wilson was, in fact, wrong about what was happening in the departments. "Race Policy Problem: Mr. Wilson Puzzled as to Appointing Negroes to Office," *WP*, September 30, 1913, 2; Sosna, "South in the Saddle," 33; "Bureau of Engraving and Printing," *WB*, May 3, 1913, 1; "Paragraphic News," *WB*, April 5, 1913, 1; "See U.S. Money Made; Mrs. Wilson and Mrs. Hopkins Visit Bureau of Engraving," *WP*, April 3, 1913, 5; "Notes," *WB*, May 24, 1913, 1; CHD, March 12, 1914, p. 106; *PWW*, 28:476; CHD, November 30, 1914, p. 189; "From the Diary of Josephus Daniels, April 11, 1913," in *PWW*, 27:290–91; Daniels and Cronon, *Cabinet Diaries*, 32–33; Cooper, *Woodrow Wilson*, 205.

8. Woodrow Wilson to Oswald Garrison Villard, July 23, 1913, container 4234, OGVP.

9. Rodgers, "In Search of Progressivism."

10. "Demand for Places; Democrats Suggest Dismissal of Republicans from Treasury," *WES*, May 26, 1913, 3.

11. William Howard Taft to Executive Order 1388, July 31, 1911; Frank Hitchcock to Memorandum, August 12, 1911; both in Thomas Richardson, PF NPRC.

12. M. O. Chance to Postmaster General, April 19, 1913; Ruskin McArdle to Roland M. Baker, July 8, 1920; both in ibid.; Fourteenth Census of the United States, 1920, Claiborne, Mississippi, E.D. 35, available at http://www.ancestry.com.

13. Stephen O. Plummer to NAACP, June 10, 1915, box 39-25, folder 512, AGC.

14. Swan M. Kendrick to Ruby Moyse, April 25, 1915, box 5, folder 5, KBFP.

15. Lafayette M. Hershaw to May Childs Nerney, September 11, 1913, Part I: C403, RNAACP.

16. A. L. Tilghman to Archibald Grimké, June 4, 1914, box 39-25, folder 499, AGC.

17. Ibid.

18. Joseph E. Ralph to John Skelton Williams, May 6, 1913, entry 12, box 5, BEPGCF.

19. John Skelton Williams to Joseph E. Ralph, April 3, 1913, entry 12-A1, box 6, ibid.

20. CHD, March 12, 1914, p. 106.

21. "New Head of Bureau," *WES*, May 11, 1908, 4; Joseph E. Ralph, PF NPRC; Charlotte Hopkins to Mrs. Ellen Wilson, March 31, 1913, box 3, Charlotte Hopkins Papers, LC.

22. South Carolina Segregation Act of 1915 quoted in Hall, Korstad, Daly, and Jones, *Like a Family*, 66.

23. Ralph reported the "trouble" to Assistant Secretary of the Treasury Charles Hamlin a year later. CHD, March 12, 1914, p. 106.

24. Joseph E. Ralph to John Skelton Williams, April 4, 1913, entry 12-A1, box 6, BEPGCF.

25. CHD, March 12, 1914, p. 106; Oswald Garrison Villard to Woodrow Wilson, October 14, 1913, container 4234, OGVP; May Childs Nerney to Woodrow Wilson, September 30, 1913, box 129, RWPP.

26. John Skelton Williams to William G. McAdoo, July 25, 1913, box 103, WGMP; James L. Wilmeth, PF NPRC.

27. Thomas H. R. Clarke to Jessie Fauset, September 10, 1913, Part I: C403, RNAACP.

28. One exception was in the Railway Mail Service, a division of the Post Office Department, where white workers did sign a petition insisting on segregated bathroom facilities on trains, a change that appears to have been granted. "Race Issue Up to Burleson; Postmaster General Will Today Receive Petition Asking for Segregation," WP, May 24, 1913, 3; F. B. Lehane to Joseph E. Ralph, November 13, 1914, entry 12-A1, box 15, BEPGCF; white railway postal clerks to T. P. Elam, n.d., box 39-10, folder 217, AGC; R. McCants Andrews to W. E. B. Du Bois, November 14, 1914, box 39-25, folder 505, AGC.

29. Although Ralph had assured Williams that the new building would be segregated, MacVeagh was, according to Hamlin, known as a liberal when it came to race. "New Edifice Opens with Flag-Raising; Transfer of Bureau of Engraving and Printing into Modern Quarters," WES, March 19, 1914, 4; CHD, March 12, 1914, p. 107; Joseph E. Ralph to John Skelton Williams, April 5, 1913, entry 12, box 5, BEPGCF.

30. Joseph E. Ralph to Charles Hamlin, March 7, 1914, entry 12-A1, box 15, BEPGCF.

31. In every reference to the March 9 order in both his diary and a November 1914 letter to McAdoo, Hamlin refers to it as a "draft" or "prepared letter" and makes no indication of ever having promulgated it. He did not send it to Ralph, and no copy of the letter exists in the bureau papers, although a copy of Ralph's March 7 letter to Hamlin does exist in those files. Word somehow reached the NAACP that Hamlin had barred segregation on March 7, two days before Hamlin prepared his letter doing so. Regardless of Hamlin's beliefs, the NAACP and newspaper reports, and the claims of some administrative officials, segregation was not forbidden in the Treasury Department. The confusion has led to a misunderstanding among historians. Arthur Link's published volumes of the *Papers of Woodrow Wilson* reproduce a news report of Hamlin's order as well as the NAACP's "thank you" letter without any discussion of the fact that Hamlin's order was not issued or that Wilson did not intend to stop segregating employees. CHD, March 9-10, 1914, pp. 100; Charles S. Hamlin to Joseph E. Ralph, March 9, 1914, box 346, Charles S. Hamlin Papers, LC; Oswald Garrison Villard to Charles S. Hamlin, March 7, 1914, box 113, WGMP; Charles S. Hamlin to William G. McAdoo, November 21, 1914, box 126, WGMP; Patler, *Jim Crow*, 197; PWW, 28:500, 29:105.

32. CHD, March 10, 1914, pp. 101-3.

33. Ibid., March 12, 1914, pp. 104-5; March 16, 1914, p. 109. Ralph had told Williams that as of July 1913, segregation existed but was not yet enforced consistently. Joseph E. Ralph to John Skelton Williams, July 12, 1913, entry 12-A1, box 6, BEPGCF.

34. CHD, March 12, 1914, pp. 107-8.

35. Ibid., March 13, 1914, p. 108.

36. Ibid., March 16, 1914, p. 110.

37. Ibid., pp. 110-12. Ralph had explained the skin irritations to Williams in May 1913. Joseph E. Ralph to John Skelton Williams, May 17, 1913, entry 12, box 2, BEPGCF; anonymous letter, June 5, 1913, box 3, Charlotte Hopkins Papers, LC.

38. CHD, March 15, 1914, pp. 109-13.

39. Ralph to Williams, July 12, 1913.

40. On April 1, 1914, Hamlin told Reverend Francis Grimké that he planned to act "quietly and slowly," reminding him that "Rome was not built in a day." CHD, March 27, 1914, pp. 115–17; April 1, 1914, pp. 117–18.

41. Ibid., March 16, 1913, p. 113.

42. In October 1911, for example, white bricklayers working in the Government Printing Office walked off the job when a black government employee was assigned to work with them. Though the white bricklayers insisted the issue was about union wages, Public Printer Donnelly announced publicly that the issue was racism and that he would refuse to accommodate the white workers' demands. "Will Not Work with Negro," WES, September 14, 1911, 18; "Union Bricklayers Strike," WP, September 15, 1911, 11; "Donnelly Strikes Back," WES, October 20, 1911, 7; "Call Donnelly Biased," WP, September 19, 1911, 2; "Donnelly's Ouster May Be Requested of President Taft," Washington Times, October 24, 1911, 2; "Local Labor Bodies after Public Printer," WES, September 21, 1911, 5; "Public Printer Donnelly," WB, September 30, 1911, 4; "Donnelly's Scalp to be Subject of Labor Union War," Washington Times, November 19, 1911, 6; "'Enemy of Unionism,'" WP, October 17, 1911, 12.

43. While differences between departments persisted, depending on the actions of individual administrators, the way in which Hamlin managed to continue segregation but bury the evidence suggests that other claims about the removal of segregation during these years must be viewed with suspicion. For example, in 1916, the Bee reported that the War Department had rescinded its segregation order. "Segregation Order Rescinded," WB, September 9, 1916, 4.

44. CHD, March 12, 1914, pp. 106–7; March 9, 1914, p. 100.

45. Clarke's demotion made the front page of the Washington Bee, along with the demotions of eight other Treasury employees. "Colored Men Reduced," WB, August 1, 1914, 1.

46. U.S. Civil Service Commission, Thirtieth Annual Report, 141.

47. U.S. Civil Service Commission to Secretary of the Treasury, February 4, 1913; Franklin MacVeagh to Thomas H. R. Clarke, February 10, 1913; James F. Curtis to U.S. Civil Service Commission, February 11, 1913; John C. Black to Secretary of the Treasury, February 21, 1913; all in Thomas H. R. Clarke, PF NPRC.

48. I have no information on who Simmons was, other than that he was a Democrat and almost certainly white. C. E. Simmons to John Skelton Williams, June 21, 1913, ibid.

49. Thomas H. R. Clarke to John Skelton Williams, August 2, 1913; James L. Wilmeth to Committee on Personnel, November 5, 1913; J. E. Harper to James L. Wilmeth, November 6, 1913; Broughton to File, November 6, 1913; all in ibid.

50. Thomas H. R. Clarke to May Childs Nerney, September 6, 1913; Thomas H. R. Clarke to May Childs Nerney, September 8, 1913; Clarke to Fauset, September 10, 1913; Thomas H. R. Clarke to May Childs Nerney, September 11, 1913; Thomas H. R. Clarke to May Childs Nerney, September 19, 1913; all in Part I: C403, RNAACP.

51. Wilmeth to Personnel, November 5, 1913; Charles S. Hamlin to Thomas H. R. Clarke, July 3, 1914; Thomas H. R. Clarke to Secretary of the Treasury, August 31, 1914; all in Thomas H. R. Clarke, PF NPRC.

52. Clarke joined Whitefield McKinlay's real estate business. McKinlay had been

Taft's collector of customs for the Port of the District of Columbia and, out of office, had become a successful realtor and landlord.

53. The Federal Employees Retirement Act (FERA), enacted in May 1920, established seventy as the mandatory retirement age and fifteen years as the minimal service required to earn a pension. Benefits were determined by years of service. Thomas H. R. Clarke to J. E. Harper, January 8, 1930; Robert F Wagner to F. A. Birgfeld, March 23, 1935, both in Thomas H. R. Clarke, PF NPRC; Clark, Craig, and Wilson, *History of Public Sector Pensions*, 157, 165.

54. Clarke's brother spelled his name without the *e*. Thomas listed David on his Treasury personnel form, and census records confirm that that the two were brothers. Assistant Secretary of the Treasury to David A. Clark, June 27, 1913, David A. Clark, PF NPRC; James L. Wilmeth to Assistant Secretary of the Treasury, October 3, 1913, ibid.; Tenth Census of the United States, 1880, District of Columbia, E.D. 38, available at http://www.ancestry.com.

55. "Daniels and Burleson Are Made Defendents," *WES*, January 12, 1915, 1; "No Rights in Job, Say P.O. Officials," *WES*, January 26, 1915, 1; "Towner Denounces Veterans' Discharge," *WES*, February 5, 1915, 4.

56. Simmons to Williams, June 21, 1913; anonymous to John Skelton Williams, November 8, 1913; both in Thomas H. R. Clarke, PF NPRC.

57. National Democratic Fair Play Association to William G. McAdoo, May 11, 1913, Richard W. Thompson, PF NPRC; Private Secretary to Alexander Walters, June 3, 1913, ibid.; "R. Wordy Thompson," *WB*, May 31, 1913, 1.

58. Though Williams did make the usual claims about efficiency, for example, in his plans to reform the various auditors' divisions within the Treasury Department. William G. McAdoo to John Skelton Williams, February 24, 1914, box 480-3, vol. 9, WGMP.

59. Nerney to Wilson, September 30, 1913.

60. Chief Clerk and Superintendent to William G. McAdoo, October 30, 1913, box 108, WGMP.

61. Nerney to Wilson, September 30, 1913; Charles A. Kram to William G. McAdoo, October 28, 1913, box 108, WGMP.

62. Heclo, *Government of Strangers*, 2. For the relationship between scientific management and early-twentieth-century politics, see Jordan, *Machine-Age Ideology*, 37, 40–42. For the history of management and Taylorism in white-collar offices and in industrial production, see Zunz, *Making America Corporate*; and Gillespie, *Manufacturing Knowledge*.

63. Indeed, white clerks regularly balked at "efficiency" drives that reduced pay or employment for them too. "Reaction on Economy Seen in Departments," *WES*, January 8, 1917, 16.

64. "Big Clerical Shakeup: Employes in 3 Departments Get Changed Positions," *WP*, July 19, 1914, 8; "Another Stab," *WB*, July 25, 1914, 4.

65. "Clerk Becomes Inventor," *New York Age*, March 30, 1911, 3; "To Practice before the US Supreme Court," *Chicago Defender*, October 26, 1912, 1.

66. Fouché, *Black Inventors*, 169–77; Shelby J. Davidson to William H. Lewis, January 27, 1912, box MS 83–1228, folder 1, Shelby Davidson Papers, MSRC; Thomas Wallace

Swann to Byron Newton, June 26, 1917; Franklin MacVeagh to Shelby J. Davidson, March 27, 1913; both in Shelby Davidson, PF NPRC.

67. Davidson to Lewis, January 27, 1912.

68. Shelby J. Davidson to Charles A. Kram, March 18, 1912; Shelby J. Davidson to Franklin MacVeagh, March 18, 1912; Charles A. Kram to Franklin MacVeagh, March 20, 1913; Post Office Department Auditor to Assistant Secretary Andrew, December 9, 1911; all in Shelby Davidson, PF NPRC; "Mr. Davidson's Appointment," *WT*, February 3, 1923, 8; Fouché, *Black Inventors*, 169–77.

69. John H. Paynter, "Finds Race Prejudice; J. H. Paynter Says Civil Service Rules Are Evaded," *WP*, March 9, 1913, FF7.

70. These counts are for all changes, including those affecting the same individual.

71. Reductions and dismissals were a standard part of government employment for white and black employees, particularly for temporary workers brought in to fulfill orders or congressional mandates. What matters here is that the prospects for black clerks changed so dramatically with the new administration. The *Civil Service Advocate* claimed that prospects in federal offices were quite good in September 1914. Indeed, the civil service had an acute "need for bodies" throughout the Wilson years. "Opportunities for Employment in the Washington Departmental Service," *Civil Service Advocate*, September 1914, 1065–66; Van Riper, *History of the United States Civil Service*, 243, 251.

72. I have excluded from this number those who were reduced first and then promoted much later (often not even to their previous salary). For promotions in all cases, fourteen of my selection's 97 black civil servants earned them in Wilson's first term. William Twine appears to be the only postal worker who received a series of promotions during Wilson's presidency, moving from $600-a-year clerk in 1912 to $1,100 by 1920 — an impressive record given the circumstances, but $1,100 after the wartime inflation was terrible pay. Complaints of racial prejudice were rarer in the Interior, Commerce, War, and Labor, and Agriculture Departments. It was also no accident that the secretaries of the Interior, Commerce, War, and Labor were the only non-southerners in Wilson's cabinet. William B. Wilson (Labor) and Franklin Lane (Interior) were actually born outside the United States.

73. The acting chief clerk claimed that in June 1914, the segregation was broken up when a building addition was completed. Yet when Walter White of the NAACP toured the government departments to study segregation, Dent and another black clerk, Joseph McDuffie, were the only black clerks in the Division of Statistics and were segregated into their own room. John S. Collins to Dr. Pratt, March 11, 1915, box 332, Department of Commerce, Office of the Secretary, RG 40, NARA; Walter White and W. T. Andrews to NAACP, August 1928, Part I: C403, RNAACP.

74. A tabulation of all "colored employees" in the District of Columbia and beyond collected by the chief clerk of the Department of Agriculture in 1914 showed that only 6 of the department's 447 black employees were earning more than $1,200 a year, and they were all veterinary inspectors probably working outside of Washington. In fact, only six employees total were employed as full clerks. In his summation of Wilson's first term, former recorder of deeds Henry Lincoln Johnson noted the phenomenon of keeping black clerks below Class 4. Johnson went so far as to suggest that Wilson

cut the number of black clerks in half. That seems a bit exaggerated. Department of Agriculture Chief Clerk to Chiefs of Bureaus, Divisions, and Offices, July 14, 1914, entry 17, box 1, Correspondence Relating to Negroes, Records of the Department of Agriculture, General Correspondence Relating to Negroes, 1909–1955, RG 16, NARA; H. Johnson, *Negro under Wilson*, 7–8.

75. As scholars Paul Pierson and Theda Skocpol have observed, "inequalities of power, perhaps modest initially, are reinforced and can become deeply embedded in organizations, institutions, and dominant modes of political understanding." Paul Pierson and Theda Skocpol, "Historical Institutionalism in Contemporary Political Science," in Katznelson and Milner, *Political Science*, 700.

76. See Fenwick Bush, John H. Cook, Charles R. Douglass, Robert A. Pelham, Robert Culley, Lawrence Wooden, Laura Joiner, and Lucretia Mott Kelly, all in PF NPRC. See also CEHP.

77. "Government Hours and Pay," *WES*, October 22, 1916, section 2, p. 4

78. Kendrick's letter is undated, but its placement in the files and the fact that he addressed the letter to Ruby Kendrick suggest it was written sometime in 1916. Swan M. Kendrick to Ruby M. Kendrick, n.d., box 6, folder 1, KBFP.

79. W. H. Love, L. M. Ferguson, and O. W. Dudley to Theodore Roosevelt, April 24, 1902; Memorandum to Director of the Census, May 23, 1902; John Dancy to William R. Merriam, June 18, 1902; James S. Clarkson to S. N. D. North, May 20, 1903; Booker T. Washington to E. Dana Durand, June 14, 1909; all in William Jennifer, PF NPRC.

80. Memorandum to Director of the Census, January 4, 1914; William Jennifer to Chief Clerk, February 21, 1914; both in ibid.

81. William Jennifer to William Harris, July 31, 1914, ibid.

82. Charles E. Hall to William L. Austin, November 27, 1916, CEHP.

83. Francille R. Wilson, *Segregated Scholars*, 131.

84. Charles E. Hall to William L. Austin, December 19, 1916, CEHP.

85. William Jennifer to William L. Austin, November 27, 1916, William Jennifer, PF NPRC.

86. F. Wilson, *Segregated Scholars*, 131.

87. Daniel C. Roper to Samuel S. Rogers, March 11, 1921; William Jennifer to William L. Austin, January 10, 1934; William Jennifer to William L. Austin, February 4, 1937; all in William Jennifer, PF NPRC; Fourteenth Census of the United States, 1920, District of Columbia, E.D. 94; Fifteenth Census of the United States, 1930, District of Columbia, E.D. 40; Fifteenth Census of the United States, 1930, Detroit City, Michigan, E.D. 82-116; all available at http://www.ancestry.com; William L. Austin to Mrs. William Jennifer, March 28, 1939, William Jennifer, PF NPRC.

88. Quiller, an officer in the black elite's Mu-So-Lit Club, had regularly volunteered for extra duties in the Library's Music Division. "Mu-So-Lit Club Elects Officers," *WB*, March 1, 1919, 5; W. R. Whittlesey to Executive Assistant, November 26, 1929, Bernard Quiller, PF NPRC.

89. Swan M. Kendrick to State War and Navy Bldg. Superintendent, May 12, 1919, box 8, folder 8, KBFP.

90. "Deplorable Condition," *WB*, December 2, 1916, 4. Even the usual fallback, teaching in segregated black schools, could not provide the steady paycheck that the

civil service had been offering these men and women. E. Glenn, *Unequal Freedom*, 81–82, 106–9; J. Jones, *American Work*, 302–3, 306, 309.

91. Communications scholar Marsha Witten has noted the ways in which narratives flow through workplaces, creating a "social construction of organizational reality." Witten, "Narrative," 101.

92. Ralph W. Tyler, "Letter to the Editor: Treasury Race Segregation," *WES*, August 7, 1913, 20.

CHAPTER 6

1. The transcriptions of Trotter and Wilson's two meetings were recovered by Arthur Link's Papers of Woodrow Wilson Project team and published in Lunardini, "Standing Firm." Trotter quoted in ibid., 255.

2. L. M. Strayer to Woodrow Wilson, September 19, 1913, file 152a, reel 230, WWP; Bruce, *Archibald Grimké*, 189; "A Righteous Protest," *The Independent*, September 4, 1913, 533–34.

3. Ralph W. Tyler, "Against Segregation Plan," *WB*, May 3, 1913, 2; Ralph W. Tyler to Woodrow Wilson, May 12, 1913, file 152a, reel 230, WWP.

4. Resistance always encompasses a "diversity" of forms of varying scale, because people struggling under oppression can become extremely creative in their efforts. As sociologists Jocelyn Hollander and Rachel Einwohner have shown, resistance is a protean concept in social scientific scholarship. While they are greatly concerned with this definitional sloppiness, I am not. Racism in federal offices in the early twentieth century was simultaneously a blunt bludgeon and an all-encompassing attack on black personhood: African Americans had a clear sense of their enemy and the ways in which their opportunities were being curtailed by white supremacy. Racism constituted a direct attack on black existence. Thus, I am willing to count as resistance just about anything that sought to preserve the dignity and legitimacy of black federal employment. Hollander and Einwohner, "Conceptualizing Resistance," 535–37.

5. Weinstein, *Bureaucratic Opposition*, 5; Aron, *Ladies and Gentlemen*, 79; Mills, *White Collar*.

6. Edward L. Scott to Secretary of the Treasury, January 17, 1920, Edward L. Scott, PF NPRC.

7. As Frances Fox Piven and Richard Cloward have argued in their now-famous study of social movements, not everyone has the freedom to participate in mass protest all the time. Protest itself is subject to contextual limitations. This chapter is, in part, an analysis of a mass movement that did not really happen, though there were triumphant moments of protest. Social movement scholar Charles Tilly made a similar point about the "repertoires" of social movements. Piven and Cloward, *Poor People's Movements*, 3, 6–14; Tilly, "Social Movements," 308.

8. James Tucker has offered a typology of "employee resistance" that includes non-aggression, collective action, and formal grievance, all of which federal employees undertook. Robin Kelley has applied James Scott's notion of "infrapolitics" to some forms of resistance to racism in the United States, and Tera Hunter has documented the ways in which African American female domestics in Atlanta used dance halls to

express ownership over their bodies after long days of forced subservience. Both Kelley and Hunter address, in particular, the resistance of working-class African Americans. Tucker, "Everyday Forms," 26; J. Scott, *Domination*, 183–201; Kelley, *Race Rebels*, 8; Hunter, *To 'Joy My Freedom*, 87. See also Prasad and Prasad, "Everyday Struggles"; and Scott E. Schaffer, "Hegemony and the Habitus." For a possible example of stealing as resistance, see William L. Johnson, PF NPRC.

9. Protests against this racial hostility poured into the White House and the mailboxes of the NAACP and its officials. See file 152a, WWP. Oswald Garrison Villard claimed to be receiving a torrent of protests against the "hostile attitude of the administration in regard to colored employees in the government departments." Oswald Garrison Villard to Woodrow Wilson, July 21, 1913, container 4234, OGVP.

10. In this way, we might see the resistance of African Americans as "productive" in the Foucaultian sense: it created a new form of power of which it then became a victim. Pickett, "Foucault," 458. For the most famous of Michel Foucault's treatises on the "productive" nature of power, see Foucault, *Discipline and Punish*.

11. Wilson quoted in Lunardini, "Standing Firm," 257.

12. William G. McAdoo to Oswald Garrison Villard, October 27, 1913, box 108, WGMP.

13. Sociologist Deena Weinstein refers to the belief that bureaucracies are merely "efficient and effective instruments for the realization of publicly proclaimed goals" as the "myth of administration." In reality, writes Weinstein, all organizations are sites of political contestation. Weinstein, *Bureaucratic Opposition*, ix; Bourdieu, *Outline*, 191, 196. See also J. Scott, *Domination*, ix–16, 49; and Tilly, "Domination."

14. Andrew F. Hilyer to Archibald Grimké, December 4, 1913, box 39-5, folder 96, AGC; Gatewood, *Aristocrats of Color*, 28–29, 223–24. See chronology of life in Andrew F. Hilyer Papers, MSRC.

15. In 1909, black women joined a white worker, Gertrude McNally, in a protest against working conditions in the BEP; in 1924, Nannie Helen Burroughs organized charwomen and messengers against the Personnel Classification Act; and in 1928, a black woman named Gretchen McRae in the Pension Bureau led a series of protests against segregation. "Gov't Workers Protest Act," *WT*, July 26, 1924, 1; "Gov't Workers to Hold Mass Meeting Monday at Cleveland School," *WT*, September 20, 1924, 1; Rung, *Servants of the State*, 39; Murphy, "Mapping African American Women's Activism."

16. All three had been appointed under the civil service and had been working in the bureau for nine or more years. Mrs. Anan E. Ball to Joseph E. Ralph, April 29, 1913, entry 12-A1, box 6, BEPGCF.

17. "Bureau of Engraving and Printing," *WB*, May 3, 1913, 1.

18. "The Protest," *The Crisis*, October 1913, 275–81; Joseph E. Ralph to Belle C. LaFollette, July 24, 1913, entry 12-A1, box 6, BEPGCF; Belle C. La Follette, "The Color Line," *La Follette's Magazine*, August 23, 1913, 6–7, republished in Unger, "Belle La Follette."

19. Joseph Stewart to Joseph H. Paghe, June 12, 1913, entry 102, box 9, Records of the Department of the Post Office, Office of the Second Assistant Postmaster General, RG 28, NAB.

20. L. Walker, "Struggles and Attempts," 73; Membership Report to NAACP, November 20, 1918, Part I: G34, RNAACP.

21. Thomas H. R. Clarke to Jessie Fauset, September 10, 1913, Part I: C403, RNAACP.

22. This letter writer became a member of the NAACP and by 1916 was openly conducting an audit of the government's treatment of black employees. It is unclear whether or not he had left government employment by 1916, freeing him to protest more overtly. James C. Waters Jr. to Oswald Garrison Villard, November 19, 1913, ibid.; James C. Waters Jr. to Secretary of Commerce, April 1, 1916, entry 6, box 68, General Correspondence, General Records of the Department of Commerce Office of the Secretary, Record Group 40, NARA.

23. D. V. Chisholm to Henry T. Brian, June 20, 1914, Raymond Fisher, PF NPRC; "Ford an Old Printer," WP, June 15, 1913, 14; A. L. Tilghman to Archibald Grimké, June 4, 1914, box 39-25, folder 499, AGC.

24. Raymond Fisher to Public Printer, June 20, 1914, Raymond Fisher, PF NPRC; Fifteenth Census of the United States, 1930, Boston, Mass., E.D. 13-125, available at http://www.ancestry.com.

25. Swan M. Kendrick to Ruby Moyse, August 7, 1913, box 5, folder 2, KBFP.

26. Kelley, Race Rebels, 18.

27. John A. Davis to H. J. Brian, March 18, 1914, John A. Davis, PF NPRC.

28. John A. Davis to Samuel B. Donnelly, May 16, 1913, ibid.

29. Woodruff, American Congo, 4–5. For the ways in which the civil rights movement has influenced American ideas about the Constitution, see Harding, "Wrestling toward the Dawn."

30. Houston was William LePre Houston's brother, who nine years earlier had left government service for a legal career. Theophilus J. Houston to Merritt O. Chance, April 21, 1916, Theophilus J. Houston, PF NPRC. For the Houston family tree, see McNeil, Groundwork.

31. Bo Sweeney to John E. Rattley, July 15, 1914; J. Milton Waldron to Gaylord M. Saltzgaber, June 18, 1914; both in John E. Rattley, PF NPRC.

32. John E. Rattley to Gaylord M. Saltzgaber, February 22, 1915; depositions of John E. Rattley, John W. Wheeler, Orpha L. Van Horn, Emilio E. Merino, Raymond B. Harding, and Helen Garrett, taken by R. W. Reed, Special Examiner of the Bureau of Pensions, June 10, 1921; all in ibid.

33. Randall Kennedy, "Racial Passing," 1170–71.

34. Terrell, Colored Woman, 266–67.

35. In his 1926 novel, Howard University librarian Edward C. Williams describes how some black Washingtonians were able to enjoy Washington's whites-only spaces while others were left to find their work and entertainment in the black enclave on U Street and in Howardtown. E. Williams, When Washington Was in Vogue, 48; "Threat to Use Vitriol," WES, February 4, 1915, 14.

36. William T. Ferguson to William G. McAdoo, February 22, 1915, box 133, WGMP.

37. For example, in 1916, Wilson promoted a white messenger to a clerkship. "Promoted to Clerkship," WES, January 8, 1917, 7. William McAdoo also recommended an executive order to promote a black messenger, Richard Green, to a clerkship as a "en-

couragement to every faithful colored employe[e] in the service." William G. McAdoo to Woodrow Wilson, June 26, 1914, box 518, WGMP. In that first term, Wilson signed significantly more orders than Taft and just five fewer than Roosevelt did in both of his administrations. According to Lewis Mayers, the increase may have been related to a general strengthening of civil service rules, thus leading to a need for more exceptions. Mayers, *Federal Service*, 70.

38. "Hold the Fort," *WB*, September 27, 1913, 4.

39. James L. Curtis to William G. McAdoo, July 17, 1914, box 119, WGMP.

40. In the minds of white supremacists, "social equality" came freighted with images of black men raping white women and an overturning of the South's class relations, thereby endangering both the livelihoods and the purity of white southerners. Opposing "social equality" was politically necessary for everyone, black or white, in this period. Painter, *Southern History*, 112–15.

41. Robert N. Wood to Woodrow Wilson, August 5, 1913, file 152a, reel 230, WWP.

42. Ibid.

43. Oswald Garrison Villard to Archibald Grimké, November 11, 1913, box 39-25, folder 492; Oswald Garrison Villard to Alexander Walters, November 11, 1913, box 39-25, folder 491, both in AGC; "Race Discrimination at Washington," *The Independent*, November 20, 1913, 330.

44. For Patterson's story, see chapter 3. James A. Ross to William G. McAdoo, December 21, 1914, box 129; Alexander Walters to William G. McAdoo, December 17, 1914, box 128; both in WGMP.

45. Wm. Monroe Trotter to William G. McAdoo, May 8, 1913, box 100; Wm. Monroe Trotter to William G. McAdoo, July 29, 1913, box 103; both in ibid.; Patler, *Jim Crow*, 129–30.

46. Wm. Monroe Trotter to Joseph P. Tumulty, August 15, 1913, file 152a, reel 230, WWP.

47. Wm. Monroe Trotter to Woodrow Wilson, August 25, 1913, ibid.

48. For more on manliness at the turn of the twentieth century, see Bederman, *Manliness*; and Martin Summers, *Manliness and its Discontents*.

49. "Committee of Colored Men Sees President Wilson and Protests against Race Segregation," *WB*, November 15, 1913, 1; Fox, *Guardian of Boston*, 175–76; Schechter, *Ida B. Wells-Barnett*, 136, 306 (n. 188); C. Reed, *Chicago NAACP*, 19.

50. Lunardini, "Standing Firm," 246–49.

51. Ibid., 249.

52. Ibid., 249–50. Lunardini credits Trotter with this last statement, but Nicholas Patler has, through the *Boston Guardian*, shown that it was Wells-Barnett who spoke the brief but moving finale. Patler, *Jim Crow*, 66.

53. "Committee of Colored Men," 1.

54. Swan M. Kendrick to Ruby Moyse, November 8, 1913, box 5, folder 2, KBFP; "City News in Brief," *WP*, November 8, 1913, 2.

55. Fox, *Guardian of Boston*, 175–79.

56. McGerr, *Decline of Popular Politics*, 184–210; McCormick, *Party Period*, 279, 274. See also Clemens, *People's Lobby*.

57. McCartin, *Labor's Great War*, 15, 34.

58. In 1913, black postal workers established the National Alliance of Postal Employees (NAPE) to push back against discrimination, but they had almost no presence in Washington and did little to help clerks outside of the Post Office Department. NAPE did not receive federal recognition until the mid-1920s. Rung, *Servants of the State*, 35, 39; H. Walker, "Formation of the National Federation"; E. Johnson, "General Unions"; "Federal Employes Organize Union," *WES*, April 8, 1916, section 1, p. 4; Spero, "Employer and Employee," 208. For black postal workers and labor organizing, see A. Glenn, *History of the National Alliance*; and Rubio, *There's Always Work*.

59. Swan Kendrick refers to his NFFE membership in a letter in 1919, but I have found little evidence that union membership played much of a role for black employees in the 1910s and 1920s. Grace Palladino, co-director of the Samuel Gompers Papers, confirmed that there is no mention of the black NFFE local in the Gompers Papers. I. Reid, *Negro Membership*, 85; Swan M. Kendrick to Waiters' Union Local 781, March 30, 1919, box 8, folder 2, KBFP; T. Roberts, "Negro in Government," 370.

60. Black Americans had real reasons to be wary of the labor movement, beyond any "misrecognition" or inability to embrace a structural critique of American society. J. C. Cunningham, "Government Governed," *WB*, March 18, 1916, 1; H. Hill, "Problem of Race," 189; J. Jones, *American Work*, 302; I. Reid, *Negro Membership*, 101; Bates, *Pullman Porters*, 54.

61. Social movement scholar Charles Tilly refers to those who joined a social movement during and after the nineteenth century as "a set of people who voluntarily and deliberately commit themselves to a shared identity, a unifying belief, a common program, and a collective struggle to realize that program." Tilly, "Social Movements," 303.

62. LaFayette McNeill Jr. to Charles Nagel, May 21, 1912, box 39-8, folder 159, AGC.

63. LaFayette McNeill Jr. to Archibald Grimké, January 8, 1914; LaFayette McNeill Jr. to Archibald Grimké, January 13, 1914; both in ibid.

64. Villard forwarded the letter on to McAdoo. Victor P. Thomas to W. E. B. Du Bois, March 18, 1913, box 98, WGMP.

65. Swan M. Kendrick to Ruby Moyse, October 30, 1913, box 5, folder 2, KBFP.

66. In addition, Wilson had reneged on an agreement with Villard to form a national race commission. R. H. Leavell to Woodrow Wilson, February 20, 1912, container 2221; Oswald Garrison Villard to R. H. Leavell, May 15, 1913, container 4234; Oswald Garrison Villard to Woodrow Wilson, August 27, 1913, container 4234; all in OGVP.

67. D. Lewis, *W. E. B. Du Bois*, 386–434; Sullivan, *Lift Every Voice*, 1–24.

68. D. Lewis, *W. E. B. Du Bois*, 416.

69. Mary White Ovington to Joel E. Spingarn, July 29, 1913, Part I: G34, RNAACP.

70. May Childs Nerney to Joel E. Spingarn, July 31, 1913, ibid.

71. May Childs Nerney to Jessie Fauset, September 11, 1913, Part I: C403, ibid.

72. Nerney expressed her frustration to Minnesota senator Moses Clapp. May Childs Nerney to Moses Clapp, September 27, 1913, Part I: C70, reel 6, ibid.; May Childs Nerney to Joseph E. Ralph, July 26, 1913, entry 12-A1, box 6, BEPGCF; May Childs Nerney, "Race Segregation in Government Departments — Report of an Invesitgation," *WB*, November 22, 1913, 1.

73. D. Lewis, *W. E. B. Du Bois*, 472.

74. Berg, *Ticket to Freedom*, 14.

75. Risa Goluboff has shown the ways in which the NAACP narrowed civil rights activism down to race as "the only cause" of discrimination. Goluboff, "'We Live's in a Free House,'" 2010. See also Goluboff, *Lost Promise*.

76. Belle La Follette reported that Murraye's alleged insubordination was a brief argument with a supervisor as she left work early, with permission, to attend to an eye injury. Thomas H. R. Clarke to May Childs Nerney, September 8, 1913, Part I: C403, RNAACP; Belle C. La Follette, "Color Line to Date," *La Follette's Magazine*, January 24, 1914, 6–7, republished in Unger, "Belle La Follette."

77. Lafayette M. Hershaw to May Childs Nerney, September 11, 1913, Part I: C403, RNAACP.

78. May Childs Nerney to Archibald Grimké, December 10, 1913, box 39-25, folder 493, AGC.

79. Janken, *White*, 150.

80. Moorfield Storey, W. E. B. Du Bois, and Oswald Garrison Villard to Woodrow Wilson, August 15, 1913, file 152a, reel 230, WWP.

81. Paul Bolin to Woodrow Wilson, August 21, 1913, ibid.

82. H. M. Beard to Woodrow Wilson, September 25, 1913, ibid.

83. Swan M. Kendrick to Ruby Moyse, October 22, 1913, box 3, folder 4, KBFP.

84. The Metropolitan's elite status spoke to the way in which church spaces could bind black protest in the early twentieth century: however militantly protesters objected to white supremacy, patriarchal and class conventions remained intact. Higginbotham, *Righteous Discontent*, 7–13; Frederick C. Harris, "Religious Institutions and African American Political Mobilization," in Paul E. Peterson, *Classifying by Race*, 279; Materson, *For the Freedom of Her Race*, 36–38.

85. Oswald Garrison Villard recalled later a total attendance, inside and outside, of closer to 5,000 people. "Race Segregation: The Greatest Meeting in the History of This City," *WB*, November 1, 1913, 1; "Protest against Race Segregation; Monster Mass Meeting Held at the Metropolitan A.M.E. Church," *WES*, October 28, 1913, 8; Villard, *Fighting Years*, 240.

86. Mass Meeting Program to D.C. Metropolitan A.M.E. Church of Washington, October 27, 1913, box 39-25, folder 491, AGC; "Race Segregation," 1; "Protest against Race Segregation," 8.

87. "Protest against Race Segregation," 8. A few weeks later, Villard would put much of this speech in print in the *North American Review*, extending further the NAACP's reach. Villard, "President and the Segregation."

88. Alfred Redman Hussey to Oswald Garrison Villard, October 21, 1913, container 1836, OGVP.

89. Kaye, "Colonel Roscoe Conkling Simmons," 82–83; Kilson, "Political Change."

90. Grimké's daughter, the poet Angelina Weld Grimké, also lived in Washington, having stayed with Francis while he was abroad. Bruce, *Archibald Grimké*, xiii, 70–78; L. Walker, "Struggles and Attempts," 60, 100.

91. L. Walker, "Struggles and Attempts," 25–26, 33, 36; Nerney to Spingarn, July 31, 1913; Bruce, *Archibald Grimké*, 187, 190–93.

92. Grimké became concerned about the interaction of race and class in the 1880s, after reading Timothy Thomas Fortune's *Black and White: Land, Labor, and Politics in*

the South. Fortune's book applied Henry George's theories about eradicating land monopoly to relations between black and white southerners. Bruce, *Archibald Grimké*, 56; Fortune, *Black and White*, 95.

93. Bruce, *Archibald Grimké*, 70–73.

94. Charles S. Hamlin to William G. McAdoo, March 11, 1914, box 114, WGMP.

95. Charles S. Hamlin to Archibald Grimké, June 16, 1914, box 39-25, folder 499, AGC. For the regular correspondence between Grimké and Hamlin, see the AGC.

96. "Colored Men Dismissed; City Postmaster Dismissing and Reducing Colored Men," *WB*, June 6, 1914, 1.

97. I was not able to locate the personnel file for Samuel Browne, so I do not have similar employment data for him. He was mentioned in the letters in Wilkinson's and Butler's files and in the article in the *Bee*. Postmaster to First Assistant Postmaster General, May 27, 1914; F. E. Frazier to Postmaster, June 2, 1914; Postmaster to Horace Springer, June 3, 1914; all in William L. D. Wilkinson, PF NPRC. See also Charles M. Butler, PF NPRC.

98. Archibald Grimké to Charles S. Hamlin, June 2, 1914, box 39-25, folder 499, AGC.

99. Ibid., May 14, 1914, folder 498.

100. In 1915, Wilkinson was dismissed from the service altogether for failure to pay his debts. By 1930, Wilkinson had found work as a government messenger, nowhere near the status he once held as a clerk with twenty years of experience. Grimké to Hamlin, June 2, 1914; F. E. Frazier to Charles S. Hamlin, June 8, 1914, box 39-25, folder 499, AGC; Postmaster to First Assistant Postmaster General, February 19, 1915, William L. D. Wilkinson, PF NPRC; Robert H. Terrell to Merritt O. Chance, June 22, 1916, William L. D. Wilkinson, PF NPRC; Postmaster to Robert H. Terrell, June 24, 1916, William L. D. Wilkinson, PF NPRC; Fifteenth Census of the United States, 1930, District of Columbia, E.D. 75, available at http://www.ancestry.com.

101. Mabel P. Phillips to Archibald Grimké, November 23, 1915, box 39-25, folder 517, AGC.

102. Grimké's work was noted both by Calvin Chase in the pages of the *Bee* and by the national office of NAACP. May Nerney, in fact, marveled at Grimké's maneuvers, and *The Crisis* crowed of his successes, even into 1916, well after the last public rally against segregation. "Archibald H. Grimke, Publicist," *WB*, July 25, 1914, 4; May Childs Nerney to NAACP, July 7, 1914, Part I: A8, RNAACP; "The Fight against Segregation," *The Crisis*, May 1916, 37–38.

103. Walter E. Hawkins to Joel E. Spingarn, July 14, 1915, box 39-25, folder 513, AGC.

104. U.S. Congress, House Select Committee on Reform in the Civil Service, *Hearing on Segregation of Clerks*, 3–4.

105. Ibid., 4, 12.

106. Archibald Grimké to May Childs Nerney, March 8, 1914, Part I: C403, RNAACP; Bruce, *Archibald Grimké*, 194; "The NAACP: The President of the Local Branch of the NAACP Opposes Aswell and Edwards Bills," *WB*, March 14, 1914, 1.

107. U.S. Congress, House Select Committee on Reform in the Civil Service, *Hearing on Segregation of Clerks*, 20–21.

108. Madden's death in 1928 made room for the candidacy and election of Republi-

can Oscar De Priest, the first black congressman elected in the twentieth century. Bullard, "From Businessman to Congressman," i–ii, 143–44; Patler, *Jim Crow*, 16; "Democrats to Run Earl B. Dickerson against Madden," *WT*, June 28, 1924, 1; Bates, *Pullman Porters*, 56.

109. Cooper, *Woodrow Wilson*, 213–36; McGerr, *Fierce Discontent*, 280; Painter, *Standing at Armageddon*, 275–78.

110. Cooper, *Woodrow Wilson*, 25.

111. Thompson, *Woodrow Wilson*, 96; Wilson quoted in A. Link, *Wilson*, 462–64; Cooper, *Woodrow Wilson*, 261, 263; Charles E. Neu, "Woodrow Wilson and Colonel House: The Early Years, 1911–1915," in Cooper and Neu, *Wilson Era*, 257–58, 260.

112. Fox, *Guardian of Boston*, 178–79.

113. Van Riper, *History of the United States Civil Service*, 238. In 1914, the NAACP had 6,000 members around the country. *The Crisis* had a circulation of over 30,000, earning enough to support the association's full-time staff in New York. Fox, *Guardian of Boston*, 178.

114. Lunardini, "Standing Firm," 255–56; Oswald Garrison Villard to Frank J. Garrison, December 11, 1914, container 1465, OGVP.

115. Lunardini, "Standing Firm," 256–57.

116. Renda, *Taking Haiti*, 109. For Renda's brilliant paternalist reading of the Trotter/Wilson meeting, see pp. 108–15. On fundamental dissonances in Wilson's liberalism, see Skowronek, "Reassociation."

117. Dorothy Ross and other students of Wilson have concluded that his particular psychological makeup encouraged him to "project his anger onto those outside the circle of his own identity." Renda, *Taking Haiti*, 111; Ross, "Woodrow Wilson," 667.

118. For an incisive history of the term "race relations," see West, *Education*.

119. Lunardini, "Standing Firm," 257–68.

120. While historians have noted Wilson's desire to avoid "racial friction," their accounts have yet to fully explore the discursive work and assumptions embedded in this key word. Samuel Lonsdale Schaffer, "New South Nation," 271–89; Ring, *Problem South*, 184–93. On key words in political discourse, see R. Williams, *Keywords*; and Rodgers, *Contested Truths*.

121. W. Wilson, "Study of Administration," 203.

122. "What Efficiency Means to Ten Efficient Men," *The Independent*, November 30, 1914, 326–36; Mosher, *Democracy and the Public Service*, 70–73; Waldo, *Administrative State*, 186–96; Jordan, *Machine-Age Ideology*, 68–90; Rodgers, *Atlantic Crossings*, 207.

123. "Friction," or, rather, the German word "reibungsflächen" (sources or surfaces of friction), appears throughout Weber's famed writing on bureaucracy. Indeed, political scientist Alvin Gouldner critiqued Weber for being more concerned about "friction" than actual power relations. Gouldner, "Industrial Sociology," 397. For an example in German, see Weber, *Wirtschaft und Gesellschaft*, 560.

124. Weber, *Economy and Society*, 973–74.

125. Weyl, *New Democracy*, 291–92; Louis Brandeis, "Efficiency and Social Ideals," *The Independent*, November 30, 1914, 327.

126. In 1907, Calvin Chase noted that white racism was causing "friction" in the Census Office. The same year, Census clerk Darwin Moore hoped that he would be as-

signed to fieldwork in a way that would avoid "friction." In 1910, John Dancy assured President Taft that he had performed his function as recorder of deeds "without the slightest friction." "Call a Halt Mr. Director," *WB*, March 23, 1907, 1; Darwin D. Moore to S. N. D. North, July 31, 1907, Darwin D. Moore, PF NPRC; John Dancy to William Howard Taft, February 26, 1910, file 547, reel 331, WHTP.

127. McAdoo to Villard, October 27, 1913.

128. Daniels quoted in Samuel Lonsdale Schaffer, "New South Nation," 367–68. For more on Daniels's reforms in the Navy Department, see pp. 316–85.

129. "Legislators Plan School Probe," *WP*, January 22, 1911, 1.

130. Garner, "Problems of Race Friction"; Royce, *Race Questions*, 51; Mecklin, *Democracy and Race Friction*.

131. Edward Earle Purinton, "Efficiency and Life — First Paper: What Is Efficiency?," *The Independent*, November 30, 1914, 321.

132. Woodrow Wilson, "An Address on Tariff Reform to a Joint Session of Congress," April 8, 1913, in *PWW*, 27:271.

133. "Wilson at Luncheon Champions Daniels," *NYT*, May 18, 1915, 5.

134. Woodrow Wilson to William G. McAdoo, October 24, 1913, box 518, WGMP.

135. Woodrow Wilson, "An Annual Message to Congress," December 2, 1913, in *PWW*, 29:6.

136. Woodrow Wilson, "Remarks upon Signing the Federal Reserve Bill," December 23, 1913, in ibid., 65.

137. Lunardini, "Standing Firm," 259.

138. Ibid., 259–60.

139. Ibid., 261–62.

140. *New Republic*, November 21, 1914, 5.

141. "Friction," *The Independent*, November 23, 1914, 269.

142. CHD, November 30, 1914, p. 189; Charles S. Hamlin to William G. McAdoo, November 21, 1914, box 126, WGMP; *PWW*, 31:309 (n. 2).

143. "President Resents Negro's Criticism," *NYT*, November 13, 1914, 1; "Mail Car Race Problem," *NYT*, May 25, 1913, 4; "Race Protest to Wilson: Constitution League Objects to Segregation of Negro Clerks," *NYT*, October 19, 1913, 15; Fox, *Guardian of Boston*, 181–82.

144. Grimké, *Excerpts from a Thanksgiving Sermon*, 4.

145. "Public Men and Things," *WB*, November 21, 1914, 4. According to Ralph Tyler, Bruce wrote his "Public Men and Things" column under the nom de plume "Sage of the Potomac." Ralph Tyler to Emmett Scott, March 1, 1914, in Harlan, *Booker T. Washington Papers*, 12:464.

146. "The White House Incident: Verdict of the Negro Press — Jim Crow Government Not Endorsed," *WB*, November 28, 1914, 6; "Mr. Trotter and President," *WB*, November 21, 1914, 4.

147. "Segregation Denounced; Colored Americans Assert Their Independence," *WB*, November 21, 1914, 1; "Insult Charge Denied: Colored Orators Say Leader Did Not Offend President," *WP*, November 16, 1914, 2.

148. "President Rebukes Negro Spokesman," *WES*, November 12, 1914, 1.

149. Julius Rosenwald to Woodrow Wilson, September 4, 1913, file 152a, reel 230;

Julius Rosenwald to Woodrow Wilson, November 13, 1914, file 152a, reel 231; both in WWP.

150. Mary S. Smith, "Letters to 'The Times': 'My White Chile,'" *Los Angeles Times*, November 19, 1914, II5.

151. Claude G. Stotts to John Skelton Williams, November 13, 1914, box 126, WGMP.

152. I. W. L. Roundtree to Woodrow Wilson, November 13, 1914, file 152a, reel 231, WWP.

153. Salem Tutt Whitney to Woodrow Wilson, November 15, 1914, ibid.

154. K. Miller, *Segregation*, 1–2.

155. Robert H. Terrell to Joseph P. Tumulty, December 9, 1914, file 152a, reel 231, WWP; Osborn, "Woodrow Wilson," 482; D. Lewis, *W. E. B. Du Bois*, 428; Charles W. Anderson to W. J. Martin, March 10, 1914, box 114, WGMP.

156. Charles W. Anderson to Joseph P. Tumulty, December 22, 1914, file 152a, reel 231, WWP.

157. The phrase "our friend" appears to have been used facetiously by Bookerites who knew that Washington had no actual influence in the Wilson White House. Charles W. Anderson to Booker T. Washington, December 29, 1914 in Harlan, *Booker T. Washington Papers*, 13:205.

158. R. R. Moton to Woodrow Wilson, November 16, 1914, file 152a, reel 231, WWP; Booker T. Washington to Charles Ellis Mason, November 24, 1914 in Harlan, *Booker T. Washington Papers*, 13:182.

159. William Monroe Trotter to Calvin Coolidge, June 30, 1928, box 93, reel 63, Calvin Coolidge Papers, LC; Fox, *Guardian of Boston*, 188, 213, 268–72.

160. Historians Thomas Sugrue and David Freund have tracked assumptions and fears about racial friction among white employers and white homeowners — and the resultant exclusion of black workers and families — to industrial cities like Detroit in the middle decades of the century. Sugrue, *Origins of the Urban Crisis*, 93, 98; Freund, *Colored Property*, 176–240.

161. Tushnet, "Politics of Equality," 891; Berg, *Ticket to Freedom*, 23–24; McAdoo to Villard, October 27, 1913; Bulletin No. 35 quoted in Chad L. Williams, *Torchbearers*, 87.

162. *Milwaukee Free Press*, reprinted in "Wilson, 'Father' of Segregation," *Chicago Defender*, April 22, 1916, 1; Lentz-Smith, *Freedom Struggles*, 33.

163. Swan M. Kendrick to President and Members, January 17, 1919, Part I: G34, RNAACP.

164. Moorfield Storey et al. to William G. McAdoo, January 6, 1916, box 152, WGMP; letter also appears in file 152a, reel 231, WWP; Patler, *Jim Crow*, 175.

165. In September 1914, Chapin Brinsmade noted the NAACP's inability to intercede into press coverage of events in Europe. Chapin Brinsmade to Archibald Grimké, September 23, 1914, box 39-25, folder 503, AGC; Patler, *Jim Crow*, 168–69.

166. Albert Pillsbury to Archibald Grimké, November 26, 1913, box 39-5, folder 100, AGC. Pillsbury was an old friend and ally of Grimké's from Boston. A former Massachusetts attorney general, he was the nephew of abolitionist Parker Pillsbury. Schneider, *Boston Confronts Jim Crow*, 138.

167. Painter, *Standing at Armageddon*, 317–18; "The Hughes Club," *WB*, November 11, 1916, 4; "Inside Story," *WB*, November 25, 1916, 1.

168. War Department Anonymous Employee to Archibald Grimké, August 10, 1916, box 39-26, folder 526, AGC; Colonel Hart to Commission in Charge of State War Navy Dept. Bldg., January 5, 1917, box 563, reel 62, Josephus Daniels Papers, LC.

169. "Party Unity," *WB*, November 13, 1915, 4.

CHAPTER 7

1. S. Gordon, *In This Temple*, 19.

2. "Harding Dedicates Lincoln Memorial," *NYT*, May 31, 1922, 1; "50,000 See Lincoln Memorial Presented to Nation When President Extols Martyr," *WES*, May 31, 1922, 4; "Huge Memorial to 'Honest Abe' Is Dedicated," *Chicago Defender*, June 3, 1922, 2; "Presented by Taft as Nation's Altar," *WP*, May 31, 1922, 2.

3. Shelby J. Davidson, "Shelby Davidson Tells Why Colored Folk Left Lincoln Memorial," *Baltimore Afro-American*, June 9, 1922, 7; "Colored Folk Defy Jim Crow at Dedication," *Baltimore Afro-American*, June 2, 1922, 1.

4. "Near Fight as Citizens Are Jim Crowed," *WT*, June 3, 1922, 1; "No Mishaps Mark Day's Ceremonies," *WP*, May 31, 1922, 2.

5. J. LeCount Chestnut, "Mock Ideal of Lincoln at Memorial," *Chicago Defender*, June 10, 1922, 1; "Near Fight as Citizens Are Jim Crowed," 1.

6. Mennell, "African-Americans and the Selective Service Act," 275; Green, *Secret City*, 184.

7. W. E. B. Du Bois, "Close Ranks," *The Crisis*, July 1918, 111.

8. C. Williams, *Torchbearers*, 53–55; S. M. Kendrick to Josephus Daniels, December 17, 1919, box 563, reel 62, Josephus Daniels Papers, LC.

9. An armed revolt against Jim Crow in Houston, Texas, in August 1917 confirmed for white supremacists, including Wilson administration officials, that African Americans should be kept out of combat roles. Lentz-Smith, *Freedom Struggles*, 59–73, 94–95; C. Williams, *Torchbearers*, 47.

10. C. Williams, *Torchbearers*, 68; D. Kennedy, *Over Here*, 160, 279–80; Green, *Secret City*, 185.

11. Lorenz, "Ralph W. Tyler."

12. Krislov, *Negro in Federal Employment*, 21; Van Riper, *History of the United States Civil Service*, 250–61.

13. "Public Men and Things," *WB*, November 17, 1917, 6.

14. T. Roberts, "Negro in Government," 371.

15. "Prof. Haynes Appointed," *WB*, May 11, 1918, 1; Reich, "Great War," 154.

16. Ruchames, *Race*, 5; Frederick P. Keppel to Carter Glass, May 5, 1919; Frederick P. Keppel to Carter Glass, May 23, 1919; both in Richard W. Thompson, PF NPRC.

17. For the most complete accounting of the Washington riots, see Krugler, "Mob in Uniform."

18. "Recent Outrages," *WB*, July 12, 1919, 4.

19. Tuttle, *Race Riot*, 14, 29–31; Krugler, "Mob in Uniform," 49, 52; Kerlin, *Voice of the Negro*, 17–18, 76–79. Kerlin's book is a collection of articles from the black press following the Washington riot.

20. Tuttle, *Race Riot*, 14.

21. Krugler, "Mob in Uniform"; L. Walker, "Struggles and Attempts," 118; Kerlin, *Voice of the Negro*, 77.

22. "Probe the Riot Tragedy!," *WES*, July 29, 1919, 6; "Race Riots and Force," *WES*, July 30, 1919, 6.

23. Thomas, "District of Columbia."

24. Warren G. Harding, "Acceptance of the Republican Presidential Nomination in 1920, Marion, Ohio," July 22, 1920, in Schlup and Hepp, *Selections*, 127.

25. Bagby, *Road to Normalcy*, 152.

26. "Harding Is Elected," *WB*, November 6, 1920, 4; *WB*, March 19, 1921, 4; Charles T. Magill, "Nation's Capital Is Ready for Harding," *Chicago Defender*, March 5, 1921, 1; Kane, "Federal Segregation," 155; Sherman, "Harding Administration," 155.

27. James Weldon Johnson, "Cause of the Negro Presented to President Harding," *The Crisis*, May 1921, 20–21.

28. Sherman, *Republican Party*, 165–69.

29. For Johnson's concerns, see Zangrando, *NAACP Crusade*, 57; and Warren G. Harding, "Speech to Congress, April 12, 1921," in Schlup and Hepp, *Selections*, 195.

30. "Inquiry on Race Row: Recorder of Deeds Promises Investigation of Office," *WP*, May 13, 1913, 16; Julius Kahn to Arthur G. Froe, December 14, 1922; Arthur G. Froe to Irene Monroe, January 14, 1926; both in Irene Monroe, PF NPRC.

31. Glenda E. Gilmore, "False Friends and Avowed Enemies: Southern African Americans and Party Allegiances in the 1920s," in Dailey, Gilmore, and Simon, *Jumpin' Jim Crow*, 222.

32. Sherman, *Republican Party*, 135; Fairclough, *Teaching Equality*, 33.

33. Lafayette M. Hershaw to James Weldon Johnson, May 9, 1923, Part I: C403, RNAACP.

34. Warren G. Harding, "Speech on Race Relations, Birmingham, Alabama," October 26, 1921, in Schlup and Hepp, *Selections*, 248–53; Parrish, *Anxious Decades*, 26. For the long history of black migration as a method of combating racial discrimination, see W. Cohen, *At Freedom's Edge*.

35. "Mr. Harding and the South," *WES*, January 14, 1921, 6.

36. "'Bearded the Lion in His Den,'" *WB*, November 5, 1921, 4; "President Harding's Speech," *WT*, October 29, 1921, 8.

37. "Harding Says Negro Must Have Equality in Political Life," *NYT*, October 27, 1921, 1.

38. Warren G. Harding to Malcolm Jennings, January 6, 1922, in Schlup and Hepp, *Selections*, 270–71.

39. "Negro 'Silent Parade' Protests Lynchings," *WES*, June 15, 1922, 9; Holden-Smith, "Lynching," 53–54; Zangrando, *NAACP Crusade*, 57, 64, 69; "Sixty Seventh Congress with Republican Majority Shows a Dismal Failure," *WT*, September 30, 1922, 1.

40. Plummer, "Afro-American Response," 132–36; Renda, *Taking Haiti*, 94–97, 115, 132. See also Schmidt, *United States Occupation*.

41. "'Link' Johnson Says He Will Be Confirmed," *WT*, September 3, 1921, 1; "A. G. Froe Expected to Be D.C. Recorder of Deeds," *WES*, February 1, 1922, 1; "West Virginian for Recorder of Deeds," *WT*, February 4, 1922, 1; "Froe Is Confirmed as Deeds Recorder," *WES*, February 16, 1922, 2; "Negro Labor Bureau," *WES*, April 7, 1921, 34; "Negro Given

High Post," *WES*, May 14, 1921, 3; C. Bascom Slemp to William M. Calder, October 5, 1925, box 93, reel 63, Calvin Coolidge Papers, LC; Sherman, *Republican Party*, 166–69. For lists of all African American appointees between 1890 and 1930, see Hiller, "Race Politics," 25, 130–32, 183, 267, 274.

42. "Special Assistants," *WT*, May 21, 1921, 8; Sherman, *Republican Party*, 168.

43. Warren G. Harding to N. D. Brascher, October 5, 1921, in Schlup and Hepp, *Selections*, 243–44.

44. "President Harding," *WT*, August 4, 1923, 6; Ferrell, *Presidency of Calvin Coolidge*.

45. "Hon. C. Bascom Slemp," *WB*, October 8, 1910, 1; C. Bascom Slemp to Washington Gardner, May 28, 1922, Ferdinand Lee, PF NPRC; "Lily Whites Receive Important Appointments," *WT*, August 18, 1923, 1; Blair, "Time for Parting," 179; Sherman, *Republican Party*, 218–21; Hathorn, "C. Bascom Slemp," 248, 260; Kousser, *Shaping of Southern Politics*, 38 (n. 47).

46. William H. Lewis to Calvin Coolidge, August 8, 1924, box 93, reel 63, Calvin Coolidge Papers, LC. Recorder of Deeds Arthur Froe had offered Slemp a similar warning earlier in the year. Arthur G. Froe to C. Bascom Slemp, November 15, 1923, ibid.; Ike Murray, "Negro Vote Is Not Safe to G.O.P.," *WT*, April 26, 1924, 1.

47. "Delegates Face Color Line in Cleveland," *WT*, June 14, 1924, 1; William L. Houston to Charles Hamilton Houston, September 4, 1924, box 8, folder 8, WLHFP.

48. On Teapot Dome, see Stratton, *Tempest over Teapot Dome*; and McCartney, *Teapot Dome Scandal*.

49. On Coolidge's modern management of his and the presidency's image, see Greenberg, *Calvin Coolidge*.

50. For the Ku Klux Klan and the faltering southern economy in this period, see MacLean, *Behind the Mask*.

51. Throughout 1924, the *Tribune* chronicled the ways in which Coolidge had proved a disappointment to African Americans. "Atty. W. H. Lewis Holds Unique Position," *WT*, April 19, 1924, 1; "Coolidge Does Little for Negro during First Year," *WT*, August 9, 1924, 8; "New Leadership Is Paramount to Racial Success. New Blood Needed," *WT*, September 6, 1924, 1; "Government Discrimination and Segregation," *WT*, September 20, 1924, 6.

52. "Office Seekers Getting Little Encouragement," *WT*, April 18, 1925, 1.

53. "Coolidge's Speech Fails to Impress Race," *WT*, August 16, 1924, 1.

54. In fact, nearly all of Howard's appointments went to Democrats. Lisio, *Hoover*, 219.

55. "Suspend Howard from U.S. Office," *WES*, July 17, 1928, 1.

56. McMillen, "Perry W. Howard."

57. "Mississippi Patronage Sold, Wilson Charges," *WES*, March 23, 1926, 42.

58. J. Grossman, *Land of Hope*, 3–4.

59. Katznelson, *Black Men*, 66; Bates, *Pullman Porters*, 55–57.

60. On African Americans in Chicago in the early twentieth century, see Baldwin, *Chicago's New Negroes*; Spear, *Black Chicago*; and Drake and Cayton, *Black Metropolis*. On New York, see T. Reed, *Not Alms*; and Osofsky, *Harlem*.

61. Chief Statistician for Agriculture to Census Director, February, 16, 1921; William L. Austin to Memorandum, March 4, 1920; both in CEHP.

62. Charles E. Hall to Herbert Hoover, March 19, 1921, ibid.

63. Samuel L. Rogers to Mr. Libbey, March 22, 1921, ibid.

64. Hoover gained a certain degree of fame (and infamy) in 1928 when he began to position himself for a presidential campaign by ordering the desegregation of Charles Hall's division. The continuous segregation apparent in Hall's personnel record suggests that the order was more political flash than substance. Arnold, "'Great Engineer'"; "Sees 'Solid South' Closed to G.O.P.," WES, April 10, 1928, 2; "Blease Scores Hoover for Lifting Color Line," WES, April 17, 1928, 3; Lisio, Hoover, 30.

65. Herbert Hoover to Andrew W. Mellon, February, 24, 1926, Joseph McDuffie, PF NPRC.

66. Roland O. Groomes, PF NPRC; Robert Pelham Jr., PF NPRC. For public acknowledgment of the Pelham group, see "Valuable Census Data on Progress of Afro-Americans," Chicago Defender, April 17, 1915, 1.

67. Census Bureau Memorandum, July 17, 1930; Daniel C. Roper to William L. Austin, June 29, 1937; William L. Austin to Charles E. Hall, May 28, 1938; all in CEHP.

68. Rung, Servants of the State, 46; Krislov, Negro in Federal Employment, 22.

69. BEP officer quoted in Johnston and Greene, Employment of Negroes, 59.

70. Classification Sheet, May 15, 1923, John A. Davis, PF NPRC.

71. F. A. Gosnell to Chief Clerk, Bureau of the Census, January 3, 1925, Roland Groomes, PF NPRC.

72. Lane was not the only person to try to quantify what had been lost financially during the Democratic administration. In a letter to the Washington Post, Uzziah Miner contended that the loss of seventeen public offices "taken from the colored race" was $65,000 in salaries. David A. Lane to H. M. Vandervort, June 7, 1921, David A. Lane, PF NPRC; Uzziah Miner, "Letter to the Editor: Alleges Colored Voters Are Now Opposed to Wilson," WP, October 30, 1916, 7.

73. Assistant Secretary of the Interior to David A. Lane, December 1, 1913; David A. Lane to G. M. Saltzgaber, December 4, 1913; Josephus Daniels to Commissioner of Pensions, May 26, 1913; Josephus Daniels to Commissioner of Pensions (Telephone Message), August 20, 1913; all in David A. Lane, PF NPRC.

74. Edward F. Arnold to Edward C. Finney, August 31, 1922; Bo Sweeney to Edward F. Arnold, July 15, 1914; Joseph S. Frelinghuysen to Pension Office Chief of Personnel, June 10, 1921; all in Edward F. Arnold, PF NPRC.

75. Botts's statement was quoted by his supervisor in a letter to D.C. City Postmaster Merritt O. Chance. C. E. Schooley to Merritt O. Chance, August 30, 1922, John M. Botts, PF NPRC.

76. Merritt O. Chance to John Minor Botts, August 31, 1922, ibid.

77. John Minor Botts to Merritt O. Chance, September 2, 1922, ibid.

78. Theodore Roosevelt Jr. to Edward C. Finney, May 16, 1923, Joseph Murray, PF NPRC.

79. William Spry to Edward C. Finney, May 17, 1923, ibid.

80. Joseph N. Murray to William Spry, September 27, 1923, and William Spry to Hubert Work, September 12, 1923, ibid.

81. Welliver was still around, though Harding had died a month earlier. I refer to

him as Harding's secretary because Coolidge would soon have him replaced. Judson C. Welliver to Hubert Work, September 28, 1923, ibid.

82. William Spry to Hubert Work, September 29, 1923, ibid.

83. Blair, "Time for Parting," 183.

84. The creation of the Personnel Classification Board in 1923 was supposed to standardize positions and pay, but its authority was deeply fractured. Ultimately, most management still resided with individual division managers. Walter White and W. T. Andrews to NAACP, August 1928, Part I: C403, RNAACP; "Departmental Segregation Must Go Now," WT, November 15, 1924, 1; "Color Discrimination in Government Service," The Crisis, November 1928, 377; "Personnel Classification," WT, July 26, 1924, 6; Skowronek, Building a New American State, 209–11; Van Riper, History of the United States Civil Service, 301–3.

85. Interior officials retracted their plan, though investigators continued to find segregation in the department. The segregation justifications appeared in an undated memo to the White House and in Work's statement to the Star. Interior Department to Memorandum, n.d. [1927?], box 93, reel 63, Calvin Coolidge Papers, LC; "Colored Workers' Charges Denied," WES, October 8, 1927, 2; Sherman, Republican Party, 218.

86. Andrew W. Mellon to James Weldon Johnson, May 16, 1928, Part I: C403, RNAACP.

87. Thomas H. Hutchins to Arthur J. Hirsch, June 28, 1923, Thomas H. Hutchins, PF NPRC.

88. Thaddeus H. Caraway to W. M. Steuart, January 8, 1924, and W. M. Steuart to Thaddeus H. Caraway, January 9, 1924, ibid.

89. Pierre Henri Davis Jr., Personnel Question Sheet, March 10, 1920; Robert A. Pelham to Memorandum for Dr. Murphy, December 12, 1924; both in Pierre H. Davis Jr., PF NPRC.

90. Pierre H. Davis Jr. to W. M. Steuart, October 24, 1929, ibid.

91. Pierre H. Davis Jr. to Lawrence Richey, October 24, 1929, and Pierre H. Davis Jr. to W. M. Steuart, July 24, 1931, ibid.

92. Herbert F. McGirt to A. S. Chadwick, August 31, 1922, Herbert F. McGirt, PF NPRC.

93. According to the report, the black federal labor force had grown from 22,540 in 1910 to 51,882 in 1928. Department of Labor to Press Release, September 1, 1928, box 93, reel 63, Calvin Coolidge Papers, LC; Green, Secret City, 203; Greene and Callis, Employment, 59.

94. Johnson and Libecap, Federal Civil Service System, 82; Van Riper, History of the United States Civil Service, 245.

95. Douglas, Real Wages, 199.

96. "Cost of Living," 60.

97. Stricker, "Affluence for Whom?"

98. Swan M. Kendrick to Ruby M. Kendrick, January 27, 1922, and January 1, 1922, box 6, folder 1, KBFP.

99. Ibid., January 3, 1922.

100. James N. House to Ruby M. Kendrick, September 13, 1923, box 7, folder 8, ibid.

101. "Investiation Reveals Deplorable Conditions in Bureau of Engraving, Part 1," *WT*, June 18, 1921, 2; "Discrimination in Bureau of Engraving Is Rank, Part 5," *WT*, July 16, 1921, 2.

102. "Investiation Reveals Deplorable Conditions in Bureau of Engraving, Part 2," *WT*, June 25, 1921, 2; "Discrimination in Bureau of Engraving Is Rank, Part 5," 2.

103. "Discrimination in Bureau of Engraving Is Rank, Part 5," 2.

104. "Final Article on Bureau Brings Out Evil of Boss System as It Now Exists, Part 6," *WT*, July 28, 1921, 2.

105. Bill McAlister, "Treasury Settles Bias Suit at Bureau of Engraving: Practices Kept Blacks in Lower-Paying Jobs," *WP*, November 21, 1990, A1.

106. In 1923, Lafayette Hershaw, a lawyer in the Interior Department, wrote to James Weldon Johnson to ask, "Has the NAACP abandoned warfare on Segregation in the Federal Civil Service? Is the association 'pussyfooting' on the question?" Lafayette M. Hershaw to James Weldon Johnson, May 9, 1923, Part I: C403, RNAACP.

107. "Gov't Workers to Hold Mass Meeting Monday at Cleveland School," *WT*, September 20, 1924, 1. On Burroughs and black women's labor organizing in Washington in the 1920s, see Murphy, "Mapping African American Women's Activism."

108. "Question of Segregation Put Squarely Up to Coolidge," *WT*, November 14, 1925, 1.

109. Some may even have been drawn to the black nationalist crusade of Marcus Garvey. Garvey spoke to enthusiastic audiences in Washington regularly between 1921 and 1924, and there was a local division of the Universal Negro Improvement Association (UNIA). But it is difficult to gauge the strength of the UNIA in the capital. I have found no evidence of government clerks being active members of the UNIA. "Speakers Protest Race Segregation," *WES*, October 26, 1927, 12; "Segregation Protested," *WES*, October 30, 1927, section 1, p. 3; Neval H. Thomas to Calvin Coolidge, August 8, 1927, box 93, reel 63, Calvin Coolidge Papers, LC; "Speech by Marcus Garvey, Washington, D.C.," November 20, 1921, in R. Hill, *Marcus Garvey*, 4:294–313; "Negroes Convene Here," *WES*, August 26, 1923, 15; "Garvey Received by Large Crowd," *WT*, November 10, 1923, 1; "Speech by Marcus Garvey, Washington, DC," January 15, 1924, in R. Hill, *Marcus Garvey*, 5:520–33; "Seeks Aid for Negroes," *WES*, April 13, 1924, 31.

110. Washington's stricter racism was connected to a "hardening" of racial nationalism that resulted, for example, in strict immigration quotas in the 1920s. Holloway, *Confronting the Veil*, 44; Green, *Secret City*, 184–217; Gerstle, *American Crucible*, 81–127; Ngai, *Impossible Subjects*, 21–55.

111. "Action by the NAACP," *WB*, November 3, 1917, 1.

112. "A Jim-Crow Beach," *WT*, December 20, 1924, 6.

113. "Big Musicale Comes to Abrupt End When Race Singers Walk Out as Protest Segregation," *WT*, May 9, 1925, 1; "A New Day Dawning," *WT*, May 9, 1925, 6.

114. "Colonel Sherrill Named," 568; U.S. Congress, House Committee on Appropriations, *District of Columbia Appropriation Bill*, 1184–89.

115. "Jim Crow Signs Posted in Rock Creek Park by Harding Appointee," *WT*, April 22, 1922, 1.

116. "Protest Beach Being Separate," *WT*, June 18, 1921, 1; "Favors Colored Golfer," *WT*, July 16, 1921, 8.

117. "Separate Bathing Beach—Never!" *WT*, January 27, 1923, 8.

118. "Bathing Beach Plans Discarded by War Dept.," *WT*, August 25, 1923, 1.

119. "Cabinet Member Segregates," *WT*, May 24, 1924, 1.

120. Ike Murray, "Jim Crow Bathing Beach Here Opposed," *WT*, April 26, 1924, 1.

121. "Senate Cuts Out Beach Items," *WT*, February 21, 1925, 1; "3 More Die in Heat Wave, 7 Overcome, with Hundreds Ill," *WP*, June 5, 1925, 1; "Warren and Madden Can Reopen Bathing Sites, Sherrill Says," *WP*, June 11, 1925, 22; "Blanton Wants Segregation in Wading Pools," *WT*, June 20, 1925, 1.

122. Green, *Secret City*, 201.

123. McQuirter, "Claiming the City," 132–77.

124. Griffith Stadium's separate bleachers were technically informal but carefully observed by the mid-1920s. "Segregation at Branch Libraries?" *WT*, March 18, 1922, 1; Snyder, *Beyond the Shadow*, xi, 12–13; "Jim-Crow Golf Course Factor in Fight on Segregation," *WT*, June 20, 1925, 1; "Pools in Potomac Park Recommended by Grant," *WP*, August 11, 1926, 8.

125. "Negroes of Washington Worry Georgia Congressman," *WT*, January 27, 1923, 1.

126. "Attempts at Residential Segregation Spreads," *WT*, April 21, 1923, 1; "Injunction against Mrs. Helen Curtis Made Permanent for Period of Twenty-One Years," *WT*, May 12, 1923, 1; "Attempted Residential Segregation in D.C.," *WT*, October 27, 1923, 1; "Residential Segregation Fight Now in D.C. Courts," *WT*, December 15, 1923, 1. On the history of racial covenants and other tools for enforcing residential segregation, see Massey and Denton, *American Apartheid*; and Freund, *Colored Property*.

127. The Court ruled that the Fourteenth Amendment barred only state discrimination, whereas racial covenants were between private citizens. 271 U.S. 323 (1926). The Court did not declare all racial covenants to be unconstitutional until *Shelley v. Kraemer*, 334 U.S. 1 (1948).

128. "Mob of Whites Visits Negro Homes," *WT*, November 10, 1923, 1. For mob intimidation in the service of residential segregation, see Sugrue, *Origins of the Urban Crisis*, 24, 73–76; and Boyle, *Arc of Justice*.

129. Geraldyn Dismond, "Capital of Nation Elaborately Fetes Proud Followers of Howard-Lincoln," *Pittsburgh Courier*, December 4, 1926, 6.

130. "Club Has Election," *WES*, January 15, 1922, 29; "Negroes Buying Homes," *WES*, June 17, 1922, 15; "Academy Session Closes," *WES*, December 29, 1922, 18; Green, *Secret City*, 208.

131. "Business Men's Parade," *WES*, April 10, 1921, 2; "Business Opportunities on U Street," *WT*, June 25, 1921, 8; "The New Bank and What It Means," *WT*, July 21, 1923, 8; Harley, "For the Good of Family and Race," 341.

132. Hughes was a descendant of the famous black Republican John Mercer Langston. Writing in *Opportunity*, Brenda Moryck disagreed, arguing that Hughes failed to see beneath the surface of Washington. Hughes, "Our Wonderful Society"; Moryck, "I, Too, Have Lived in Washington," 228–31, 243.

133. "Thrift of Colored Residents Shown," *WES*, September 2, 1922, 2.

134. "Business Opportunities on U Street," 8.

135. "Helplessness of Negro Business," *WT*, March 24, 1923, 8; "After Graduation—What?" *WT*, June 23, 1923, 8.

136. "Senator Vardaman Put on District Committee," *WES*, March 12, 1917, 3; Korn-weibel, *Investigate Everything*, 199–225; "Moen Case a Sensation," *Chicago Defender*, April 5, 1919, 15; "Society Scandal Shocks Washington," *Chicago Defender*, April 12, 1919, 1; "Washington Public Schools—'A National Disgrace,'" *WT*, August 30, 1924, 6; Green, *Secret City*, 210–12.

137. All three Kendrick children attended college. Martha graduated summa cum laude from Howard, studied at the Sorbonne, and then went on to chair Howard's Department of Romance Languages; Charlotte became a highly regarded teacher and the first black woman to be elected president of the National Council of Teachers of English; and Webster—known as Ken—became an award-winning physicist in Balti-more. Brooks and Brooks, *Kendrick Kin*, 241–60.

138. Hughes, "Our Wonderful Society"; Toomer, *Cane*, 41; Frank quoted in Mintz, "Historical Ethnography," 253. On Toomer and Frank, see M. Yellin, "Visions of Their America."

139. E. Williams, *When Washington Was in Vogue*, 121.

140. L. Walker, "Struggles and Attempts," 102. On the migration in general, see J. Grossman, *Land of Hope*; and Wilkerson, *Warmth of Other Suns*.

141. U.S. Bureau of the Census, "Table 23: District of Columbia."

142. "The South in Congress," *WES*, December 7, 1915, 6; "The South," *WES*, April 9, 1916, 6.

143. "The Recordership," *WES*, April 22, 1915, 6.

144. "Lynching," *WES*, December 20, 1921, 6.

145. Hughes, "Our Wonderful Society," 227.

146. J. Miller, "Black Washington"; Ronald M. Johnson, "Those Who Stayed." For the importance of New Negro culture in Chicago and New York, see Baldwin, *Chicago's New Negroes*; and D. Lewis, *When Harlem Was In Vogue*. For the centrality of the "international perspective" in the Harlem Renaissance, see Fabre and Feith, *Temples for Tomorrow*, 259–332.

EPILOGUE

1. "Klan Host Parades on Penn. Ave.; No Disorder; Everybody Prepared," *WT*, August 15, 1925, 1; "Sight Astonishes Capital," *NYT*, August 9, 1925, 1; "White-Robed Klan Cheered on March in Nation's Capital," *WP*, August 9, 1925, 1.

2. Barber, *Marching on Washington*; Farrar, *Building the Body Politic*.

3. For the mass movement of African Americans into the Democratic Party, see Weiss, *Farewell*.

4. Sullivan, *Days of Hope*, 136; Dalfiume, "'Forgotten Years,'" 99; Ruchames, *Race*, 20–21; Elmer W. Henderson, "The Employment of Negroes in the Federal Govern-ment," box 231, Records of the Committee on Fair Employment Practice Central Files, Administrative Division, Central Files, 1941–1946, RG 228, NARA.

5. Landis, *Segregation in Washington*, 62.

Bibliography

PRIMARY SOURCES

Archival and Manuscript Collections

Cambridge, Mass.
  Houghton Library, Harvard University
    Oswald Garrison Villard Papers
Charlottesville, Va.
  Special Collections, University of Virginia Library
    John Skelton Williams Papers
College Park, Md.
  National Archives and Records Administration
    Bureau of Employment Security (RG 183)
    Bureau of Engraving and Printing (RG 318)
    Bureau of the Census (RG 29)
    Civil Service Commission (RG 146)
    Committee on Fair Employment Practice Central Files (RG 228)
    Department of Agriculture (RG 16)
    Department of Commerce (RG 40)
    Department of Commerce and Labor (RG 257)
    Department of Justice (RG 60)
    Department of Labor (RG 174)
    Department of the Interior (RG 48)
    Department of the Treasury (RG 56)
    Government of the District of Columbia (RG 351)
    Government Printing Office (RG 149)
    Publications of the Federal Government (RG 287)
Princeton, N.J.
  Manuscripts Division, Department of Rare Books and Special Collections,
    Princeton University Library
    Records of the Woodrow Wilson Papers Project
St. Louis, Mo.
  National Personnel Records Center
    Civilian Personnel Files
Washington, D.C.
  Historical Society of Washington, D.C.
    Kiplinger Research Library Reference Collection

Howard University, Moorland-Spingarn Research Center
    Thomas H. R. Clarke Papers
    James Adlai Cobb Papers
    Shelby Davidson Papers
    Archibald Grimké Collection
    Andrew F. Hilyer Papers
Manuscript Division, Library of Congress
    Albert Burleson Papers
    Grover Cleveland Papers
    Calvin Coolidge Papers
    George B. Cortelyou Papers
    Josephus Daniels Papers
    William Dudley Foulke Papers
    Constance McLaughlin Green Papers
    Charles S. Hamlin Papers
    William Henry Harrison Papers
    Charlotte Hopkins Papers
    William LePre Houston Family Papers
    Kendrick-Brooks Family Papers
    William Gibbs McAdoo Papers
    William McKinley Papers
    Daniel Alexander Payne Murray Papers
    Records of the National Association for the Advancement of Colored People
    Theodore Roosevelt Papers
    William Howard Taft Papers
    Robert Terrell Papers
    John Sharp Williams Papers
    Woodrow Wilson Papers
    Carter G. Woodson Collection
National Archives Building
    Bureau of Naval Personnel (RG 24)
    Department of the Navy (RG 80)
    Department of the Post Office (RG 28)
    Department of War (RG 107)
    Charles E. Hall Papers

Periodicals

Atlanta Constitution
Baltimore Afro-American
Chicago Defender
Civil Service Advocate
Cleveland Gazette
The Congregationalist
Congressional Record

The Crisis
The Independent
Indianapolis Freeman
Los Angeles Times
The Nation
The New Republic
New York Age
New York Amsterdam News
New York Times
Pittsburgh Courier
Washington Bee
Washington Evening Star
Washington Herald
Washington Post
Washington Times
Washington Tribune

Government Documents

U.S. Bureau of the Census. *Bulletin 94: Statistics of Employees: Executive Civil Service of the United States, 1907.* Edited by Lewis Merriam. Washington: Government Printing Office, 1908.
———. "Historical Census of Housing Tables: Homeownership." *Housing and Household Economics Statistics Division.* Available at http://www.census.gov/hhes/www/housing/census/historic/owner.html. August 24, 2011.
———. *Historical Census Statistics on Population Totals by Race, 1790 to 1990, and by Hispanic Origin, 1970 to 1990, for Large Cities and Other Urban Places in the United States.* Available at http://www.census.gov/population/www/documentation/twps0076/twps0076.html. July 25, 2012.
———. *The Social and Economic Status of the Black Population in the United States, 1790–1978: An Historical View.* Washington: Bureau of the Census, 1979.
———. *The Statistical History of the United States, from Colonial Times to the Present.* New York: Basic Books, 1976.
———. "Table 23: District of Columbia—Race and Hispanic Origin, 1800–1990." Available at http://www.census.gov/population/www/documentation/twps0056/tab23.pdf. May 24, 2012.
U.S. Civil Service Commission. *Civil Service Act, Rules and Executive Orders.* Washington: Government Printing Office, 1912.
———. *Thirtieth Annual Report of the United States Civil Service Commission, 1913.* Washington: Government Printing Office, 1914.
U.S. Congress. House of Representatives. Committee on Appropriations. *District of Columbia Appropriation Bill for 1923.* 67th Cong., 2nd sess., December 29, 1921. Washington: Government Printing Office, 1921.
U.S. Congress. House of Representatives. Committee on the District of Columbia.

Intermarriage of White and Negro Races within the District of Columbia. 63rd Cong., 2nd sess., H. Rept. 432. Washington: Government Printing Office, 1914.

U.S. Congress. House of Representatives. Select Committee on Reform in the Civil Service. *Hearing on Segregation of Clerks and Employees in the Civil Service.* 63rd Cong., 2nd sess., March 6, 1914. Washington: Government Printing Office, 1914.

U.S. Congress. Senate. Committee on the District of Columbia. *Hearing on Inhabited Alleys in the District of Columbia and Housing of Unskilled Workingmen.* 63rd Cong., 2nd sess. March 7, 1914. Washington: Government Printing Office, 1914.

U.S. Works Progress Administration. Federal Writers' Project. *Washington: City and Capital.* Washington: Government Printing Office, 1937.

Published Works

Bancroft, Frederic, ed. *Speeches, Correspondence, and Political Papers of Carl Schurz.* Vol. 6. New York: G. P. Putnam's Sons, 1913.

Burton, David Henry, ed. *The Collected Works of William Howard Taft.* 8 vols. Athens: Ohio University Press, 2001.

"Colonel Sherrill Named as President Harding's Military Aide." *Engineering News Record* 86, no. 13 (March 31, 1921): 568.

Cuney-Hare, Maud. *Norris Wright Cuney: A Tribune of the Black People.* 1913. New York: G. K. Hall and Co., 1995.

Dancy, John C. *Sand against the Wind: The Memoirs of John C. Dancy.* Detroit: Wayne State University Press, 1966.

Daniels, Josephus, and Edmund David Cronon. *The Cabinet Diaries of Josephus Daniels, 1913–1921.* Lincoln: University of Nebraska Press, 1963.

Du Bois, W. E. B. "My Impressions of Woodrow Wilson." *Journal of Negro History* 58, no. 4 (October 1973): 453–59.

———. *The Souls of Black Folk.* 1903. New York: Penguin Books, 1996.

Dunbar, Paul Laurence. "Negro Society in Washington." *Saturday Evening Post,* December 1901, 9.

Dunning, William A. *Reconstruction, Political and Economic, 1865–1877.* New York: Harper and Brothers, 1907.

Fish, Carl Russell. *The Civil Service and the Patronage.* Cambridge, Mass.: Harvard University Press, 1904.

———. "Lincoln and the Patronage." *American Historical Review* 8, no. 1 (October 1902): 53–69.

Foltz, El Bie K. *The Federal Civil Service as a Career: A Manual for Applicants for Positions and Those in the Civil Service of the Nation.* New York: G. P. Putnam's Sons, 1909.

Fortune, Timothy Thomas. *Black and White: Land, Labor, and Politics in the South.* 1884. New York: Arno Press, 1968.

Garner, J. W. "Problems of Race Friction." *The Dial,* January 1, 1909, 19.

Gregory, T. W. *Reconstruction and the Ku Klux Klan: A Paper read before the Arkansas and Texas Bar Associations, July 10, 1906.* Austin, Tex.: n.p., 1906.

Grimké, Francis J. *Excerpts from a Thanksgiving Sermon, Delivered November 26, 1914, and Two Letters Addressed to Hon. Woodrow Wilson, President of the U.S.* Washington, D.C.: R. L. Pendleton, 1914.

Harlan, Louis R., ed. *The Booker T. Washington Papers.* 14 vols. Urbana: University of Illinois Press, 1972–89.

Hill, Robert A., ed. *The Marcus Garvey and Universal Negro Improvement Association Papers.* 11 vols. Berkeley: University of California Press, 1983.

Hughes, Langston. "Our Wonderful Society: Washington." *Opportunity,* August 1927, 226–27.

Johnson, Henry Lincoln. *The Negro under Wilson.* Washington, D.C.: Republican National Committee, 1916.

Jones, Thomas Jesse. "The Alley Homes of Washington." *Survey,* October 19, 1912, 67–69.

———. *Negro Education: A Study of the Private and Higher Schools for Colored People in the United States.* Vol. 1. Washington, D.C.: Government Printing Office, 1917.

Kerlin, Robert T. *The Voice of the Negro 1919.* 1920. New York: Arno Press, 1968.

Landis, Kenesaw Mountain, II. *Segregation in Washington, a Report.* Chicago: National Committee on Segregation in the Nation's Capital, 1948.

Leupp, Francis Ellington. *How to Prepare for a Civil-Service Examination.* New York: Hinds and Noble, 1898.

Link, Arthur S., ed. *The Papers of Woodrow Wilson.* 69 vols. Princeton: Princeton University Press, 1966–.

Logan, Mrs. John. *Thirty Years in Washington, or Life and Scenes in Our National Capital.* Hartford, Conn.: A. D. Worthington and Co., 1901.

Low, A. Maurice. "Society in Washington." *Harper's Monthly Magazine,* April 1902, 688–99.

———. "Washington: The City of Leisure." *Atlantic Monthly,* December 1900, 767–78.

———. *Woodrow Wilson, an Interpretation.* Boston: Little, Brown, and Co., 1918.

Lynch, John Roy. *The Facts of Reconstruction.* 1913. New York: Arno Press, 1968.

Mallalieu, Wilbur Vincent. "A Washington Alley." *Survey,* October 19, 1912, 69–71.

Mecklin, John Moffatt. *Democracy and Race Friction: A Study in Social Ethics.* New York: Macmillan Company, 1914.

Miller, Kelly. *Segregation: The Caste System and the Civil Service.* Washington, D.C.: Murray Bros. Co., 1914.

Morison, Elting E., ed. *The Letters of Theodore Roosevelt.* 8 vols. Cambridge, Mass.: Harvard University Press, 1951–54.

Moryck, Brenda Ray. "I, Too, Have Lived in Washington." *Opportunity,* August 1927, 228–43.

Patterson, Adam E., and M. W. Guy. *The Homeseeker's Guide.* Muskogee, Indian Territory: Commercial Industrial Association, 1907.

"Political Activity in the Presidential Campaign." *Good Government* 29, no. 4 (April 1912): 55–56.

Riis, Jacob A. "The Housing Problem Facing Congress." *Charities* 12, no. 6 (February 6, 1904): 161–66.

———. *How the Other Half Lives: Studies among the Tenements of New York.* 1890. New York: Penguin Books, 1997.

Roosevelt, Theodore. "An Object Lesson in Civil Service Reform." *Atlantic Monthly*, February 1891, 253–55.

Roper, Daniel C. *Fifty Years of Public Life*. Durham, N.C.: Duke University Press, 1941.

Royce, Josiah. *Race Questions, Provincialisms, and Other American Problems*. 1908. New York: Fordham University Press, 2009.

Schlup, Leonard, and John H. Hepp IV, eds. *Selections from the Papers and Speeches of Warren G. Harding, 1918–1923*. Lewiston, N.Y.: Edwin Mellen Press, 2008.

Sherman's Directory and Ready Reference of the Colored Population in the District of Columbia. Washington, D.C.: Sherman Directory Company, 1913.

Simmons, William J. *Men of Mark: Eminent, Progressive and Rising*. 1887. New York: Arno Press, 1968.

Slayden, Ellen Maury. *Washington Wife: Journal of Ellen Maury Slayden from 1897–1919*. New York: Harper and Row, 1962.

State of South Carolina. General Assembly. *Concurrent Resolution H. 561*. Regular sess., January 12, 1909. Columbia: Gonzalez and Bryan, State Printers, 1909.

Terrell, Mary Church. *A Colored Woman in a White World*. Washington, D.C.: Ransdell, 1940.

———. "Society among the Colored People of Washington." *Voice of the Negro*, March 1904, 150–56.

Thomas, Neval. "The District of Columbia—A Paradise of Paradoxes." *Messenger*, October 1923. In *These Colored United States: African American Essays from the 1920s*, edited by Tom Lutz and Susanna Ashton, 80–85. New Brunswick, N.J.: Rutgers University Press, 1996.

Toomer, Jean. *Cane*. 1923. New York: W. W. Norton and Company, 1988.

Turner, George Kibbe. "What Wilson Is Up Against." *McClure's Magazine*, February 1913, 148–78.

Twain, Mark, and Charles Dudley Warner. *The Gilded Age: A Tale of To-Day*. Hartford: American Publishing Company, 1873.

Tyler, Lyon G., ed. *Men of Mark in Virginia: Ideals of American Life*. Vol. 1. Washington, D.C.: Men of Mark Publishing Company, 1906.

Unger, Nancy. "How Did Belle La Follette Resist Racial Segregation in Washington D.C., 1913–1914?" In *Women and Social Movements in the United States, 1775–2000*, edited by Kathryn Sklar and Thomas Dublin, 8, no. 2. Binghamton: SUNY at Binghamton, 2004, http://www.alexanderstreet6.com/wasm/index.html. August 8, 2005.

Villard, Oswald Garrison. *Fighting Years: Memoirs of a Liberal Editor*. New York: Harcourt, Brace and Company, 1939.

———. "The President and the Segregation at Washington." *North American Review*, December 1913, 800–807.

Waldron, J. Milton, and J. D. Harkless. *The Political Situation in a Nut-Shell: Some Un-Colored Truths for Colored Voters*. Washington, D.C.: National Independent Political League, 1912.

Walters, Alexander. *My Life and Work*. New York: Fleming H. Revell Company, 1917.

Weber, Max. *Economy and Society: An Outline of Interpretive Sociology*. Edited by Guenther Roth and Claus Wittich. Vol. 3. New York: Bedminster Press, 1968.

————. *Wirtschaft und Gesellschaft.* Edited by Johannes Winckelmann. Studienausgabe Tübingen: J. C. B. Mohr [Paul Siebeck], 1980.

Weller, Charles F. *Neglected Neighbors: Stories of Life in the Alleys, Tenements and Shanties of the National Capital.* Philadelphia: John C. Winston Company, 1909.

Weyl, Walter E. *The New Democracy: An Essay on Certain Political and Economic Tendencies in the United States.* New York: Macmillan Company, 1912.

Williams, Edward Christopher. *When Washington Was in Vogue: A Love Story (A Lost Novel of the Harlem Renaissance).* New York: Amistad, 2003.

Wilson, Woodrow. "Democracy and Efficiency." *Atlantic Monthly,* March 1901, 289–99.

————. *A History of the American People.* Vol. 5. New York: Harper and Brothers, 1902.

————. "The Need of Citizenship Organization." *American City,* November 1911, 265–68.

————. *The New Freedom: A Call for the Emancipation of the Generous Energies of a People.* New York: Doubleday, Page and Company, 1913.

————. "The Reconstruction of the Southern States." *Atlantic Monthly,* January 1901, 1–15.

————. *The State: Elements of Historical and Practical Politics.* Rev. ed. 1898. Boston: D. C. Heath and Co., 1904.

————. "The States and the Federal Government." *North American Review,* May 1908, 684–701.

————. "The Study of Administration." *Political Science Quarterly* 2, no. 2 (June 1887): 197–222.

Work, Monroe N. *Negro Year Book, an Annual Encyclopedia of the Negro, 1912.* Tuskegee, Ala.: Negro Year Book Publishing Co., 1912.

SECONDARY SOURCES

Abbott, Carl. *Political Terrain: Washington, D.C., from Tidewater Town to Global Metropolis.* Chapel Hill: University of North Carolina Press, 1999.

Abinales, Patricio N. "Progressive-Machine Conflict in Early-Twentieth-Century U.S. Politics and Colonial-State Building in the Philippines." In *The American Colonial State in the Philippines,* edited by Julian Go and Anne L. Foster, 148–81. Durham, N.C.: Duke University Press, 2003.

Abrams, Richard M. "Woodrow Wilson and the Southern Congressmen, 1913–1916." *Journal of Southern History* 22, no. 4 (November 1956): 417–37.

Alexander, Shawn Leigh. *An Army of Lions: The Civil Rights Struggle before the NAACP.* Philadelphia: University of Pennsylvania Press, 2012.

Anderson, Judith Icke. *William Howard Taft: An Intimate History.* New York: W. W. Norton and Company, 1981.

Arnesen, Eric. "Up from Exclusion: Black and White Workers, Race, and the State of Labor History." *Reviews in American History* 26, no. 1 (March 1998): 146–74.

Arnold, Peri E. "The 'Great Engineer' as Administrator: Herbert Hoover and Modern Bureaucracy." *Review of Politics* 42, no. 3 (July 1980): 329–48.

Aron, Cindy S. *Ladies and Gentlemen of the Civil Service: Middle-Class Workers in Victorian America.* New York: Oxford University Press, 1987.

———. "'To Barter Their Souls for Gold': Female Clerks in Federal Government Offices, 1862–1890." In *History of Women in the United States: Historical Articles on Women's Lives and Activities*, edited by Nancy F. Cott, 47–66. Munich: K. G. Saur, 1992.

Auchincloss, Louis. *Woodrow Wilson.* New York: Viking Press, 2000.

Ayers, Edward L. *The Promise of the New South: Life after Reconstruction.* New York: Oxford University Press, 1992.

Bacote, Clarence A. "Negro Officeholders in Georgia under President McKinley." *Journal of Negro History* 44, no. 3 (July 1959): 217–39.

———. "Negro Proscriptions, Protests, and Proposed Solutions in Georgia, 1880–1908." *Journal of Southern History* 25, no. 4 (November 1959): 471–98.

Bagby, Wesley M. *The Road to Normalcy: The Presidential Campaign and Election of 1920.* Baltimore: Johns Hopkins University Press, 1962.

Baldwin, Davarian L. *Chicago's New Negroes: Modernity, the Great Migration, and Black Urban Life.* Chapel Hill: University of North Carolina Press, 2007.

Balogh, Brian. "The State of the State among Historians." *Social Science History* 27, no. 3 (Fall 2003): 455–63.

Barber, Lucy G. *Marching on Washington: The Forging of an American Political Tradition.* Berkeley: University of California Press, 2002.

Baruch, Ismar. *Position-Classification in the Public Service; a Report Submitted to the Civil Service Assembly by the Committee on Position-Classification and Pay Plans in the Public Service.* Chicago: Civil Service Assembly of the United States and Canada, 1941.

Bates, Beth Tompkins. *Pullman Porters and the Rise of Protest Politics in Black America, 1925–1945.* Chapel Hill: University of North Carolina Press, 2001.

Bederman, Gail. *Manliness and Civilization: A Cultural History of Gender and Race in the United States, 1880–1917.* Chicago: University of Chicago Press, 1995.

Benbow, Mark E. "Birth of a Quotation: Woodrow Wilson and 'Like Writing History with Lightning.'" *Journal of the Gilded Age and the Progressive Era* 9, no. 4 (October 2010): 509–33.

Benson, Susan Porter. *Counter Cultures: Saleswomen, Managers, and Customers in American Department Stores, 1890–1940.* Urbana: University of Illinois Press, 1986.

Berg, Manfred. *The Ticket to Freedom: The NAACP and the Struggle for Black Political Integration.* Gainesville: University Press of Florida, 2005.

Billingsley, Andrew. *Yearning to Breathe Free: Robert Smalls of South Carolina and His Families.* Columbia: University of South Carolina Press, 2007.

Billington, Monroe L. *Thomas P. Gore: The Blind Senator from Oklahoma.* Lawrence: University of Kansas Press, 1967.

Bimes, Terri, and Stephen Skowronek. "Woodrow Wilson's Critique of Popular Leadership: Reassessing the Modern-Traditional Divide in Presidential History." *Polity* 29, no. 1 (Autumn 1996): 27–63.

Bjelopera, Jerome P. *City of Clerks: Office and Sales Workers in Philadelphia, 1870–1920.* Urbana: University of Illinois Press, 2005.

Blair, John L. "A Time for Parting: The Negro during the Coolidge Years." *Journal of American Studies* 3, no. 2 (December 1969): 177–99.

Blakely, Allison. "Black U.S. Consuls and Diplomats and Black Leadership, 1880–1920." *UMOJA: A Scholarly Journal of Black Studies* 1, no. 1 (Spring 1977): 1–16.

Blight, David W. *Race and Reunion: The Civil War in American Memory.* Cambridge, Mass.: Harvard University Press, 2001.

Blum, John M. *Joe Tumutly and the Wilson Era.* Boston: Houghton Mifflin Company, 1951.

Blumenthal, Henry. "Woodrow Wilson and the Race Question." *Journal of Negro History* 48, no. 1 (January 1963): 1–21.

Blumin, Stuart M. *The Emergence of the Middle Class: Social Experience in the American City, 1760–1900.* New York: Cambridge University Press, 1989.

Borchert, James. *Alley Life in Washington: Family, Community, Religion, and Folklife in the City, 1850–1970.* Urbana: University of Illinois Press, 1980.

Bourdieu, Pierre. *Distinction: A Social Critique of the Judgment of Taste.* Cambridge, Mass.: Harvard University Press, 1984.

———. *Outline of a Theory of Practice.* Cambridge: Cambridge University Press, 1977.

Bourdieu, Pierre, Loic J. D. Wacquant, and Samar Farage. "Rethinking the State: Genesis and Structure of the Bureaucratic Field." *Sociological Theory* 12, no. 1 (March 1994): 1–18.

Boyer, Paul. *Urban Masses and Moral Order in America, 1820–1920.* Cambridge, Mass.: Harvard University Press, 1978.

Boyle, Kevin. *Arc of Justice: A Saga of Race, Civil Rights, and Murder in the Jazz Age.* New York: Henry Holt, 2004.

Broesamle, John J. *William Gibbs McAdoo: A Passion for Change, 1863–1917.* Port Washington, N.Y.: Kennikat Press, 1973.

Brooks, Charlotte Swan Kendrick, and Joseph Kendrick Brooks. *The Kendrick Kin: An African-American Family Saga.* Washington, D.C.: Brooks, 1995.

Brown, Elsa Barkley. "Negotiating and Transforming the Public Sphere: African American Political Life in the Transition from Slavery to Freedom." *Public Culture* 7 (1994): 107–46.

Bruce, Dickson D., Jr. *Archibald Grimké: Portrait of a Black Independent.* Baton Rouge: Louisiana State University Press, 1993.

Brundage, W. Fitzhugh. *Lynching in the New South: Georgia and Virginia, 1880–1930.* Urbana: University of Illinois Press, 1993.

Bullard, Thomas R. "From Businessman to Congressman: The Careers of Martin B. Madden." Ph.D. diss., University of Illinois, 1973.

Bunie, Andrew. *The Negro in Virginia Politics, 1902–1965.* Charlottesville: University Press of Virginia, 1967.

Butler, Leslie. *Critical Americans: Victorian Intellectuals and Transatlantic Liberal Reform.* Chapel Hill: University of North Carolina Press, 2007.

Cahill, Cathleen D. *Federal Fathers and Mothers: A Social History of the United States Indian Service, 1869–1933.* Chapel Hill: University of North Carolina Press, 2011.

Callcott, Margaret Law. *The Negro in Maryland Politics, 1870–1912.* Baltimore: Johns Hopkins University Press, 1969.

Canaday, Margot. *The Straight State: Sexuality and Citizenship in Twentieth-Century America.* Princeton: Princeton University Press, 2009.

Capozzola, Christopher. *Uncle Sam Wants You: World War I and the Making of the Modern American Citizen*. New York: Oxford University Press, 2008.

Carby, Hazel. "Policing the Black Woman's Body in an Urban Context." *Critical Inquiry* 18, no. 4 (Summer 1992): 738–55.

Carpenter, Daniel P. *The Forging of Bureaucratic Autonomy: Reputations, Networks, and Policy Innovation in Executive Agencies, 1862–1928*. Princeton: Princeton University Press, 2001.

Cary, Francine C., ed. *Washington Odyssey: A Multicultural History of the Nation's Capital*. Washington, D.C.: Smithsonian Books, 1996.

Casdorph, Paul D. "Norris Wright Cuney and Texas Republican Politics, 1883–1896." *Southwestern Historical Quarterly* 68, no. 4 (April 1965): 455–64.

———. *Republicans, Negroes, and Progressives in the South, 1912–1916*. University: University of Alabama Press, 1981.

Cell, John W. *The Highest Stage of White Supremacy: The Origins of Segregation in South Africa and the American South*. Cambridge: Cambridge University Press, 1982.

Chace, James. *1912: Wilson, Roosevelt, Taft, and Debs—the Election That Changed the Country*. New York: Simon and Schuster, 2004.

Chafe, William H. "The Negro and Populism: A Kansas Case Study." *Journal of Southern History* 34, no. 3 (August 1968): 402–19.

Chase, Hal S. "'Honey for Friends, Stings for Enemies': William Calvin Chase and *The Washington Bee*, 1882–1921." Ph.D. diss., University of Pennsylvania, 1973.

———. "'Shelling the Citadel of Race Prejudice': William Calvin Chase and the Washington 'Bee,' 1882–1921." *Records of the Columbia Historical Society, Washington, D.C.* 49 (1973/74): 371–91.

Clark, Herbert L. "The Public Career of James Carroll Napier, Businessman, Politician, and Crusader for Racial Justice, 1845–1940." D.A. diss., Middle Tennessee State University, 1980.

Clark, Kathleen Ann. *Defining Moments: African American Commemoration and Political Culture in the South, 1863–1913*. Chapel Hill: University of North Carolina Press, 2008.

Clark, Robert L., Lee A. Craig, and Jack W. Wilson. *A History of Public Sector Pensions in the United States*. Philadelphia: University of Pennsylvania Press, 2003.

Clark-Lewis, Elizabeth. *Living In, Living Out: African-American Domestics in Washington, D.C., 1910–1940*. Washington, D.C.: Smithsonian Institution Press, 1994.

———. "'This Work Had a End': African-American Domestic Workers in Washington, D.C., 1910–1940." In *"To Toil the Livelong Day": America's Women at Work, 1780–1880*, edited by Carol Groneman and Mary Beth Norton, 196–212. Ithaca: Cornell University Press, 1987.

Clemens, Elisabeth S. *The People's Lobby: Organizational Innovation and the Rise of Interest Group Politics in the United States, 1890–1925*. Chicago: University of Chicago Press, 1997.

Clements, Kendrick A. *Woodrow Wilson, World Statesman*. Rev. ed. Chicago: I. R. Dee, 1999.

Cohen, Harvey G. *Duke Ellington's America*. Chicago: University of Chicago Press, 2010.

Cohen, William. *At Freedom's Edge: Black Mobility and the Southern White Quest for Racial Control, 1861–1915.* Baton Rouge: Louisiana State University Press, 1991.

Cooper, John Milton, Jr. *The Warrior and the Priest: Woodrow Wilson and Theodore Roosevelt.* Cambridge, Mass.: Harvard University Press, 1983.

———. *Woodrow Wilson: A Biography.* New York: Alfred A. Knopf, 2009.

———, ed. *Reconsidering Woodrow Wilson: Progressivism, Internationalism, War, and Peace.* Baltimore: Johns Hopkins University Press, 2008.

Cooper, John Milton, Jr., and Charles E. Neu, eds. *Wilson Era: Essays in Honor of Arthur S. Link.* Arlington Heights, Ill.: Harlan Davidson, 1991.

"Cost of Living of Federal Employees in Five Cities." *Monthly Labor Review* 29 (August 1929): 41–69.

Crowder, Ralph L. *John Edward Bruce: Politician, Journalist, and Self-Trained Historian of the African Diaspora.* New York: New York University Press, 2004.

Dabney, Lillian G. "The History of Schools for Negroes in the District of Columbia, 1807–1947." Ph.D. diss., Catholic University of America, 1949.

Dailey, Jane E. *Before Jim Crow: The Politics of Race in Postemancipation Virginia.* Chapel Hill: University of North Carolina Press, 2000.

Dailey, Jane E., Glenda E. Gilmore, and Bryant Simon, eds. *Jumpin' Jim Crow: Southern Politics from Civil War to Civil Rights.* Princeton: Princeton University Press, 2000.

Dalfiume, Richard M. "The 'Forgotten Years' of the Negro Revolution." *Journal of American History* 55, no. 1 (June 1968): 90–106.

Daniel, Pete. *The Shadow of Slavery: Peonage in the South, 1901–1969.* Urbana: University of Illinois Press, 1972.

Davies, Margery. *Woman's Place Is at the Typewriter: Office Work and Office Workers, 1870–1930.* Philadelphia: Temple University Press, 1982.

Dawley, Alan. *Struggles for Justice: Social Responsibility and the Liberal State.* Cambridge, Mass.: Harvard University Press, 1991.

Degler, Carl N. *In Search of Human Nature: The Decline and Revival of Darwinism in American Social Thought.* New York: Oxford University Press, 1991.

De La Fuente, Alejandro. *A Nation for All: Race, Inequality, and Politics in Twentieth-Century Cuba.* Chapel Hill: University of North Carolina Press, 2000.

De Santis, Vincent P. "Negro Dissatisfaction with Republican Policy in the South, 1882–1884." *Journal of Negro History* 36, no. 2 (April 1951): 148–59.

———. *Republicans Face the Southern Question: The New Departure Years, 1877–1897.* Westport, Conn.: Greenwood Press, 1969.

Donald, David Herbert. *Lincoln Reconsidered: Essays on the Civil War Era.* 3rd ed. New York: Vintage Books, 2001.

Douglas, Paul H. *Real Wages in the United States, 1890–1926.* Boston: Houghton Mifflin, 1930.

Drake, St. Claire, and Horace R. Cayton. *Black Metropolis: A Study of Negro Life in a Northern City.* 1945. Chicago: University of Chicago Press, 1993.

Dyer, Thomas G. *Theodore Roosevelt and the Idea of Race.* Baton Rouge: Louisiana State University Press, 1980.

Edwards, Rebecca. *Angels in the Machinery: Gender in American Party Politics from the Civil War to the Progressive Era.* New York: Oxford University Press, 1997.

Evans, Peter B., Dietrich Rueschemeyer, and Theda Skocpol, eds. *Bringing the State Back In*. Cambridge: Cambridge University Press, 1985.

Fabre, Geneviève, and Michel Feith. *Temples for Tomorrow: Looking Back at the Harlem Renaissance*. Bloomington: Indiana University Press, 2001.

Fairclough, Adam. *Teaching Equality: Black Schools in the Age of Jim Crow*. Athens: University of Georgia Press, 2001.

Farrar, Margaret E. *Building the Body Politic: Power and Urban Space in Washington, D.C.* Urbana: University of Illinois Press, 2008.

Feimster, Crystal N. *Southern Horrors: Women and the Politics of Rape and Lynching*. Cambridge, Mass.: Harvard University Press, 2009.

Ferrell, Robert H. *The Presidency of Calvin Coolidge*. Lawrence: University Press of Kansas, 1992.

Finegold, Kenneth. *Experts and Politicians: Reform Challenges to Machine Politics in New York, Cleveland, and Chicago*. Princeton: Princeton University Press, 1995.

Fink, Leon. *In Search of the Working Class: Essays in American Labor History and Political Culture*. Urbana: University of Illinois Press, 1994.

Fitzpatrick, Michael Andrew. "Shaw, Washington's Premier Black Neighborhood: An Examination of the Origins and Development of a Black Business Movement, 1880–1920." M.A. thesis, University of Virginia, 1989.

Fitzpatrick, Sandra, and Maria R. Goodwin. *The Guide to Black Washington: Places and Events of Historical and Cultural Significance in the Nation's Capital*. New York: Hippocrene Books, 1990.

Foner, Eric. *The Fiery Trial: Abraham Lincoln and American Slavery*. New York: W. W. Norton, 2010.

———. *Reconstruction: America's Unfinished Revolution, 1863–1877*. New York: Harper and Row, 1988.

Foster, Gaines M. *Ghosts of the Confederacy: Defeat, the Lost Cause, and the Emergence of the New South, 1865 to 1913*. New York: Oxford University Press, 1987.

Foucault, Michel. *Discipline and Punish: The Birth of the Prison*. New York: Vintage Books, 1979.

Fouché, Rayvon. *Black Inventors in the Age of Segregation: Granville T. Woods, Lewis H. Latimer, and Shelby J. Davidson*. Baltimore: Johns Hopkins University Press, 2003.

Fox, Stephen R. *The Guardian of Boston: William Monroe Trotter*. New York: Atheneum Press, 1970.

Franke, Katharine M. "Becoming a Citizen: Reconstruction Era Regulation of African American Marriages." *Yale Journal of Law and the Humanities* 11 (1999): 251–309.

Franklin, John Hope. *Mirror to America: The Autobiography of John Hope Franklin*. New York: Farrar, Straus and Giroux, 2005.

Freund, David. *Colored Property: State Policy and White Racial Politics in the Modern American Suburb*. Chicago: University of Chicago Press, 2007.

Friedman, Milton, and Anna Jacobson Schwartz. *A Monetary History of the United States 1867–1960*. Princeton: Princeton University Press, 1963.

Gaines, Kevin K. *Uplifting the Race: Black Leadership, Politics, and Culture in the Twentieth Century*. Chapel Hill: University of North Carolina Press, 1996.

Gatewood, Willard B. *Aristocrats of Color: The Black Elite, 1880–1920*. Bloomington: Indiana University Press, 1990.

———. "Theodore Roosevelt and the Indianola Affair." *Journal of Negro History* 53, no. 1 (January 1968): 48–69.

———. "William D. Crum: A Negro in Politics." *Journal of Negro History* 53, no. 4 (October 1968): 301–20.

Gaughan, Anthony. "Woodrow Wilson and the Legacy of the Civil War." *Civil War History* 43, no. 3 (September 1997): 225–42.

Gerstle, Gary. *American Crucible: Race and Nation in the Twentieth Century*. Princeton: Princeton University Press, 2001.

Gillespie, Richard. *Manufacturing Knowledge: A History of the Hawthorne Experiments*. Cambridge: Cambridge University Press, 1991.

Gillette, Howard, Jr. *Between Justice and Beauty: Race, Planning, and the Failure of Urban Policy in Washington, D.C.* Baltimore: Johns Hopkins University Press, 1995.

Gilmore, Glenda. *Defying Dixie: The Radical Roots of Civil Rights, 1919–1950*. New York: W. W. Norton, 2009.

———. *Gender and Jim Crow: Women and the Politics of White Supremacy in North Carolina, 1896–1920*. Chapel Hill: University of North Carolina Press, 1996.

———. "One of the Meanest Books: Thomas Dixon, Jr. and the Leopard's Spots." *North Carolina Literary Review* 2, no. 1 (Spring 1994): 87–101.

Glassie, Henry H. "Victorian Homes in Washington." *Records of the Columbia Historical Society, Washington, D.C.* 63/65 (1963/65): 320–65.

Glenn, A. L. *History of the National Alliance of Postal Employees, 1913–1955*. Cleveland: National Association of Postal Employees, 1956.

Glenn, Evelyn Nakano. *Unequal Freedom: How Race and Gender Shaped American Citizenship and Labor*. Cambridge, Mass.: Harvard University Press, 2002.

Godshalk, David Fort. *Veiled Visions: The 1906 Atlanta Race Riot and the Reshaping of American Race Relations*. Chapel Hill: University of North Carolina Press, 2005.

Goings, Kenneth W., and Raymond A. Mohl, eds. *New African American Urban History*. Thousand Oaks, Calif.: Sage, 1996.

Goldstein, Michael L. "Race Politics in New York City, 1890–1930: Independent Political Behavior." Ph.D. diss., Columbia University, 1973.

Goluboff, Risa L. *The Lost Promise of Civil Rights*. Cambridge, Mass.: Harvard University Press, 2007.

———. "'We Live's in a Free House Such as It Is': Class and the Creation of Modern Civil Rights." *University of Pennsylvania Law Review* 151, no. 6 (June 2003): 1977–2018.

———. "'Won't You Please Help Me Get My Son Home': Peonage, Patronage, and Protest in the World War II Urban South." *Law and Society Inquiry* 24, no. 4 (Autumn 1999): 777–806.

Gordon, Ian. *Comic Strips and Consumer Culture, 1890–1945*. Washington, D.C.: Smithsonian Institution Press, 1998.

Gordon, Suzanne. *In This Temple: A Guide Book to the Lincoln Memorial*. Washington, D.C.: Museum Press, 1973.

Gosnell, Harold F. *Negro Politicians: The Rise of Negro Politics in Chicago.* 1935. Chicago: University of Chicago Press, 1967.

Gould, Lewis L. *The William Howard Taft Presidency.* Lawrence: University Press of Kansas, 2009.

Gouldner, Alvin W. "Industrial Sociology: Status and Prospects: Discussion." *American Sociological Review* 13, no. 4 (August 1948): 396–400.

Graham, Lawrence Otis. *The Senator and the Socialite: The True Story of America's First Black Dynasty.* New York: HarperCollins, 2006.

Green, Constance McLaughlin. *The Secret City: A History of Race Relations in the Nation's Capital.* Princeton: Princeton University Press, 1967.

———. *Washington: Capital City, 1879–1950.* Princeton: Princeton University Press, 1962.

Greenberg, David. *Calvin Coolidge.* New York: Henry Holt and Company, 2006.

Greene, Lorenzo Johnston, and Myra Callis. *The Employment of Negroes in the District of Columbia.* Washington, D.C.: Association for the Study of Negro Life and History, 1931.

Greenwood, Janette Thomas. *Bittersweet Legacy: The Black and White "Better Classes" in Charlotte, 1850–1910.* Chapel Hill: University of North Carolina Press, 1994.

Grossman, James R. *Land of Hope: Chicago, Black Southerners, and the Great Migration.* Chicago: University of Chicago Press, 1989.

Grossman, Lawrence. *The Democratic Party and the Negro: Northern and National Politics, 1868–92.* Urbana: University of Illinois Press, 1976.

———. "Democrats and Blacks in the Gilded Age." In *Democrats and the American Idea: A Bicentennial Appraisal,* edited by Peter B. Kovler, 127–45. Washington, D.C.: Center for National Policy Press, 1992.

Hahn, Steven. *A Nation under Our Feet: Black Political Struggles in the Rural South from Slavery to the Great Migration.* Cambridge, Mass.: Harvard University Press, 2003.

Hale, Grace Elizabeth. *Making Whiteness: The Culture of Segregation in the South, 1890–1940.* New York: Vintage Books, 1999.

Hall, Jacquelyn Dowd. "The Long Civil Rights Movement and the Political Uses of the Past." *Journal of American History* 91, no. 4 (March 2005): 1233–63.

———. "'The Mind That Burns in Each Body': Women, Rape, and Racial Violence." In *Powers of Desire: The Politics of Sexuality,* edited by Ann Snitow, Christine Stansell, and Sharon Thompson, 328–49. New York: Monthly Review Press, 1983.

———. *Revolt against Chivalry: Jessie Daniel Ames and the Women's Campaign against Lynching.* New York: Columbia University Press, 1979.

Hall, Jacquelyn Dowd, Robert Korstad, Christopher B. Daly, and Lu Ann Jones. *Like a Family: The Making of a Southern Cotton Mill World.* Chapel Hill: University of North Carolina Press, 2000.

Halttunen, Karen. *Confidence Men and Painted Women: A Study of Middle-Class Culture in America, 1830–1870.* New Haven: Yale University Press, 1982.

Harding, Vincent G. "Wrestling toward the Dawn: The Afro-American Freedom Movement and the Changing Constitution." *Journal of American History* 74, no. 3 (December 1987): 718–39.

Harlan, Louis R. *Booker T. Washington: The Making of a Black Leader, 1856–1901.* New York: Oxford University Press, 1972.

———. *Booker T. Washington: The Wizard of Tuskegee, 1901–1915.* New York: Oxford University Press, 1983.

Harley, Sharon. "Beyond the Classroom: The Organizational Lives of Black Female Educators in the District of Columbia, 1890–1930." *Journal of Negro Education* 51, no. 3 (Summer 1982): 254–65.

———. "Black Women in a Southern City: Washington, D.C., 1890–1920." In *Sex, Race, and the Role of Women in the South,* edited by Joanne V. Hawks and Sheila L. Skemp, 59–74. Jackson: University Press of Mississippi, 1983.

———. "For the Good of Family and Race: Gender, Work, and Domestic Roles in the Black Community, 1880–1930." *Signs* 15, no. 2 (Winter 1990): 336–49.

———. "When Your Work Is Not Who You Are: The Development of a Working-Class Consciousness among Afro-American Women." In *Gender, Class, Race, and Reform in the Progressive Era,* edited by Noralee Frankel and Nancy S. Dye, 42–55. Lexington: University Press of Kentucky, 1991.

Harrison, Robert. *Congress, Progressive Reform, and the New American State.* Cambridge: Cambridge University Press, 2004.

Hartog, Hendrik. "The Constitution of Aspiration and 'The Rights That Belong to Us All.'" *Journal of American History* 74, no. 3 (December 1987): 1013–34.

Hathorn, Guy B. "C. Bascom Slemp — Virginia Republican Boss, 1907–1932." *Journal of Politics* 17, no. 2 (May 1955): 248–64.

Hayes, Laurence J. W. "The Negro Federal Government Worker: A Study of His Classification Status in the District of Columbia, 1883–1938." M.A. thesis, Howard University, 1941.

Hays, Samuel P. "The Changing Political Structure of the City in Industrial America." *Journal of Urban History* 1, no. 1 (November 1974): 6–38.

Heclo, Hugh. *A Government of Strangers: Executive Politics in Washington.* Washington, D.C.: Brookings Institution, 1977.

Hedstrom, Margaret L. "Beyond Feminisation: Clerical Workers in the United States from the 1920s through the 1960s." In *The White-Blouse Revolution: Female Office Workers since 1870,* edited by Gregory Anderson, 145–69. Manchester: Manchester University Press, 1989.

Helg, Aline. *Our Rightful Share: The Afro-Cuban Struggle for Equality, 1886–1912.* Chapel Hill: University of North Carolina Press, 1995.

Henretta, James A. "The Study of Social Mobility: Ideological Assumptions and Conceptual Bias." In *The Labor History Reader,* edited by Daniel J. Leab, 28–41. Urbana: University of Illinois Press, 1985.

Higginbotham, Evelyn Brooks. *Righteous Discontent: The Women's Movement in the Black Baptist Church, 1880–1920.* Cambridge, Mass.: Harvard University Press, 1993.

Hill, Herbert. "The Problem of Race in American Labor History." *Reviews of American History* 24, no. 2 (1996): 189–208.

Hiller, Marsha Hurst. "Race Politics in New York City, 1890–1930." Ph.D. diss., Columbia University, 1972.

Hodes, Martha E. *White Women, Black Men: Illicit Sex in the Nineteenth-Century South.* New Haven: Yale University Press, 1997.

Holden-Smith, Barbara. "Lynching, Federalism, and the Intersection of Race and Gender in the Progressive Era." *Yale Journal of Law and Feminism* 8, no. 1 (Spring 1996): 31–78.

Hollander, Jocelyn A., and Rachel L. Einwohner. "Conceptualizing Resistance." *Sociological Forum* 19, no. 4 (December 2004): 533–54.

Holloway, Jonathan Scott. *Confronting the Veil: Abram Harris Jr., E. Franklin Frazier, and Ralph Bunche, 1919–1941.* Chapel Hill: University of North Carolina Press, 2002.

Holt, Thomas C. *Black over White: Negro Political Leadership in South Carolina during Reconstruction.* Urbana: University of Illinois Press, 1979.

———. "Marking: Race, Race-Making, and the Writing of History." *American Historical Review* 100, no. 1 (February 1995): 1–20.

Hoogenboom, Ari Arthur. *Outlawing the Spoils: A History of the Civil Service Reform Movement, 1865–1883.* Urbana: University of Illinois Press, 1961.

Hunter, Tera W. *To 'Joy My Freedom: Southern Black Women's Lives and Labors after the Civil War.* Cambridge, Mass.: Harvard University Press, 1997.

Jacob, Kathryn Allamong. *Capital Elites: High Society in Washington, D.C., after the Civil War.* Washington, D.C.: Smithsonian Institution Press, 1995.

Jacobs, Meg. *Pocketbook Politics: Economic Citizenship in Twentieth-Century America.* Princeton: Princeton University Press, 2005.

James, Felix. "Robert Russa Moton and the Whispering Gallery after World War I." *Journal of Negro History* 62, no. 3 (July 1977): 235–42.

Janken, Kenneth. *White: The Biography of Walter White, Mr. NAACP.* New York: New Press, 2003.

Johnson, Eldon L. "General Unions in the Federal Service." *Journal of Politics* 2, no. 1 (February 1940): 23–56.

Johnson, Joan Marie. "'Ye Gave Them a Stone': African American Women's Clubs, the Frederick Douglass Home, and the Black Mammy Monument." *Journal of Women's History* 17, no. 1 (Spring 2005): 69–78.

Johnson, Ronald M. "Those Who Stayed: Washington Black Writers in the 1920s." *Records of the Columbia Historical Society of Washington, D.C.* 50 (1980): 484–99.

Johnson, Ronald N., and Gary D. Libecap. *The Federal Civil Service System and the Problem of Bureaucracy: The Economics and Politics of Institutional Change.* Chicago: University of Chicago Press, 1994.

Johnson, Russell L. "'Great Injustice': Social Status and the Distribution of Military Pensions after the Civil War." *Journal of the Gilded Age and the Progressive Era* 10, no. 2 (April 2011): 137–60.

Johnston, Lorenzo, and Myra Callis Greene. *The Employment of Negroes in the District of Columbia.* Washington, D.C.: Association for the Study of Negro Life and History, 1931.

Jones, Jacqueline. *American Work: Four Centuries of Black and White Labor.* New York: W. W. Norton, 1998.

———. *Labor of Love, Labor of Sorrow: Black Women, Work, and the Family, from Slavery to the Present.* New York: Vintage Books, 1985.

Jordan, John M. *Machine-Age Ideology: Social Engineering and American Liberalism, 1911–1939.* Chapel Hill: University of North Carolina Press, 1994.

Justesen, Benjamin R. *Broken Brotherhood: The Rise and Fall of the National Afro-American Council.* Carbondale: Southern Illinois University Press, 2008.

Kane, Richard D. "The Federal Segregation of the Blacks during the Presidential Administrations of Warren G. Harding and Calvin Coolidge." *Pan-African Journal* 7, no. 2 (Summer 1974): 153–71.

Kantrowitz, Stephen D. *Ben Tillman and the Reconstruction of White Supremacy.* Chapel Hill: University of North Carolina Press, 2000.

———. "'Intended for the Better Government of Man': The Political History of African American Freemasonry in the Era of Emancipation." *Journal of American History* 96, no. 4 (March 2010): 1001–26.

Katz, Michael B., Mark J. Stern, and Jamie J. Fader. "The New African American Inequality." *Journal of American History* 92, no. 1 (June 2005): 75–108.

Katznelson, Ira. *Black Men, White Cities: Race, Politics, and Migration in the United States, 1900–30 and Britain, 1948–68.* New York: Oxford University Press, 1973.

———. "The 'Bourgeois' Dimension: A Provocation about Institutions, Politics, and the Future of Labor History." *International Labor and Working-Class History* 46 (Fall 1994): 7–32.

Katznelson, Ira, and Helen V. Milner, eds. *Political Science: The State of the Discipline.* New York: W. W. Norton, 2002.

Kaufman, Herbert. "The Growth of the Federal Personnel System." In *The Federal Government Service,* edited by Wallace S. Sayre, 7–69. Englewood Cliffs, N.J.: Prentice-Hall, 1965.

Kaye, Andrew. "Colonel Roscoe Conkling Simmons." *Journal of American Studies* 37, no. 1 (2003): 79–98.

Kazin, Michael. *A Godly Hero: The Life of William Jennings Bryan.* New York: Alfred A. Knopf, 2006.

Keller, Morton. *Affairs of State: Public Life in Late Nineteenth Century America.* Cambridge, Mass.: Harvard University Press, 1977.

Kelley, Robin D. G. *Race Rebels: Culture, Politics, and the Black Working Class.* New York: Free Press, 1994.

Kennedy, David M. *Over Here: The First World War and American Society.* Oxford: Oxford University Press, 1980.

Kennedy, Randall. "Racial Passing." *Ohio State Law Journal* 62 (2001): 1145–73.

Kenzer, Robert C. *Enterprising Southerners: Black Economic Success in North Carolina, 1865–1915.* Charlottesville: University Press of Virginia, 1997.

Kerber, Linda K. "The Meanings of Citizenship." *Journal of American History* 84, no. 3 (December 1997): 833–54.

Kilson, Martin. "Political Change in the Negro Ghetto, 1900–1940s." In *Key Issues in the Afro-American Experience,* vol. 2, edited by Nathan I. Huggins, Daniel M. Fox, and Martin Kilson, 167–92. New York: Harcourt Brace Jovanovich, 1971.

King, Desmond S. "The Racial Bureaucracy: African Americans and the Federal Government in the Era of Segregated Race Relations." *Governance: An International Journal of Policy and Administration* 12, no. 4 (October 1999): 345–77.

———. *Separate and Unequal: Black Americans and the U.S. Federal Government.* Oxford: Oxford University Press, 1995.

———. "A Strong or Weak State? Race and the U.S. Federal Government in the 1920s." *Ethnic and Racial Studies* 21, no. 1 (January 1998): 21–47.

King, Desmond S., and Rogers M. Smith. "Racial Orders in American Political Development." *American Political Science Review* 99, no. 1 (February 2005): 75–92.

King, Desmond S., and Stephen Tuck. "De-centering the South: America's Nationwide White Supremacist Order after Reconstruction." *Past and Present* 194 (February 2007): 213–53.

Kirby, Jack Temple. *Darkness at the Dawning: Race and Reform in the Progressive South.* Philadelphia: Lippincott, 1972.

Klarman, Michael J. *From Jim Crow to Civil Rights: The Supreme Court and the Struggle for Racial Equality.* New York: Oxford University Press, 2004.

Kocka, Jürgen. *White Collar Workers in America, 1890–1940: A Social-Political History in International Perspective.* London: Sage, 1980.

Kornweibel, Theodore. *Investigate Everything: Federal Efforts to Compel Black Loyalty during World War I.* Bloomington: Indiana University Press, 2002.

Kousser, J. Morgan. *The Shaping of Southern Politics: Suffrage Restriction and the Establishment of the One-Party South, 1880–1910.* New Haven: Yale University Press, 1974.

Kramer, Paul A. "Empires, Exceptions, and Anglo-Saxons: Race and Rule between the British and United States Empires, 1880–1910." *Journal of American History* (March 2002): 1315–53.

Krislov, Samuel. *The Negro in Federal Employment: The Quest for Equal Opportunity.* Minneapolis: University of Minnesota Press, 1967.

Krugler, David F. "A Mob in Uniform: Soldiers and Civilians in Washington's Red Summer, 1919." *Washington History* 21 (2009): 48–77.

Lamon, Lester C. *Black Tennesseans 1900–1930.* Knoxville: University of Tennessee Press, 1977.

Lasswell, Harold. *Politics: Who Gets What, When, How.* New York: McGraw-Hill, 1936.

Lears, Jackson. *Rebirth of a Nation: The Making of Modern America, 1877–1920.* New York: HarperCollins, 2009.

Lentz-Smith, Adriane. *Freedom Struggles: African Americans and World War I.* Cambridge, Mass.: Harvard University Press, 2009.

Lessoff, Alan. *The Nation and Its City: Politics, Corruption, and Progress in Washington, D.C., 1861–1902.* Baltimore: Johns Hopkins University Press, 1994.

Leuchtenburg, William E. "The Pertinence of Political History: Reflections on the Significance of the State in America." *Journal of American History* 73, no. 3 (December 1986): 585–600.

Lewis, David Levering. *District of Columbia: A Bicentennial History.* New York: W. W. Norton, 1976.

———. *W. E. B. Du Bois — Biography of a Race, 1868–1919.* New York: Henry Holt, 1993.

———. *When Harlem Was in Vogue.* 1981. New York: Penguin Books, 1997.

Lewis, Earl. *In Their Own Interests: Race, Class, and Power in Twentieth-Century Norfolk, Virginia.* Berkeley: University of California Press, 1991.

Link, Arthur S. *The Higher Realism of Woodrow Wilson, and Other Essays.* Nashville: Vanderbilt University Press, 1971.

————. "The Negro as a Factor in the Campaign of 1912." *Journal of Negro History* 32, no. 1 (January 1947): 81–99.

————. *Wilson: The New Freedom.* Vol. 2. Princeton: Princeton University Press, 1947.

————. *Woodrow Wilson and the Progressive Era, 1910–1917.* New York: Harper and Brothers, 1954.

————. "Woodrow Wilson: The American as Southerner." *Journal of Southern History* 36, no. 1 (February 1970): 3–17.

Link, William A. *The Paradox of Southern Progressivism, 1880–1930.* Chapel Hill: University of North Carolina Press, 1992.

Lisio, Donald J. *Hoover, Blacks, and Lily Whites: A Study of Southern Strategies.* Chapel Hill: University of North Carolina Press, 1985.

Litwack, Leon F. *Trouble in Mind: Black Southerners in the Age of Jim Crow.* New York: Alfred A. Knopf, 1998.

Logan, Rayford W. *The Betrayal of the Negro, from Rutherford B. Hayes to Woodrow Wilson.* New York: Collier Books, 1969.

Lorenz, Alfred Lawrence. "Ralph W. Tyler: The Unknown Correspondent of World War I." *Journalism History* 31, no. 1 (Spring 2005): 2–12.

Luker, Ralph E. *The Social Gospel in Black and White: American Racial Reform, 1885–1912.* Chapel Hill: University of North Carolina Press, 1991.

Lunardini, Christine A. "Standing Firm: William Monroe Trotter's Meetings with Woodrow Wilson, 1913–1914." *Journal of Negro History* 64, no. 3 (Summer 1979): 244–64.

Lutz, Tom, and Susanna Ashton, eds. *These Colored United States: African American Essays from the 1920s.* New Brunswick, N.J.: Rutgers University Press, 1996.

Mack, Kenneth W. "Law, Society, Identity, and the Making of the Jim Crow South: Travel and Segregation on Tennessee Railroads, 1875–1905." *Law and Society Inquiry* 24, no. 2 (Spring 1999): 377–409.

MacLean, Nancy. *Behind the Mask of Chivalry: The Making of the Second Ku Klux Klan.* New York: Oxford University Press, 1994.

————. "White Women and Klan Violence in the 1920s: Agency, Complicity, and the Politics of Women's History." *Gender and History* 3, no. 3 (Autumn 1991): 285–303.

Mandle, Jay R. *The Roots of Black Poverty: The Southern Plantation Economy after the Civil War.* Durham, N.C.: Duke University Press, 1978.

Manela, Erez. *The Wilsonian Moment: Self-determination and the International Origins of Anticolonial Nationalism.* Oxford: Oxford University Press, 2007.

Massey, Douglas S., and Nancy A. Denton. *American Apartheid: Segregation and the Making of the Underclass.* Cambridge, Mass.: Harvard University Press, 1993.

Masur, Kate. *An Example for All the Land: Emancipation and the Struggle over Equality in Washington, D.C.* Chapel Hill: University of North Carolina Press, 2010.

Materson, Lisa G. *For the Freedom of Her Race: Black Women and Electoral Politics in Illinois, 1877–1932.* Chapel Hill: University of North Carolina Press, 2009.

Mayers, Lewis. *The Federal Service: A Study of the System of Personnel Administration of the United States Government.* New York: D. Appleton and Company, 1922.

McCartin, Joseph A. "Bringing the State's Workers In: Time to Rectify an Imbalanced US Labor Historiography." *Labor History* 47, no. 1 (February 2006): 73–94.

———. *Labor's Great War: The Struggle for Industrial Democracy and the Origins of Modern American Labor Relations, 1912–1921.* Chapel Hill: University of North Carolina Press, 1997.

McCartney, Laton. *The Teapot Dome Scandal: How Big Oil Bought the Harding White House and Tried to Steal the Country.* New York: Random House, 2009.

McCormick, Richard L. *The Party Period and Public Policy: American Politics from the Age of Jackson to the Progressive Era.* New York: Oxford University Press, 1986.

McGerr, Michael E. *The Decline of Popular Politics: The American North, 1865–1928.* New York: Oxford University Press, 1986.

———. *A Fierce Discontent: The Rise and Fall of the Progressive Movement in America, 1870–1920.* New York: Free Press, 2003.

McMillen, Neil R. *Dark Journey: Black Mississippians in the Age of Jim Crow.* Urbana: University of Illinois Press, 1989.

———. "Perry W. Howard, Boss of Black-and-Tan Republicanism in Mississippi, 1924–1960." *Journal of Southern History* 48, no. 2 (May 1982): 205–24.

McMurry, Donald L. "The Bureau of Pensions during the Administration of President Harrison." *Mississippi Valley Historical Review* 13, no. 3 (December 1926): 343–64.

McNeil, Genna Rae. *Groundwork: Charles Hamilton Houston and the Struggle for Civil Rights.* Philadelphia: University of Pennsylvania Press, 1983.

McPherson, James M. "Grant or Greeley? The Abolitionist Dilemma in the Election of 1872." *American Historical Review* 71, no. 1 (October 1965): 43–61.

McQuirter, Marya Annette. "Claiming the City: African Americans, Urbanization, and Leisure in Washington, D.C., 1902–1957." Ph.D. diss., University of Michigan, 2000.

Meier, August. "The Negro and the Democratic Party, 1875–1915." *Phylon* 17, no. 2 (1956): 173–91.

———. *Negro Thought in America, 1880–1915: Racial Ideologies in the Age of Booker T. Washington.* Ann Arbor: University of Michigan Press, 1969.

Meier, August, and Elliott Rudwick. "The Rise of Segregation in the Federal Bureaucracy, 1900–1930." *Phylon* 28, no. 2 (1967): 178–84.

Mennell, James. "African-Americans and the Selective Service Act of 1917." *Journal of Negro History* 84, no. 3 (Summer 1999): 275–87.

Merton, Robert K. *Social Theory and Social Structure.* New York: Free Press, 1968.

Miller, Edward A., Jr. *Gullah Statesman: Robert Smalls from Slavery to Congress, 1839–1915.* Columbia: University of South Carolina Press, 1995.

Miller, George Mason. "'A This Worldly Mission': The Life and Career of Alexander Walters." Ph.D. diss., SUNY at Stony Brook, 1984.

Miller, James A. "Black Washington and the New Negro Renaissance." In *Composing Urban History and the Constitution of Civic Identities,* edited by John J. Czaplicka, Blair A. Ruble, and Lauren Crabtree, 219–41. Washington, D.C.: Woodrow Wilson Center Press, 2003.

Miller, M. Sammye. "An Early Venture in Black Capitalism: The Capital Savings Bank in the District of Columbia, 1888–1902." *Records of the Columbia Historical Society of Washington, D.C.* 50 (1980): 359–66.

Mills, C. Wright. *White Collar: The American Middle Classes.* 1951. New York: Oxford University Press, 2002.

Mintz, Steven. "Historical Ethnography of Black Washington, D.C." *Records of the Columbia Historical Society, Washington, D.C.* 52 (1989): 235–53.

Mitchell, Michele. *Righteous Propagation: African Americans and the Politics of Racial Destiny after Reconstruction.* Chapel Hill: University of North Carolina Press, 2004.

Moore, Jacqueline M. *Leading the Race: The Transformation of the Black Elite in the Nation's Capital, 1880–1920.* Charlottesville: University Press of Virginia, 1999.

Moore, James T. "Black Militancy in Readjuster Virginia, 1879–1883." *Journal of Southern History* 41, no. 2 (May 1975): 167–86.

Morris, Edmund. *Colonel Roosevelt.* New York: Random House, 2010.

———. *Theodore Rex.* New York: Random House, 2001.

Mosher, Frederick C., ed. *Basic Documents of American Public Administration, 1776–1950.* New York: Holmes and Meier, 1976.

———. *Democracy and the Public Service.* New York: Oxford University Press, 1968.

Moss, Alfred A. *The American Negro Academy: Voice of the Talented Tenth.* Baton Rouge: Louisiana State University Press, 1981.

Murphy, Mary-Elizabeth. "Mapping African American Women's Activism: Politics and Organizing in Washington, D.C., 1920–1930." Ph.D. diss., University of Maryland, College Park, 2012.

Needham, David Charles. "William Howard Taft, the Negro, and the White South, 1908–1912." Ph.D. diss., University of Georgia, 1970.

Ngai, Mae M. *Impossible Subjects: Illegal Aliens and the Making of Modern America.* Princeton: Princeton University Press, 2004.

Norrell, Robert J. *Up from History: The Life of Booker T. Washington.* Cambridge, Mass.: Harvard University Press, 2009.

Novak, William J. "The Myth of the 'Weak' American State." *American Historical Review* 113 (June 2008): 752–72.

Omori, Kazuteru. "Race-Neutral Individualism and the Resurgence of the Color Line: Massachusetts Civil Rights Legislation, 1855–1895." *Journal of American Ethnic History* 22, no. 1 (Fall 2002): 32–58.

Osborn, George C. "Woodrow Wilson Appoints a Negro Judge." *Journal of Southern History* 24, no. 4 (November 1958): 481–93.

Osofsky, Gilbert. *Harlem, the Making of a Ghetto: Negro New York, 1890–1930.* New York: Harper and Row, 1966.

Painter, Nell Irvin. *Exodusters: Black Migration to Kansas after Reconstruction.* New York: Alfred A. Knopf, 1977.

———. *The History of White People.* New York: W. W. Norton, 2010.

———. "'Social Equality,' Miscegenation, Labor, and Power." In *The Evolution of Southern Culture,* edited by Numan V. Bartley, 47–67. Athens: University of Georgia Press, 1988.

———. *Southern History across the Color Line*. Chapel Hill: University of North Carolina Press, 2002.

———. *Standing at Armageddon: United States, 1877–1919*. New York: W. W. Norton, 1987.

Parrish, Michael E. *Anxious Decades: America in Prosperity and Depression, 1920–1941*. New York: W. W. Norton, 1992.

Patler, Nicholas. *Jim Crow and the Wilson Administration: Protesting Federal Segregation in the Early Twentieth Century*. Boulder: University Press of Colorado, 2004.

Penningroth, Dylan C. "African American Divorce in Virginia and Washington, D.C., 1865–1930." *Journal of Family History* 33, no. 1 (2008): 21–35.

Perman, Michael. *Struggle for Mastery: Disfranchisement in the South, 1888–1908*. Chapel Hill: University of North Carolina Press, 2001.

Peterson, Merrill D. *Lincoln in American Memory*. New York: Oxford University Press, 1994.

Peterson, Patti McGill. "Colonialism and Education: The Case of the Afro-American." *Comparative Education Review* 15, no. 2 (June 1971): 146–57.

Peterson, Paul E., ed. *Classifying by Race*. Princeton: Princeton University Press, 1995.

Pickett, Brent L. "Foucault and the Politics of Resistance." *Polity* 28, no. 4 (Summer 1996): 445–66.

Pinkett, Harold T. "The Keep Commission, 1905–1909: A Rooseveltian Effort for Administrative Reform." *Journal of American History* 52, no. 2 (September 1965): 297–312.

Piven, Frances Fox, and Richard A. Cloward. *Poor People's Movements: Why They Succeed, How They Fail*. New York: Pantheon Books, 1977.

Plummer, Brenda Gayle. "The Afro-American Response to the Occupation of Haiti, 1915–1934." *Phylon* 43, no. 2 (2nd qtr., 1982): 124–43.

———. *Haiti and the Great Powers, 1902–1915*. Baton Rouge: Louisiana State University Press, 1988.

Prasad, Anshuman, and Pushkala Prasad. "Everyday Struggles at the Workplace: The Nature and Implications of Routine Resistance in Contemporary Organizations." *Research in the Sociology of Organizations* 15 (1998): 225–57.

Rabin, Jack, and James S. Bowman, eds. *Politics and Administration: Woodrow Wilson and American Public Administration*. New York: Marcel Dekker, 1984.

Rauchway, Eric. "The High Cost of Living in the Progressives' Economy." *Journal of American History* 88, no. 3 (December 2001): 898–924.

Reed, Adolph A., Jr. "The Study of Black Politics and the Practice of Black Politics: Their Historical Relation and Evolution." In *Problems and Methods in the Study of Politics*, edited by Ian Shapiro, Rogers M. Smith, and Tarek E. Masoud, 106–36. Cambridge: Cambridge University Press, 2004.

Reed, Christopher Robert. *The Chicago NAACP and the Rise of Black Professional Leadership, 1910–1966*. Bloomington: Indiana University Press, 1997.

Reed, Touré F. *Not Alms but Opportunity: The Urban League and The Politics of Racial Uplift, 1910–1950*. Chapel Hill: University of North Carolina Press, 2008.

Reich, Steven A. "The Great War, Black Workers, and the Rise and Fall of the NAACP in the South." In *The Black Worker: Race, Labor, and Civil Rights since Emancipation*, edited by Eric Arnesen, 147–77. Urbana: University of Illinois Press, 2007.

Reid, George W. "Four in Black: North Carolina's Black Congressmen, 1874–1901." *Journal of Negro History* 64, no. 3 (Summer 1979): 229–43.

Reid, Ira DeA., ed. *Negro Membership in American Labor Unions*. 1930. New York: Negro Universities Press, 1969.

Renda, Mary A. *Taking Haiti: Military Occupation and the Culture of U.S. Imperialism, 1915–1940*. Chapel Hill: University of North Carolina Press, 2000.

Ring, Natalie J. *The Problem South: Region, Empire, and the New Liberal State, 1880–1930*. Athens: University of Georgia Press, 2012.

Roberts, Samuel Kelton, Jr. *Infectious Fear: Politics, Disease, and the Health Effects of Segregation*. Chapel Hill: University of North Carolina Press, 2009.

Roberts, Thomas N. "The Negro in Government War Agencies." *Journal of Negro Education* 12, no. 3 (Summer 1943): 367–75.

Robinson, Henry S. "The M Street High School, 1891–1916." *Records of the Columbia Historical Society of Washington, D.C.* 51 (1988): 119–43.

Rodgers, Daniel T. "An Age of Social Politics." In *Rethinking American History in a Global Age*, edited by Thomas Bender, 250–73. Berkeley: University of California Press, 2002.

———. *Atlantic Crossings: Social Politics in a Progressive Age*. Cambridge, Mass.: Harvard University Press, 1998.

———. *Contested Truths: Keywords in American Politics since Independence*. New York: Basic Books, 1987.

———. "In Search of Progressivism." *Reviews in American History* 10 (1982): 113–32.

Roediger, David. *The Wages of Whiteness: Race and the Making of the American Working Class*. London: Verso, 1999.

Ross, Dorothy. "Woodrow Wilson and the Case for Psychohistory." *Journal of American History* 69, no. 3 (December 1982): 659–68.

Rotella, Elyce J. *From Home to Office: U.S. Women at Work, 1870–1930*. Ann Arbor: UMI Research Press, 1981.

Rubio, Philip F. *There's Always Work at the Post Office: African American Postal Workers and the Fight for Jobs, Justice, and Equality*. Chapel Hill: University of North Carolina Press, 2010.

Ruchames, Louis. *Race, Jobs, and Politics: The Story of FEPC*. New York: Columbia University Press, 1953.

Rung, Margaret C. *Servants of the State: Managing Diversity and Democracy in the Federal Workforce, 1933–1953*. Athens: University of Georgia Press, 2002.

Sanders, Elizabeth. *Roots of Reform: Farmers, Workers, and the American State, 1877–1917*. Chicago: University of Chicago Press, 1999.

Sarasohn, David. *The Party of Reform: Democrats in the Progressive Era*. Jackson: University Press of Mississippi, 1989.

Saville, Julie. *The Work of Reconstruction: From Slave to Wage Laborer in South Carolina, 1860–1870*. Cambridge: Cambridge University Press, 1994.

Schaffer, Samuel Lonsdale. "New South Nation: Woodrow Wilson's Generation and the Return of the South, 1880–1920." Ph.D. diss., Yale University, 2010.

Schaffer, Scott E. "Hegemony and the Habitus: Gramsci, Bourdieu, and James Scott on the Problem of Resistance." *Research and Society* 8 (1995): 29–53.

Schechter, Patricia A. *Ida B. Wells-Barnett and American Reform, 1880–1930*. Chapel Hill: University of North Carolina Press, 2001.

Scheiner, Seth M. "President Theodore Roosevelt and the Negro, 1901–1908." *Journal of Negro History* 47, no. 3 (July 1962): 169–82.

Schmidt, Hans. *The United States Occupation of Haiti, 1915–1934*. New Brunswick, N.J.: Rutgers University Press, 1971.

Schneider, Mark R. *Boston Confronts Jim Crow, 1890–1920*. Boston: Northeastern University Press, 1997.

Schweninger, Loren. *Black Property Owners in the South, 1790–1915*. Urbana: University of Illinois Press, 1990.

Scott, Anne Firor. "A Progressive Wind from the South, 1906–1913." *Journal of Southern History* 29, no. 1 (February 1963): 53–70.

Scott, James C. *Domination and the Arts of Resistance: Hidden Transcripts*. New Haven: Yale University Press, 1990.

———. *Weapons of the Weak: Everyday Forms of Peasant Resistance*. New Haven: Yale University Press, 1985.

Shaffer, Donald Robert. *After the Glory: The Struggles of Black Civil War Veterans*. Lawrence: University Press of Kansas, 2004.

Shapiro, Ian, Stephen Skowronek, and Daniel Galvin, eds. *Rethinking Political Institutions: The Art of the State*. New York: New York University Press, 2006.

Shefter, Martin. "Party and Patronage: Germany, England, and Italy." *Politics and Society* 7, no. 4 (1977): 403–52.

———. *Political Parties and the State: The American Historical Experience*. Princeton: Princeton University Press, 1994.

Sherman, Richard B. "The Harding Administration and the Negro: An Opportunity Lost." *Journal of Negro History* 49, no. 3 (July 1964): 151–66.

———. *The Republican Party and Black America from McKinley to Hoover, 1896–1933*. Charlottesville: University Press of Virginia, 1973.

———. "Republicans and Negroes: The Lessons of Normalcy." *Phylon* 27, no. 1 (1st qtr., 1966): 63–79.

Silberman, Bernard S. *Cages of Reason: The Rise of the Rational State in France, Japan, the United States, and Great Britain*. Chicago: University of Chicago Press, 1993.

Skocpol, Theda. *Protecting Soldiers and Mothers: The Political Origins of Social Policy in the United States*. Cambridge, Mass.: Harvard University Press, 1992.

Skowronek, Stephen. *Building a New American State: The Expansion of National Administrative Capacities, 1877–1920*. Cambridge: Cambridge University Press, 1982.

———. *The Politics Presidents Make: Leadership from John Adams to George Bush*. Cambridge, Mass.: Harvard University Press, 1993.

———. "The Reassociation of Ideas and Purposes: Racism, Liberalism, and the American Political Tradition." *American Political Science Review* 100, no. 3 (August 2006): 385–401.

Smith, Kathryn Schneider, ed. *Washington at Home: An Illustrated History of*

Neighborhoods in the Nation's Capital. Northridge, Calif.: Windsor Publications, 1988.

Snyder, Brad. *Beyond the Shadow of the Senators: The Untold Story of the Homestead Grays and the Integration of Baseball*. Chicago: Contemporary Books, 2003.

Socolofsky, Homer E., and Allan B. Spetter. *The Presidency of Benjamin Harrison*. Lawrence: University Press of Kansas, 1987.

Sosna, Morton P. "The South in the Saddle: Racial Politics during the Wilson Years." *Wisconsin Magazine of History* 54 (Autumn 1970): 30–49.

Spear, Allan H. *Black Chicago: The Making of a Negro Ghetto, 1890–1920*. Chicago: University of Chicago Press, 1967.

Spero, Sterling D. "Employer and Employee in the Public Service." In *Problems of the American Public Service: Five Monographs on Specific Aspects of Personnel Administration*, edited by Carl Joachim Friedrich et al., 171–239. New York: McGraw-Hill, 1935.

Sproat, John G. *"The Best Men": Liberal Reformers in the Gilded Age*. New York: Oxford University Press, 1968.

Stanley, Amy Dru. *From Bondage to Contract: Wage Labor, Marriage, and the Market in the Age of Slave Emancipation*. Cambridge: Cambridge University Press, 1998.

Stratton, David H. *Tempest over Teapot Dome: The Story of Albert B. Fall*. Norman: University of Oklahoma Press, 1998.

Stricker, Frank. "Affluence for Whom?—Another Look at Prosperity and the Working Classes in the 1920s." In *The Labor History Reader*, edited by Daniel J. Leab, 288–316. Urbana: University of Illinois Press, 1985.

Sugrue, Thomas J. *The Origins of the Urban Crisis: Race and Inequality in Postwar Detroit*. Princeton: Princeton University Press, 1996.

Sullivan, Patricia. *Days of Hope: Race and Democracy in the New Deal Era*. Chapel Hill: University of North Carolina Press, 1996.

———. *Lift Every Voice: The NAACP and the Making of the Civil Rights Movement*. New York: New Press, 2009.

Summers, Mark Wahlgren. *Rum, Romanism, and Rebellion: The Making of a President, 1884*. Chapel Hill: University of North Carolina Press, 2000.

Summers, Martin. *Manliness and Its Discontents: The Black Middle Class and the Transformation of Masculinity, 1900–1930*. Chapel Hill: University of North Carolina Press, 2004.

Thompson, J. A. *Woodrow Wilson*. London: Longman, 2002.

Thornbrough, Emma Lou. "American Negro Newspapers, 1880–1914." *Business History Review* 40, no. 4 (Winter 1966): 467–90.

———. "The Brownsville Episode and the Negro Vote." *Mississippi Valley Historical Review* 44, no. 3 (December 1957): 469–93.

Thorsen, Niels. *The Political Thought of Woodrow Wilson, 1875–1910*. Princeton: Princeton University Press, 1988.

Thurber, Bert H. "The Negro at the Nation's Capital, 1913–1921." Ph.D. diss., Yale University, 1973.

Tilly, Charles. "Domination, Resistance, Compliance . . . Discourse." *Sociological Forum* 6, no. 3 (September 1991): 593–602.

———. "Social Movements and National Politics." In *Statemaking and Social Movements: Essays in History and Theory*, edited by Charles Bright and Susan Harding, 297–317. Ann Arbor: University of Michigan Press, 1984.

Tuck, Stephen G. N. *We Ain't What We Ought to Be: The Black Freedom Struggle, from Emancipation to Obama*. Cambridge, Mass.: Harvard University Press, 2010.

Tucker, James. "Everyday Forms of Employee Resistance." *Sociological Forum* 8, no. 1 (March 1993): 25–45.

Tushnet, Mark. "The Politics of Equality in Constitutional Law: The Equal Protection Clause, Dr. Du Bois, and Charles Hamilton Houston." *Journal of American History* 74, no. 3 (December 1987): 884–903.

Tuttle, William M., Jr. *Race Riot: Chicago in the Red Summer of 1919*. New York: Atheneum Press, 1977.

Urofsky, Melvin I. *Louis D. Brandeis: A Life*. New York: Random House, 2009.

Valelly, Richard M. *The Two Reconstructions: The Struggle for Black Disfranchisement*. Chicago: University of Chicago Press, 2004.

Van Riper, Paul P. *History of the United States Civil Service*. Evanston, Ill.: Row Peterson, 1958.

Veblen, Thorstein *The Theory of the Leisure Class*. New York: Modern Library, 2001.

Wailoo, Keith. *Dying in the City of Blues: Sickle Cell Anemia and the Politics of Race and Health*. Chapel Hill: University of North Carolina Press, 2001.

Waldo, Dwight. *The Administrative State: A Study of the Political Theory of American Public Administration*. 2nd ed. New York: Holmes and Meier, 1984.

Walker, Harvey. "Employee Organizations in the National Government Service: The Formation of the National Federation of Federal Employees." *Public Personnel Studies* 10, no. 4 (October 1941): 130–35.

———. "Employee Organizations in the National Government Service: The Period Prior to the World War." *Public Personnel Studies* 10, no. 3 (August 1941): 67–73.

Walker, Lewis Newton, Jr. "The Struggles and Attempts to Establish Branch Autonomy and Hegemony: A History of the District of Columbia Branch National Association for the Advancement of Colored People, 1912–1942." Ph.D. diss., University of Delaware, 1979.

Walton, Hanes, Jr. *Black Republicans: The Politics of the Black and Tans*. Metuchen, N.J.: Scarecrow Press, 1975.

Wang, Xi. *The Trial of Democracy: Black Suffrage and Northern Republicans, 1860–1910*. Athens: University of Georgia Press, 1997.

Weiner, Jonathan M. "Class Structure and Economic Development in the American South, 1865–1955." *American Historical Review* 84, no. 4 (October 1979): 970–92.

Weinstein, Deena. *Bureaucratic Opposition: Challenging Abuses at the Workplace*. New York: Pergamon Press, 1979.

Weiss, Nancy J. *Farewell to the Party of Lincoln: Black Politics in the Age of FDR*. Princeton: Princeton University Press, 1983.

———. "The Negro and the New Freedom: Fighting Wilsonian Segregation." *Political Science Quarterly* 84, no. 1 (March 1969): 61–79.

Welch, Richard E., Jr. *The Presidencies of Grover Cleveland*. Lawrence: University Press of Kansas, 1988.

West, Michael R. *The Education of Booker T. Washington: American Democracy and the Idea of Race Relations.* New York: Columbia University Press, 2006.

White, Deborah G. *Too Heavy a Load: Black Women in Defense of Themselves, 1894–1994.* New York: W. W. Norton, 1999.

White, Leonard D. *The Republican Era, 1861–1901: A Study in Administrative History.* New York: Macmillan, 1958.

White, Richard D., Jr. *Roosevelt the Reformer: Theodore Roosevelt as Civil Service Commissioner, 1889–1895.* Tuscaloosa: University of Alabama Press, 2003.

Wiebe, Robert. *The Search for Order, 1877–1920.* New York: Hill and Wang, 1967.

Wilkerson, Isabel. *The Warmth of Other Suns: The Epic Story of America's Great Migration.* New York: Random House, 2010.

Williams, Chad L. *Torchbearers of Democracy: African American Soldiers in the World War I Era.* Chapel Hill: University of North Carolina Press, 2010.

Williams, Raymond. *Keywords: A Vocabulary of Culture and Society.* New York: Oxford University Press, 1976.

Williamson, Joel. *The Crucible of Race: Black/White Relations in the American South since Emancipation.* New York: Oxford University Press, 1984.

Wilson, Francille R. *The Segregated Scholars: Black Social Scientists and the Creation of Black Labor Studies, 1890–1950.* Charlottesville: Unversity of Virginia Press, 2006.

Witcover, Jules. *Party of the People: A History of the Democrats.* New York: Random House, 2003.

Witten, Marsha. "Narrative and the Culture of Obedience at the Workplace." In *Narrative and Social Control: Critical Perspectives,* edited by Dennis K. Mumby, 97–118. Newbury Park, Calif.: Sage, 1993.

Wolgemuth, Kathleen Long. "Woodrow Wilson and Federal Segregation." *Journal of Negro History* 44, no. 2 (April 1959): 158–73.

———. "Woodrow Wilson's Appointment Policy and the Negro." *Journal of Southern History* 24, no. 4 (November 1958): 457–71.

Woodruff, Nan Elizabeth. *American Congo: The African American Freedom Struggle in the Delta.* Cambridge, Mass.: Harvard University Press, 2003.

Woods, Randall B. "C. H. J. Taylor and the Movement for Black Political Independence, 1882–1896." *Journal of Negro History* 67, no. 2 (Summer 1982): 122–35.

Woodward, C. Vann. *Origins of the New South, 1877–1913.* Baton Rouge: Louisiana State University Press, 1971.

———. *The Strange Career of Jim Crow.* 3rd ed. New York: Oxford University Press, 1974.

Yellin, Eric Steven. "In the Nation's Service: Racism and Federal Employees in Woodrow Wilson's Washington." Ph.D. diss., Princeton University, 2007.

Yellin, Michael. "Visions of Their America: Waldo Frank's Jewish-Modernist Influence on Jean Toomer's 'Fern.'" *African American Review* 43, no. 2/3 (Summer/Fall 2009): 427–42.

Zangrando, Robert L. *The NAACP Crusade against Lynching, 1909–1950.* Philadelphia: Temple University Press, 1980.

Zunz, Olivier. *Making America Corporate, 1870–1920.* Chicago: University of Chicago Press, 1990.

Index

and racial discrimination in Treasury, 117–20, 123–25

Wilmeth, James L., 119

Wilmington, N.C., 98

Wilson, Ellen Axson, 103, 118, 159, 239 (n. 7)

Wilson, Margaret, 103

Wilson, William B., 243 (n. 72)

Wilson, Woodrow, 2, 6, 61, 81–82, 140, 175; progressive politics of, 3, 5, 83–86, 92–93, 108, 135, 145, 158, 161, 177; involvement in federal segregation, 3, 96, 105, 112, 115, 120, 143, 150, 166; and administration of bureaucracy, 6–7, 82, 84–85, 114, 125–26, 161–64; and Reconstruction, 72, 87, 94, 99; and South, 72, 87, 97, 99, 105; and 1912 election, 75, 76, 77, 83; racism of, 104–5, 160–61, 209 (nn. 6, 7); presidential appointments by, 107–11, 142; defense of segregation, 115, 135, 144–45, 159, 161–65, 190; 1913 meeting with Trotter, 132, 136, 144–45; 1914 meeting with Trotter, 159–70

Wilson administration, 6, 38, 60; white southerners in, 82, 96–100; relations with black Democrats, 105–8, 141–43. See also Racism: in Wilson administration; Wilson, Woodrow

Wilsonian praxis, 114, 123, 133, 135, 141, 142, 165, 190

Woman suffrage, 181

Wood, Robert N., 142–43

Work, Hubert, 192

World War I, 30, 110, 139, 140, 159, 170, 171, 178; African American involvement in, 177–78, 182

Young, Charles, 178

CPSIA information can be obtained at www.ICGtesting.com
Printed in the USA
LVOW08s1614020616

490959LV00004B/616/P

JUL 0 6 2016